W9-ANQ-039

Freedom's Journal

Freedom's Journal

The First African-American Newspaper

Jacqueline Bacon

LEXINGTON BOOKS

A division of
ROWMAN & LITTLEFIELD PUBLISHERS, INC.
Lanham • Boulder • New York • Toronto • Plymouth, UK

LEXINGTON BOOKS

A division of Rowman & Littlefield Publishers, Inc.
A wholly owned subsidary of The Rowman & Littlefield Publishing Group, Inc.
4501 Forbes Boulevard, Suite 200, Lanham, MD 20706

Estover Road, Plymouth PL6 7PY, United Kingdom

Copyright © 2007 by Lexington Books

All rights reserved. No part of this publication may be reproduced, stored in a
retrieval system, or transmitted in any form or by any means, electronic,
mechanical, photocopying, recording, or otherwise, without the prior permission
of the publisher.

British Library Cataloguing in Publication Information Available

Library of Congress Cataloging-in-Publication Data

Bacon, Jacqueline, 1965–
   Freedom's journal : the first African-American newspaper / Jacqueline Bacon.
      p. cm.
   Includes bibliographical references and index.
   ISBN-13: 978-0-7391-1893-1 (cloth : alk. paper)
   ISBN-10: 0-7391-1893-5 (cloth : alk. paper)
   ISBN-13: 978-0-7391-1894-8 (pbk. : alk. paper)
   ISBN-10: 0-7391-1894-3 (pbk. : alk. paper)
 1. Freedom's journal (New York, N.Y. : 1827) I. Title.
   PN4899.N42F743 2007
   071'.471--dc22

                                        2006035865

Printed in the United States of America

∞™ The paper used in this publication meets the minimum requirements of
American National Standard for Information Sciences—Permanence of Paper for
Printed Library Materials, ANSI/NISO Z39.48-1992.

For my brothers and sisters in faith and fellowship
at Christ United Presbyterian Church, San Diego

God is good—*all the time.*

Contents

Part III

Acknowledgments

This book has been the product of a decade's thought, research, and writing. For various forms of support, encouragement, and assistance, I am indebted to many people.

My husband, Glen McClish, is truly remarkable. He encourages and supports me, engages in lively exchanges with me about research, provides thoughtful suggestions, reads and comments on my work, sustains me through my failures, celebrates with me my successes, and is a wonderful father to our children. Our sons, Roger and Henry, bring me indescribable joy and happiness and continually revitalize me with their energy, affection, and humor. Living in a home with these three sustains and fulfills me.

My father, Gary Bacon, has been an extraordinary research assistant, visiting microfilm rooms and library stacks on various assignments related to this project. The information and resources he turned up inform this study throughout; frequently he also made unexpected discoveries that enhanced the book in various ways. My mother, Wynne Bacon, read the entire manuscript enthusiastically as well as analytically and made many important suggestions. Both of my parents have been cheerleaders and supporters. My sister, Shelley Bacon Kazliner, has rooted for my success and brought me delight with her unique sense of humor. My parents-in-law, Leonard and Elaine McClish, encouraged me and took an interest in my work. For over two decades, they have treated me as a daughter.

I am grateful to various people who have been, to use my son Roger's phrase, "on my team" in diverse ways, from reading and commenting on my work to caring about and for me and my family. They know the ways that they have helped; I hope also that they know my appreciation: Suzanne Bordelon, Linda Ferreira-Buckley, Andy and Christa Goldblatt, David Gold, Hedda Fish, Ann and David Johns, Gregory LaDue, Ellen Quandahl, Stephen Sobel, and Chris Werry. During the initial research for the book, I was blessed to be a part of the faith community of St. James Episcopal Church in Austin, Texas; I am grateful for their love and support.

I thank my editor at Lexington Books, MacDuff Stewart, for her enthusiasm and dedication to the book. From the start, her optimism enabled me to believe that it would be published, and her advocacy and assistance made that dream a reality. I am grateful to the anonymous reader for Lexington Books for feedback and suggestions.

No book of this nature is possible without the generous help of librarians. I thank the staffs of the libraries of Southwestern University (Georgetown, Texas), the University of Texas at Austin, and San Diego State University—particularly these institutions' interlibrary loan departments. I am grateful for assistance from the librarians at the Historical Society of Pennsylvania; the Library Company of Philadelphia; the Boston Public Library; The Schomburg Center for Research in Black Culture at the New York Public Library; the Presbyterian Church (U.S.A.) Department of History and Records Management Services, Philadelphia; and Sarah Huggins of the Library of Virginia.

Every week for the past few years, I have had the honor and pleasure of worshiping, celebrating, and enjoying fellowship with the congregation of Christ United Presbyterian Church in San Diego. They uplift me, sustain me, encourage me, nurture me, teach me, and help me order my steps. I dedicate this book to them, with love.

Above all, I thank God, who leads me and guides me. *Psalm 19:14.*

*   *   *

Introduction:
"A Clap of Thunder"

In an 1837 speech to the New York State Anti-Slavery Society, African-American abolitionist Theodore Wright recalled the support of many white Americans during the previous two decades for the colonization movement, particularly the American Colonization Society (ACS). The ACS's proposals that free African Americans should be encouraged to emigrate to Africa were opposed by most people of color, Wright related, but "they could not gain access to the public mind: for the press would not communicate the facts in the case—it was silent." In fact, the "press came out against" African Americans, suggesting that it was "proper to make them go, whether they would or not."[1]

In this "dark and gloomy period" of "despair," a major positive event occurred. On March 16, 1827, *Freedom's Journal*, the first African-American newspaper, began publication in New York. Wright described the significance of this periodical, which gave the African-American community a voice in the debate over colonization. "The united views and intentions of the people of color were made known," he asserted, "and the nation awoke as from a slumber. The *Freedom's Journal* . . . announced the facts in the case, our entire opposition. . . . [I]t came like a clap of thunder!"[2]

To African Americans, oppressed, silenced, and long denied the opportunity to publish their views in most white newspapers, the appearance of *Freedom's Journal* in 1827 must indeed have seemed like the sudden onset of a storm. And, as Wright's metaphor suggests, its publication changed the atmosphere irrevocably. *Freedom's Journal* was a new forum edited and controlled by African Americans in which they could articulate their concerns; and, unlike the more limited opportunities for publishing books or

1

pamphlets previously available to them, a newspaper could bring a variety of voices into civic debates. National in scope and distributed in several countries, the paper connected African Americans beyond the boundaries of city or region and engaged international issues from their perspective. Arguments in the newspaper shaped the activism of both African-American and white leaders and reformers for generations to come, and the community activism fostered by the periodical catalyzed the abolition movement. Although many historians of abolition focus on the period beginning in the 1830s, white leaders such as William Lloyd Garrison, and organizations such as the American Anti-Slavery Society (AASS),[3] *Freedom's Journal* demonstrates that African-American activists were already engaged in protests in the 1820s, addressing slavery as well as the many other problems and concerns of free people of color and their future as citizens of the United States. In fact, the rhetoric and activism of African Americans reflected in the columns of *Freedom's Journal* both predated and influenced whites' involvement with the struggles for antislavery and civil rights. In an 1855 editorial in *Frederick Douglass' Paper*, New York physician James McCune Smith emphasized the pre-1830s activism of African Americans, including the publication of *Freedom's Journal*, asserting that they "almost began the present [antislavery] movement; they certainly antedated many of its principles."[4]

Although *Freedom's Journal* ceased publication in 1829, the African-American community would never again be without a newspaper for long. *Freedom's Journal* established that an independent press had a central role in black activism, that it was central to the struggle for freedom, self-determination, and civil rights. An 1837 editorial by former *Freedom's Journal* editor Samuel Cornish in the weekly newspaper the *Colored American* asserted that a strong African-American press had become fundamental to the agenda of community leaders. Exhorting African Americans to support the periodical, Cornish declared, "The maintenance of a Public Journal, as the organ of 'COLORED AMERICANS,' the Editor considers as essential to our respectability and elevation. We can never rise to a level in society without it. It is one of the principal engines, by which our rights are to be *obtained and maintained*." Cornish summarized the perspective of African-American editors who built on his and John Russwurm's pioneering efforts: "Colored men . . . must establish and maintain the PRESS, and through it, speak out in THUNDER TONES, until the nation repent and render to every man that which is just and equal. . . ."[5] Cornish's choice of words is notable. If, in Wright's terms, *Freedom's Journal* represented a "clap of thunder," the African-American press continued to charge the atmosphere, creating storms that resonated throughout the nation.

But like the onset of a thunderstorm, the publication of the first African-American newspaper, though it must have seemed sudden, was influenced by factors that had been building in the environment. Since the Revolution, African Americans had been creating powerful community institutions and arguing forcefully for civil rights, and by the 1820s, black activism was particularly strong. Protesting oppression and asserting their right to determine their own destinies, African Americans developed a national political consciousness that linked citizens throughout the country. African Americans of the 1820s were dedicated to establishing and supporting community institutions and to using the power of writing to gain freedom and self-determination. It was in this context that *Freedom's Journal* emerged.

Despite its significance, *Freedom's Journal* has not been investigated comprehensively. Historians who have examined *Freedom's Journal* in the context of African-American history or the history of the press have considered it only briefly, often making assumptions about the periodical—its founding, its focus, its goals, its editors—that overlook important facts or that do not fully account for the publication's richness and depth. Many questions concerning significant facets of *Freedom's Journal*'s history and mission have been left largely unanswered or have been only partially or inaccurately addressed by scholars. Why was the paper created? Was it aimed at white or African-American readers? How was it financed? How did it address compelling issues of the day? Why did it only last two years? What were readers' responses to it? How did later editors build on its goals? In addition, *Freedom's Journal* is a rich but understudied source of information about African-American thought and life of the late 1820s, a crucial period of community building and political protest. What can we discover by reading the columns of *Freedom's Journal* and examining the information and arguments they contain?

This study engages these and other questions. Part I examines in depth the history of *Freedom's Journal*. I begin with a chapter devoted to African-American history, activism, and rhetoric from the Revolution to the 1820s, providing crucial context for understanding *Freedom's Journal* and its time. Chapter 2 presents a thorough historical account of the periodical's founding, development, and demise. In chapter 3, I focus on the goals of *Freedom's Journal* in order to give a sense of the periodical's scope, mission, and overall content. Part II consists of five chapters examining *Freedom's Journal*'s coverage of various subjects critical to antebellum African Americans—self-help, morality, and racial uplift; gender roles; the histories, present conditions, and futures of Africa and Haiti; colonization and emigration; and slavery and abolition. In Part III, I address the impact and legacy of *Freedom's Journal*; chapter 9 examines its influence in the antebellum period and beyond.

As this overview suggests, this book does not constitute what we might call a "traditional" historical narrative, which advances chronologically and attempts to place particular characters, events, and themes into a unified, seamless account. Although I relate stories that fit a more conventional model within the study, particularly in the first two chapters, much of the book is structured thematically around *Freedom's Journal*'s coverage of particular issues and events. This approach reflects my vision of how we can best understand *Freedom's Journal*—by realizing its place both in its own time and in American history, and approaching it as a resource for better understanding the African-American community of the late 1820s. Any detailed account of the periodical is incomplete without a sense of what its editors and supporters hoped to accomplish—aims that were complex and multifaceted, ranging from providing ordinary African Americans with vital information about contemporary issues and everyday concerns to showcasing the rhetorical and literary efforts of emerging and established talents. Yet an examination of these concerns does not fit neatly into a chronological narrative; indeed, to try to integrate them into a sequential account would be reductive if not misleading. Instead I explore these goals fully in a chapter that seeks to examine and illustrate the multiple ways that the periodical served African Americans of the late 1820s (chapter 3).

Similarly, the middle section of the book is arranged thematically, analyzing the coverage of specific subjects in *Freedom's Journal*. Indeed, I would argue that the impressive depth and diversity of the newspaper's treatment of various topics demands such a framework. The rich range of material on, for example, slavery or self-help does not conform readily to a chronological narrative. On crucial issues, the editors' inclusion of articles from a variety of sources created a complex *dialogue*, with voices countering and interacting with one another, rather than a simple *progression* from one perspective to another. As John Ernest explains, in African-American newspapers "various voices, from all walks of life, are placed in dynamic relation with one another and with the representatives of the white community that influence African American experience."[6] For *Freedom's Journal* in particular, the dialogic aspect of the material in its columns is also a result of the periodical's short tenure, making it less fruitful to examine changes over time than to probe the range of perspectives represented in the paper during this important period of African-American history. In other words, explorations of the coverage of particular issues reflect the vibrancy and range of African Americans' views on important topics and demonstrate the editors' attempts to give voice to a variety of viewpoints in the paper's columns.

Although an appreciation of developments of the late 1820s, as scholars have noted, is crucial for understanding antebellum African-American history,[7] few studies delve deeply into this era.[8] *Freedom's Journal* is a particularly rich source for examining this period and for exploring the issues important to African Americans of the time. Because a newspaper serves as a forum for the ideas of people whose views may not be published elsewhere, discussions and debates in *Freedom's Journal* provide a more comprehensive view of African Americans' responses in the late 1820s to subjects such as colonization or women's roles than is available in pamphlets or speeches. As Walter Daniel remarks, *Freedom's Journal* is "one of the most unimpeachable resources for black American life in the urban North in the first half of the nineteenth century." More generally, Henry Louis Gates notes that in the pages of black newspapers can be found "a remarkable amount of information about the world's impact every day upon African-Americans, and their impact upon the world, [which] can be scrutinized by scholars, thus filling in lacunae that even the most subtle intellectual history cannot otherwise address."[9]

By focusing in depth on the newspaper's coverage of various important issues, we can use *Freedom's Journal* as a unique lens through which to view African Americans' perspectives on various subjects during the period in which it was published. In the newspaper, we will discover the views of famous, as well as unknown and even unnamed, African Americans who communicated through letters and speeches as well as in advertisements and reports. We will find that the editors and contributors to the periodical addressed issues that we usually associate with antebellum African-American activism, such as slavery and abolition, yet we will explore the coverage of many other subjects in *Freedom's Journal* as well. This exploration helps create an inclusive, genuine picture of African-American life in the late 1820s. As Frances Smith Foster argues, the fact that antebellum African-American writers engaged subjects other than slavery "demonstrates a sense of empowerment and social awareness beyond that which some might ordinarily attribute to persons enslaved"—and, by extension, those oppressed by slavery's shadow.[10]

The legacy of *Freedom's Journal* also deserves full exploration. Just as the history of the periodical does not begin in 1827, but must be seen in the context of developments in the late eighteenth and early nineteenth centuries, it does not end in 1829 when the newspaper ceased publication. *Freedom's Journal* influenced antebellum African Americans and white reformers, and its relevance extends to later periods as well. *Freedom's Journal* is a necessary part of the historical context that illuminates debates that continued after the publication's demise—and that indeed continue to resonate today—about issues such as integration versus separatism, the intersections of race and gender, and the place of Africa in African-American life.

This study, then, both creates a historical account of the periodical and uses the texts that were published in its columns to illuminate African-American life in the late 1820s. Because of my approach to *Freedom's Journal* and the structure of this book, readers will find that certain issues and themes reappear throughout my analysis. The issue of colonization, for example, is featured in various chapters, as is the perspective of African Americans in the late 1820s about the United States, its ideals, and their roles in the nation. Such reverberation is beneficial, allowing subjects to be illuminated in different ways in a variety of contexts. We discover different implications of the colonization movement, for example, by examining the newspaper's coverage from different angles, relating the issue to the editors' goals, to contemporary views of Africa, and to the links and conflicts between African-American and white reformers. A consequence of the reappearance of key issues is that, to some extent, chapters can stand on their own, and readers need not take them in order. At the same time, I make important connections throughout the book between different chapters, noting associations among various goals, subjects, articles, and authors. In a sense, my study shares this characteristic with *Freedom's Journal* itself, in which various contributions were self-contained but frequently related to one another.

I am guided by other considerations and assumptions, both practical and theoretical. Although my research has uncovered facts that have not been mentioned in previous discussions of *Freedom's Journal*—and which, in many cases, contradict standard interpretations—I could not definitively answer all the questions that arise about the periodical. My research has taken me to New York, Philadelphia, and Boston; and I have pored over manuscript and microfilm collections of the papers of various individuals and organizations. As with all archival research, my searches were sometimes fruitful, yet frequently I encountered dead ends. In some cases, I offer speculative answers based on the sources I have located. Although I have tried to pursue every avenue that came to mind, the uncertainty that remains suggests that future researchers may find new material that will add to our understanding of *Freedom's Journal*. This book is not intended to be the last word on *Freedom's Journal* but to foster fresh interest in the periodical.

In concert with various scholars, I work from the premise that the African-American community is not and has never been monolithic.[11] Indeed, dissent was an important part of the mission of *Freedom's Journal*. Thus, although I use the term "community" and phrases such as "community concerns," I do not mean to diminish this diversity. I follow the lead of James and Lois Horton, who explain, "We use the term 'community' to include both institutions (social, political, economic, and religious) and sentiments based on shared experience and a sense of common destiny that bound community members together. . . . [Eighteenth- and nineteenth-century African Americans] were highly diverse in background, experience, and opinion, linked to one another across regions by communications that helped them join their communities in a common struggle." James Blackwell aptly describes the African-American community as one that promotes "unity without uniformity."[12]

My approach is also grounded in the view that, as scholars endeavor to examine African-American history, we must give agency to its primary actors—to blacks themselves. Significant events have often been framed as responses or reactions to forces outside the African-American community, particularly to the actions or provocations of white Americans. It is, of course, true that African Americans are an integral part of American society, and thus are affected by it. Yet to focus primarily on the influence of whites' opinions and conduct when examining historical events is reductive, assuming at least to some extent that blacks are passive rather than active and diminishing the importance of self-directed action among African Americans. As Gary Nash maintains, "It has not been easy for historians to recognize how vibrant and multifaceted were the northern urban centers of black life in the antebellum period. Mostly they have focused on what happened *to* black communities, not what transpired *within* them." Craig Steven Wilder similarly warns against a simplistic historical approach that "limits the investigation to what was happening to [African Americans] and ignores what they were constructing for themselves." Recent studies have challenged this traditional historiography, closely examining historical factors that demonstrate the power within the African-American community. This new approach, Nash explains, assumes that "alongside a history of discrimination and oppression must be placed the internal history of a people striving to live life as fully, as freely, as creatively, and as spiritually rich as their inner resources and external circumstances allowed."[13]

An example of these competing historiographical trends—which we might describe in shorthand as casting African Americans as *objects* rather than as *subjects* of history—illustrates Nash's and Wilder's points. The rise of independent African-American churches in the late eighteenth century has often been attributed to prejudice within white churches, particularly in the form of defining events such as the walkout of black parishioners of St. George's Methodist Church in Philadelphia after they were ordered to move to a segregated section of the recently constructed gallery. It is often assumed that because of this incident and the racism that motivated it, Philadelphia African Americans established their own churches.[14] Yet scholars recently have developed a more complex view of the factors influencing the development of independent African-American churches in Philadelphia. They point to institutions such as the influential Free African Society that arose in Philadelphia during the period of intense community development of the late eighteenth century. In addition, they have found that African-American parishioners at St. George's were already developing plans for their own church prior to the incident provoking the walkout. Without denying that white racism existed or was one of many factors that fueled enthusiasm for separate churches, they suggest that the rise of independent churches developed from within the African-American community, drawing on the strength of its leadership and institutions.[15] I approach the history of *Freedom's Journal* in this spirit. Although I do not diminish the racism of the late 1820s and its influence on the periodical, I emphasize forces within the African-American community itself and the self-directed action of its members.

In addition, as a historian who is fundamentally interested in language as well as culture, texts as well as events, I am compelled to examine closely the way rhetorical strategies are deployed and how discourse reflects and shapes experiences and perspectives. In my analysis of *Freedom's Journal*'s columns, I explore not only what was said and what that tells us about the era of the late 1820s, but also how African Americans during this period used language and to what ends, to whom they were arguing and how that shaped their discourse, and what factors influenced their persuasive strategies.

In addition, because the editors published articles by a variety of writers, African-American leaders and white reformers as well as those who were not famous and who often were unnamed, the periodical offers us a unique historical vantage point. This study expands the history of African-American rhetoric of the late 1820s through consideration of the voices of people who might not have been well known or influential but who were able, through the newspaper's columns, to contribute to discussions and debates about issues important to them. While we are often accustomed to encountering the well-established opinions of leaders on issues such as gender roles, emigration, or Africa's history and future, an examination of the rhetoric in *Freedom's Journal* reveals a range and depth of opinion on these subjects that may otherwise be overlooked.

Even given this diversity, we must remain aware of the fact that *Freedom's Journal*, like the African-American newspapers that followed it, was produced and financed by middle-class members of the community. As we shall see, *Freedom's Journal*'s editors were well educated and connected with supporters who could fund their project, and their social class shaped their work. Those who wrote articles for the newspaper similarly would have had both the skills and the leisure time to do so. Yet although it is important to understand the impact of the position of the editors and contributors on the newspaper, we should not assume that its significance both in its own time and as a historical tool is diminished as a result. Those who were influenced by *Freedom's Journal*, we shall discover, were not necessarily part of the African-American middle or upper classes; we cannot even assume that they were literate by traditional definitions. Because of the ways printed material was distributed, shared, and read aloud, the newspaper's readership likely included people who did not have traditional education or means, including those who could not read, those who were learning to read, and slaves.

Nor should we oversimplify the range of goals and opinions among those who contributed to its columns. As Elizabeth McHenry argues, "the perspectives of the black middle and upper classes" have often been treated reductively and inaccurately "as assimilationist or accommodationist." I similarly believe that we need to address the "complexity" within this group of African Americans and what McHenry describes as their "acts of resistance to the hostile racial climate that made the United States an uncomfortable and unequal place for all black Americans, regardless of their social or economic condition." In many ways, as Ira Berlin and Leslie Harris note of antebellum African-American New Yorkers, the elite and the poor were allied, coming together in public spaces and sharing culture and ideology, so that "most black people lived in both worlds."[16]

I draw on secondary sources throughout this study, and I am indebted to the work of those who have researched various aspects of eighteenth- and nineteenth-century African-American history and the history of the press. In addition, various scholars have studied particular aspects of *Freedom's Journal*; and although at times I challenge or modify historical claims in light of the primary evidence I have uncovered, I do not mean to minimize the importance of their contributions to my work. These studies have laid necessary groundwork for my scholarship, providing particular insights into the periodical and directing me to resources for further study. Yet my principal sources, whenever possible, are the voices of those connected to *Freedom's Journal*, found in their letters, manuscripts, and the columns of the newspaper itself. In these texts, those African Americans who established, supported, contributed to, and were influenced by *Freedom's Journal* spoke for themselves. It is my goal that, as I explore their discourse, their words will be not only analyzed but *heard*— and that we can understand and appreciate the intensity and impact of the thunderstorm that was *Freedom's Journal*.

NOTES

*The following abbreviations are used in notes throughout the book:

CA   *Colored American*
FJ   *Freedom's Journal*
RA   *Rights of All*

1. Theodore S. Wright, "The Progress of the Antislavery Cause," in *Negro Orators and Their Orations*, ed. Woodson, 87–88.
2. Wright, "Progress," 88.
3. See, for example, Dumond, *Antislavery*; Lawrence J. Friedman, *Gregarious Saints*; Barnes, *Antislavery Impulse*; Kraditor, *Means and Ends*; Walters, "Boundaries"; Walters, *Antislavery Appeal*; Scott, "Abolition"; Perry, *Radical Abolitionism*; Arkin, "Federalist Trope." There has been a body of scholarship that has challenged these

views, redefining the historiography of the abolition movement to take into account the significant work of African Americans prior to and after 1830; see Quarles, *Black Abolitionists*; Pease and Pease, *They Who Would Be Free*; Levesque, "Black Abolitionists"; Dick, *Black Protest*; Jacobs, *Courage and Conscience*; Yee, *Black Women Abolitionists*; Logan, *"We Are Coming"*; Ripley et al., *Black Abolitionist Papers*; Hinks, *To Awaken*; Swartz, "Emancipatory Narratives," 347–52; Bacon, *Humblest*; Timothy Patrick McCarthy, "To Plead."

4. Communipaw [James McCune Smith], "From Our New York Correspondent" [letter to editor], *Frederick Douglass' Paper*, 26 January 1855.

5. Samuel E. Cornish, "A Statement and a Call," *CA*, 17 June 1837; Samuel E. Cornish, "Why We Should Have a Paper," *CA*, 4 March 1827.

6. Ernest, *Liberation*, 292.

7. Dixon, *African America*, 15; McHenry, *Forgotten Readers*, 38–42; Finseth, "David Walker," 344; Hinks, *To Awaken*, 91–112; Harding, *Other American Revolution*, 29–32; Goodman, *Of One Blood*, 23–26.

8. It is true, of course, that a variety of studies, including James Oliver Horton and Lois Horton's *In Hope of Liberty*, Leonard Curry's *The Free Black in Urban America*, and Gary Nash's *Forging Freedom*, discuss African-American life in the 1820s. However, because they consider a longer time span, they do not focus extensively on this period.

9. Daniel, *Black Journals*, 185; Gates, introduction to *African-American Newspapers*, x. On the role of African-American newspapers in allowing ordinary citizens to have their viewpoints printed, see Belt-Beyan, *Emergence*, 167–68.

10. Frances Smith Foster, *Written by Herself*, 24.

11. See, for example, Blackwell, *Black Community*, xi; Horton and Horton, *In Hope*, xi; Clarence E. Walker, *Deromanticizing Black History*, xvi–xviii; Leonard Sweet, *Black Images*, 3; Horton and Horton, *Black Bostonians*, xi; Horton, *Free People*, 2–3, 15–16, 200; Curry, *Free Black*, xvi; Winch, *Philadelphia's Black Elite*, 3; Hutton, *Early Black Press*, 3; Shane White, *Somewhat More Independent*, 182; McHenry, *Forgotten Readers*, 14–15.

12. Horton and Horton, *In Hope*, xi; Blackwell, *Black Community*, 3.

13. Nash, *Forging Freedom*, 7; Wilder, *In the Company*, 3–4.

14. Richardson, *Dark Salvation*, 65; Lammers, "Rev. Absalom Jones," 164–67; Foner, *History . . . Cotton Kingdom*, 563–64; Franklin and Moss, *From Slavery*, 114; Wilmore, *Black Religion*, 105–6; Henry Young, *Major Black Religious Leaders*, 28–29. This emphasis on racism at St. George's is probably due in part to a misdating of the walkout, as Gary Nash explains. Because the incident was traditionally dated as 1787, it has been assumed that the parishioners left St. George's before the founding of the Free African Society that year, which solidified the Philadelphia African-American community. Scholars have determined, though, that 1792 is a more accurate date, suggesting that when the parishioners left St. George's important African-American community institutions, such as the Free African Society, were already established (*Forging Freedom*, 118–19).

15. See Gravely, "Rise," 304–5; Winch, *Philadelphia's Black Elite*, 9–10; George, "In the Beginning," 43–44; Lincoln and Mamiya, *Black Church*, 50–51; Horton and Horton, *In Hope*, 138; Nash, *Forging Freedom*, 118–19.

16. McHenry, *Forgotten Readers*, 17; Berlin and Harris, "Uncovering," 21.

PART I

1

~

"The Time Has Now Arrived": The African-American Community of the Late 1820s

In the inaugural issue of *Freedom's Journal*, published March 16, 1827, editors Samuel Cornish and John Russwurm clearly outlined their intentions: "We wish to plead our own cause. Too long have others spoken for us." To claim their rights as Americans and determine their own destinies, they suggested, African Americans needed a voice in civic debates. It was a "real necessity" that they have "a public channel" shaped and controlled by African Americans themselves, "devoted exclusively to their improvement" and reflecting their "sentiments" on subjects affecting them. "Often has injustice been heaped upon us," they asserted, "but we believe that the time has now arrived, when the calumnies of our enemies should be refuted by forcible arguments."[1]

The time had indeed arrived. The racism that Cornish and Russwurm identified, although not new, translated into severe restrictions on African Americans' civil rights, access to employment and education, and personal safety. In the face of these obstacles, free African Americans in various cities throughout the United States in the 1820s "built the black community from within," in the words of Vincent Harding, engaging in a concerted effort to achieve "self-determination, self-improvement, and freedom." In this struggle, African Americans focused on the power of the written and spoken word, challenging the notion that others could speak for them. A national newspaper allowed them unprecedented access to public debates. As Cornish and Russwurm explained, African Americans needed a forum for the "dissemination of knowledge . . . in the community," for "the moral, religious, civil, and literary improvement of [their] injured race," and for the circulation of "communication between [African

Americans] and the public." "Experience teaches us," the editors re-marked in the periodical's first issue, "that the Press is the most economical and convenient method by which this object is to be obtained."[2]

Many factors rendered 1827 an opportune time for the birth of the first African-American newspaper. Yet although developments of the 1820s were influential, previous generations of African Americans had laid the foundation for the work of leaders such as Cornish and Russwurm. Since the Revolution, African Americans had engaged in political, social, and cultural activities that made the development of a national newspaper possible and that cultivated the sense of community and black identity expressed in its columns.

BEYOND THE REVOLUTION: 1780–1800

The decades following the American Revolution were critical to the development of the free African-American community.[3] Beginning in the 1780s, a first generation of leaders began to address issues of identity, self-determination, and group consciousness. They did so against a backdrop of racism, oppression, violence, and tension within the new republic about slavery and the place of free African Americans in the nation. The views and actions of the author of the Declaration of Independence illustrate the complexities inherent in post-Revolutionary Americans' views of race, slavery, and freedom. Though apprehensive about slavery, Jefferson maintained his status as a slaveholder and offered pronouncements in his 1787 treatise *Notes on the State of Virginia* about the inferiority of people of African descent that influenced racial thought for generations to come.[4]

Slavery was abolished throughout most of the North in the late eighteenth and early nineteenth centuries, constitutionally in states such as Vermont (1777) and Massachusetts (1783), and through gradual abolition laws in states such as Pennsylvania (1780), Rhode Island (1784), and New York (1799). Yet gradual emancipation left out many African Americans who would never have the right to be free, and some Northern slaveholders attempted to thwart gradual abolition laws by selling their slaves to other states. Joanne Pope Melish speculates that masters in certain states may have kept slaves ignorant of their dates of birth in order to keep them from attaining freedom under *post nati* statutes freeing all slaves born after a specific year.[5]

Nor did freedom from slavery bring with it basic rights of citizenship such as equal opportunity, civil rights, or safety. Free African Americans were restricted or excluded by legislation from entering various Northern states, and they confronted discrimination and segregation that dictated where they could work, live, and worship. Throughout the North, they faced the danger of abduction by those who would sell them into slavery, a pervasive threat magnified by the indifference of most white officials and heightened by the Fugitive Slave Law of 1793, denying due process to victims of kidnappings who were said to be fugitive slaves. As gradual abolition and immigration of manumitted slaves from the South increased the free African-American population in cities such as New York and Philadelphia, white hostility intensified. Because African Americans were more likely to be arrested than whites, were apprehended for violations for which whites often were not cited, were given longer prison terms, and were more frequently driven by poverty to property crimes, they were overrepresented in the prison population—a fact often cited by whites as evidence of their "degraded" status.

At the same time, the Revolution fostered antislavery sentiment and spurred efforts to aid African Americans in many parts of the United States. Early antislavery societies such as the Pennsylvania Abolition Society (established in 1775) and the New York Manumission Society (founded in 1785)[6] sought to improve the treatment of slaves; to create access to education for African Americans, such as that provided by New York's African Free School, founded by the Manumission Society in 1787; to free slaves held illegally; to prevent kidnappings; and to end the importation of slaves. The question of exactly how to end slavery, however, was not easily answered even by those white Americans who opposed the system. The approach of early antislavery societies to abolition was moderate, frequently hesitant, and often contradictory. They often focused more on freeing particular individuals through legal or financial action than on a national end to slavery. Advocating gradualist means for eradicating the institution, they assumed that any plan of abolition should proceed over time and with consideration to conciliating—and, in some cases, compensating—slaveholders.[7] African Americans were excluded from membership in early antislavery organizations, while both the Pennsylvania Abolition Society and the New York Manumission Society admitted slaveholders as members in their early years.[8] In addition, many antislavery whites in the early republic feared the consequences of emancipation, believing, like Jefferson, that free African Americans and whites could not coexist peacefully in the United States.[9]

In addition, the rhetoric of white Americans in the early republic was at best paternalistic or unresponsive to the experiences, needs, and concerns of African Americans and at worst malevolent and intolerant. Even many whites who opposed slavery held racist views and supported abolition more out of concern for its effects on white Americans than on those it was meant to liberate. In a report to a convention of delegates from various abolition societies, held May 3, 1797, the New York Manumission Society declared that slavery in New York was "very tolerable" and claimed that people of color faced few problems in the state. After the yellow fever epidemic of 1793 in Philadelphia, throughout which African Americans served as nurses to their neighbors (despite great danger to themselves), bookseller and printer Mathew Carey published an account of the plague denigrating the work of the African-American nurses and accusing them of theft and exploitation.[10] Like Jefferson, early American writers from both the North and the South assumed the inferiority of African Americans, often arguing that physical differences were markers of subordinate status and buttressing their views with Scripture. As gradual emancipation unfolded in post-Revolutionary America, Melish demonstrates, "a genre of humorous and (often savagely) satirical anecdotes, cartoons, and broadsides" emerged which suggested people of color were incompetent, behaved inappropriately, and were unfit for the responsibilities of citizenship.[11]

In the face of legal and societal restrictions, misrepresentations, racist rhetoric, and threats to their safety, African Americans in the late eighteenth century established a network of independent community organizations and developed a political consciousness. Mutual aid societies such as the Free African Union Society of Newport, Rhode Island (1780); Philadelphia's Free African Society (1787); and the African Society of Boston (1796) assisted members during times of need. Beyond this practical function, these organizations were instrumental in creating a generation of leaders, fostering civic consciousness, and allowing African Americans to define their identity and goals. Black freemasonry, organized by Massachusetts minister Prince Hall, also served to unite African Americans and to allow them to develop and promote a political agenda. In 1775 Hall and other Boston African Americans joined a British Masonic lodge, whose members were soldiers living in the city. When the British left, they wished to retain their fraternity. Refused recognition by white American Masons, African-American Masons were chartered by the Grand Lodge of England in 1787. Lodges in various cities were influential political organizations, counting among their members prominent black leaders such as Absalom Jones and Richard Allen. African-American Masons agitated against slavery and kidnappings, petitioned for abolition, promoted education, and often used their lodges as stations on the Underground Railroad. Also in the late eighteenth century, independent African-American churches were established in Northern cities, often in connection with mutual aid societies. Their functions, Gayle Tate maintains, "crossed sacred and secular lines," spurring community building, protest, and the development of a growing political consciousness.[12]

Activism among African Americans against slavery and oppression also evolved in the late eighteenth century. African-American antislavery efforts in the seventeenth and much of the eighteenth centuries were primarily individual in nature, seeking freedom for particular slaves. With the rise of community organizations, group action developed. Some ventures were practical and often informal in nature, such as sheltering runaway slaves. As the work of the Masons demonstrates, African-American fraternal and mutual aid organizations also assisted fugitives and addressed slavery as one of the issues critical to the community. Petitioning was also an important part of African Americans' early group activity against slavery and other forms of oppression. Through antislavery petitions of the 1770s (as well as broadsides and poetry), African Americans developed an empowering rhetoric for asserting their rights and defining their needs and concerns in the face of misrepresentations and paternalism. Allowing African Americans "to directly utilize the power of language," Harry Reed maintains, petitions demonstrate "the beginning process of self-identity" and the creation of "a community of common interest and the potential for united action."[13]

Although petitions assumed the rhetorical form of requests, they also functioned as political arguments, addressing the rights and status of African Americans in the early republic, often in bold language. A 1779 petition of Connecticut African Americans asserted, "We perceive by our own Reflection, that we are endowed with the same Faculties with our masters, and there is nothing that leads us to a Belief . . . that we are any more obliged to serve them, than they us. . . . [W]e are Convinced of our Right . . . to be free . . . and can never be convinced that we were made to be Slaves." In 1780, brothers Paul and John Cuffe, along with five other African Americans living in Dartmouth, Massachusetts, petitioned their state's legislature, declaring that they should not be subject to taxation without representation. African Americans were denied "the Privilage [*sic*] of freemen of the State having no influence in the Election of those that Tax us," they protested, even though many served "in the field of Battle" to oppose "a similar Exertion of Power (in Regard to taxation)" in the Revolutionary War.[14]

In the 1780s and 1790s, African Americans developed even more forceful arguments about rights and identity, combining honor for their African heritage, affirmation of their status as Americans, and refutations of negative representations of them. "An Essay on Negro Slavery," written by a free African American under the name Othello and published in 1788 in the *American Museum,* called on Americans to abolish a practice "inconsistent with the declared principles of the American Revolution," deplored the effect of the slave trade on Africa, and warned that God would punish Americans "with a dreadful attention to justice" if they persisted in countenancing slavery. Beginning in the 1790s, as Richard Newman, Patrick Rael, and Phillip Lapsansky demonstrate, pamphlets assumed an important role in "the broader struggle by black Americans to assert themselves in the public sphere." In 1794, for example, Philadelphia African-American leaders and clergymen Absalom Jones and Richard Allen published *A Narrative of the Proceedings of the Black People, During the Late Awful Calamity in Philadelphia, in the Year 1793: And a Refutation of Some Censures Thrown Upon Them in Some Late Publications*, a direct response to the aspersions cast by Mathew Carey on the work of African-American nurses during the yellow fever epidemic. Beyond their defense of the nurses' efforts, Jones and Allen argued for African-American rights and freedom, demonstrating that blacks could and should assume the agency to define their own concerns and to assert their identity.[15]

In these late-eighteenth-century pamphlets, Newman, Rael, and Lapsansky argue, "black activists self-consciously dedicated themselves to creating a literary voice which could reach beyond any local African-American community." The activities of mutual aid organizations, Masonic lodges, and religious denominations also helped foster connections among African Americans in different cities in the last decades of the eighteenth century. Interest in emigration also linked African Americans with their counterparts throughout the North. In the late eighteenth century, organizations began to form in various cities to explore the possibility of emigration to Africa. As these groups corresponded with one another, discussions about African Americans' cultural identity and their future in America or elsewhere created bridges between local communities. Although specific plans never materialized from these deliberations, Peter Hinks notes that the discussion of potential emigration ventures brought various African-American leaders in different cities "into contact," in many cases "probably for the first time." Thus during the 1780s and 1790s, Elizabeth Rauh Bethel asserts, "an emerging translocal moral community" developed.[16]

African Americans could also look for inspiration to another region beyond America's borders at the end of the eighteenth century. The successful slave rebellion in Saint Domingue beginning in 1791—which would eventually lead to the abolition of slavery there in 1794 and the creation of the independent black republic of Haiti in 1804—resonated deeply with Americans in the last decade of the eighteenth century. For whites, the revolution was cause for anxiety and concern. White Saint Dominguans who immigrated to cities such as New York and Philadelphia brought with them anti-black attitudes and stories of rebellion that stirred white Americans' fears and fostered hostility toward abolition and black civil rights. For African Americans, the revolution was a source of pride, an example of the potential of blacks to assert their freedom, and a representation of black nationalism that contributed to a growing militancy. In a Masonic sermon given in 1797 to the African lodge in Menotomy, Massachusetts, Prince Hall drew on events in Saint Domingue for inspiration and hope:

My brethren, let us not be cast down . . . let us remember what a dark day it was with our African brethren six years ago, in the French West-Indies. . . . [A]ll manner of tortures [were] inflicted on those unhappy people for nothing else but to gratify their masters [*sic*] pride, wantonness, and cruelty: but blessed be God, the scene is now changed; they now confess that God hath no respect of persons. . . . Thus does Ethiopia begin to stretch forth her hand, from a sink of slavery to freedom and equality.[17]

Such a powerful symbol of the potential of struggle to bring freedom helped shape the consciousness of a generation of African Americans as the nineteenth century dawned.

GROWTH OF A NATIONAL CONSCIOUSNESS: 1800–1820

The first two decades of the nineteenth century brought new obstacles for African Americans.[18] The status of free African Americans in Northern cities in the early nineteenth century generally worsened. Living in often substandard conditions in increasingly segregated cities, they were frequently denied employment. White workers resented African Americans trained by educational efforts begun in the previous century, whom they perceived as competition for jobs. As African-American institutions established at the end of the eighteenth century solidified community consciousness and as more institutions were created—such as the New York African Society for Mutual Relief, founded in 1808; and the African Baptist Church of Boston, organized in 1806, which became a forum for protest and a station on the Underground Railroad—white hostilities increased. African Americans in Northern cities continued to face the persistent threats of kidnapping and violence perpetrated by white mobs. Notions of white supremacy and allegiances to slavery, both in the North and the South, were strong. The antislavery sentiment that had attracted some whites after the Revolution weakened, particularly by the second decade of the nineteenth century.

Various states considered and often enacted legislation which restricted African Americans' rights. Between 1805 and 1814, the Pennsylvania state legislature considered laws to restrict black immigration into the state, to require African Americans to carry certificates of freedom, to levy special taxes on them, and even to allow those who were not registered with the state or who were convicted of crimes to be jailed or sold. Although these campaigns were not successful, the level of support they received illustrates, as Gary Nash remarks, that "racial prejudice continued to congeal" in the early nineteenth century.[19] As legislation expanded the franchise for white males, African Americans' voting rights were restricted. In New York in 1811, a law was passed requiring that African Americans who wished to vote present a certificate proving their freedom. Because this certificate had to be obtained through a judge of the Supreme Court or a county court or from the mayor or recorder of a city, potential African-American voters had to pay for the services of a lawyer—an obstacle that disenfranchised many. New Jersey restricted the franchise to free white men in 1807, as did Connecticut in an 1814 law that became part of the state constitution in 1818.

Despite this widespread oppression, significant events in the early nineteenth century furthered the development of the "translocal" connections among African-American communities in different cities that arose at the end of the previous century. Two events in particular held promise for African Americans—the creation of the independent state of Haiti in 1804 and the abolition of the international slave trade to the United States in 1808. The former, as Mitch Kachun asserts, had a "profound meaning for antebellum African Americans" as an "example of black self-liberation and independence."[20] The latter brought anticipation of the end of slavery within the United States, and African Americans commemorated it throughout the early nineteenth century. Public celebrations were important for all Americans at this time, but for African Americans they were particularly political events, furthering their sense of community; functioning as opportunities for protest; honoring their African heritage; and facilitating the expression of their rights and ideals, particularly their opposition to slavery. Through the themes and imagery featured in orations at celebrations commemorating the 1808 slave trade abolition, they addressed issues that connected them to free African Americans in other cities as well as to those who were still enslaved. Print culture enhanced and complemented these oral arguments, as Newman, Rael, and Lapsansky maintain; as orators published speeches and sermons as pamphlets, often with the support of community organizations, "print carried black voices through space . . . so that a broader national community of black leaders and white citizens could see African-American arguments."[21]

The rhetoric of the period demonstrates how these events helped African Americans assert their political position, their desire for self-determination, and their focus on national concerns. Speaking in 1808 at a commemoration of the abolition of the international slave trade at the New York African Church, the Reverend Peter Williams Jr. vividly described the destruction of Africa brought on by the traffic in human beings. Significantly, Williams compared the assertion of the "inherent rights of man" affirmed by the outlawing of the slave trade to the declaration of freedom of America's Founding Fathers. Williams's speech demonstrates the powerful emerging identity of early-nineteenth-century African Americans, which William Gravely describes as a "dialectic" seeking to honor their ties to Africa while proclaiming their right to be given full equality and freedom as Americans. In an 1809 sermon giving thanks for the abolition of the international slave trade in Philadelphia's St. Thomas's African Episcopal Church, Absalom Jones harshly chastised those who owned slaves and proposed that one of the duties incumbent upon African Americans was to implore God "to dispose the hearts of our legislatures to pass laws" that would help end slavery in the United States. In an 1818 speech at the founding of Philadelphia's Augustine Society, an organization devoted to mutual aid and education, Prince Saunders referred to Haiti as one of many examples of the power of "the blessings of instruction." When African Americans assert their right to strive for knowledge, Saunders suggested, it can be a militant act.[22]

National consciousness among African Americans gained strength in the second decade of the nineteenth century as they responded to the idea of African colonization. As at the end of the previous century, some African Americans continued to be interested in emigration to Africa. The plans of Paul Cuffe in particular, Floyd Miller indicates, "helped stimulate a new awareness of Africa among both blacks and whites."[23] A ship captain, Cuffe was interested in emigration to expand his commercial interests, to bring Christianity to Africa, and to further the cause of black independence. African Institutions, organizations to support emigration, were created in various cities, and in 1815 Cuffe set sail for Sierra Leone with thirty-eight emigrants.

Cuffe's efforts inspired many white Americans to look to colonization in Africa—but often for reasons that differed from those of African-American emigrationists. The ACS, founded in 1816, represented for many white Americans a "solution" to racial problems in the United States. Proposing that free African Americans should be encouraged to remove themselves to a colony in Africa, the ACS campaigned for government support for this venture. The membership of the organization was heterogeneous, bringing together antislavery whites who were uncomfortable with the presence of free African Americans; missionaries who wanted to "civilize" and bring Christianity to Africa; those who believed colonization would help end the slave trade and encourage manumissions among American masters; and slaveholders and their supporters.

Although some African Americans supported the ACS, most found its agenda extremely problematic and opposed it strongly. Dominated by whites, the ACS did not represent a perspective on emigration that would appeal to African Americans' desire for self-determination and independence. Whereas "the early African-American proponents of colonization formed an identity that was self-assertive and non-ascriptive," Dickson Bruce explains, "a 'national identity' was not something to be imposed by others, and, when the Colonization Society sought to do just that, the appeal of the program ended."[24] In fact, the ACS incited not only opposition but often anger and hostility among African Americans. Most expressed a desire to stay in the United States, and many feared that participation in the ACS's plans would not be entirely voluntary.[25]

There was also great suspicion that the ACS actually intended to help strengthen slavery by removing "troublesome" free people of color who could help fight for freedom, a belief supported by the membership of many slaveholders in the ACS. As John Randolph noted in his comments to the 1816 founding meeting of the organization, colonization "must materially tend to secure the property of every master in the United States over his slaves." "The existence of this mixed and intermediate population of free negroes," Randolph asserted, "was viewed by every slave holder as one of the greatest sources of insecurity. . . . [T]hey excite in their fellow beings a feeling of discontent . . . and . . . they act as channels of communication not only between different slaves but between the slaves of different districts." In his speech to the same gathering, Kentucky politician and slaveholder Henry Clay remarked that he and other "gentlemen from the south and the west" had agreed to participate in the meeting only "upon th[e] condition" that those assembled would not "deliberate on, or consider at all, any question of emancipation, or that was connected with the abolition of slavery."[26]

Although not always as explicitly proslavery as Randolph's remarks, the racist rhetoric of the ACS offended African Americans and undermined their quest for freedom and rights in the United States. Speaking at the 1816 organizational meeting of the ACS, Elias Caldwell maintained that providing African Americans with education and rights was counterproductive:

> The more you endeavour to improve the condition of these people . . . the more miserable you make them in their present state. You give them a higher relish for those privileges which they can never attain. . . . No, if they must remain in their present situation, keep them in the lowest state of degradation and ignorance. The nearer you bring them to the condition of brutes, the better chance do you give them of possessing their apathy.

In an 1818 published letter to Caldwell, General Robert Goodloe Harper of Maryland declared that regardless of the "industry" and "conduct" of free African Americans, "they could never hope, to see the two races placed on a footing of perfect equality with each other." The result, he argued, is that free people of color must always be "an idle worthless and thievish race," a "nuisance and burden" who "contribute greatly to the corruption of the slaves" and inevitably "sink for the most part into a state of sloth wretchedness and profligacy."[27]

In response to the ACS and its rhetoric, African Americans gathered in protest in various cities. These events were African Americans' "first widespread use of mass meetings," Lerone Bennett asserts, beginning as early as 1817 in cities such as Richmond, New York, and Philadelphia. The January 1817 meeting in Philadelphia, which attracted a crowd of three thousand, "assumed the proportions of a national protest demonstration," Ottley and Weatherby indicate. Demonstrators in other cities similarly expressed their opposition to the ACS and its plans. An August 1817 anticolonization meeting in Philadelphia adopted an address to white Philadelphians written by James Forten, who presided over the gathering, and Russell Parrott, its secretary. Forten and Parrott maintained that colonization would separate free African Americans from their slave brethren, lead to "assured perpetual slavery and augmented sufferings" of those still in bondage, and send colonists to an arduous situation for which they were "unprepared."[28] The demonstrations against the ACS, which included oratory and resolutions, enabled the already "translocal" African-American community to develop national connections. As Hinks explains, a "grid of communication among blacks" in different parts of the country had grown as a result of links between benevolent societies and within religious denominations, and reaction to the ACS "began to weave these strands into an organized network."[29] Declaring themselves unwilling to leave their enslaved brethren and asserting their rights as Americans, African Americans continued their militant stand in pursuit of freedom.

Although there was great opposition to the ACS's agenda, not all African Americans gave up the notion of emigration. By 1818, leaders who had supported Cuffe were discussing the option of emigration to Haiti. In contrast to the ACS's plans, John Saillant explains, "emigration to Haiti was a free choice, orchestrated by American and Haitian blacks."[30] Interest in Haitian emigration was also strengthened by African-American pride in the Haitian Revolution and the creation of an independent black nation. In the next decade, this nascent support for Haitian emigration would take concrete shape.

SELF-DETERMINATION, RESISTANCE, AND THE POWER OF WRITING: THE 1820S

The trends that characterized the first two decades of the nineteenth century—community organization, an incipient militancy, and increasing oppression—came to a head during its turbulent third decade.[31] African Americans further developed a community infrastructure that allowed them to determine their own agendas, debate important issues, create strong rhetoric, and develop unique forms of cultural expression. As Shane White maintains, "in the first third of the nineteenth century,

New York (and, to a lesser extent, Philadelphia) became innovative and creative African American cultural centers, witnessing, in particular, a veritable explosion of black music and dance." In both New York and Philadelphia in the 1820s, James and Lois Horton demonstrate, "a uniquely American musical art form" arose that combined "European and African styles."[32] Also during the 1820s, New York's African Theatre presented performances, including Shakespearean plays, ballets, and operas, which were attended by both African Americans and whites.

Despite their continuing general opposition to the ACS, African Americans also continued to discuss the possibility of emigration. The budding Haitian emigration movement of the previous decade gained strength in the mid-1820s. As we have seen, the Haitian Revolution helped shape the consciousness of those African Americans who came of age in the 1820s. Unrealized hopes for equality in the United States spurred interest in making a home in Haiti. African Americans in various cities formed organizations such as the Haytien Emigration Society of Philadelphia, established in 1824, among whose leaders were Richard Allen and James Forten. They were encouraged by the president of Haiti, Jean-Pièrre Boyer, who sent Jonathan Granville to the United States in 1824 as an agent of Haiti to motivate potential emigrants. Thousands of African Americans emigrated that year.[33] However, many were not satisfied with their new homeland, and about a third returned, disillusioned, by 1826. The negative experiences of many emigrants reinforced opposition to African colonization and the ACS among free African Americans.

As most African Americans committed themselves to creating vital communities within the United States rather than emigrating, they further developed the network of institutions built over previous generations. They strengthened already established African-American churches and mutual aid societies and created new organizations. In particular, African Americans in many cities founded literary societies, libraries, and reading rooms. African Americans realized, Elizabeth McHenry argues, that "text, identity, and public access" were "linked," and by the 1820s they perceived "reading and writing as a means of forming durable communities and asserting their right to American citizenship" and to recognition "in the national public sphere."[34] In literary societies, African Americans learned formal rhetorical principles and were given the opportunity to reshape traditional rhetorical strategies in ways that empowered them. Those who could not read could have texts read to them by other literary society members, giving them access to ideas and arguments. Because literacy was linked to freedom for African Americans, a weapon against white domination that allowed them to develop strategies of resistance, the act of joining together to read, write, and help others become literate was a way of fighting oppression.[35]

As members spoke on and debated issues of importance in literary gatherings, antislavery activism was nurtured. Other organizations were founded whose agendas demonstrated the increasingly radical spirit of the 1820s, particularly on the subject of abolition. As we have seen, African Americans were protesting and organizing against slavery prior to the 1820s as well as assisting and sheltering fugitives. This activism continued and gained strength. African Americans created organizations such as the Massachusetts General Colored Association (MGCA), founded in 1826, which adopted antislavery as one of its goals.

By the late 1820s, African-American antislavery rhetoric was forceful and often militant.[36] Speaking to the MGCA in 1828, the abolitionist David Walker asserted that "inactivity" in the face of oppression was unacceptable, and called on African Americans "to try every scheme that [they] think will have a tendency to facilitate [their] salvation." Explicitly arguing for the abolition of slavery, he remarked, "Will anyone be so hardy as to say, or even to imagine, that we are incapable of effecting any object which may have a tendency to hasten our emancipation?" Walker's dynamic and controversial 1829 *Appeal to the Coloured Citizens of the World* vehemently condemned slavery and colonization. Using harsh jeremiadic language, Walker exhorted white Americans to end slavery or to endure God's harsh punishment for their oppression of African Americans. Walker asserted that violent antislavery action by African Americans was justified and perhaps necessary, insisting, "It is not to be understood . . . that I mean for us to wait until God shall take us . . . and drag us out of abject wretchedness and slavery." He underscored his call for resistance with a bold challenge: "The man who would not fight under our Lord and Master Jesus Christ, in the glorious and heavenly cause of freedom and of God . . . ought to be kept with all of his children or family, in slavery, or in chains, to be butchered by his *cruel enemies*."[37]

Although Walker's *Appeal* was one of the most well publicized and controversial texts of the era, it should not be seen as atypical of its time. By the late 1820s, other black leaders were strongly condemning slavery and calling upon African Americans to take action against it. Nor should the rhetoric of the period be perceived as an abrupt change from that of earlier eras. As we have seen, African Americans had been arguing against slavery since the late eighteenth century. Walker and his contemporaries built upon the work of previous generations, drawing upon and intensifying resonant themes such as the eventual judgment of God and America's unfulfilled promise of liberty.[38] In an 1828 address to the Colored Reading Society of Philadelphia, a literary organization, William Whipper asked, "Where is the slaveholder who professes to love his God that has not a lie in his mouth when he says that he does unto others as he would that they should do unto him. . . . Yes, and I am sorry to say that the seat of our government contains a majority of these misanthropists." Whipper denounced the hypocrisy of Americans who celebrated the moment "when their fathers declared themselves free from British tyranny," but countenanced the "barbarity and injustice of slavery." Whipper also called upon free African Americans to agitate against slavery, condemning those who were "satisfied with their situation, and [would] not meddle with the cause."[39]

African Americans also argued strongly against colonization, often challenging white supporters of the ACS directly. In his *Appeal*, Walker castigated Henry Clay and Elias Caldwell for their support for colonization. Colonizationist arguments merely served slaveholders' interests, Walker asserted, suggesting that Clay and his ilk deserved God's punishment "for advocating the murderous cause of slavery." "America is more our country than it is the whites," he declared, "we have enriched it with our *blood and tears*." Writing in 1828 to Benjamin Lundy, the editor of the antislavery newspaper the *Genius of Universal Emancipation* (and a supporter of gradual abolition and colonization), William Watkins asked why the members of the ACS "take upon themselves to represent, prejudicially the interests of thousands who had never delegated them any such power." "If they are so misguided as to believe that we are anxious to remove from this highly favoured land, to the sun-burnt shores of Africa," Watkins remarked, "let them call public meetings of our people and find out their true sentiments relative to colonization in Africa. They will then learn, that we deprecate, as a great evil, those [procolonization] orations, and collections [for the ACS]."[40]

Yet African Americans' efforts to strengthen their community organizations and resist oppression were met by increased hostility and violence from whites. American racial attitudes assumed a hard edge, and racism became more blatant. The Missouri Compromise extended the reach of slavery, and theories based on the presumed innate inferiority of those of African descent were developed to justify the institution. A Scottish traveler in New York in 1822 described in his diary the daily treatment of African Americans, whom whites considered "inferior creature[s]." They were shunned by whites who believed it "disgraceful" to "associate with them in any form," forced to sit in church in "back benches in the gallery and not allowed to come near a white mans [*sic*] person," and called "niggar" by "young and old." "If a teacher should take a black pupil into his school," the diarist recorded, "the whole of the whites would in a moment leave it."[41]

Throughout the North, African Americans faced increasing legal restrictions, institutional oppression, and violence. Reforms aimed at empowering the "common (white) man" politically were accompanied by increasing limitations on African Americans' political participation. Voting rights were further curtailed in Northern states in which African Americans were not already completely disenfranchised. In Rhode Island, African Americans were disenfranchised in 1822. New York's new state constitution of 1821 eliminated property qualifications for white voters while maintaining for black voters the requirement that they possess property worth more than 250 dollars. When the few suffrage restrictions remaining for whites were eliminated in 1826, the New York Democratic-controlled state legislature voted to keep property qualifications for African Americans. Blacks continued to face harassment and limits on their employment, particularly as an influx of poor white immigrants in Northern cities in the 1820s led to competition for jobs.

Racial tension and animosity against African Americans often led to violence. Horton and Horton maintain, "Harassment and mob violence against African Americans became more blatantly racially motivated in the East and the Midwest throughout the 1820s and into the 1830s." In 1825, for example, a violent Boston mob wearing blackface invaded the North End, an African-American section of town. Mobs did not restrict themselves to "disreputable" targets such as brothels and gambling houses. They also disrupted productions at the African Theatre and attacked African-American churches, small businesses, community institutions, and celebrations. The police closed performances at the African Theatre, often throwing actors in jail, and routinely swept through black neighborhoods, citing people for any number of offenses. African Americans were frequently arrested and imprisoned for different criminal activities than were whites. "Police forces," Leonard Curry explains, "found minor infractions by persons of color, or sometimes, their mere presence in the vicinity of a disturbance, cause for arrest. And juries, from which blacks were rigorously excluded, considered the arrest of Negroes to be, at the very least, prima facie evidence of guilt."[42]

In this context of widespread racism and hostility, it is not surprising that white Americans of the 1820s were generally opposed to the abolition of slavery. Antislavery sentiment among white Americans had declined by the 1820s; and those whites who continued to hold antislavery views tended, as had their predecessors, to be reluctant to offend Southerners and to favor gradual rather than immediate abolition. We hear this hesitant tone in an 1823 letter from Edwin Atlee, Chairman of the Acting Committee of the American Convention for Promoting the Abolition of Slavery, an interstate organization of white philanthropists, to "benevolent individuals in those States where slaves are held in hereditary bondage." Atlee asserted, "We disclaim, on the part of the Convention, any intention of meddling improperly with the policy of those states, or what may be deemed the rights of individual slave holders . . . yet we believe we are acting the part of sincere friends, both to their temporal and eternal interests, in calling upon them to reflect on their conduct as men and as christians. . . ."[43]

In addition, many white individuals and organizations who opposed slavery supported colonization. The ACS gained strength and became more aggressive during the decade, garnering support from political figures and Southern legislatures. Funds were solicited for the cause, and the ACS often appropriated the Fourth of July as an occasion to promote its agenda. The blatant rhetoric of ACS members and supporters played on white Americans' fears and prejudices. Speaking at an 1824 meeting in New Jersey to form a state colonization society, James M. Green described free African Americans as "a mass of ignorance, misery, and depravity," a "dangerous foe." Even if they were given rights, they could never be the equals of whites in America, Green asserted, since "with a few honourable exceptions, they degenerate in proportion as they are indulged." In an 1825 sermon, New York pastor William McMurray claimed free African Americans were "low and immoral" because they were "doomed, by the indelible mark which the hand of God has placed upon them, to be contemned and despised." The existence of free African Americans in the United States was an "evil," Henry Clay maintained in an 1827 speech to the ACS. "Contaminated themselves," he asserted, "they extend their vices to all around them, to the slaves and the whites. . . . A common evil confers a right to consider and apply a common remedy."[44] Such portrayals inevitably discouraged efforts to improve education or to secure civil rights for African Americans.

Nor were supporters of colonization alone in denigrating African Americans. In the late 1820s, African Americans were mocked, denounced, and ridiculed in white theatricals, broadsides, and newspapers. White actors in blackface parodied African Americans on the stage and in street performances.[45] The vicious caricatures in broadsides and cartoons created since the Revolution became more elaborate. Beginning around 1815 or 1816, broadsides ridiculing African-American freedom celebrations were produced in Boston, constituting what Phillip Lapsansky describes as perhaps "the earliest consistent pattern of American racist caricature." An "enormous volume of such material" followed these early productions, Lapsansky demonstrates, such as the "satirical etchings denigrating blacks" created by Philadelphia artists.[46] One of these caricaturists, Edward Clay, produced the series of etchings *Life in Philadelphia* in 1828. These extremely popular cartoons, which portrayed well-off African Americans as buffoons, mocking their speech and dress, spawned a *Life in New York* series with an analogous focus. Clay's focus on upper-class rather than on working-class African Americans is significant, Emma Jones Lapsansky notes, fitting a pattern of white resentment and hostility toward those who they felt were "stepping out of their 'places.'" Yet it was not just those who had achieved some success who were objects of derision. When African Americans appeared before magistrates, Curry describes, "court reporters made them figures of fun—exaggerating (or fabricating) their mannerisms, dialect, and ignorance of legal forms."[47]

The publications of Mordecai Manuel Noah, a playwright, essayist, politician, and editor of various New York newspapers including the *New-York Enquirer* and the *New-York National Advocate*, were notorious examples of the treatment of African Americans in the white press. In an 1821 editorial, "Africans," Noah took a decidedly Jeffersonian view of race, questioning African Americans' intelligence and exaggerating physical features. Reviewing the 1821 production of *Richard III* at the African Theatre in the *National Advocate*, Noah mocked and parodied the performance. Noah opposed slavery in his early years, yet he became much more tolerant of the institution after the Missouri Compromise, aligning himself with the views of Southerners. Writing in 1826, Noah remarked that Southerners "held and now hold slaves; it is an evil entailed upon them, from which there is no escape and no remedy; their slaves are constitutionally recognized and guaranteed to them." "The people of the south have been designedly abused and misrepresented," Noah argued in an 1827 editorial, "in relation to their treatment of slaves."[48]

More blatantly, Noah's rhetoric demonstrated his extreme antipathy toward free African Americans. Mocking the "high life" of free black New Yorkers, Noah made them the objects of scorn and ridicule. In his 1825 "High Life Below Stairs," Noah remarked, "The fashion of servants aping their masters and mistresses is becoming very prevalent. . . . They make great personal sacrifices to purchase a hat and feathers, and other becoming ornaments. The coloured folks are dipping deep in these bon ton touches." He described a boisterous party attended by "several strapping black gentlemen and ladies," who, upon being startled by a white neighbor, took him "instantly for a ghost, and the guests set up a scream so loud and shrill, as to awaken the [police] watch." His "High Life Among the Coloured Folks," also published in 1825, similarly depicted a social gathering broken up by the police, parodying the speech of the party "manager" to the magistrate: "He desired to know 'for what dey disturb peaceable black people cause dey had a party—dey hab rights—dey pay dare money and dey behave as vell as the vite gentlemen vat go to de City Hall—and dey hand de vine and cake about on a vaiter like dem vite folks at de Washington Hall and de Greek Ball.'" In his editorials and in articles reprinted from other papers, Noah endorsed the requirement that African Americans carry free papers, denigrated the Manumission Society for its aid to fugitive slaves, and condemned those who tried to prevent the kidnappings of blacks for their "interference" with laws designed to protect "property."[49]

Because he was both a prolific and influential editor, Noah's writings were particularly detrimental to African Americans. In addition, Noah was a prominent New York Democratic politician who played a role in garnering support for the 1821 suffrage restrictions on African Americans. Yet Noah's racism was not unusual. White newspaper coverage of African Americans in the 1820s often mocked them, placed excessive emphasis on criminal acts, or focused on reports of illicit activity.[50] Correspondent H. to the New York *Statesman*, which printed both proslavery and antislavery articles, decried in an 1826 piece the "extravagant and often useless commiseration" given to slaves, whose condition "is their own misfortune, which we cannot relieve, any more than we can change the condition of children born with any other defects or liabilities." An untitled 1827 article originally published in Philadelphia's *National Gazette and Literary Register* and reprinted in the *New-York American* argued that the fact that the mortality rate is higher among free African Americans in New York and Philadelphia than among slaves in Baltimore is due to "the care bestowed on the slaves, and shows the effects of temperate habits, contrasted with the idleness, intemperance, and improvidence which characterise the free blacks."[51] Other whites derided and parodied African-American speech and social life in print. An article originally published in the *Boston Daily Advertiser* and reprinted in the *New-York Evening Post* reported on the toasts ostensibly offered by African Americans celebrating the abolition of slavery in Massachusetts. The article's vulgar parodies included toasts to *"De Presidum ob de Day"* ("May his health be preserve, and may he lib longer dan Gen. Washington, Goberner Strong, and all de other heroes of antiquity") as well as to the *"Missouri Question"* ("If you ax me, I say no question at all").[52]

It was in this atmosphere of the 1820s that African-American leaders saw both a need and an opportunity to create a forum directed and controlled by African Americans that would air their views. *Freedom's Journal*, as we shall see, was not simply a reaction to the oppression of the time; it was also an outgrowth of the community building that had developed since the Revolution and that coalesced in the 1820s. A newspaper would allow African Americans to respond to attacks by whites, but it would do much more. It would enable them to connect with those in other cities, to debate important issues, to determine their own agendas, and to further communal goals. In the columns of *Freedom's Journal*, African Americans could plead their own cause.

NOTES

1. Samuel E. Cornish and John B. Russwurm, "To Our Patrons," *FJ*, 16 March 1827; Samuel E. Cornish and John B. Russwurm, "Prospectus," *FJ*, 16 March 1827. The "Prospectus" was also published in other issues.

2. Harding, *Other American Revolution*, 30; Cornish and Russwurm, "Prospectus."

3. My overview in this section is informed by the following studies and sources: Wilson, *Freedom at Risk*; Wilson, "Active Vigilance"; Ottley and Weatherby, *Negro in New York*; Thomas Morris, *Free Men All*; Needles, *Historical Memoir*; Alice Dana Adams, *Neglected Period*; Foner, *History . . . Cotton Kingdom*; Rowe, "Black Offenders"; Horton and Horton, *In Hope*; Payne, "Negro"; Nash, *Race and Revolution*; Wright, *African Americans*; Horton and Horton, *Black Bostonians*; Curry, *Free Black*; Nash, *Forging Freedom*; Phillip Lapsansky, "Abigail"; Bacon, "Rhetoric and Identity"; Swan, "John Teasman"; Zilversmit, *First Emancipation*; Wesley, "Negro's Struggle"; Wesley, "Concept"; Lincoln and Mamiya, *Black Church*; Hunt, *Haiti's Influence*; Lerone Bennett, *Confrontation*; Bethel, *Roots*; Bethel, "Images of Hayti"; Vincent Thompson, "Leadership"; Woodson, *Education*; Andrews, "African Methodists"; Lindsay, "Economic Condition"; Hirsch, "Negro"; Gilje, *Road*; Shane White, *Somewhat More Independent*; Shane White, "Impious Prayers;" Mabee, *Black Education*; McManus, *History*; Horton, *Free People*; Lerone Bennett, *Shaping*; Harding, *Other American Revolution*; Levesque, "Inherent Reformers"; Michael Levine, *African Americans*; Arthur O. White, "Black Leadership"; Hinks, *To Awaken*; Winch, *Philadelphia's Black Elite*; David Brion Davis, "Emergence"; Reed, *Platform*; Bruce, "National Identity"; Berry and Blassingame, *Long Memory*; Horton and Horton, *Hard Road*; Hodges, *Root & Branch*; Shade, "Though We Are Not Slaves"; Melish, *Disowning Slavery*; Melish, "Condition"; Rury, "Philanthropy"; *Proceedings of the Free African Society*; Egerton, *He Shall Go Out Free*, 43–46; Newman, *Transformation*; John Wood Sweet, *Bodies Politic*; Newman, "Protest," 182–90; Rael, "Long Death"; Bay, "See Your Declaration"; Forbes, "Truth Systematised"; Newman, "Chosen Generation."

4. Jefferson, *Notes*, 137–43.

5. Melish, *Disowning Slavery*, 91.

6. These societies are generally known by these abbreviated titles; their full names are, respectively, the Pennsylvania Society, for Promoting the Abolition of Slavery, for the Relief of Free Negroes Unlawfully Held in Bondage, and for Improving the Condition of the African Race; and the New York Society for Promoting the Manumission of Slaves, and Protecting Such of Them as Have Been, or May Be Liberated. The former, when organized, was known simply as the Society for the Relief of the Free Negroes, Unlawfully Held in Bondage, a name which describes its agenda at the time. It reconvened in 1784 after a nine-year lapse, and was reorganized in 1787 with the abolition of slavery as part of its name and one of its goals. See Needles, *Historical Memoir*, 14–15; Nash, *Forging Freedom*, 43, 91, 100–104.

7. On the "inconsistency on racial issues" that characterized antislavery organizations of the late eighteenth century, see also Harrold, *Subversives*, 17.

8. Horton and Horton, *In Hope*, 56; Foner, *History . . . Cotton Kingdom*, 366, 574; Zilversmit, *First Emancipation*, 166.

9. Jefferson, *Notes*, 137–38.

10. New York Society for Promoting the Manumission of Slaves, "Report from the New York Society for Promoting the Manumission of Slaves &c. made to the Convention of Delegates, from the Abolition Societies, to be held at Philadelphia, the third of May, 1797," Pennsylvania Abolition Society Papers, Box 8A; Carey, *Short Account*, 34–35, 78–79.

11. Melish, *Disowning Slavery*, 165–71; see also Phillip Lapsansky, "Graphic Discord," 216; Shane White, *Stories*, 56.

12. Tate, "Free Black," 771; see also Lammers, "Rev. Absalom Jones," 162.

13. Reed, *Platform*, 11–12. Documentary evidence suggests that while individual African Americans petitioned for freedom prior to the American Revolution, collective petitioning arose in the 1770s (Aptheker, *Documentary History*, 5–12).

14. Petition of Connecticut African Americans to General Assembly of State of Connecticut (1779), in Aptheker, *Documentary History*, vol. 1, 11; Petition of Dartmouth African Americans to Massachusetts legislature (1780), in Aptheker, *Documentary History*, vol. 1, 15. For an analysis of the rhetoric of early African-American petitions, see Bacon and McClish, "Descendents," 3–14.

15. Othello, "Essay on Negro Slavery," *American Museum* 4 (1788), 412–15, 509–12, reprint in Ducas and Van Doren, *Great Documents*, 30–38; Newman, Rael, and Lapsansky, "Introduction," 2–3; Jones and Allen, *Narrative*. For further analysis of Jones and Allen's *Narrative* and its importance as protest rhetoric, see Phillip Lapsansky, "Abigail"; Bacon, "Rhetoric and Identity"; Bruce, *Origins*, 85–86; Newman, "Chosen Generation," 59–60; Brooks, *American Lazarus*, 166–74.

16. Newman, Rael, and Lapsansky, "Introduction," 4; Hinks, *To Awaken*, 96; Bethel, *Roots*, 76. On the development in the late eighteenth century of connections between African Americans in different cities, see also McHenry, *Forgotten Readers*, 38, 45.

17. Prince Hall, "Pray God Give Us the Strength to Bear Up Under All Our Troubles," in Foner, *Lift Every Voice*, 49.

18. I draw in this section from Wesley, "Negro Suffrage"; Gravely, "Dialectic"; Ripley et al., *Black Abolitionist Papers*, 3–7; Hinks, *To Awaken*; Mehlinger, "Attitude"; Bruce, "National Identity"; Lerone Bennett, *Confrontation*; Bethel, *Roots*; Quarles, "Antebellum Free Blacks"; Quarles, *Black Abolitionists*; Vincent Thompson, "Leadership"; Bethel, "Images of Hayti"; Swift, "Black Presbyterian"; Swift, *Black Prophets*; Floyd Miller, *Search*; Freeman, "Free Negro"; Ottley and Weatherby, *Negro in New York*; Hirsch, "Negro and New York"; Gilje, *Road to Mobocracy*; Bloch, *Circle of Discrimination*; Meier and Rudwick, *From Plantation to Ghetto*; Shane White, "Death"; Condit and Lucaites, *Crafting Equality*; Nash, *Race and Revolution*; Leonard Sweet, *Black Images*; Wright, *African Americans*; Horton and Horton, *Black Bostonians*; Foner, *History . . . 1850*; Horton and Horton, *In Hope*; Franklin and Moss, *From Slavery to Freedom*; James Truslow Adams, "Disfranchisement"; Curry, *Free Black*; Michael Levine, *African Americans*; Tise, *Proslavery*; Nash, *Forging Freedom*; Winch, *Philadelphia's Black Elite*; McGraw, "Richmond"; Rosen, "Abolition"; Friedman, "Purifying"; Kinshasa, *Emigration*; George, *Segregated Sabbaths*; Jordan, *White Over Black*; Hutton, "Economic Considerations"; Kachun, *Festivals*, 25–41; Shane White, *Stories*; Williams-Myers, "Some Notes"; Bay, "See Your Declaration."

19. Nash, *Forging Freedom*, 181.

20. Kachun, "Antebellum African Americans," 252. Kachun argues that although the Haitian Revolution held great significance for African Americans, the evidence does not support the common assumption that it was regularly commemorated publicly. He speculates that African Americans realized the risks of "publicly identifying with the bloody slave rebellion and revolution" and thus

"consciously avoided connecting their public demonstrations to the Haitian Revolution" (250).

21. Newman, Rael, and Lapsansky, "Introduction," 3–4; see also Newman, *Transformation*, 90–96. For an analysis of the rhetoric of orations at celebrations commemorating the 1808 slave trade abolition, see Bacon and McClish, "Descendents," 15–25.

22. Peter Williams Jr., "Abolition of the Slave Trade," in Foner, *Lift Every Voice*, 67–71; Gravely, "Dialectic," 302, 307–8; Absalom Jones, "A Thanksgiving Sermon," in Foner, *Lift Every Voice*, 77–78; Prince Saunders, *An Address, Delivered at Bethel Church, Philadelphia; on the 30th of September, 1818. Before the Pennsylvania Augustine Society, for the Education of People of Colour*, in Porter, *Early Negro Writing*, 87–95.

23. Floyd Miller, *Search*, 21; see also Bruce, *Origins*, 129–34.

24. Bruce, "National Identity," 28.

25. This concern seems to have had some validity. Penelope Campbell describes an 1835 incident in which a group of freed Maryland slaves was threatened with transportation to Pennsylvania, "where, in all probability, they would either starve, be sent to the penitentiary, or be hanged," if they did not emigrate to Africa (*Maryland*, 104–5).

26. Randolph's and Clay's comments in American Colonization Society, *View*, 9.

27. Caldwell's comments in American Colonization Society, *View*, 5, 7; Harper, *Letter*, 7, 9–10, 17.

28. Lerone Bennett, *Confrontation*, 47; Ottley and Weatherby, *Negro in New York*, 69; James Forten and Russell Parrott, *Address*, ii–iii. Forten's views on colonization were complex, evolving from early interest to later rejection; see Foner, *History . . . Cotton Kingdom*, 589–92; Sterling, *Speak Out*, 24–27; Horton and Horton, *In Hope*, 188; Nash, *Forging Freedom*, 184–85, 235–37; Winch, *Philadelphia's Black Elite*, 35–38; Winch, *Gentleman of Color*, 178–206; Bay, "See Your Declaration," 38–39; James Forten to Paul Cuffe, Philadelphia, 25 January 1817, in Moses, *Classical Black Nationalism*, 50–52.

29. Hinks, *To Awaken*, 98; see also Bay, "See Your Declaration," 35–37; Condit and Lucaites, *Crafting Equality*, 77.

30. Saillant, "Circular," 486.

31. My discussion in this section is informed by Foner, *History . . . Cotton Kingdom*; Foner, *History . . . 1850*; Porter, "Organized"; David Brion Davis, "Emergence"; Shane White, "Death"; Shane White, *Somewhat More Independent*; Shane White, *Stories*; Charles Foster, "Colonization"; Alice Dana Adams, *Neglected Period*; Samuel Hay, *African American Theatre*, 5–11; Dewberry, "African Grove"; Marshall and Stock, *Ira Aldridge*, 28–36; Hodges, *Root & Branch*; Dodson et al., *Black New Yorkers*; George Thompson, *Documentary History*; McAllister, *White People*; Bacon and McClish, "Reinventing"; Cottrol, *Afro-Yankees*; Dick, *Black Protest*; Rammelkamp, "Providence"; Bethel, *Roots*; Wilson, *Freedom at Risk*; Emma Jones Lapsansky, "Since They Got"; Emma Jones Lapsansky, *Neighborhoods*; Nash, "Reverberations of Haiti"; Nash, *Forging Freedom*; Lincoln and Mamiya, *Black Church*; George E. Walker, "Afro-American"; Freeman, "Free Negro"; Ottley and Weatherby, *Negro in New York*; Hirsch, "Negro and New York"; Gilje, *Road to Mobocracy*; Bloch, *Circle of Discrimination*; Sorin, *New York Abolitionists*; Wright, *African Americans*; Lerone Bennett, *Shaping*; Levesque, "Inherent Reformers"; Levesque, "Black

Abolitionists"; Horton and Horton, *In Hope*; Leonard Sweet, "Fourth of July"; James Truslow Adams, "Disfranchisement"; Curry, *Free Black*; Aptheker, *"One Continual Cry"*; Hinks, *To Awaken*; McHenry, "Dreaded Eloquence"; McHenry, *Forgotten Readers*; Takaki, "Black Child-Savage"; Stewart, "Emergence"; Tise, *Proslavery*; Wilentz, introduction to *David Walker's Appeal*; Pride and Wilson, *History*; Winch, *Philadelphia's Black Elite*; Floyd Miller, *Search*; Staudenraus, *African Colonization*; Friedman, "Purifying"; Dick, "Negro Oratory"; George, *Segregated Sabbaths*; Reed, *Platform for Change*; Boylan, "Benevolence"; Logan, "Literacy"; Shade, "Though We Are Not Slaves"; Melish, *Disowning Slavery*; Newman, *Transformation*, 11–13; Hill and Hatch, *History*, 24–36.

32. Shane White, "Death," 764; Horton and Horton, *In Hope*, 161–62.

33. Although the official number of settlers sponsored by the Haitian government was 6,000, the number of emigrants was probably higher. Some estimates propose that as many as 13,000 emigrated by the end of the 1820s (Horton and Horton, *In Hope*, 194; Floyd Miller, *Search*, 81; Bethel, *Roots*, 153).

34. McHenry, *Forgotten Readers*, 23–24; see also Peterson, "Black Life," 213; Vogel, *ReWriting White*, 16–17, 22.

35. For discussions of the education in African-American literary societies and of the connections between literacy and freedom, see Belt-Beyan, *Emergence*, 14, 115–23; Tony Martin, "Banneker Literary Institute"; Gates, *Figures in Black*, 11–13, 108; Cornelius, *"When I Can Read,"* 2–3, 17, 61; Bacon and McClish, "Reinventing"; Bacon, *Humblest*, 108; McHenry, "Forgotten Readers," 151; Warren, *Culture*, 121–27; Fox, "From Freedom," 52–57; Royster, *Traces*, 104–42; Williams, *Self-Taught*, 7–29.

36. The history of antislavery activism among African Americans challenges traditional views of the abolition movement, which have often suggested that radical abolitionism began in the 1830s under the leadership of William Lloyd Garrison and other white reformers. See Bacon, *Humblest*, 15–50; Franklin and Moss, *From Slavery*, 199–200; Quarles, *Black Abolitionists*; Levesque, "Black Abolitionists"; Michael Bennett, *Democratic Discourses*, 2–3; Ripley et al., *Black Abolitionist Papers*, vol. 3, 3–9.

37. David Walker, "Address, Delivered Before the [Massachusetts] General Colored Association at Boston, by David Walker," *FJ*, 20 December 1828; *David Walker's Appeal*, 11–12.

38. For further discussion of the context for *Walker's Appeal* and other antislavery rhetoric of the late 1820s, see also Hinks, *To Awaken*, 108–9, 173–95; Dick, *Black Protest*, 3; Finseth, "David Walker."

39. William Whipper, *An Address Delivered in Wesley Church on the Evening of June 12, Before the Colored Reading Society of Philadelphia, for Moral Improvement*, in Porter, *Early Negro Writing*, 113–15.

40. *David Walker's Appeal*, 45–51, 65; A Colored Baltimorean [William Watkins], letter to editor, *Genius of Universal Emancipation*, 28 June 1828.

41. 6 March 1822 entry in BV Diary, 1821–1824.

42. Horton and Horton, *In Hope*, 164–65; Curry, *Free Black*, 114. See also Horton, "Urban Alliances," 31; Kachun, *Festivals*, 26–27.

43. Edwin Atlee to benevolent individuals in those States where slaves are held in hereditary bondage, Philadelphia, May 7, 1823, Pennsylvania Abolition Society Papers, box 9, folder 10.

44. *Proceedings of a Meeting Held at Princeton*, 15–17; McMurray, *Sermon*, 18; Clay, *Speech*, 6, 12.

45. Sandra Sandiford Young, "John Brown Russwurm's Dilemma," 102, 105; Toll, *Blacking Up*, 26–28; Lott, *Love and Theft*, 22, 40–62; Horton and Horton, *In Hope*, 159–60; McAllister, *White People*, 150–62; Winch, *Elite of Our People*, 36–38; Saxton, "Blackface Minstrelsy"; Malcomson, *One Drop of Blood*, 322–23; Cockrell, *Demons*, 30–33.

46. Phillip Lapsansky, "Graphic Discord," 216–20; see also Kachun, *Festivals*, 27; Emma Jones Lapsansky, *Neighborhoods*, 145–48; Winch, *Elite of Our People*, 36; Nash, *Forging Freedom*, 253–59; McAllister, *White People*, 151–58; John Wood Sweet, *Bodies Politic*, 378–90.

47. Emma Jones Lapsansky, "Since They Got," 61–67; Curry, *Free Black*, 93.

48. Mordecai Manuel Noah, "Africans," *National Advocate*, 3 August 1821; Manuel Mordecai Noah, review of performance of *Richard III*, *National Advocate*, 21 September 1821; Manuel Mordecai Noah, "Mr. Clay and the Sulpher Springs," *New-York Enquirer*, 19 September 1826; Manuel Mordecai Noah, "Slavery," *New-York Enquirer*, 24 April 1827. For biographical information on Noah, see Simonhoff, *Jewish Notables*, 207–10; Kleinfeld, "Manuel Mordecai Noah"; Sarna, *Jacksonian Jew*; Goldberg, *Major Noah*; Rael, "Long Death," 141.

49. Mordecai Manuel Noah, "High Life Below Stairs," *New-York National Advocate*, 2 March 1825; Manuel Mordecai Noah, "High Life Among the Coloured Folks," *New-York National Advocate*, 18 March 1825; "From the Richmond Enquirer," *New-York Enquirer*, 26 September 1826; Manuel Mordecai Noah, "Blacks," *New-York Enquirer*, 20 September 1826; Manuel Mordecai Noah, "Colored Folks," *New-York Enquirer*, 21 September 1826; Manuel Mordecai Noah, "Case of Gilbert Horton," *New-York Enquirer*, 4 January 1827.

50. This focus can be seen in the columns of various newspapers such as the *New-York Evening Post*, the *New-York American*, and the *National Gazette and Literary Register* (Philadelphia).

51. H., "Slavery," *Statesman*, 1 December 1826; *New-York American*, 22 November 1827.

52. "From the Boston Daily Advertiser, July 17," *New-York Evening Post*, 19 July 1822.

2

~

The History of
Freedom's Journal

C ertain historical facts about *Freedom's Journal* are well established. The
weekly newspaper began publication on March 16, 1827, in New
York City, initially edited by two free-born African Americans, Samuel E.
Cornish and John B. Russwurm. In September 1827, Cornish resigned,
leaving Russwurm to assume sole editorship of the periodical. *Freedom's
Journal* was published on Fridays, with its office first on Varick Street and
later on Church Street.[1] The paper was originally four pages of four
columns each, with the motto "Righteousness Exalteth a Nation" on the
masthead; beginning with the issue of March 28, 1828, Russwurm
changed the format to eight pages of three columns each, with the motto
"Devoted to the Improvement of the Coloured Population."[2] The paper's
columns contained domestic and foreign news, correspondence, editorials, literary offerings, and advertisements. Distributed throughout the
North and parts of the South, *Freedom's Journal* also had agents in Haiti,
England, and Canada. The newspaper was plagued with financial problems; in addition, Russwurm received criticism about his editing. On
March 28, 1829, just two years after *Freedom's Journal*'s founding, Russwurm published the final issue.

Yet this is the briefest of histories, and it raises many questions. What
led to the establishment of the first African-American newspaper at this
time? Why did *Freedom's Journal* originate in New York and not, for example, Philadelphia, which also nurtured a vibrant African-American
community? How was it financed? Who was the target audience for the
periodical, and who actually read it? Why did editor Samuel Cornish resign after only six months on the job? What changes were made by editor

John Russwurm when he assumed sole responsibility for the periodical, and what were his motivations? And, finally, why did the paper cease publication in 1829? Although in some cases we cannot find definitive answers to these queries, a close analysis of available sources provides information that enriches and often challenges traditional accounts of the periodical.

CHALLENGING THE NOAH THESIS

A brief account of the founding of *Freedom's Journal* appears in an 1891 history written by late-nineteenth-century African-American journalist I. Garland Penn:

> There was a local paper published in New York City in 1827 and 1828 by an Afro-American-hating Jew, which made the vilest attacks upon the Afro-Americans. It encouraged slavery and deplored the thought of freedom for the slave. It seems to have been a power in that direction. Against this *The Journal* was directed. . . .
> . . . [T]he inception of *The Journal* was the result of a meeting of Messrs. Russwurm, Cornish and others at the house of M. Boston Crummell (Rev. Dr. [Alexander] Crummell's father,) in New York, called to consider the attacks of the local paper mentioned above.[3]

There is no reason to doubt certain aspects of Penn's story. His account appears to be at least in part the result of discussion with people who had firsthand knowledge of events, whom he referred to as "those few who now live and remember anything about the matter." It is probable that the idea for *Freedom's Journal* developed within a gathering of African-American leaders in New York. Boston Crummell, a successful oysterman and a prominent member of New York's African-American community, was connected with many of its leaders and would likely have opened his home for such a meeting.[4] But Penn himself suggested that we should not assume his account is definitive or even completely accurate since, as he noted, there was a "conflict of opinion" on certain matters even among his sources who remembered the era of *Freedom's Journal*.[5]

Despite this caveat, Penn's account has been accepted, in part or in full, by most historians of the African-American press. In particular, many descriptions of the origins of *Freedom's Journal* follow Penn in singling out Mordecai Noah—the "Afro-American-hating Jew"—as the primary force motivating African Americans to create their own newspaper.[6] As we have seen, Noah was indeed no friend of African Americans, and he often printed racist propaganda in his newspapers. As a prominent New Yorker, his influence made his views all the more dangerous to African

Americans, particularly in that city. Yet there are problems with what we might call as the Noah thesis—the assumption that his "vile attacks" were the main impetus for the creation of *Freedom's Journal.*

By emphasizing the attacks of one particular editor, we run the risk of decontextualizing Noah's racist rhetoric. Although Noah's views had wide circulation, they were hardly anomalous, as we have seen. Other editors also wrote and/or published defenses of slavery, disparaging accounts of African-American life, and racist parodies. Various newspapers frequently featured detailed and sensationalized reports of crimes by African Americans, caricatured and parodied them, and denigrated their concerns. Vicious satirical broadsides and cartoons targeting free African Americans circulated widely, drawing on and fueling whites' resentment and prejudice and attempting to discredit people of color by portraying them as pretentious fools incapable of behaving as respectable citizens. And colonizationist rhetoric—often in the form of sermons by prominent clergymen—was frequently explicitly racist, employing highly charged language to describe African Americans as dangerous and inferior.

Indeed, Cornish and Russwurm's own statement of their concerns and the responses to racist rhetoric in the columns of *Freedom's Journal* demonstrate that the editors (and contributors) were not disturbed by Noah alone. In their first editorial, they described the attacks against them: "There are [those] who make it their business to enlarge upon the least trifle, which tends to the discredit of any person of colour; and pronounce anathemas and denounce our whole body for the misconduct of this guilty one." In their "Prospectus" in the same issue, they declared that "often has injustice been heaped upon" them by their "enemies."[7] These descriptions fit Noah's treatment of African Americans, but they also apply to other racist rhetoric.

In fact, the responses to the white press in *Freedom's Journal* reveal that the editors and contributors indeed had wider concerns than the publications of one individual. The paper's columns do contain specific references to—and refutations of—Noah's rhetoric. A correspondent cleverly writing under the name Mordecai, for example, described Noah's *New-York Enquirer* as one of the "many engines, whose object it is to keep alive the prejudice of the whites against the coloured community of this city" through "unceasing and unprincipled attacks." In an editorial seconding the remarks of Mordecai, Cornish and Russwurm noted strikingly that Noah, as a Jew, should be able to understand and "sympathize with the oppressed of every hue." Yet the editors featured similarly strong rebuttals to attacks by other editors of major newspapers. Among others, they cited the editor of the *New-York Evening Post* for attempting to "palliat[e] the crime of slavery" by proposing that Southern slaves generally lived a life of "contentment, of gaiety and happiness" and the editor of the New

York *Morning Chronicle*, who represented New York African Americans as a nuisance, suggested that the condition of Southern slaves had been "misrepresented," and feared an increase in the black population of the city. A two-part article by Philadelphia African Americans took to task the editor of the Philadelphia periodical the *Ariel*, who described blacks in that city as "lazy" and "pampered" and supported the efforts of colonizationists to rid the country of them.[8]

Cornish and Russwurm also stated their concern with the racist nature of other influential rhetoric. "From the press and the pulpit we have suffered much by being incorrectly represented," they asserted. The editors specifically identified rhetoric emanating from the "pulpit," such as the many popular sermons that disparaged African Americans, promoted colonization, and supported slavery. As an 1827 correspondent to *Freedom's Journal* remarked, "Even our pious clergymen, in their exhortations and religious consolations, when they condescend to favour the coloured people with attentions, are always careful to represent them as an inferior race of beings. They exhort them to resignation, but are careful not to afford them any prospect of elevating their condition by virtue and merit.— Such advice is more injurious than beneficial." In an early issue of *Freedom's Journal*, the editors cited the arguments of a colonizationist clergyman in Newark who maligned the character of free African Americans. Cornish and Russwurm responded in a detailed two-part series.[9]

The editors also maintained that they wished to respond to misrepresentations of purported friends. "Men, whom we equally love and admire have not hesitated to represent us disadvantageously," they lamented, "without becoming personally acquainted with the true state of things. . . ." Indeed, as we have discovered, many who professed to oppose slavery or favor civil rights often expressed fear or distrust of African Americans and were ignorant of their true concerns. The editors explicitly noted, in fact, that many ostensible supporters held racist views: "Our friends, to whom we concede all the principles of humanity and religion . . . seem to have fallen into the current of popular feeling and are imperceptibly floating on the stream—actually living in the practice of prejudice, while they abjure it in theory, and feel it not in their hearts." *Freedom's Journal*, they suggested, would serve to correct these perceptions as well as more overtly racist views: "Is it not very desirable that such should know more of our actual condition, and of our efforts and feelings, that in forming or advocating plans for our amelioration, they may do it more understandingly?"[10]

It is unrealistic, then, to assume that *Freedom's Journal* owed its creation to the malignant rhetoric of one man. But there are problems also with an extension of the Noah thesis that would posit that white rhetoric generally was the principal force behind the periodical. Various historians suggest in particular that *Freedom's Journal* developed in response to the popularity of the colonization movement among whites or the increasing power of slaveholding interests in the United States.[11] That white leaders, clergy, and editors were racist is not to be disputed; nor would it be valid to deny that African-American leaders wished to have a forum to respond to their bigoted rhetoric and to institutional oppression. One function of *Freedom's Journal*, as we have seen, was to counter attacks on African Americans—to see to it that they were, in the words of the editors, "refuted by forcible arguments."[12] It is also clear that the colonization movement galvanized African Americans to protest publicly and to express their opposition. Yet to suggest that any of these influences was the *primary reason* the periodical was created is reductive. This assumption diminishes the agency of the African-American community, suggesting that this pivotal accomplishment was a response to white society rather than a self-directed effort of African Americans themselves, and undervalues the forces within the black community that contributed to this momentous event.

To fully understand the creation of *Freedom's Journal*, we must look *within* the African-American community to examine the interaction of racism and oppression with myriad factors, most influentially the organizational structures already in place in free black communities and the awareness of the crucial power of writing as a tool of freedom. As Frances Smith Foster asserts, the creation of "the African-American press owed as much, if not more, to the desire to create a positive and purposeful self-identified African America as to any defensive gestures responding to racist attacks and libel."[13] Generations of leaders had laid the groundwork for the periodical by building community institutions, demonstrating the power of rhetoric in forming a national consciousness, and asserting the right to determine their own destinies.

COMMUNITY, LITERACY, AND THE POWER OF THE PRESS

As we have explored in detail, the period from the American Revolution to the appearance of *Freedom's Journal* was characterized by intense community development for African Americans in various cities. "By the late 1820s," Peter Hinks maintains, "the free black communities of the North had come of age. Resting on a settled infrastructure . . . black communities, especially in such major centers as Boston, New York City, and Philadelphia, had not only become fully aware of themselves as distinctive entities with their own specific needs, but were much more assertive in pronouncing that difference publicly and pursuing their own ends."[14]

Indeed, Cornish and Russwurm placed far greater emphasis on African Americans' self-determination and collective identity than on white racism.

They noted in their "Prospectus" that African Americans were "daily slandered" and described themselves as "champions in defence of oppressed humanity" who would refute "the calumnies of [their] enemies"; and responses to white rhetoric, as we have seen, were included in the periodical. Yet the editors explicitly pointed to community concerns as their primary motivation in publishing *Freedom's Journal*. "We deem it expedient to establish a paper," they remarked, "and bring into operation all the means with which our benevolent CREATOR has endowed us, for the moral, religious, civil and literary improvement of our race. . . . [T]he diffusion of knowledge, and raising our community into respectability, are the principal motives which influence us in our present undertaking." The editors articulated the desire of African Americans to have a forum that was theirs, allowing them to "plead [their] own cause" rather than being "spoken for" by others. Because free African Americans had previously had "no public channel" for their voices, they discerned a "real necessity, at present, for the appearance of the FREEDOM'S JOURNAL."[15] The content of the periodical also indicates that it was the concerns of the African-American community itself, rather than the attacks of others, that were most salient to the editors and contributors. The paper's columns, as we shall see, contained a diverse array of articles and essays, a great number of which did not respond to the rhetoric of Noah or other white detractors, but rather advocated causes from an African-American perspective.

Other factors created a climate favorable to the creation of *Freedom's Journal*. By the 1820s, as we have seen, links among those in different locales were forged and common objectives were identified. Thus there was a social infrastructure that could support a national newspaper. The editors placed their efforts into this context of developing affiliations among African Americans separated geographically:

> It is our earnest wish to make our Journal a medium of intercourse between our brethren in the different states of this great confederacy: that through its columns an expression of our sentiments, on many interesting subjects which concern us, may be offered to the publick: that plans which apparently are beneficial may be candidly discussed and properly weighed; if worthy, receive our cordial approbation; if not, our marked disapprobation.[16]

The development of the periodical was also vitally connected to the value placed on reading and writing as keys to empowerment in African-American communities in the North. Cornish and Russwurm specifically identified *Freedom's Journal* as part of a collective drive for literacy and education, affirming that they considered it "part of [their] duty to recommend to [their] young readers, such authors as will not only enlarge their stock of useful knowledge, but such as will also serve to stimulate them to higher attainments in science." Their comments reflect the climate of the late 1820s, in which, as we have seen, literary societies developed in various cities to encourage reading and writing and to give members opportunities to develop and practice rhetorical skills. "As early as the first decade of the nineteenth century," Elizabeth McHenry maintains, "some mutual aid societies began to call for the revision and expansion of their functions to include more deliberate writing and public presentation of their condition." Both the formation of African-American literary societies and the institution of a black press in the late 1820s, she demonstrates, evolved from this desire for "association with literature, as readers and writers."[17] *Freedom's Journal* was one such venue. In addition, this emphasis on literacy nurtured a readership for the periodical.

The emergence of *Freedom's Journal* should also be seen in the context of the larger journalistic climate. In the late 1820s, other marginalized groups created periodicals that would allow them to voice their perspectives. The first labor newspaper, the Philadelphia *Journeyman Mechanic's Advocate*, was published in 1827, and the *Mechanic's Free Press* followed in 1828. The Cherokee nation founded the first Native-American periodical, the *Cherokee Phoenix*, in Georgia in 1828. In addition, as industrialization made paper less expensive to produce, periodicals could be made available widely and economically.[18] Cornish and Russwurm alluded to these developments in their "Prospectus." After stating their central goal of improving their community, they asserted, "Experience teaches us that the Press is the most economical and convenient method by which this object is to be obtained."[19]

We find, then, that the establishment of *Freedom's Journal* depended fundamentally on the sense of community, the drive for education, the recognition of the power of the press, and the emphasis on rhetoric and self-determination that had been nurtured by generations of African Americans prior to its publication. The leaders who emerged in the 1820s had been influenced by the developments of their predecessors. Thus it was that Cornish and Russwurm were prepared to undertake what they called "a new and untried line of business"—and African Americans were ready to give them their support.[20]

THE EDITORS

The lives and careers of Cornish and Russwurm were different in many respects, yet in 1827 they came together for a short period of time as senior and junior editor, respectively, of *Freedom's Journal*. Samuel Cornish was born free in Delaware about 1795.[21] He moved to Philadelphia in 1815. There he taught in a school run by John Gloucester, a former slave who was the dynamic minister of First African Presbyterian Church, the first African-American Presbyterian congregation in the country. Cornish became interested in becoming a Presbyterian minister, and starting in 1817, he undertook studies with ministers in the Philadelphia Presbytery. As David Swift notes, he was the first African American "to undergo the normal exacting training and testing procedures required for Presbyterian ordination." Licensed to preach by the Philadelphia Presbytery in 1819, he was a missionary to slaves on the Eastern shore of Maryland during the summer and fall of 1820. He later described his repugnance for the "Christian slave-holders" at whose homes he stayed, who professed their religious convictions while mistreating their slaves.[22] It is not surprising that he left this post and moved to New York City.

Still affiliated with the Philadelphia Presbytery, Cornish undertook a ministry in 1821 with the New-York Evangelical Missionary Society of Young Men, preaching and ministering to black New Yorkers. He founded the first African-American Presbyterian church in New York— the First Colored Presbyterian Church—about a year after his arrival in the city, and was installed as pastor in 1824. In 1822, Cornish requested to be dismissed from the care of the Philadelphia Presbytery and ordained by the New York Presbytery. Although he was recruited to return to Philadelphia to take over the leadership of First African Church after the death of Gloucester in 1823, he decided to stay in New York.

Cornish was active in the African-American community of New York City. He was a member of the Haytian Emigration Society but became opposed to the idea of leaving the country after many emigrants to Haiti returned, dissatisfied, to the United States. In particular, he was strongly averse to African colonization. Although Cornish was a successful minister, his church was plagued by financial problems and he requested to be relieved of his duties there, but the Presbytery of New York asked him instead to endeavor to raise funds. He retained his ministry when he accepted the post of senior editor of *Freedom's Journal* in 1827. He worked on the periodical for only six months before resigning and leaving it under the sole editorship of his partner John Russwurm.

Russwurm was born in Jamaica in 1799, the son of a black woman and a white plantation owner, a Virginian who had been educated in England.[23] His father sent him to a boarding school in Quebec in 1807, and he returned to the United States to live with his father in Maine when he was thirteen. He was educated at a private school there, graduating in 1819. He then moved to Boston, where he was a teacher at a school for African-American youth. In 1824, he was admitted to Bowdoin College in Maine, its first African-American student. He accepted an invitation to join the college's Athenaean Society, a literary fraternity whose president was Nathaniel Hawthorne.

At Bowdoin, Russwurm began to make plans to study medicine in Boston, become a doctor, and eventually emigrate to Haiti to practice there. When he graduated in 1826—one of the first African-American college graduates in the United States[24]—he spoke at his commencement ceremony on "The Condition and Prospects of Haiti." Russwurm's remarks demonstrate that the Haitian Revolution and the independence of the black nation inspired him:

> When Liberty, when once Freedom struck [the Haitians'] astonished ears, they became new creatures, stepped forth as men, and showed to the world, that though slavery may benumb it, it cannot entirely destroy our faculties. . . .
>
> May we not indulge in the pleasing hope, that the independence of Haiti has laid the foundation of an empire that will take rank with the nations of the earth . . . that a country . . . possessing a free and well-regulated government . . . containing an enterprising and growing population which is determined to live free or die gloriously will advance rapidly in all the arts of civilization.[25]

In the fall of 1826, Russwurm studied anatomy at the Bowdoin College Medical School. Still interested in emigration, he shifted his focus to Liberia. In late 1826, he expressed interest in emigrating there to take a position as a teacher or assistant to the resident agent to the colony. However, when the ACS offered him a position later that year, he declined. Writing to R. R. Gurley, the corresponding secretary of the ACS, in February 1827, Russwurm noted that, after consulting with friends, he had decided that, for reasons he did not specify, "it would not be advisable" to accept the ACS's offer.[26] Instead he settled in New York, where he undertook the position as junior editor of *Freedom's Journal*.

FINANCES

Of course, for Cornish and Russwurm to undertake such an effort required the support of many others who could assist them not only by promoting and distributing the paper but also by raising and contributing money beyond the funds paid by subscribers (which, as we shall see, could not alone keep the paper solvent). Since no financial records from *Freedom's Journal* have been found, it is impossible to ascertain definitively who initially funded the venture. Yet the evidence suggests that, contrary to the assumptions of some historians, both African Americans and whites provided financial support.[27] To determine who in the African-American community might have given money to the project, it is instructive to examine the list of agents for the paper—those who promoted the paper and obtained subscribers in various cities—printed at the end of each issue. Penn notes that these included many "remarkable men,"[28] and, indeed, the list at the end of each issue of *Freedom's Journal* featured many prominent and well-connected African Americans. David Walker was agent for Boston, as was the Reverend Thomas Paul, pastor of Boston's African Baptist Church. There were other influential agents as well, including the Reverend Nathaniel Paul, Thomas Paul's brother and the founder of the Union Street Baptist Church in Albany and the First African Society there; Theodore Wright, a student at Princeton Seminary who replaced Cornish as minister of New York's First Colored Presbyterian Church in 1829; and the Reverend Benjamin Hughes of Newark, New Jersey, who had previously served as the pastor of Philadelphia's First African Presbyterian Church when Cornish declined the call in 1824.[29]

It seems that various agents for the paper either helped to raise money to finance the paper or donated their own. Nearly a month before *Freedom's Journal's* first issue appeared, David Walker hosted a meeting at his home in Boston "for the purpose of taking into consideration the expediency of giving aid and support to the FREEDOM'S JOURNAL." The attendees at the meeting included Thomas Paul and a Mr. Hilton, probably John T. Hilton, leader of the African-American Masons in the city. Having already received a prospectus for *Freedom's Journal*, they resolved to "freely and voluntarily . . . give it [their] aid and support, and to use [their] utmost exertions to increase its patronage."[30] It is likely that this "aid and support" included seeking or providing financial backing.

Some agents would have been in a position to donate funds themselves. Booker T. Washington indicated that David Walker and Stephen Smith, the paper's agent for Columbia, Pennsylvania, from its founding, were also "contributors" to the paper.[31] Smith was an extremely successful lumber merchant and, as Philip Foner notes, "one of the leading black capitalists of the nineteenth century, if not the leading one." He was also an activist who often gave money as well as time to causes he believed in. He was involved with the Underground Railroad, and when John Brown was in Philadelphia in 1858, he met with African-American leaders in Smith's home, where he stayed during his visit.[32] Washington did not elaborate on the specific contributions made by Walker and Smith, but it seems that he was referring to monetary support, since he noted Smith's "considerable fortune" and his financial donations to "a home for aged and infirm Negroes in Philadelphia."[33] Boston Crummell's comfortable financial situation might also have allowed him to provide financial backing. Other well-off African Americans, such as John Remond, a successful hairdresser and community leader in Salem, Massachusetts, who joined the list of agents a month after the newspaper began publication, might also have been contributors.

In addition, leaders who could not give money themselves nonetheless would have been connected to others in the African-American community who could. In 1816, the Reverend Peter Williams Jr. wrote to Thomas Tucker, a member of the New York Manumission Society, apparently in response to a request by Tucker to report how many New York African Americans held property in land and houses. (This information would have been relevant because of New York's requirement that African Americans possess property worth at least 250 dollars in order to vote.) Historian Harry Reed speculates that Williams may have drawn on this list eleven years later to garner support for *Freedom's Journal* from those in the African-American community who possessed resources.[34]

White individuals who provided funds to establish *Freedom's Journal* appear to have included philanthropists and antislavery reformers. Thomas Hale, a member of the New York Manumission Society, wrote in January 1827 to Isaac Barton, a Philadelphia merchant and a member of the Pennsylvania Abolition Society, alerting him that Hale's "friend the Revd Samuel E. Cornish" would soon be in New York. Cornish, Hale related, "is devoting a portion of his time means and talents to promote . . . a Periodical Paper to be published in this City, and to be principally intended to meliorate the Condition of the Colored people, [and] with this view he intends a visit to your place in a few days." Hale commented that he had provided Cornish with "a few lines to [Barton] by way of Introduction" because he perceived that Barton would be supportive of "any measure tending to the advancement of the Happiness of African descendents." It seems probable that Cornish's trip was to raise funds for *Freedom's Journal* among abolitionists in Philadelphia, including white supporters such as Barton.[35]

Cornish's visit apparently was successful in gaining at least the interest and likely the financial support of Barton and possibly other white abolitionists with whom he was connected. In October 1827, Cornish and Russwurm wrote Barton thanking him for a letter he had sent them. They suggest that the support of white abolitionists was instrumental to their project: "The enterprize in which we are engaged is of so novel a nature, that it will require some time to elapse, before our people can set a true value upon the Journal; in the meanwhile, we must look to our friends in different parts of the Globe to stay our feeble hands." It is not clear why Cornish and Russwurm expressed disappointment to Barton about African Americans' support of *Freedom's Journal*, but perhaps they were referring to the lack of payment by many who received the paper, which was, as we shall see, a constant problem. White New York philanthropist Gerrit Smith also may have contributed money in addition to subscribing to *Freedom's Journal*. In an 1827 letter to Gurley, Smith recalled that when the paper appeared, he was "disposed to patronize" it as well as "take" it, suggesting that he gave financial support beyond its subscription cost.[36]

Revenue was also raised through fees from advertisements and subscriptions. Advertisements of under twelve or of twelve to twenty-two lines cost fifty or seventy-five cents, respectively, with each repetition of the advertisement costing twenty-five or thirty-eight cents, respectively. Advertising space of more than twenty-two lines was priced proportionally. There was a six, twelve, or fifteen percent reduction in these rates for those advertising for three, six, or twelve months, respectively. Most advertisements fell into the twelve- to twenty-two-line category. A variety of merchants and businesses located in various cities advertised in *Freedom's Journal*, including clothing stores, grocers, tailors, schools, boarding houses, pharmacies, and medical practitioners. Many entrepreneurs took advantage of the discount for repetition of their advertisements. Some of the most intriguing are "Indian Doctress" Sarah Green's notice of her cure for the "Piles, Dysentary, all kinds of Wounds and Bruises; also a remedy for the growing in of the toe nails, for oppression of the lungs, felons, fistulas, and the bite of a mad dog"; Nicholas Pierson's announcement of his New York "MEAD GARDEN . . . for the accommodation of genteel and respectable persons of colour," with "no admittance for unprotected females"; a notice for a New York school run by a Mr. Gold, whose "new and improved" plan for teaching English grammar would enable "a pupil of ordinary capacity" to "obtain a correct and thorough knowledge of the principles of the English language, by attending to the study thereof, two hours in a day in six weeks"; and David Walker's advertisement for his new and used clothing store in Boston.[37]

A yearly subscription to *Freedom's Journal* cost three dollars, and subscriptions were not to be accepted for less than one year. Although the official terms stated that this amount was "payable half yearly in advance"—with a reduction to two dollars and fifty cents for those paying for a full year at the time of subscription—it is clear that the editors were not strict about these arrangements and sent papers to subscribers in advance of receiving these amounts. They noted that those subscribers "who are not prepared to pay the amount of their subscriptions at this time, are informed that we shall expect they will do so as early as they possibly can."[38] This leniency did not benefit the newspaper financially. It appears that many who received the paper regularly were negligent in their payments—a common problem for newspapers in the eighteenth and nineteenth centuries.[39] In the issue published May 25, 1827, the editors politely remarked that they were "sorry to be under the necessity of saying" that many subscribers had not paid "their several dues" to the paper. In a note appearing in the August 24 and 31, 1827, issues, the editors "remind[ed] [their] delinquent subscribers, of the necessity of their paying" and informed them that they would no longer deliver papers to those who had not settled their accounts by September 7. It appears that these reminders were not sufficient; many notices appeared in the latter part of 1827 appealing to subscribers to pay their overdue half-yearly installments.[40]

It seems that the problems only worsened in 1828 and 1829. Russwurm's 1828 "Prospectus" was identical to that published in the first issue of *Freedom's Journal*, with one exception. In a new paragraph added at the end, Russwurm mentioned the paper's "encouraging success" in gaining a "number of subscribers" but noted that the "loss having ensued from subscribers in different parts of the country" forced him "to make another appeal to his brethren, for their continued patronage to the arduous undertaking in which he has embarked." Indeed, it appears that by March 1828, some subscribers had received the paper for a full year but had made no payments. Russwurm suggested in a notice published two months later that he might resort to publishing the names of those in debt, although it was "against [his] feelings," because he had "lost so much by delinquent subscribers." Those who were "in arrears for their last year's subscription," he warned, should "govern themselves accordingly." Russwurm also relied on more creative appeals for payment. In a vignette titled "The Subscription List—A Farce," reprinted from the *Berkshire Press*, an editor "conjur[es] up the ghosts of delinquent subscribers," including the aptly named Lemuel Love-the-bottle and Anthony Scurvypocket. All have excuses why they have not paid, after which "the editor, all out of patience, thrusts the subscription list into the fire" while the ghosts "dance a fandango at his disappointment and mortification." These appeals, however entertaining, do not appear to have elicited the funds owed to the paper. At the end of November 1828, Russwurm was forced to skip an issue of the paper solely because of lack of payment by subscribers.[41]

The paper also lost support and ultimately money when some white readers expressed their opposition to the paper's initial position against colonization. In June 1827, the editors reprinted in *Freedom's Journal* part of an editorial from the *Georgetown Columbian and District Advertiser*. *Freedom's Journal*, the *Advertiser*'s editor proclaimed, attempted to make people of color "distrustful of [the ACS's] object and suspicious of the motives of those wise and philanthropic men, composing the Society." In a letter published in June 1827, a correspondent to *Freedom's Journal* described an instance of a published criticism: "The correspondent of the N[ew] J[ersey] Patriot says, that [*Freedom's Journal*] will lose all its patrons among the friends of colonization; that it need not look any longer for support through them. . . ." In an October 1827 letter to Gurley, Gerrit Smith, at that time a supporter of colonization, lamented that "the Editors of the Freedom's Journal" were against what he considered the "patriotic duty of contributing to relieve our country of its black population." Although he remarked that he "still take[s]" the paper, Smith declared that Cornish and Russwurm's position showed that "the turn that *Negro-learning* takes in this country is not always favourable," ominously echoing the sentiments of many ACS members that educating African Americans would only make it harder to convince them to leave the United States. Indeed, Smith mused, they might "prefer staying at home to unite with others to defeat [the ACS's] objects."[42]

Other white subscribers went farther than Smith by canceling their subscriptions because of the colonization issue. Professor Samuel Miller of Princeton Seminary wrote a letter to the editors of the *New-York Observer,* which Russwurm reprinted in *Freedom's Journal* in late September 1827, renouncing *Freedom's Journal*'s efforts "to defeat the success of the friends of the colonization system." Miller asserted that although he had "been a subscriber to [*Freedom's Journal*] from its commencement," he could "no longer reconcile it with [his] sense of duty to be found among its patrons." As an article reprinted in *Freedom's Journal* a month later reported, Miller also denounced the paper from the pulpit. Other faculty and students at Princeton Seminary, a school with strong connections to the ACS, canceled their subscriptions as well.[43]

Given these financial difficulties, it might seem surprising that *Freedom's Journal* survived for two full years. In part, it was able to continue, albeit precariously, through the magnanimity of the editors, who clearly lost money—Russwurm described "debts to a considerable amount due [him]" in an 1829 letter. In addition, African Americans and possibly white reformers also contributed money to alleviate some of the newspaper's financial difficulties. In the issue of December 21, 1827, Russwurm thanked those "kind friends who have generously come forward" to offer assistance to the paper. Writing to Cornish in 1837, African-American abolitionist John B. Vashon of Pittsburgh recalled that "eight or ten years earlier," when *Freedom's Journal* was "sinking for the want of six or seven hundred dollars . . . some five or six individuals amongst our brethren, one of whom was your correspondent, stepped forward and advanced the required amount."[44]

Sorely needed funds might also have been raised through the use of the newspaper's printing press. Beginning in late August 1827, issues of *Freedom's Journal* featured notices that orders for printing could be left at the office of the newspaper. Armistead Pride and Clint Wilson infer that "the newspaper owned and operated its own printing press, along with the necessary cases of type and auxiliary equipment for producing a newspaper and handling printing jobs."[45] Additional printing assignments may have provided financing beyond subscription and advertising revenues for the periodical's operation.

READERSHIP AND DISTRIBUTION

It is estimated that the number of subscribers to *Freedom's Journal* was at least 800. I use the term *subscriber* here in the technical sense, referring to those who made arrangements to receive the periodical regularly rather than only to those who actually paid for the paper in part or in full. The editors assumed this meaning, referring, for example, to "delinquent subscribers" who had not paid for papers they had received. In addition, the more restricted definition would not be practical (since we can more accurately estimate the number of copies distributed rather than the number of paying customers), nor would it fully capture the paper's reach.

The figure of 800 is based on subscription numbers for the *Rights of All*, the newspaper edited by Samuel Cornish in 1829 after the demise of *Freedom's Journal*.[46] By 1829, as we shall see, there was dissatisfaction with the ultimate direction taken by *Freedom's Journal*. Thus Bella Gross argues that "there must have been many more" than 800 subscribers to *Freedom's Journal* because "quite a number of the old subscribers refused to subscribe to the *Rights of All* because of their disappointment in the management of [*Freedom's*] *Journal*."[47] Although it is impossible to determine if there were truly more than 800 subscribers—and, if so, how many—scholars generally use the 800 figure as an estimate, which would make the circulation of *Freedom's Journal* close to that of other weekly papers of the time.[48]

This number, however, should not be interpreted as the number of *readers* of the periodical, which would have been much larger. Frankie Hutton notes that for antebellum African-American newspapers, "actual readership was probably considerably wider than circulation figures suggest" because copies were often shared.[49] Editors, naturally concerned with funds, were not always happy with those who wished to read newspapers without subscribing. An 1827 piece in *Freedom's Journal* remarked, "We have frequently frowned when the following question has been put to us by the newspaper borrowing gentry: 'Will you lend me your last paper? I only want to read it.' . . . [I]f they want [newspapers] why don't they pay for them, and thus remunerate the printer? A man might with the same propriety go to a baker and say, 'Sir, won't you lend me a loaf of bread—I only want to eat it.'" An 1829 article reprinted by Russwurm suggested that nonsubscribers were not always so forthright about their intentions: "Newspaper Borrowers . . . generally come out before breakfast in the morning . . . and carry off the newspaper before the owner or his family have had an opportunity of reading it themselves."[50] There is no evidence that *Freedom's Journal* in particular was commonly "borrowed" in this manner, but clearly Russwurm and other editors of his time suspected that this practice lowered their revenues. In addition, organizations subscribed to or were given copies of *Freedom's Journal*, giving nonsubscribing individuals access to the paper. *Freedom's Journal* was in the library of the Colored Reading Society of Philadelphia, for example; the American Convention for Promoting the Abolition of Slavery resolved to subscribe to two copies of the periodical for the Acting Committee to give "such circulation as they may think best"; and it was distributed for free to the library of the African Free School.[51]

It is clear, then, that *Freedom's Journal* had many African-American readers. Some historians have incorrectly assumed that the newspaper was aimed primarily at white readers because the literacy rate for African Americans at the time was too low to support a readership for the periodical.[52] In fact, there were a significant number of blacks with reading and writing skills in Northern and some Southern cities in the first part of the nineteenth century. Schools in various cities, such as the African Free Schools of New York, as well as mutual aid organizations and literary societies, provided African Americans with opportunities to receive an education.[53] In 1816, Peter Williams Jr. wrote to Quaker preacher Stephen Grellet, outlining "the present condition and prospects of the African race" in New York. Williams reported, "In Literature our prospects are excellent. We have a number of respectable talents & the bulk of our young people can read. We have a free school under the direction & patronage of the manumission Society. . . . We also have a number of private schools in different parts of the city. Besides, our people have admission into all, or most at least . . . sunday schools, of which there are a great number; so that all whether rich or poor, young or old, have an opportunity of being instructed."[54] Additionally, those who could not read could still have obtained information from *Freedom's Journal*. It was common practice for literate African Americans to read newspapers and other texts to those who could not read.[55] As Tony Martin asserts, those who established *Freedom's Journal* "did not operate in a vacuum" but rather within "a highly disciplined, remarkably productive constituency of literate, socially conscious African Americans."[56]

The availability of educational opportunities such as those described by Williams may shed some light in part on a question that cannot be definitively answered—why did the periodical originate in New York rather than in another city? New York was not the only center of African-American political and intellectual life at the time, nor did other cities lack strong black leadership. As we have seen, African Americans in Philadelphia and Boston created vital community institutions, held public protests and celebrations, and promoted literary and political activities. Boston was home to the MGCA and David Walker, while Philadelphia was the location of what appears to have been the first African-American literary society, the Colored Reading Society, organized in 1828.[57] Yet there were attributes of New York that would have made it particularly fertile ground for the first African-American newspaper. As Pride and Wilson explain, it "had the largest free Black population of any Northern center, as well as the largest concentration of Negroes with education."[58] It is important, though, not to conclude that because the paper was published in New York it did not involve the efforts of African Americans in many cities. Noting the great support for the paper in Boston, Hinks remarks, "[*Freedom's Journal*] was the creation of the members of a number of black communities, not simply of the editors in New York City."[59]

Cornish and Russwurm's statements in *Freedom's Journal* suggest that they envisioned these African-American communities throughout the country as the primary audience for the periodical. In their first editorial, they noted the "interesting fact that there are FIVE HUNDRED THOUSAND free persons of colour, one half of whom might peruse, and the whole be benefitted by the publication of the Journal." Yet they welcomed the support of their white subscribers and readers as well. They remarked that they intended for African Americans' concerns and opinions to be communicated "to the publick" through the columns of the paper, and they referred to their hope that their "colored brethren" would "strengthen [their] hands by their subscriptions and that their "numerous friends" would "assist by their communications."[60]

Freedom's Journal's network of agents rapidly grew, expanding the reach of the periodical outside the North and beyond the United States. The original list was itself impressive, with representatives in Portland, Maine; Salem and Boston, Massachusetts; Providence, Rhode Island; New London, Connecticut; Philadelphia and Columbia, Pennsylvania; Baltimore, Maryland; Albany, New York; Princeton, New Brunswick, and Newark, New Jersey, and Washington, D. C. An agent in Port-au-Prince, Haiti, was listed beginning in the second issue. Agents were added rapidly in cities throughout the United States and abroad, including North Yarmouth, Maine (April 1827); Flushing, Long Island (June 1827); Fredericksburg, Virginia (July 1827); Liverpool, England (November 1827); Elizabethtown, North Carolina (January 1828); and Waterloo, Canada (May 1828).

As with circulation figures, though, we need to look beyond the printed record to grasp the geographical reach of the periodical. After the publication of *David Walker's Appeal* in 1829, the pamphlet was discovered in cities in Virginia, Louisiana, and Georgia, in the possession of slaves as well as free African Americans. Black sailors from the North had developed contacts in the South, creating underground channels in various cities for the distribution of antislavery information and texts, such as Walker's *Appeal*. Urban slaves who were hired out by their masters to work for others were able to acquire money and "participate in the market economy of the urban South," explains Douglas Egerton, "creating an illicit network . . . in which information moved as easily as stolen goods."[61] Networks for such material also depended upon runaways, itinerant laborers, longshoremen, sailors, and churches and other religious organizations.[62] It is probable that *Freedom's Journal* enjoyed similar distribution, particularly given David Walker's prominent role as an agent of the paper.

In fact, there is evidence that *Freedom's Journal* found its way to and was read by slaves. In an 1831 letter to William Lloyd Garrison's *Liberator*, correspondent V. revealed,

> A few years since, being in a slave state, I chanced one morning, very early, to look through the curtains of my chamber window, which opened upon a back yard. I saw a mulatto with a newspaper in his hand, surrounded by a score of colored men, who were listening, open mouthed, to a very inflammatory article the yellow man was reading. Sometimes the reader dwelt emphatically on particular passages, and I could see his auditors stamp and clench their hands. I afterwards learned that the paper was published in New-York, and addressed to the blacks.

The description suggests that the paper in question was indeed *Freedom's Journal*; and the context of V.'s remarks—a discussion of the impracticability of enforcing laws preventing slaves from learning to read—implies that at least some among the reader and his auditors were slaves.[63]

CORNISH'S DEPARTURE

In September 1827, Cornish announced his resignation in *Freedom's Journal*. "Six months of our Editorial labours having expired," he declared, "by mutual consent, and good wishes for the prosperity and usefulness of each other, our connection in the 'JOURNAL,' is this day dissolved, and the right and prerogatives exclusively vested in the Junior Editor, J. B. Russwurm." Cornish cited his "health and interest" as his reasons for resigning, noting that he wished to "remove to the country" and to "devote [him]self exclusively to the work of the Ministry, as a Missionary, or otherwise."[64]

Scholars have speculated that other factors led Cornish to this decision. In particular, because Russwurm, as we shall see, eventually announced in *Freedom's Journal* in February 1829 his support for the ACS and its plans in Liberia, many have assumed that Cornish's decision to leave the paper was the result of disagreement with Russwurm over colonization.[65] However, Lionel Barrow notes that there is no evidence for this claim.[66] Indeed, available information indicates that the dissolution of Cornish and Russwurm's partnership was amicable and that the senior editor's departure was due to causes other than dissension with his junior colleague. In his farewell statement, Cornish expressed confidence in Russwurm: "I . . . recommend [*Freedom's Journal*], in the hands of its present Editor, whose education and talents so amply qualify him for its duties, to the liberal patronage of our brethren and friends." This statement does not appear to have been mere politeness. In the issue which contains Cornish's resignation, Russwurm noted that Cornish would continue to be associated with *Freedom's Journal* as a "General Agent," who was "authorized to transact any business relating to it."[67] Beginning with the issue published two weeks later and continuing to the end of the paper's run, Cornish's name appeared on the list of agents at the end of the newspaper. Announcements of weddings performed by Cornish continued to appear in the paper's columns, as they did before his departure. In January 1828, Russwurm announced in the paper Cornish's appointment as the New York Manumission Society's General Visiting Agent for the African Free Schools, charged with calling on families in order to encourage enrollment and attendance.[68]

It appears, in fact, that Cornish was surprised when Russwurm announced his support for African colonization in 1829. Reflecting on Russwurm's support for colonization in the *Rights of All* in May 1829, Cornish asserted that Russwurm's "sudden change" on this issue was "equally strange" to him as it was "to others." It seems that while the two worked together, Russwurm kept any interest he might have had in colonization from his editorial partner. In addition, Russwurm did not for some time change the paper's official editorial position against colonization. Although Russwurm published in *Freedom's Journal* articles written by others in favor of colonization, this was not in itself a change in policy. As we shall explore in some detail in the next chapter, Cornish and Russwurm established from the outset that differing positions on important subjects should be represented in their columns, and colonization was no exception. In the last issue Cornish and Russwurm coedited, they offered the first of a series of procolonization pieces written by white Philadelphian John H. Kennedy, Gurley's assistant. The editors asserted, "We can assure our readers that, though we have expressed [*sic*] our decided disapprobation of the [American Colonization] Society, we wish to see the subject fully discussed in our columns, being truly anxious to make a few converts among our friends."[69]

In addition, although Russwurm might have retained some of his earlier interest in emigration even before his public announcement of support in 1829, it appears that he was not yet certain at the time of Cornish's departure in 1827 about the wisdom of the ACS's Liberian venture. In an editorial published in January 1828, Russwurm affirmed that he was "opposed to the plans of the American Colonization Society" and questioned whether the glowing reports from Liberian colonists were written by "impartial men" or by "those, who having formed visionary theories, are determined to try the experiment, no matter how many lives are sacrificed." Russwurm endorsed the comments of an author in 1828: "When we reflect on the vast sums which infatuation is wasting on Colonization, which will never profit but the few; we have lamented that philanthropists should be so misled. Were half the amount expended in emigration to Hayti and Africa, devoted to the subject of African Education, it would bring about a new era in the history of our coloured population."[70]

It appears unlikely, then, that Russwurm and Cornish's editorial partnership dissolved over colonization. The particulars of Russwurm's varying sentiments about colonization are impossible to determine, but apparently he vacillated and was often conflicted over the issue. His response represents what Vincent Bakpetu Thompson describes as "the contradictions and ambivalence" among African Americans from the eighteenth to the twentieth centuries about "their destiny—whether it was to be in the Americas or elsewhere, including Africa."[71]

RUSSWURM'S EDITING

By 1828, some readers expressed discontent with Russwurm's editing of *Freedom's Journal*. An article published in the paper in April 1828 reported that a meeting was held in Boston the previous month "for the purpose of enquiring whether the Freedom's Journal had been conducted in a manner satisfactory to the subscribers and to the Coloured community at large." Although those present at the meeting, including John T. Hilton and David Walker, strongly pledged their continuing support for the periodical, Hilton noted "opposition" by some who were "hostile to the interest of the Journal." Russwurm's comments in the paper's columns in December 1828 also indicated that he had received complaints; he noted somewhat bitterly that if "some of [his] learned advisors" would "undertake the publication of a journal; they will then find, that it is invariably easier to advise than to perform."[72]

For some readers, the criticism of Russwurm's editing may have stemmed from the effect of his shifting attitudes about colonization on the paper's content.[73] Although Russwurm did not express public support for African colonization until February 1829, his attitude, as we shall discuss, began to change prior to his announcement. Indeed, when publicly announcing his altered opinion, Russwurm commented that it was not "the hasty conclusion of a moment" and that he had "pondered much on this interesting subject."[74] As we shall explore in detail in chapter 7, the effects of this contemplation are evident in the paper. Pieces opposing colonization continued to be published during 1828, but in smaller numbers, and by late 1828 the number of positive articles about Liberia and its settlers had increased.

Other readers, however, may not have been concerned with Russwurm's growing emphasis on news from Liberia or even with the increasing number of procolonization pieces. In their opening editorial, the editors proposed that "every thing that relates to Africa, shall find a ready admission into [their] columns."[75] As we shall explore in detail in chapter 6, news about Liberia was no exception, even when such information emanated from colonizationist sources. Thus even in 1827 news provided by members of the ACS and others favoring colonization was published in *Freedom's Journal* and would no doubt have been appreciated by readers, even those opposed to the ACS, who wished to learn about the African continent. Even explicitly procolonization pieces might not have troubled all readers. At least early in 1828, it seems, some attributed Russwurm's inclusion of procolonization material to the editorial commitment to publish both sides of controversial issues. Veritas asserted in the first of a three-part article on colonization, "I have remarked, with no inconsiderable exultation, that pieces have been published in this paper, that I knew where [*sic*] in direct opposition to the sentiment of the Editors; thus proving that their sole object was clearly to elicit truth, by throwing open its columns to a free and candid investigation." Textual clues in Veritas's essays suggest a white writer who was nonetheless strongly opposed to colonization; however, it is not unreasonable to assume that African-American readers would also have lauded the editors' inclusive policy. Indeed, many readers apparently did not suspect prior to Russwurm's official declaration that his attitude toward colonization was changing. In an editorial published three weeks after the controversial announcement, Russwurm remarked, "The change in our views on colonization, seems to be a 'seven days wonder' to many of our readers."[76]

Some readers expressed concerns with Russwurm's editing that were unconnected to the issue of colonization. A letter to Russwurm published in the final issue suggested that Russwurm's harsh remarks on the subject of economy in the previous issue offended some in his audience. Russwurm also discussed complaints he received without mentioning particular subjects. He indicated, for example, that he had drawn criticism about his increasing inclusion of material from other sources in *Freedom's Journal* rather than pieces original to the paper. "Did we consider the usefulness and respectability of the Journal to consist in the *quantity* of its original matter," he asserted, "we assure our readers, we could fill our columns weekly with matter, considered by the writers as original, but in our humble opinion, unworthy even of a place in our columns." It also appears that Russwurm was not immune to the complaints that editors inevitably endure from readers who feel that their particular concerns are not addressed. An article he reprinted from the *Lichfield Post* in February 1829 declared that because each reader has a unique opinion as to what "constitute[s] proper matter to fill a paper," if all of a newspaper's subscribers "should have a hand in compiling" it, the resulting publication would be "as spacious as heaven's canopy."[77]

Even though some readers began to be less than satisfied with *Freedom's Journal*, we should be skeptical about the judgments of many historians that the quality of the periodical declined under Russwurm's leadership.[78] These assessments often rely on present journalistic standards and assume that we can ascertain definitively what nineteenth-century readers wanted and expected from *Freedom's Journal*, an impossible task. Although some readers were concerned about the inclusion of material from other sources, it was a common and accepted practice at the time to reprint stories from other periodicals and would not have been considered unusual in and of itself.[79] Elizabeth McHenry notes that even the "miscellaneous material" that "was unrelated to the immediate lives of [*Freedom's Journal*'s] readers" served an important purpose. By furnishing free African Americans with "interesting and diverse reading material consumable by a readership of various ages and literacy levels," the editors "facilitat[ed] the continual practice of literacy and encourag[ed] the development of literary sophistication."[80] Indeed, it seems that originality was not a major concern for all readers. In the report of the Boston meeting supportive of the paper, David Walker commented upon "the disadvantages the people of Colour labour under, by the neglect of literature."[81] In the context of a meeting about *Freedom's Journal*, Walker's remark suggests that he would likely have approved of the inclusion of a variety of material in the paper, including the frequent literary pieces that Russwurm favored.

In addition, our contemporary emphasis on "news" items differs from early-nineteenth-century perspectives. Historians of the press emphasize that contemporary distinctions such as "news" versus "editorials" do not apply to this era; and periodicals frequently mixed literary, political, and commercial content.[82] Gayle Berardi and Thomas Segady aptly note,

> Early [African-American] newspapers were not entirely devoted to articles that contained purely news items. Articles about local community and church activities were plentiful, as well as articles describing the best method for cleaning soiled shirts or remedies that would cure the common cold. This content should not be dismissed as trivial, however; it provided valuable information regarding everyday concerns of a growing, increasingly literate African-American population.[83]

Indeed, it appears that criticism of Russwurm's editing cannot be traced to one single concern. Instead it constituted a complex response to his leadership and his work on the paper. We neglect the diversity of opinion in the African-American community at the time if we fail to acknowledge that readers would have had varying expectations for *Freedom's Journal*.

The opposition he encountered, whatever its source, clearly took a toll on Russwurm. As his somewhat caustic responses to his critics indicate, by 1829 he was growing weary of his editorial position, which he described as a "most trying" job.[84] The many appeals for money to sustain the paper indicate as well that his patience with delinquent subscribers wore thin. More generally, he became dissatisfied with what he perceived to be the opportunities for African Americans in the United States and explored alternatives for his future. As its editor pondered his own prospects, the future of *Freedom's Journal* was at stake.

"UNVANQUISHED WE RETIRE": THE END OF *FREEDOM'S JOURNAL*

If it appears that Russwurm was deliberating about colonization in late 1828, by January 1829 he had indeed shifted to a procolonization position. He had also made a fateful decision. In a letter written to Gurley in January 1829, Russwurm announced:

> I deem it expedient to advise you, that I am on the eve of relinquishing the publication of Freedom's Journal, with my views on the subject of Colonization *materially* changed. My reasons for this change, I shall not set forth at present. I am willing to be employed in the colony [of Liberia] in any business, for the performance of which you may deem me qualified. If unqualified, I am willing to qualify myself in this country under the patronage of the society.[85]

Although some historians have held that he was somehow forced or coerced by the Colonization Society to emigrate,[86] Russwurm's solicitation of employment by the ACS demonstrates otherwise.

Russwurm's comments to Gurley—made a few weeks before his public announcement in the paper of his change of heart—similarly belie the common presumption that Russwurm was forced to retire after his altered views on colonization became publicly known.[87] Russwurm had freely determined that he would resign from his post in April 1829 in preparation for emigration to Liberia. He informed Gurley that his "present engagement with the Journal" would end at that time, presumably meaning that he would have finished the second full year of the paper pledged to subscribers.[88]

By February 1829, Russwurm had determined that he had to go public with his new perspective. "A day or two prior to the arrival of your letter [of February 11]," he explained in correspondence to Gurley, "I had come to the conclusion, that as a change had taken place in my views on the subject of Colonization, I was in duty bound, situated as I am, to publish the same to the community, as I had been the instrument of leading many into the wrong way. . . ." His February 14, 1829, editorial in *Freedom's Journal* fulfilled this perceived obligation. After commenting on news from Liberia, he declared,

> As our former sentiments have always been in direct opposition to the plan of colonizing us on the coast of Africa: perhaps so favorable an opportunity may not occur, for us to inform our readers, in an open and candid manner, that our views are materially altered. We have always said, that when convinced of our error, we should hasten to acknowledge it—that period has now arrived. The change which has taken place, has not been the hasty conclusion of a moment; we have pondered much on this interesting subject . . . and we come out from this examination, a decided supporter of the American Colonization Society.
>
> We know, that in making this avowal, we advance doctrines in opposition to the majority of our readers . . . but however unpopular soever they may be, *we know* they are conscientious ones—formed from no sordid motives; but having for their basis, the good of our brethren.[89]

As we have seen, many were surprised by Russwurm's position. His announcement was also met with anger and suspicion. "Th[e] few words I have written," he remarked to Gurley in a letter written just ten days after his announcement was published, "have caused me some persecution already, from the more influential of our people . . . but . . . I am determined, that nothing shall be kept back from the fear of men's frowns." The hostility persisted. Corresponding with Gurley in May, Russwurm related, "A violent persecution which is not considerably subsided, has been raging against me, in [Philadelphia], on account of my change. Two meetings have been held, which were numerously attended; & in fulfillment of my prediction, ended in useless declamation."[90]

Remarks made in the *Liberator* during the 1830s suggested the charges of Russwurm's critics. In an 1831 letter to the editor, R. asserted, "[Russwurm's] ingratitude is but too deeply stamped on the minds of many. . . . After he subverted the pledge he made to his colored brethren, he left, to our satisfaction, his country—suffused with shame—and branded with the stigma of disgrace—to dwell in that land for which the tempter MONEY caused him to avow his preferment." Correspondent C. D. T. remarked that "when [Russwurm's] patrons failed to support the Journal, he, not being able to live without other subscribers, converted the people's paper to the use of the Colonization Society, by which change he worked himself into their employ." C. D. T. was willing to pardon Russwurm to some degree, contending that had he "been in flourishing circumstances," Russwurm would not "have gone to Africa even on a visit." Yet he did not mince words about Russwurm's views, calling his claim that there was "no other home" for African Americans "than Africa" a "palpable falsehood." Like R., C. D. T. implied that money was a motivating force in Russwurm's decision, describing Russwurm's acceptance of colonization as an example of "the change which this world's goods are calculated to make in the principles of man." And even those who did not explicitly accuse him of changing his views for financial reasons implied that he had nonetheless sold out. Commenting on Russwurm's motivations in the *Liberator* in 1831, Garrison noted dryly, "A man is bought in more ways than one."[91]

Russwurm was aware that some were suspicious of his change of heart, but he asserted that he was motivated by principle. In his March 14, 1829, editorial in *Freedom's Journal*, he countered those who would accuse him of "improper motives," asking, "Who has made half the sacrifices we have to oppose the Colonization society? who has labored half so much by *night* and by day for the same end? who has had to bear the brunt of the battle. . . ? who has suffered so much for conscience's sake?" Writing to Gurley, he observed, "I have offered [*sic*] my poor services to the society; and though some may be suspicious of the motives, still, all who know me, will do me the justice to say, that the change in my views, is a real one—arising from a conviction of error in my former opinions."[92]

Although those angry with Russwurm may have focused on his pro-colonization perspective, his view constituted, as Kenneth Nordin maintains, more than a mere change of opinion on one subject. Russwurm had shifted from believing that African Americans could achieve equality and full citizenship as Americans to concluding that it was vain to seek opportunity and justice in the United States.[93] He expressed this view strongly in the editorial in which he announced his endorsement of the ACS, asserting, "We consider it mere waste of words to talk of ever enjoying citizenship in this country; it is utterly impossible in the nature of things; all therefore who pant for these, must cast their eyes elsewhere." His comments over the following weeks echoed this position. The United States, he remarked, "is a land in which we cannot enjoy the privileges of citizens, for certain reasons which are known and felt daily; but [Liberia] is one where we may enjoy all the rights of freemen. . . ." In another comparison, he asserted that in Liberia there is "every incentive to virtuous action," while in the United States, "the mere name of colour, blocks up every avenue. . . . [I]f [an African American] have the feelings of a man, he must be sensible of the degraded station he holds in society; and from which it is impossible to rise, unless he can change the Ethiopian hue of his complexion."[94] As we shall see when we examine the periodical's goals in the next chapter, this rejection of the United States was also a repudiation of one of the original objectives of *Freedom's Journal* and of the philosophical perspectives of many African Americans, who wished to be accepted as Americans and to work toward a future of equality in the United States.

Russwurm no doubt also provoked anger when, in his procolonization rhetoric, he to some extent excused restrictions of African Americans' civil rights. In his editorial of March 14, 1829, he argued,

> The subject of Colonization is certainly important, as having a great bearing on that of slavery: for it must be evident that the universal emancipation so ardently desired by us & by all our friends, can never take place, unless some door is opened whereby the emancipated may be removed as fast as they drop their galling chains, to some other land besides the free states; for it is a fact, that prejudices now in our part of the country, are so high, that it is often the remark of liberal men from the south, that their free people are treated better than we are, in the boasted free states of the north. If the free states have passed no laws as yet forbidding the emigration of free persons of colour into their limits; it is no reason that they will not, as soon as they find themselves a little more burdened. We will suppose that a general law of emancipation should be promulgated in the state of Virginia, under the existing statutes which require every emancipated slave to leave the state, would not the other states, in order to shield themselves from the evils of having so many thousands of ignorant beings thrown upon them, be obliged in self-defence to pass prohibitory laws? Much as we may deplore the evils of slavery—much as we may desire the freedom of the enslaved; who could reproach the free states from enacting such laws?[95]

"We hope none of our readers," Russwurm added, "will . . . think that we approve in the least of the present prejudices . . . far from it, we deplore them as much as any man; but they are not of our creation, and they are not in our power to remove." This rather lukewarm denunciation of racism hardly mitigated his basic point that African Americans should not waste their time fighting oppressive laws, his apology for those who would enact such legislation, and his use of racist phrases ("burdened," "evils," "ignorant beings thrown upon them") popular with white colonizationists. Russwurm did not go as far as some white colonizationists who, as we have seen, argued explicitly for curtailing free African Americans' civil rights so that they would not be tempted to remain in the United States. Yet he clearly went far enough to offend many readers.

The History of Freedom's Journal 63

Despite the anger that he encountered, we should not oversimplify the response of African Americans to Russwurm. Cornish's reaction to his former partner's decision to emigrate, for example, was complex. In an 1838 article in the *Colored American*, Cornish expressed great anger about Russwurm's decision. The doctrine "Take care of N[umber] ONE," Cornish lamented, "carried Mr. Russwurm to Liberia." Cornish also noted that this doctrine "made Arnold sell his country" and "plunged the South into all the guilt and shame of a cruel system of slavery," placing Russwurm in traitorous and detestable company indeed. Yet in 1829, he assisted his former partner, giving the ACS a positive recommendation of Russwurm as they examined his fitness for employment in the colony. Charles Andrews, who contacted Cornish on behalf of the ACS to inquire about Russwurm's fitness for employment in Liberia, informed Gurley in an 1829 letter that Cornish "considers Mr. R. worthy of all confidence, and is willing to bear full testimony as to R's correct habits and exemplary deportment."[96] Cornish's public criticism and private aid suggest that although he was strongly opposed to Russwurm's decision, he still had some admiration for his talents and character, at least in 1829.

It appears that other influential African-American leaders shared Cornish's sentiments. David Walker continued to be listed as an agent of the paper through its final issue, a notable endorsement given Walker's vehement denunciation of colonization in his *Appeal*, first published in 1829. In a letter written in late February 1829, Russwurm informed Gurley (hoping to expedite the decision of the ACS board about his employment in Liberia) that "the people of colour in Boston" were "making an effort to replace [him] in [his] old situation in the Free School," indicating that an important position in the African-American community was available to Russwurm even after his public procolonization announcement. Not all African Americans shared this confidence in Russwurm; his correspondence with Gurley mentions one case in which a person contacted by the ACS responded with a negative assessment of Russwurm's character. Yet it seems that many still valued Russwurm's contributions, although they opposed his views.[97]

Russwurm bade farewell to his patrons in the final issue of the periodical, published March 28, 1829. Not hiding his disillusionment, he expressed both frustration with the practical problems he encountered and disappointment over the response of many to his work:

We commenced the Journal under the impression that the whole of our time would be devoted to the editorial department—that none of the manual labor of the office would fall upon us; but how disappointed we have been, we need not mention. . . . Generally speaking, an editor's office is a thankless one; and if so, among an enlightened people; what could *we* expect? We are therefore

not in the least astonished, that we have been slandered by the villainous—that
our name is byword among the more ignorant, for what less could we expect?

Yet Russwurm did not admit defeat—far from it. "Prepared, we entered
the lists," he asserted, "and unvanquished we retire, with the hope that
the talent committed to our care, may yet be exerted under more favorable auspices, and upon minds more likely to appreciate its value."[98] Indeed "unvanquished," Russwurm left for Liberia in September 1829,
committed to remaining in public life.

Thus the era of *Freedom's Journal* came to a close. But Russwurm's hope
that the first African-American newspaper would be followed by others
was indeed realized. In fact, his former partner Cornish would be a major
force in African-American journalism for years to come. And as we shall
see, despite its short life, *Freedom's Journal* had a significant impact, both
in the antebellum period and beyond, influencing African-American journalism, the abolition movement, and generations of American reformers.

NOTES

1. The dates of the last ten issues of *Freedom's Journal* (January 24, 1829 to March
28, 1829) are actually Saturdays. The issue prior to January 24, 1829, is dated on
the masthead as January 16, a Friday, and on the sixth page as January 17, a Sat-
urday. (Such inconsistencies within an issue occasionally occur on other dates as
well.) However, the publication information at the end of these issues still notes
that "THE FREEDOM'S JOURNAL IS PRINTED & PUBLISHED EVERY FRIDAY."
The exact reason for this discrepancy is unclear.

2. The issue of March 28, 1828, does not appear to be extant. It is absent from the
microfilmed version of the periodical; historian Arthur Schomburg's report on his
efforts to locate a complete run of the periodical indicates that it was not found
("Freedom's Journal," in *Arthur A. Schomburg Papers* [microfilm collection], reel 7,
frames 1066–69). The pagination of the subsequent number (April 4, 1828) indicates that the missing issue was eight pages long.

3. Penn, *Afro-American Press*, 28. Booker T. Washington's 1909 account of *Freedom's Journal's* founding is almost identical to Penn's (*Story*, vol. 1, 292).

4. On Boston Crummell, see Moses, *Alexander Crummell*, 12–13.

5. Penn, *Afro-American Press*, 26. In fact, there are various errors in Penn's account;
he asserted, for example, that *Freedom's Journal* suspended publication in 1828 and
that the short-lived *Rights of All* began publication in 1828 with Russwurm as its editor (*Afro-American Press*, 30). Actually, as we shall discuss in chapter 9, the first issue of the *Rights of All*, edited by Cornish, was dated May 29, 1829.

6. See, for example, Gross, "*Freedom's Journal*," 242–43; Bryan, "Negro Journalism," 7–8; Dann, *Black Press*, 16; Gore, *Negro Journalism*, 5; Tripp, *Origins*,
12–13; Wolseley, *Black Press*, 24–25; Finkle, *Forum*, 17–18; Simmons, *African-
American Press*, 9–10; Kessler, *Dissident Press*, 27–28; Pride and Wilson, *History*,
6–10; Detweiler, *Negro Press*, 36; Wilson, *Black Journalists*, 25; Lerone Bennett, *Pioneers*, 59; Emery and Emery, *Press*, 181; Brewer, "John B. Russwurm," 414;

Gronowicz, *Race*, 57; Murphy, *Other Voices*, 79; Berardi and Segady, "Development," 96; Sagarin, *John Brown Russwurm*, 49–50.

7. Samuel E. Cornish and John B. Russwurm, "To Our Patrons," *FJ*, 16 March 1827; Samuel E. Cornish and John B. Russwurm, "Prospectus," *FJ*, 16 March 1827.

8. Mordecai, letter to editors, *FJ*, 17 August 1827; Samuel E. Cornish and John B. Russwurm, "Major Noah's 'Negroes,'" *FJ*, 24 August 1827; Samuel E. Cornish and John B. Russwurm, "Slavery in the West-Indies," *FJ*, 11 May 1827; Samuel E. Cornish and John B. Russwurm, untitled editorial, *FJ*, 29 June 1827; F. C. Webb et al., "Philadelphia Report" (part I), *FJ*, 18 July 1828; F. C. Webb et al., "Philadelphia Report" (part II), *FJ*, 30 July 1828. For other examples of responses in *Freedom's Journal* to articles in white periodicals, see Spectator, letter to editors, *FJ*, 7 September 1827; "From the Pennsylvania Gazette," *FJ*, 14 March 1828; "The Jurist," *FJ*, 25 July 1828.

9. Cornish and Russwurm, "To Our Patrons"; anonymous letter to Samuel E. Cornish, *FJ*, 13 July 1827; Samuel E. Cornish and John B. Russwurm, untitled editorial (part I), *FJ*, 30 March 1827; Samuel E. Cornish and John B. Russwurm, untitled editorial (part II), *FJ*, 13 April 1827.

10. Cornish and Russwurm, "To Our Patrons."

11. See, for example, Lerone Bennett, *Confrontation*, 57; Ottley and Weatherby, *Negro*, 89; Swift, *Black Prophets*, 27; Carter, "Black," 146; Thompson, *Africans*, 139.

12. Cornish and Russwurm, "Prospectus."

13. Frances Smith Foster, "Narrative," 718.

14. Hinks, *To Awaken*, 91.

15. Cornish and Russwurm, "To Our Patrons"; Cornish and Russwurm, "Prospectus."

16. Cornish and Russwurm, "To Our Patrons." On the desire of Cornish and Russwurm to connect African Americans in different parts of the nation through *Freedom's Journal*, see also Robert Levine, "Circulating the Nation," 22; Goodman, *Of One Blood*, 26; Belt-Beyan, *Emergence*, 142–44.

17. Cornish and Russwurm, "To Our Patrons"; McHenry, *Forgotten Readers*, 48, 85. On African Americans' utilization of print and its key role in their activism, see also Newman, "Chosen Generation," 71–74; Newman, "Protest," 181–82; Timothy Patrick McCarthy, "To Plead," 116–18.

18. On these developments, see Emery and Emery, *Press*, 115, 131–35; Humphrey, *Press*, 144–45; Horton and Horton, *In Hope*, 206–7; Brown, *Knowledge*, 8–9; Murphy, *Other Voices*, 60.

19. Cornish and Russwurm, "Prospectus."

20. Cornish and Russwurm, "To Our Patrons."

21. My biographical sketch of Cornish draws from the following sources: Presbytery of Philadelphia, Minutes, 21 October 1817–1 July 1823; Presbytery of New York, Minutes, 16 April 1822–12 October 1826; Swift, *Black Prophets*, 2–3, 19–41; Swift, "Black Presbyterian," 433; Sorin, *New York*, 92–93; Cincinnati, "Belleville"; Moore, "Righteousness," 224–25; New-York Evangelical Missionary Society, *Fifth Annual Report*, 115–16; New-York Evangelical Missionary Society of Young Men, *Brief View*, 17; Mohl, *Poverty*, 205; Reed, *Platform*, 83; Floyd Miller, *Search*, 77, 82–83; Murray, *Presbyterians*, 42; Emma Jones Lapsansky, *Neighborhoods*, 121; Pride and Wilson, *History*, 11–12.

22. Swift, *Black Prophets*, 19; Samuel E. Cornish, "A Few of the Abominations of Slavery," *CA*, 1 April 1837.

23. My biographical sketch of Russwurm draws from Floyd Miller, *Search*, 84–88; Sagarin, *John Brown Russwurm*; Borzendowski, *John Russwurm*; Foner, "John Browne Russwurm"; Foner, *History . . . 1850*, 226–27; Pride and Wilson, *History*, 12–13; Horton and Horton, *In Hope*, 196–97; Beyan, *African American Settlements*; Sandra Sandiford Young, "John Brown Russwurm's Dilemma"; extract from a report of proceedings of the Maine Genealogical Society, John Brown Russwurm folder, box 7, Miscellaneous American Letters and Papers, New York Public Library, Schomburg Center; John Brown Russwurm to William Russwurm, 9 January 1826, *John Sumner Russwurm Papers*.

24. Russwurm, who graduated from Bowdoin on September 6, 1826, was the third African-American college graduate in the United States, preceded by Alexander Lucius Twilight from Middlebury College, Vermont, in August 1823, and Edward Jones from Amherst College on August 23, 1826. See Hileman, "Iron-Willed Schoolmaster," 6, 12; Foner, *History . . . 1850*, 226; Franklin and Moss, *From Slavery*, 181; Horton and Horton, *In Hope*, 290.

25. John Brown Russwurm, "The Condition and Prospects of Haiti," in Foner, *Lift Every Voice*, 103–4.

26. John B. Russwurm to R. R. Gurley, New York, 26 February 1827, *Records of the American Colonization Society*, reel 1.

27. Roland Wolseley assumes that whites must have been the main supporters of the periodical; see *Black Press*, 25. Bella Gross, conversely, suggests that whites did not support the paper except through subscriptions; see *"Freedom's Journal,"* 250.

28. Penn, *Afro-American Press*, 30.

29. For more information on Thomas and Nathaniel Paul, Wright, and Hughes, see Hinks, *To Awaken*, 95–97; Murray, *Presbyterians*, 35.

30. Untitled report of Boston meeting, *FJ*, 16 March 1827.

31. Washington, *Story*, vol. 1, 292–93.

32. Foner, *History . . . 1850*, 266, 483; see also Delany, *Condition*, 95; Horton and Horton, *In Hope*, 265; Quarles, *Allies*, 40.

33. Washington, *Story*, vol. 1, 292–93.

34. Peter Williams Jr. to Thomas Tucker, New York, 10 June 1816, *Black Abolitionist Papers* [microfilm collection], reel 17, frame 152; Reed, *Platform*, 101–2.

35. Thomas Hale to Isaac Barton, New York, 25 January 1827, Pennsylvania Abolition Society Papers, box 10, folder 1.

36. Samuel E. Cornish and John B. Russwurm to Isaac Barton, New York, 2 October 1827, Pennsylvania Abolition Society Papers, box 10, folder 4; Gerrit Smith to R. R. Gurley, Peterboro, New York, 10 October 1827, *Records of the American Colonization Society*, reel 2.

37. These advertisements appear in the following issues of *Freedom's Journal* as well as in others: 1 June 1827; 8 June 1827; 16 November 1827; 31 October 1828. The information about advertising rates is listed at the end of each issue.

38. Information about subscriptions and payment was provided at the end of each issue. The note to subscribers unable to pay in advance appears in the first five issues only.

39. Leonard, *News for All*, 37.

40. Samuel E. Cornish and John B. Russwurm, editorial notice, *FJ*, 25 May 1827; Samuel E. Cornish and John B. Russwurm, editorial notice, *FJ*, 24 August 1827;

Samuel E. Cornish and John B. Russwurm, editorial notice, *FJ*, 31 August 1827; Samuel E. Cornish and John B. Russwurm, editorial notice, *FJ*, 14 September 1827; John B. Russwurm, editorial notice, *FJ*, 21 September 1827; John B. Russwurm, editorial notice, *FJ*, 28 September 1827; John B. Russwurm, "Our Own Concerns," *FJ*, 16 November 1827; John B. Russwurm, "Our Own Concerns," *FJ*, 23 November 1827; John B. Russwurm, "Our Own Concerns," *FJ*, 30 November 1827; John B. Russwurm, editorial notice, *FJ*, 21 December 1827; John B. Russwurm, "Our Own Concerns," *FJ*, 21 December 1827.

41. John B. Russwurm, "Prospectus," *FJ*, 25 April 1828 (as well as in other issues); John B. Russwurm, "Our Own Concerns," *FJ*, 21 March 1828; John B. Russwurm, editorial notice, *FJ*, 23 May 1828; "The Subscription List—A Farce," *FJ*, 9 January 1829; John B. Russwurm, editorial notice, *FJ*, 5 December 1828.

42. Samuel E. Cornish and John B. Russwurm, "Colonization Society," *FJ*, 8 June 1827; A Man of Colour, letter to the editors, *FJ*, 8 June 1827; Smith to Gurley, Peterboro, New York, 10 October 1827.

43. Samuel Miller, letter to editors of the *New-York Observer*, *FJ*, 21 September 1827; "Freedom's Journal," *FJ*, 26 October 1827. On white criticism of *Freedom's Journal*'s position and the opposition at Princeton, see Swift, *Black Prophets*, 36–40; Bella Gross, "Life and Times," 134; Horton and Horton, *In Hope*, 197–98; Goodman, *Of One Blood*, 27.

44. John B. Russwurm to R. R. Gurley, New York, 24 February 1829, *Records of the American Colonization Society*, reel 5; Russwurm, "Our Own Concerns," *FJ*, 21 December 1827; J[ohn] B. Vashon, letter to editor, *CA*, 18 November 1837.

45. Pride and Wilson, *History*, 18.

46. Cornish referred to the distribution of 800 copies monthly in an issue of the *Rights of All* ("The Rights of All," *Rights of All*, 7 August 1829). (Although 7 August 1829 is the date on the masthead of this issue, within its pages the date is given as 14 August 1829. Here and elsewhere in this book, I use the date on the masthead in notes when there is variation within an issue.)

47. Gross, "*Freedom's Journal*," 249.

48. Barrow, "Our Own Cause," 229; Pride and Wilson, *History*, 18.

49. Hutton, *Early Black Press*, xv; see also Kinshasa, *Emigration*, 2; McHenry, *Forgotten Readers*, 89.

50. "Borrowing," *FJ*, 23 November 1827; "Newspaper Borrowers," *FJ*, 2 January 1829.

51. William Whipper, "Address," *FJ*, 20 June 1828; "Minutes, &c. of the American Convention. [Continued.]," *FJ*, 8 February 1828; "New-York African Free School," *FJ*, 9 November 1827.

52. See, for example, Wolseley, *Black Press*, 25; Murphy, *Other Voices*, 79; Berardi and Segady, "Development," 96–97; O'Kelly, "Black Newspapers," 1.

53. Woodson, *Education*, 98–150; McHenry, *Forgotten Readers*, 337; Belt-Beyan, *Emergence*; Frances Smith Foster, "Narrative," 720–23.

54. Peter Williams Jr. to Stephen Grellet, New York, 1 June 1816, Grellet Manuscript Collection, Volume I.

55. McHenry, "Dreaded Eloquence," 46; McHenry, *Forgotten Readers*, 34–35; Levesque, "Inherent," 492; Hinks, *To Awaken*, 153–54; Kinshasa, *Emigration*, 114–17; Frances Smith Foster, "Narrative," 715, 726–27; Peterson, "Black Life," 213.

56. Tony Martin, "Banneker Literary Institute," 309.

57. Porter, "Organized," 558.

58. Pride and Wilson, *History*, 7; see also Gross, "*Freedom's Journal*," 254–55.

59. Hinks, *To Awaken*, 75.

60. Cornish and Russwurm, "To Our Patrons." The editors cite 500,000 free people of color while the 1830 census only listed 319,599; the reason for the discrepancy, Philip Foner explains, is that "undoubtedly the editors, like other blacks of
the period, were aware that many escaped slaves hid from the census takers" (*History . . . 1850*, 251).

61. Egerton, *He Shall Go*, 54, 68.

62. See Hinks, *To Awaken*, 54–55, 116–72, 238–41; Wilentz, introduction to David
Walker's Appeal, vii, xiv; Aptheker, "*One Continual Cry*," 45; Horton and Horton, *In
Hope*, 203–4; Egerton, *He Shall Go*, 98, 225; McHenry, *Forgotten Readers*, 25–26,
30–31.

63. V., "Walker's Appeal. No. 2," *Liberator*, 14 May 1831. Janet Duitsman Cornelius and Phyllis Belt-Beyan indicate that many slaves gained a basic ability to
read and write (Cornelius, following historian Carter G. Woodson, estimates
the number at ten percent), allowing them to read literature such as *Freedom's
Journal* (Cornelius, "*When I Can Read*," 6–8; Belt-Beyan, *Emergence*, 109; see
also Hinks, *To Awaken*, 154–58; Gross, "*Freedom's Journal*," 253). As V.'s account
suggests, others had the periodical read aloud to them, a common practice
among slaves and free African Americans in the South (Hinks, *To Awaken*,
154–56).

64. Samuel E. Cornish, "To the Patrons and Friends of 'Freedom's Journal,'" *FJ*,
14 September 1827.

65. See Bryan, "Negro Journalism," 9; Wolseley, *Black Press*, 25; Hutton, *Early
Black Press*, 5; Dann, *Black Press*, 250; Simmons, *African-American Press*, 10; Kessler,
Dissident Press, 28–29; Rouse, "We Can Never," 133.

66. Barrow, "'Our Own Cause,'" 121; see also Borzendowski, *John Russwurm*, 56;
Sagarin, *John Brown Russwurm*, 67.

67. Cornish, "To the Patrons and Friends"; "Notice," *FJ*, 14 September 1827.

68. John B. Russwurm, "City Free Schools," *FJ*, 11 January 1828.

69. Samuel E. Cornish, "To Our Patrons, and the Publick Generally," *Rights of
All*, 29 May 1829; Samuel E. Cornish and John B. Russwurm, "Colonization Society," *FJ*, 14 September 1827.

70. John B. Russwurm, "Liberian Circular," *FJ*, 25 January 1828; untitled and unsigned response to F.A., letter, *FJ*, 15 February 1828.

71. Vincent Bakpetu Thompson, *Africans*, 201.

72. "Freedom's Journal," *FJ*, 25 April 1828; John B. Russwurm, "Our Labours,"
FJ, 5 December 1828.

73. Horton and Horton, *In Hope*, 198.

74. John B. Russwurm, "Liberia," *FJ*, 14 February 1829.

75. Cornish and Russwurm, "To Our Patrons."

76. Veritas, "Colonization Society," *FJ*, 22 February 1828; John B. Russwurm,
"Our Vindication," *FJ*, 7 March 1829.

77. A Subscriber But No Press Stock Holder, letter to editor, *FJ*, 28 March 1828;
Russwurm, "Our Labours"; "Newspaper Readers," *FJ*, 28 February 1829. Kenneth

Nordin analyzes the paper's "growing reliance on feature material borrowed from other sources" ("In Search," 124).

78. See, for example, Simmons, *African-American Press*, 10; Finkle, *Forum for Protest*, 19; Bryan, "Negro Journalism," 9; Borzendowski, *John Russwurm*, 56; Foner, *History*, 255.

79. Tripp, *Origins*, 14.

80. McHenry, *Forgotten Readers*, 92–93.

81. *Freedom's Journal*, 25 April 1828.

82. Schudson, *Discovering*, 4–16; Baldasty, *Commercialization*, 6.

83. Berardi and Segady, "Development," 97.

84. Russwurm, "Our Labours."

85. Russwurm to Gurley, New York, 26 January 1829.

86. Payne, "Negro," 61; Oak, *Negro Newspaper*, 122; Wolseley, *Black Press*, 18; Bryan, "Negro Journalism," 9–10.

87. See, for example, Gross, "*Freedom's Journal*," 249, 279; Lerone Bennett, *Pioneers*, 65; Lerone Bennett, "Founders," 100; Sagarin, *John Brown Russwurm*, 71; Horton and Horton, *Black Bostonians*, 98; Borzendowski, *John Russwurm*, 65; Pride and Wilson, *History*, 17; Horton and Horton, *In Hope*, 198; Foner, *History . . . 1850*, 255, 299; Finkle, *Forum*, 19; Quarles, *Black Abolitionists*, 7; Sagarin, *John Brown Russwurm*, 71; Timothy Patrick McCarthy, "To Plead," 132.

88. Russwurm to Gurley, New York, 26 January 1829.

89. Russwurm to Gurley, New York, 24 February 1829; Russwurm, "Liberia," *FJ*, 14 February 1829.

90. Russwurm to Gurley, New York, 24 February 1829; John B. Russwurm to R. R. Gurley, Philadelphia, 7 May 1829, *Records of the American Colonization Society*, reel 5.

91. R., letter to editor, *Liberator*, 16 April 1831; C. D. T., letter to editor, *Liberator*, 30 April 1831; William Lloyd Garrison, untitled editorial comments, *Liberator*, 21 March 1831.

92. John B. Russwurm, "Colonization," *FJ*, 14 March 1829; Russwurm to Gurley, New York, 24 February 1829.

93. Nordin, "In Search," 127; see also Hutton, "Democratic Idealism," 7; Hutton, *Early Black Press*, 7; Foner, *History . . . 1850*, 298; Hodges, *Root & Branch*, 199; Sagarin, *John Brown Russwurm*, 71–72.

94. Russwurm, "Liberia," 14 February 1829; John B. Russwurm, "Liberia," *FJ*, 21 February 1829; Russwurm, "Our Vindication."

95. Russwurm, "Colonization."

96. Samuel E. Cornish, "Take Care of Number One!" *CA*, 27 January 1838; C. C. Andrews to R. R. Gurley, New York, 1 July 1829, *Records of the American Colonization Society*, reel 6.

97. Russwurm to Gurley, New York, 24 February 1829; Russwurm to Gurley, New York, 3 July 1829, *Records of the American Colonization Society*, reel 6.

98. John B. Russwurm, "To Our Patrons," *FJ*, 28 March 1829.

3

❧

"Whatever Concerns Us as a People": The Goals of *Freedom's Journal*

The objectives that Cornish and Russwurm set out to accomplish through the columns of *Freedom's Journal* have at times been misunderstood. As we have seen, scholars have often incompletely portrayed the periodical's founding primarily as a means of responding to white rhetoric, thereby implying that this goal was of paramount importance to its editors and contributors. Others have suggested that the periodical's central aim was to fight slavery.[1] Yet although the paper featured arguments against white racism and slavery, overemphasizing these objectives diminishes the scope and magnitude of *Freedom's Journal*. The editors did not have a monolithic focus; their comprehensive goals were directed by the needs and concerns of African Americans themselves. "The end of slavery and social justice for free blacks were major objectives of the newspaper," Kenneth Nordin argues, "but . . . its editors also had a broader journalistic objective: to produce a nationally circulated newspaper which would develop a sense of fraternity, a black consciousness" among African Americans throughout the United States.[2]

Cornish and Russwurm explicitly stated this inclusive approach to the periodical's goals: "In short, whatever concerns us as a people, will ever find a ready admission into the FREEDOM'S JOURNAL." As this description implies, *Freedom's Journal* covered many issues of concern to African Americans, such as colonization, education, self-improvement, women's and men's ideal roles in the home and in society, and slavery. On these subjects, *Freedom's Journal* allowed African Americans to "plead their own cause," to speak for themselves, to define these issues in their own terms, and to create powerful arguments. We shall, at length, explore the coverage of particular subjects in subsequent chapters. But there were also more general objectives that the paper set out to accomplish that were a result of what Russwurm described as "the invaluable benefits likely to accrue to [African Americans] as a body, from possessing a channel of public communication."[3] These "invaluable benefits" included practical results that improved everyday living as well as the more intangible effects of furthering community consciousness and identity, fostering racial pride, and empowering African Americans to take control of the ways they were represented in the press and in society.

"USEFUL KNOWLEDGE"

In their first editorial, Cornish and Russwurm asserted that their paper would be "devoted to the dissemination of useful knowledge among [their] brethren" and that "useful knowledge of every kind . . . shall find a ready admission into [their] columns."[4] At first glance, the editors' description may seem to emphasize practical concerns, and indeed much of the "useful knowledge" featured in the periodical's columns was directed toward improving the day-to-day lives of African Americans. Yet this information in *Freedom's Journal* had a significance that should not be underestimated. The practical knowledge that African Americans found on its pages could help nurture group identity and community consciousness, empower them to take control of their lives and destinies, connect communities divided by geography, and mobilize activism.

In addition to generating revenue for *Freedom's Journal*, advertisements functioned to disseminate information about the community unavailable in other venues. African-American consumers could learn from the newspaper where they could buy clothing, sell their used garments, obtain various types of instruction for themselves and their children, and purchase medicines for various ailments. These advertisements may appear mundane, but they played an important role in the community. As Harry Reed explains, "Only a few black businesses were able to advertise in white papers, and that privilege was usually restricted to black businesses that catered to a white clientele. Absence of an advertising venue constituted a double jeopardy for blacks. Black entrepreneurs were denied one of the basic avenues to advertising their products and maximizing their profits. Black consumers, on the other hand, were limited in their knowledge of and access to black merchants." *Freedom's Journal* enabled African Americans to use their economic power and to take control of their material needs in ways that would give them self-determination and build the community. The many advertisements for lodging are of particular significance. Housing for nineteenth-century urban African Americans "was pretty restrictive," Reed notes, and available quarters were often substandard. The commentary included in lodging advertisements could help steer African Americans moving or traveling to various cities to appropriate accommodations. Charles Short's notice that his Philadelphia Union Hotel was "a House of the first-rate kind," F. Wiles's description of his clientele for his New York boardinghouse as "genteel persons of colour," and Eliza Johnson's remark that her "house is in a healthy and pleasant situation" demonstrate how such advertisements addressed African Americans' concerns for safety and respectability.[5]

Announcements about matters of practical importance often appeared in the columns of *Freedom's Journal*. An article in the issue of May 25, 1827, informed readers about an organization created to oversee a fund that would help poor New York City residents with their fuel costs. In preparation for the expensive winter months, citizens could contribute monthly to the fund, which the society would use "to lay in a supply of fuel at those periods of the year, when it may be purchased at cheaper rates." From December to March, they would then be eligible to buy fuel "at its summer cost." The editors suggested that those who took advantage of the opportunity would gain more than the tangible benefit: "It would not only contribute to our present comforts, but it would enable us the better to provide for our offspring, and at the same time be placing before them an example of frugality, that could not fail to have its influence upon their future lives and conduct."[6] A solution to an everyday problem became for the editors more than a way of helping individuals to survive—it was also an opportunity to demonstrate how the community could be enriched when members developed means for creating autonomy and self-respect.

Many African Americans faced another everyday challenge—providing clothing for their families. An 1828 notice in *Freedom's Journal* addressed one of the consequences of this problem for children attending New York's African Free Schools—"owing to want of suitable clothing," many were forced to "absent themselves from school." A meeting of African-American women, ministers, and Manumission Society members, the announcement reported, led to the formation of the African Dorcas Association, which would "afford relief in clothing, hats, and shoes" by soliciting donations. As with the notice of the fuel savings fund, this announcement stressed that the implications for the community went beyond practical results. "We individually consider it a great blessing for our children," the organization's constitution proclaimed, "and those of our friends of Colour, to enjoy the advantages of a good education . . . so that the rising generation amongst us, may freely participate in the good which their and our benefactors are so liberally tendering them."[7]

Other announcements in the newspaper called attention to educational opportunities available to African Americans in various cities. These notices often took the form of advertisements, listing prices for instruction. African-American adults in New York could learn from the columns of *Freedom's Journal* that the African Mutual Instruction Society operated an evening school that would teach reading, writing, and arithmetic; that B. F. Hughes's school accepted "coloured children of both sexes"; and that those desiring musical instruction could attend St. Philip's Church Music School, open Tuesday and Friday evenings. A notice from New York's African Free School informed those who could not afford tuition (between twenty-five cents and one dollar per quarter, depending upon a family's finances) that their children would be educated at the school free of charge. A notice placed by Jeremiah Gloucester of Philadelphia notified readers that the subjects taught in his school included "Reading, Writing, Cyphering, Geography, English Grammar, and Natural Philosophy" as well as "Needle Work" for "the females." Notices also informed African-American residents of various cities about the formation of community organizations, such as the Colored Reading Society of Philadelphia, New York's African Mutual Relief Society, and the Rush Education Society of Philadelphia, and announced their events and meetings.[8]

As we shall explore in detail in chapter 8, some practical announcements gave urgent and critical information that could literally preserve individuals' freedom. *Freedom's Journal* frequently featured warnings about the continual threat of kidnapping faced by African Americans in Northern cities, reports that could potentially help liberate those who were victims of this outrage, and measures to escape kidnappers. Beyond their immediate value in helping individual African Americans live safer and more fulfilling lives, practical information in the paper's columns served to strengthen the bonds among African Americans within various cities that, as we have seen, had been fostered and nurtured since the Revolution. Notices about education, mutual relief, cultural events, and personal safety strengthened African Americans' sense of solidarity and empowered them to control their lives and destinies. The announcements often functioned rhetorically to argue strongly for civil rights. We shall see, for example, that Russwurm's strongly worded warnings to fugitives unequivocally asserted slaves' right to take their freedom. In addition, James Oliver Horton indicates, concrete information was often part of an effort to mobilize activism by bringing people together to address important concerns and issues such as personal safety and slavery.[9]

The significance of information and announcements about the concerns of African Americans in particular locations went beyond the benefit to one particular city or community. Cornish and Russwurm intended the paper to be "a medium of intercourse between our brethren in the different states of this great confederacy," and information about a particular locale made readers aware that their everyday concerns were shared by others in different cities, nurturing the national consciousness that, as we have seen, had been developing since the turn of the century.[10] Russwurm's 1828 "Travelling Scraps" columns, chronicling his travels between New York and Washington, D.C., described for readers in various locations the conditions—from available educational opportunities to the effects of slavery—that influenced the daily lives of their counterparts in cities such as Philadelphia and Baltimore.[11] Beyond creating an awareness of a national community, these sources of information reinforced a fundamental premise of the periodical and of black identity and activism in general—the freedom and self-determination of African Americans was a communal rather than an individual enterprise.[12] Slavery and abolition, for example, were not issues that affected only those in certain states; as Cornish and Russwurm asserted in their opening editorial, they wished for their readers to be continually aware of their ties to their "brethren who are still in the iron fetters of bondage." Announcements that the Friendship Society of Baltimore, an African-American benevolent organization, and a "respectable number of the Coloured Inhabitants of Fredericksburgh," Virginia, celebrated the abolition of slavery in New York on July 4, 1827, underscored the communal nature of freedom and slavery.[13]

Notices of developments in various cities could also serve as models for those in other locations trying to deal with pressing issues. A piece giving the details of an "Infant School for Coloured children" in Philadelphia, for example, demonstrated how residents of one locale addressed the need for care for the children of working mothers, a concern of many African-American women. Explicitly suggesting that this institution should be replicated in other cities, Russwurm noted that interested New Yorkers should work toward a similar end. Similarly, he commented in a notice about kidnapping, "The members of our Manumission Society have been unwearied in their labours . . . but the duty has been so constant and pressing, we think something should be done by us. . . . Perhaps the formation of such a society as the Protecting Society, of Philadelphia for the preventing of kidnapping and man-stealing, might be of incalculable benefit. . . ."[14] "Useful knowledge" about the lives and activities of their counterparts throughout the North did more than create a sense of national unity among African Americans—it suggested new possibilities for community building and activism.

"ALL THE PRINCIPAL NEWS OF THE DAY"

As the announcements in *Freedom's Journal* about kidnapping and slavery demonstrate, "useful knowledge" that directly influenced African Americans' daily lives was frequently connected to larger events in the United

States and the world—in other words, to news. As we have noted, nineteenth-century periodicals did not always draw a rigid distinction between news and other types of articles.[15] Indeed, Cornish and Russwurm suggested in their opening editorial the interconnected nature of news and practical information, noting that "whatever concerns [them] as a people" would be "interwoven" in the periodical "with all the principal news of the day."[16]

To this end, the paper featured both national and international news stories, usually reprinted from other sources. Although many news stories in *Freedom's Journal* had been published before, their inclusion in the publication was significant, bringing together in one forum information that readers otherwise might not have encountered and placing it in a context that emphasized its import for African Americans. As we shall explore in detail in subsequent chapters, a variety of news stories addressed slavery, abolition, Haiti, and Africa. Other subjects of interest to African Americans were covered as well. Like their selection of practical information, Cornish and Russwurm's choice of news items went beyond merely informing African Americans about the nation and the world. The "principal news of the day" that Cornish and Russwurm selected presented alternatives to the general coverage of white periodicals of the day and fostered racial pride by reporting on the achievements of African Americans.

Freedom's Journal provided contrasting views to the sensationalized stories in the white press about the perpetration of crimes by free blacks by reporting news about crimes *against* free African Americans—a phenomenon that white Americans often ignored. In addition to warnings about kidnappings, for example, the periodical also published accounts of this crime, in cities from Philadelphia to Norfolk (and, in some fortunate cases, reported the return of those who had been abducted).[17] Other crimes against people of color were also noted. A "Domestic News" item in the second issue of the periodical reported, "G. W. Steele, of the schooner Harden . . . has been committed to prison in Boston, on a charge of cruelly beating Allen Cooper, a coloured man, on board that vessel. . . . Cooper's back was lacerated in a most shocking manner. Steele to be tried this month."[18]

In August 1827, the editors reprinted a piece from the *Genius of Universal Emancipation* under the title "Horrible! Most Horrible!" The article recounted the "BURNING OF A HUMAN BEING!!! with merely a resemblance of legal process"—in other words, a lynching. The account is, in fact, the first known newspaper report of a lynching.[19] When "a Mr. McNeily" of Alabama "lost some great value," the article related, "the slave of a neighboring planter was charged with theft." When the slave was found "driving his master's wagon" by McNeily and his brother, he stabbed McNeily. Although the slave was "taken before the Justice of the

Peace," that official "waved his authority," giving over the prisoner to a "mob" which had gathered near the justice's home and which voted that "he should be immediately executed by being *burnt to death*." The account noted that this incident was not an anomaly: "This is the second negro who has been thus put to death, without Judge or Jury in that county."[20] Such articles provided African-American readers with a perspective often unavailable in other periodicals. Crimes against them were not to be ignored, but were to be taken seriously, the editors of *Freedom's Journal* established; and readers deserved an alternative to the one-sided coverage of most white publications.

An account of a horrible offense against an African-American child, published in *Freedom's Journal* on December 5, 1828, served another function as well. "Sarah, a coloured woman," embarking upon "an errand" with a white woman, left her infant in the care of the white woman's son, nearly five. Returning, Sarah found her "dead and awfully mangled" child "lying about twenty feet from the door," the victim of great brutality: "Its head was deeply gashed and bruised, apparently with several blows of an axe; the left leg was chopped off close to the foot; and wounds were seen upon the other foot, and various parts of the body." The five-year-old reported that "a drunken black man" had killed the baby, but the next day the boy confessed that it was he who had murdered the infant after it cried for its mother.[21] Beyond reporting a ghastly crime, the article demonstrated how prejudice could lead to false charges against African Americans—and, shockingly, the early age at which whites develop the biases that underlie these accusations.

African Americans were not only victims, though, in *Freedom's Journal's* news coverage. Numerous items offered positive accounts of African Americans and their successes. An article published on February 22, 1828, remarked on the sixty-ninth birthday of Richard Allen, celebrated in Philadelphia by "a number of respectable ladies and gentlemen." The piece listed Allen's prestigious accomplishments: "Bishop Allen was the first person that formed a Religious Society among the People of Colour in the United States. . . . He was also the first person that established a Benevolent Society among us for the grand purpose of relieving one another in time of distress. He was also the founder of the first African Church in the United States of America. . . ."[22] These achievements, the article noted, motivated many others in their religious and community efforts.

News of the activities of less prominent figures was no less a source of inspiration. A brief piece published in August 1827, for example, reported that "great numbers of negroes have settled, within a few years, in the western parts of Upper Canada, where they have introduced the culture of tobacco, and in six years raised the export from almost nothing to 500 or 600 hogsheads." An article about African Americans in Highland

County, Ohio, related that they were not passive in the face of the opposition of white citizens to their settling there. At a "large meeting" in Chillicothe, they formulated "an exposition of their grievances" to be "laid before the legislature at its next session, signed by the people of colour, petitioning that body to grant them the full privileges of citizens."[23] These articles about the efforts of African Americans to take control of their destiny and to assert their rights portrayed them not as passive victims of white oppression or as a powerless group unable to advance in American society, but as a strong and industrious community.

"DAILY SLANDERED"

In their opening editorial, Cornish and Russwurm remarked that if African Americans were to "to plead [their] own cause," they would have to, at least in part, address the "misrepresentations" and attacks of whites. Even purported supporters often portrayed African Americans negatively, as we have seen, and others were more explicitly malicious. One of the goals of *Freedom's Journal* was to give a public voice to those who wished to respond to racist rhetoric: "Daily slandered, we think that there ought to be some channel of communication between us and the public: through which a single voice may be heard, in defence of *five hundred thousand free people of colour.*"[24]

Articles in *Freedom's Journal* that responded to white rhetoric, however, were not merely defensive. They went beyond refuting enemies to assume an active role that allowed them to take control of the way they were represented, advocate strongly for the rights of African Americans, and expose the foundations of racism in American society. Just as *Freedom's Journal* itself was not merely a forum for reacting to white society, the rhetoric in the periodical that addressed whites' misperceptions and abuse of African Americans was not restricted by the arguments and assumptions of their opponents. Entering into debates about public policy, they changed the terms of these discussions to reflect African Americans' perspectives and interests. In addition, through *Freedom's Journal*, a variety of voices could enter into these discussions, rather than only those few whose positions allowed them to print pamphlets or deliver speeches.[25]

To understand the way the rhetoric in *Freedom's Journal* responding to racism replaced reaction with advocacy, consider a two-part editorial published in March and April 1827, which addressed a sermon given by a Newark preacher on behalf of the ACS. The speaker, the editors reported, argued that emancipation of slaves would not be beneficial if those freed "remain in this country." Citing "the condition" of the "free coloured population"—in particular, their great numbers in "jails and penitentiaries" and their "idle, ignorant, and depraved" state—as proof that most free African Americans could not attain "a respectable standing" in the United States, he declared that they would remain "in moral and intellectual bondage," "emancipated but not elevated." The editors responded directly to the preacher's charges, asserting that his "estimation of the condition and character of the coloured population of our towns and cities . . . is the most uncharitable and inaccurate [they] have ever seen, or heard of." "There certainly is not one fourth of our people, who justly come under the character set forth in all those strong epithets," they argued. As evidence, they offered figures from the city's almshouse, demonstrating that the percentage of African Americans who were paupers was lower than that of whites. When the editors turned to the speaker's assertions about prisoners, they went beyond refutation to make a strong argument about societal injustice. While it is true that "instances of crime are in a greater proportion among [African Americans]," they maintained, "if crime be taken in the depravity and viciousness of its character," the "advantage" would again be in their favor because "the coloured man's offence, three times out of four, grows out of the circumstances of his condition, while the white man's, most generally, is premeditated and vicious." It was for this reason that more African Americans were in prison, they argued, exposing the societal basis for a statistic commonly used against them and making an implicit argument about the effects of the entrenched prejudice that drove arrests and convictions.[26]

The preacher's accusations also led Cornish and Russwurm to characterize the activism that was needed on the part of African Americans to counter such racist rhetoric. Those who supported colonization were trying to convince them that they could not be productive members of society, thereby attempting to impede them "from making lawful efforts" to improve their lives. At the same time, "the virtuous and industrious man of colour" faced great disadvantages in education and employment. What African Americans must do in the face of these obstacles, the editors asserted, was advocate for increased opportunities and to use the black community's own power and resources to take control of their destiny. "We have the means of education and morality to considerable extent," they argued; "many of our youth are in excellent schools and some of our young men in the first colleges of the country. . . . [W]e think it is highly important that every means should be made use of that will have any tendency to improve the condition of our people." The editors also declared strongly that African Americans should claim the rights of American citizens rather than succumb to the pressure of the ACS:

> This is the land of our nativity, and we have claims on its inhabitants. . . . Whatever may be the success of the colonization society, there is no probability that

there ever will be a time in which the coloured population of the country, will
not exceed two millions. . . . It is high time for christians to discard the idea that
nothing effectually can be done for our people while remaining in this country.[27]

Responses to the prolific editor Mordecai Noah, who, as we have seen,
frequently assailed African Americans, also illustrate how the editors and
contributors to *Freedom's Journal* used racist rhetoric as a way to expose
the foundations and consequences of prejudice and oppression. In an 1827
letter to the editors, cleverly signed Mordecai, a correspondent noted recent attacks by Noah on the character of free African Americans. It was
true, correspondent Mordecai conceded, that there were "dissolute"
African Americans who engaged in "highly reprehensible behavior," yet
Noah ignored the fact that there were also many of his "own *caste*" who
were prone to vice. Mordecai suggested a potential reason for Noah's se-
lective attacks:

> The people of colour in New-York, are decidedly more respectable in charac-
> ter and condition at the present day, than they have hitherto been. If this is
> not indicative of their susceptibility of improvement, and ominous that in
> time, with but two-thirds the advantages in possession of their detractors,
> they will have attained a standing, equal *at least*, with their friend and advo-
> cate, the worthy Mr. N——, then there is no correspondence between Heaven
> and earth.[28]

Mordecai went beneath the surface of Noah's attacks to expose his motives, highlighting that racism is often a response to the threat of a group's
improvement and an attempt to hold them back.

In their editorial "Major Noah's 'Negroes,'" Cornish and Russwurm
similarly countered Noah's "unmanly and slanderous attack on the
coloured population of this city," in which he declared "the free negroes
of this city are a nuisance incomparably greater than a million of slaves."
Like their correspondent Mordecai, the editors briefly responded by noting that "blackguards" and "prostitutes" were often of "the Major's own
complexion" and that "the baseness of character and conduct" Noah described was "confined to a very small portion of the people of colour"
(and that they "wish it were confined to a smaller portion of the whites").
Most of the editorial explored the consequences of such rhetoric, particularly the fact that it incited violence by "increas[ing] the prejudice of the
lower orders of society." "The mob want no leader," the editors remarked.
"Blackguards among the whites, are sufficiently ready to insult decent
people of colour." In addition, they showed that in fact Noah's attacks increased the very problem he complained about, by "discourag[ing] the
virtuous" and "remov[ing] motives of inducement from the vile" in the
black community. Using their opponent's words in a new context—an

African-American rhetorical strategy which is part of "signifying," interacting with white discourse while revising it—Cornish and Russwurm declared that "the indiscriminate abuse of [their] brethren, which is too often indulged in by little minds . . . renders the *slanderer* equally a *nuisance* with the slandered."[29]

In an 1828 article, Russwurm featured a published attack on African Americans as an example of the bias that directs news reporting in the white press. Russwurm reprinted two paragraphs from an article titled "High Life Below Stairs," which was published in the *Pennsylvania Gazette*. The *Gazette* article described a "Coloured Fancy Ball" which attracted the "attention of boys and idlers," leading to a mob attacking the guests at the ball. Implicitly blaming the African Americans attending this event for this outcome, the editors of the *Gazette* remarked that some "serious attention" should be "paid to [their] conduct and pursuits," which may lead to "masters and servants chang[ing] places."[30]

"We are really sorry that the *fanciful* ideas of the Editors [of the *Gazette*] should lead them to deviate so far from facts," Russwurm declared. He countered the *Gazette*'s descriptions of the costumes and deportment of the guests at the event, showing that it was actually a "plain subscription Ball" at which no guest "appeared in any dress which could with propriety be termed a 'Fancy' one." And, indeed, "who was blamable" for the disorder, Russwurm asked, "the noisy mob, or the decent and reputable persons who composed the assembly?" Russwurm also put the event in a new context by remarking on the fact that much attention was paid to disturbances involving African Americans while other events went unnoticed:

> From a friend . . . we learn, that at a Ball given by persons who were not *coloured* that same evening, in the said city of Philadelphia, the company commenced quarrelling and fighting, and one or more broken heads were the result of their broil. But how comes it that the ever watchful and over scrupulous Editors of the Pennsylvania Gazette, are silent on the subject—*why they were not coloured people, and are therefore unworthy even of a passing notice.*[31]

Russwurm offered a profound statement about contemporary news reporting and its connection to prejudice, inviting readers not only to question the particular article he mentioned but all coverage of African Americans in the white press.

The editors also considered an important philosophical question about racist rhetoric—do attacks, particularly those which are especially hostile, even merit a response or should they be ignored? In their 1827 editorial "Propriety of Conduct," Cornish and Russwurm touched on this issue in a two-part argument. People of color should avoid "indecorous conduct," they asserted; but, at the same time, the "sweeping judgment" of those who assumed all African Americans behaved inappropriately was unfair and unreasonable. "We wish not to hide the faults of our brethren—but to correct them," the editors maintained, and "to be champions in their defence against the attacks of open and manly foes." What if, though, an enemy was less than "open and manly"—should African Americans respond to such opponents or not? The complexities of this issue were revealed in articles published the following year. In July 1828, Russwurm published a two-part "Philadelphia Report," a response by a committee of African Americans to attacks against them in the Philadelphia newspaper the *Ariel*. Russwurm revealed his mixed feelings about the exchange:

> I am glad our Philadelphia brethren feel so sensibly this vile attempt to injure our body at large, but I question whether they have taken the wisest steps to counter it, whether coming from so contemptible a source, it deserved to be so highly honored. For my part I believe it generally to be best to suffer all such vile publications to descend to obscurity unanswered whenever they emanate from such *obscure* sources.[32]

Perhaps, Russwurm implied, responding to racist arguments, particularly those which may not have circulated too widely, gave an opponent more attention than was deserved. He thus addressed a profound issue about how African Americans could best advance their cause in the face of opposition and about the advantages of, in some cases, *not* reacting to racist attacks and instead focusing on the community itself, its needs and concerns.

TO "CIRCULATE FAR AND NEAR": AFRICAN-AMERICAN RHETORIC AND LITERATURE

As we have seen, African Americans in the 1820s were intensely aware of the power of literacy and the connection of rhetoric to citizenship. In keeping with this perspective, *Freedom's Journal* represented a forum in which important rhetorical and literary texts by African Americans could be disseminated to a wide audience. As Peter Hinks remarks, the "scarc[ity]" of "material written and printed by blacks . . . in the first three decades of the nineteenth century" made *Freedom's Journal* "profoundly important for the literate members of the North's free black communities." It was, Dickson Bruce proposes, "a pioneering outlet for African American writers—poets, story writers, and essayists."[33] In addition to providing a forum for original contributions, *Freedom's Journal* printed sermons and speeches, extending the reach of these orations beyond their initial audiences, and republished texts that might otherwise have been available only to a limited audience, such as those who might have access to a copy of an essay published in pamphlet form.

In 1828, Russwurm reprinted in *Freedom's Journal* two important works written by African Americans of previous decades. He published an excerpt from Othello's 1788 "An Essay on Negro Slavery," which first appeared in the *American Museum* and constitutes, as we have seen, an example of the strong protest rhetoric of the 1780s and 1790s. Arguing powerfully against slavery, Othello called upon Americans to honor their Revolutionary history—a theme that, as we shall see, resonated deeply for antebellum African Americans. Russwurm also reprinted *A Series of Letters by a Man of Color*, written by James Forten in 1813. First published in pamphlet form, this text addressed restrictions against African Americans proposed (but ultimately not passed) that year in the Pennsylvania state legislature. Although Forten argued against this particular legislation, his rhetoric went beyond this context to advocate for African-American rights in general. He remarked, for example, that among the free African Americans in Pennsylvania were many "men of merit," such as those who had organized and worked in "benevolent organizations," and "men of property" who had "accumulated" their wealth through "years of honest industry." These citizens should be able to trust that the law will provide them "protection" rather than "oppress" them.[34] Like Othello, Forten appealed to the spirit of the country's founding, arguing that blacks were entitled to the freedom and equality for which Revolutionary Americans, including many African Americans, fought.

Russwurm suggested through his republication in *Freedom's Journal* of Othello's and Forten's dynamic arguments that readers of the 1820s should be aware of the historical context for the activism and rhetoric of contemporary leaders. In a headnote to the first of Forten's letters, Russwurm declared,

> We invite the attention of our readers to the perusal of the following essays . . . from the pen of one of our most intelligent and respectable citizens of Colour in the U. States. They were originally published in the year 1813 . . . when a proposition came before the Legislature of Pennsylvania, to register all free persons of Colour within the state, and also to prevent others from the different states settling within her borders. For our ourselves [*sic*], we are so pleased with them, that we are anxious that they will circulate far and near, and be perused by friend and foe.[35]

African Americans and their "friends" needed to be aware that the discourse of the 1820s, including *Freedom's Journal* itself, was part of a strong tradition of which they could be proud and on which they could draw for inspiration. "Foes" as well should take note of the powerful rhetoric of previous generations and be aware that the desire to "plead their own cause" was not a new or anomalous development among African Americans, but a longstanding force.

The publication in *Freedom's Journal* of speeches delivered in various cities connected African Americans separated by geography, giving readers a sense that their concerns were shared by those in other cities and that they were part of a national community with common interests and goals. This rhetoric could also serve as models for those who were becoming empowered to speak for themselves of persuasion that was strong, even militant. Consider, for example, Albany minister Nathaniel Paul's oration on July 5, 1827, celebrating the abolition of slavery in the state of New York, published in *Freedom's Journal* the following month. Arguing that slavery must end, Paul noted examples of its abolition throughout the world, including the "catastrophe, and exchange of power in the Isle of Hayti." This precedent, along with "the restless disposition of both master and slave in the southern states" and the "irrevocable decrees of Almighty God," suggested that "the power of tyranny must be subdued, the captive must be liberated, the oppressed go free, and slavery must . . . be forever annihilated from the earth."[36] Paul's implications were militant, anticipating in some ways the striking arguments made by David Walker two years later in his *Appeal to the Coloured Citizens of the World*— God is on the side of the oppressed and may even dictate that slavery must be ended by force, as it was in Haiti.

Notably, *Freedom's Journal* featured Walker's rhetoric prior to the appearance of the *Appeal*. Russwurm published Walker's 1828 address to the MGCA, in which he raised many of the issues and themes of the *Appeal*, urging his brethren to unite to fight for their advancement, their rights, and the liberty of slaves. Walker asserted, for example, that African Americans must determine their own course and be active in pursuing their goals. Even though they had many "white brethren and friends" who made "mighty efforts, for the amelioration of [their] condition," African Americans could not "stand as neutral spectators of the work," Walker argued. They must both "co-operate with" these supporters and work within their own community organizations: "Ought we not to form ourselves into a general body, to protect, aid, and assist each other to the utmost of our power. . . ?" In striking terms that suggest the jeremiadic themes and the potential for militant action that are central to his *Appeal*, Walker urged African Americans to work for the freedom of all. "Mighty deeds" can be accomplished if they worked together, Walker informed his audience, assuring them, "God has something in reserve for us, which . . . will repay us for all our suffering and miseries."[37]

By featuring models of strong persuasion by African Americans, *Freedom's Journal* provided its readers with a kind of rhetorical education. Just as the literary societies that arose in the 1820s emphasized the role of persuasion in the fight for social justice and educated African Americans about rhetorical principles,[38] so too did the publication of *Freedom's Jour-*

nal demonstrate the link between rhetorical expertise and public activism. In some cases, the goals of the literary societies and those of the newspaper became one and the same. In December 1828, Russwurm published in *Freedom's Journal* an extract of an oration by William Whipper before the Colored Reading Society of Philadelphia, in which he laid out the principles that he believed should underlie the study and practice of rhetoric. Although Whipper's address was also printed in pamphlet form, its publication in *Freedom's Journal* significantly increased its availability. This accessibility was in keeping with the goals of African-American literary societies, which provided education to many who might not otherwise receive it. Whipper's statement of the goals of the Colored Reading Society, for example—also published in *Freedom's Journal*—noted that because many, particularly in the "rising generation," had only "limited opportunities of improvement," a literary organization was of particular importance in preparing them to "qualify themselves, for future usefulness."[39] *Freedom's Journal* extended the opportunities that such an institution could provide beyond geographical boundaries.

In addition to reprinting poems from white newspapers and by canonical authors such as Lord Byron, *Freedom's Journal's* poetry column also published works by African-American poets such as Phillis Wheatley and George Moses Horton.[40] Beyond providing quality literary material that would benefit "young readers" (instead of the "works of trivial importance" on which, the editors believed, many wasted their time),[41] these contributions served to demonstrate that African Americans could and did produce important literary works worthy of study. An 1827 article by contributor J. on Phillis Wheatley discussed the significance of her work for African Americans. In doing so, J. entered a debate about Wheatley's work that had more than literary significance—the assessment of her poetry was linked by eighteenth- and nineteenth-century commentators to the question of African Americans' mental capabilities.[42] J.'s article demonstrated an understanding of the implications of this debate. Wheatley's great "aptitude for learning" and her "zeal to improve herself in all useful knowledge," J. asserted, disproved common perceptions: "It was a matter of wonder and amazement in those days, that the brain of an African slave should be capacious enough to harbor an idea, and most of all to express it in poetry." Many may "sneer" at her work, J. remarked; although J. did not explicitly name him, the scathing assessment of Thomas Jefferson, who claimed Wheatley's work was "below the dignity of criticism," comes to mind. Those who denigrated Wheatley, J. suggested, did not base their views on her work itself but on the racist belief that "fleecy locks and black complexion, are sufficient to forfeit nature's claim." J. dismissed these critics—the "merit of [Wheatley's] poetry" had already been acknowledged by "the public, who are the only judges."[43]

Freedom's Journal also published poems that were original to the newspaper, written by readers.[44] Other literary features written for the newspaper included short stories such as "Seduction" and essays such as "The Slanderer" that took up moral subjects.[45] Russwurm's column "The Observer," a regular feature in the second half of 1827, was written in the style of eighteenth-century British journalists such as Defoe, Steele, and Addison and devoted to subjects such as music, proper behavior in church, and marriage.[46] In a sense, the newspaper created a sort of larger literary society among its readers, providing a forum for their original productions. As with the literary societies created in different cities, one of the expressed goals of the periodical was readers' "literary improvement."[47] Publishing readers' work, like sharing compositions in literary organizations, put theoretical principles into practice.

AMERICA: KNOWLEDGE, LANGUAGE, COMMEMORATION

In their "Prospectus," Cornish and Russwurm indicated that they would take on civic issues from a particular philosophical perspective: "In the discussion of political subjects, we shall ever regard the constitution of the United States as our polar star. Pledged to no party, we shall endeavour to urge our brethren to use their right to the elective franchise as free citizens." Their statement suggests the democratic idealism to which, Frankie Hutton argues, antebellum African-American editors were committed. Like other early-nineteenth-century Americans, African Americans were influenced by the Revolution and its promises of liberty and equality. The first black editors believed that if the nation truly honored its professed commitment to democratic ideals, African Americans would be given their fundamental rights as citizens. Yet—as we might expect, given the restrictions they faced in American society—their view was not merely a blind allegiance to American ideals. Like other African Americans, early editors were troubled by America's failure to honor its professions. Antebellum African Americans' rhetoric about America and its Revolutionary history was based on a defining tension between, on the one hand, their allegiance to America's promises of freedom and equality and, on the other, their commitment to exposing the nation's hypocrisy and inconsistency with its founding goals.[48]

In the case of *Freedom's Journal*, this defining tension shaped the periodical's articles about civic matters. For the most part, the rhetoric about America published in the newspaper supported democratic ideals, emphasized African Americans' rights to citizenship, and exposed America's failure to realize its professed ideals. This focus on America did not mean that the editors asked readers to give up their identification as descendants of Africa—as we shall see, the readers and editors wished to emphasize their African heritage. Antebellum African-American identity was based upon their status as both Africans and Americans.[49] At the same time, though, the editors emphasized that African Americans had the right to be a fundamental part of the nation and to enjoy the liberty that it promised—an argument that not only empowered them but also countered colonizationist propaganda.

There was, of course, a notable exception to this approach—Russwurm's pessimistic articles about African Americans' future in the nation published in 1829 after his decision to emigrate to Africa. As we have seen, Russwurm came to doubt that America would ever live up to its ideals, and he gave up the pro-American idealism that had shaped the periodical for most of its run. Most readers did not agree with Russwurm's perspective, as we have seen, and many felt that he had betrayed a fundamental goal of the paper. *Freedom's Journal* was seen by African Americans as their organ and not just the mouthpiece for an editor, and most readers would have rejected Russwurm's ultimate assessment of America and remained committed to asserting their rights as American citizens.

Civic education was one manifestation of the defining tension between ideals and reality underlying *Freedom's Journal*'s approach to America. Knowledge about the United States and its government, the editors suggested, was fundamental for African Americans if they were to become active citizens of the nation. Yet this education about political matters constituted more than a static civics lesson. Articles gave readers information about the American legal system and made them aware of ways those in power used American policies against them. An 1827 article ironically titled "Equality," for example, explained how the disenfranchised slave population in Southern states skewed the balance of voting power in favor of the white South. "Is such a state of things *equal*?" the article asked. "But such are the advantages of slaves to the southern states. And yet slaves do not vote. A white man at the South has a representative power greater by about fifty per cent than a freeman at the North has." Similarly, an article reprinted in 1828 from the *Christian Watchman* reported on a debate in the House of Representatives over whether the owner of a slave injured in military service was entitled to receive "compensation for damages" from the government. Although the claim was excluded by the Ways and Means Committee, the piece described the "conciliating manner" toward the South of a New York representative and reported the extended defense of slavery by Congressman Randolph of Virginia.[50] These articles demonstrated the editors' position that knowledge about American politics should not promote an unquestioning patriotism but should in fact encourage African Americans to examine the nation's government critically and understand the link between political power and oppression.

The defining tension through which the editors covered the nation's politics suggested that American political power was a double-edged sword—while it could be used to bolster oppression, it could also be the means through which African Americans could change the American system from within. In particular, the editors asserted that African Americans should use the tools available to them to empower themselves as citizens, particularly by exercising the vote in cases where they could do so: "We shall . . . urge upon our brethren, (who are qualified by the laws of the different states) the expediency of using their elective franchise." An 1828 article, "Votes in the Several States,'" which outlined in detail the qualifications needed to exercise the franchise in different states, provided practical knowledge about voter eligibility. Free African Americans should see themselves as fundamentally connected to America and should use whatever political means they could to press their claims as citizens, this coverage suggested. In an 1828 oration to New York's African Society for Mutual Relief published in *Freedom's Journal*, Thomas Jinnings affirmed that African Americans must continually demand the rights to which they are entitled: "The fact is this, [our rights] have been bought at a dear rate, our liberty . . . has been obtained agreeably to the laws of the land; and we have a just right to enter our claim to justice. . . . [I]t can do no harm to be awake to our political interest. . . ."[51]

If political knowledge could empower African Americans, so too could political language, particularly the discourse of freedom and equality upon which America was founded. The defining tension between ideals and reality led to a paradoxical linguistic consequence—the language of the oppressor could become the tool of the oppressed. The Declaration and the Constitution, written by powerful white men, have a power that is not controlled by whites—and their words, appropriated by African Americans, have often been a rhetorical weapon in the fight for civil rights.[52] Articles in *Freedom's Journal* marshaled this power to articulate African Americans' particular position in American society, committed to pushing the nation to be true to its professions.

A December 1827 editorial by Russwurm about Washington, D.C., illustrated this rhetorical strategy. It would seem that this city, Russwurm argued, would be "sacred to the goddess of Liberty—to the rights of man," yet slave trading was carried out "under the immediate notice of Congress" and "many who there plead for the equal rights of man, are the very men who . . . buy and sell their brethren like beasts of burden." Referring to a resolution passed the previous May that would force African Americans in Washington to provide documentation of their freedom or risk being sent to jail as fugitive slaves, Russwurm asserted,

Professions are nothing, when contradicted by daily practice. While the Constitution declares that all men are born free and equal, the wise corporation of the city of Washington . . . see proper to proscribe the rights of a certain portion of the community. . . . Ought such laws to exist? Ought Congress to allow Washington, the spot which, alone of all others should be sacred to the rights of man . . . to be polluted by the footsteps of a slave?

Russwurm used white Americans' own language as ammunition against their oppression of people of color: "The constitution [declares] that all men have certain unalienable rights; notwithstanding, the corporation of the city of Washington would by their laws decree . . . that [all men] have not certain unalienable rights, and consequently that the same laws should not be given all."[53] We see in Russwurm's words a fundamental aspect of the periodical's message about America. While affirming the nation's principles, African Americans' arguments about America in *Freedom's Journal* were far from mild or accommodationist; indeed, they were bold, assertive, and even militant.

As they reinterpreted American revolutionary discourse, negotiating the competing demands of allegiance and protest, African Americans faced the question of whether and how to participate in America's celebration of its history. Commemoration and communal celebrations of historical events are necessarily political; and, as we have seen, early-nineteenth-century African Americans solidified their community consciousness and developed an increased political awareness as they memorialized events such as the abolition of the slave trade. But what was to be done about July Fourth, a day sacred to white Americans but fraught for African Americans with the implications of the contradiction between America's promises of freedom and the reality of oppression? Should it be honored by African Americans as well, or should an alternative commemoration be created that would combine celebration and protest? *Freedom's Journal* served as a forum for debate about this issue, allowing readers and contributors to explore the ramifications of this question for African Americans' political identity.[54]

Because July 4, 1827, was the day that slavery was officially abolished in New York State, freeing all slaves who had not already been emancipated under the 1799 gradual abolition law, African-American New Yorkers naturally felt called to celebrate the event.[55] Yet the fact that the promises of the Fourth of July had not yet been fully realized led many to propose that commemorations should take place on July 5 instead. In part, concern for safety influenced those who rejected celebrating the Fourth—white revelers often attacked African Americans on Independence Day.[56] Yet there was also concern that some type of protest should be lodged against America's uneven commitment to its founding principles. *Freedom's Journal* reported the proceedings of a meeting in Albany in March 1827, at which it was resolved that "whereas the 4th day of July is the day that the National Independence of this country is recognized by the white citizens, we deem it proper to celebrate the 5th." African-American residents of New York City, a notice published in late June announced, would hold "two CELEBRATIONS": "One party will celebrate the Fourth of July, without any public procession, and the other, the Fifth, with a Grand Procession, Oration, and Public Dinner."[57]

A response by correspondent R. to this announcement appeared in *Freedom's Journal* the following week. R. indicated that safety considerations indeed dictated to some extent the decision to hold a private event on July Fourth and to celebrate publicly on July 5. But R. also suggested that there was a clash over the appropriate way for African Americans to participate in the most patriotic of American holidays. Lamenting that African Americans were "divided" on the issue, R. maintained,

> Nothing can be more evident than that the Fourth is the proper day to be observed. . . . Is it a reason, that we should not keep this day; that our white fellow-citizens will be celebrating on it, the delivery of the country from foreign bondage? To me it appears the very reverse. The event celebrated by the whites, is one in which we are interested, and have cause to rejoice, as well as they. Indeed many of our forefathers laboured and shed their blood to produce it. And the event which we are specially called upon to celebrate, is one in which every white citizen, who has any regard to the honour, or welfare of his country, has cause to rejoice as well as we. . . . But it is thought by some, that if we have a procession on that day, we shall be in danger of being molested by vagabonds among the whites. Admitting this why cannot a procession be dispensed with? . . . I hope those who resolved upon it, will calmly re-consider the subject, and . . . join with their brethren in celebrating the proper day in a proper manner.[58]

The proposal to reject white America's day of celebration and R.'s response illustrated the tensions underlying antebellum African Americans' relationship to America. African Americans were a fundamental part of the nation and entitled to its promises—having, as R. noted, fought in many cases for its principles—yet they were confronted daily with the fact that these ideals have not been realized. Their destiny in the United States was inextricably linked to that of white Americans, as R. suggested in his remark that whites should celebrate the abolition of slavery along with African Americans. Yet many whites attempted to ignore that connection, and protest was necessary to awaken the nation's attention to African Americans' claims to full citizenship. Introducing readers to this debate by publishing different views, *Freedom's Journal* revealed that there were no easy resolutions to these tensions. Although R. may have been disappointed by the differences of opinion expressed on the issue, the divergent perspectives in the periodical helped elucidate the complexities of the debate about African Americans' relationship to American patriotism and history.

"THE PEOPLE'S PAPER"

Freedom's Journal's publication of opposing views on celebrations of July Fourth points to another central goal of the periodical—to provide a forum for differing opinions on important issues. Although articles shared a focus on issues pertinent to African Americans—"whatever concerns [them] as a people"—Cornish and Russwurm implied that that they wished to encourage debate and that the expression of diverse perspectives was both anticipated and desirable. They asked that contributors participate in "a temperate discussion of interesting subjects" and that matters facing African Americans "be candidly discussed and properly weighed." As Nordin notes, the editors suggested that civic debate would help forge connections among readers and create a sense of community among African Americans living in different cities.[59]

In their calls for the free expression of opposing views in *Freedom's Journal*, Cornish and Russwurm were in advance of many of their white counterparts. Before the 1830s, mainstream newspapers were expected to be partisan and to promote party interests. Although opposing parties supported competing newspapers in various regions, particular periodicals were not expected to give more than one side of an issue.[60] By contrast, as Hutton demonstrates, African-American editors from the beginning advocated a press that was "nonpartisan" and that promoted "fairness and truthfulness in reporting." They were "in effect harbingers of responsibility and ethics in the operation of their newspapers," she remarks.[61]

On various issues, Cornish and Russwurm published articles that represented different perspectives on important controversies, even those that clashed with the editors' stated views. As we have seen, even though the paper's official editorial stance in 1827 was against colonization, the editors featured arguments on both sides of the issue, remarking that they hoped "to see the subject fully discussed in [their] columns." They revealed, in fact, that they thought that a fair presentation of both sides of the issue was the most persuasive way to promote what they felt was best for African Americans—to, in their words, "make a few converts among [their] friends." After commenting in an editorial that "all men are *equal* by nature," citing the fact that Africans were "the inventors of the different Arts and Sciences, while the rest of the now civilized world, were sunk in darkness and ignorance," Cornish and Russwurm invited their opponents to an open debate of the issue. "Calling upon the advocates of Slavery, to disprove" their claims, the editors remarked, "To them, our columns are open to a candid investigation of the subject. We are willing to place both sides of the issue before an enlightened public."[62]

It seems that readers valued the commitment to open and free discussion that was unavailable in other newspapers. Remarking on the "subservience to popular prejudice" of Baltimore editors, correspondent Civis asserted that "there are few presses so independent as to publish what may be unpopular; and thus it is that error is so often forced upon the public mind, because to hear both sides alone can lead to a discovery of truth." Readers apparently felt that opposing views on even such a contentious issue as colonization should be presented. Veritas maintained in the first of a three-part article on colonization published in early 1828, "I have remarked, with no inconsiderable exultation, that pieces have been published in this paper, that I knew where [sic] in direct opposition to the sentiment of the Editors; thus proving that their sole object was clearly to elicit truth, by throwing open its columns to a free and candid investigation."[63] Indeed, as we have seen, even after more and more positive information about Liberia began to appear in *Freedom's Journal's* columns in late 1828 and in 1829, leaders such as Theodore Wright and David Walker, who were strongly opposed to colonization, continued to support the periodical by working as agents and, in Walker's case, buying advertisements for his clothing store. It appears that readers wanted—indeed, expected—various perspectives on issues to be represented, not just views that most of them would endorse.

Yet after Russwurm openly avowed his support for colonization, both sides of this important issue were no longer represented. Although Russwurm claimed in a March 1829 editorial that *Freedom's Journal* was still "open to a free discussion of this important subject," the paper's columns from February 14, 1829—the date he announced his change of view—until it ceased publication contained news from Liberia and reprinted material from the ACS's periodical the *African Repository*, but no articles critical of colonization. As we have discussed, the hostility directed toward Russwurm by the end of his tenure as *Freedom's Journal's* editor was not due solely to his support for colonization. Yet his perspective shaped his editing of *Freedom's Journal* in ways that limited its value as a forum for open exchange on the issue. As correspondent C. D. T. explained in an 1831 letter to Garrison's *Liberator*, Russwurm had "converted the people's paper to the use of the Colonization Society."[64] Whereas in 1827 Cornish and Russwurm had tried to present views in opposition to their own on colonization as well as other subjects—to make the periodical "the people's paper" that would allow for debate—Russwurm had allowed the paper to become a partisan vehicle for his views.

At the end of his tenure as editor of *Freedom's Journal*, then, Russwurm did not remain true to the mission of presenting a range of opinion on a very volatile issue. Yet throughout most of the periodical's existence, it offered varying perspectives on colonization as well as many other important subjects. *Freedom's Journal* was indeed, for most of its run, "the people's paper," representing the diversity and complexity within the African-American community of the late 1820s. Keeping this description in mind, let us now turn to the periodical's coverage of the issues of the day.

NOTES

1. Penn, *Afro-American Press*, 27; Bryan, "Negro Journalism," 8; Martin, "Pioneer," 527; Gore, *Negro Journalism*, 5; Wilson, *Black Journalists*, 27; Oak, *Negro Newspaper*, 122; Hirsch, "Negro and New York," 444; Berry and Blassingame, *Long Memory*, 61; Allen, *Negro*, 82.

2. Nordin, "In Search," 123. Others also argue that the conception of *Freedom's Journal* as primarily an abolitionist newspaper is too narrow; see Tripp, *Origins*, 14–15; Hutton, *Early Black Press*, ix; McHenry, *Forgotten Readers*, 88; Frances Smith Foster, "Narrative," 718–19.

3. Samuel E. Cornish and John B. Russwurm, "To Our Patrons," *FJ*, 16 March 1827; John B. Russwurm, "Our Own Concerns," *FJ*, 21 December 1827.

4. Cornish and Russwurm, "To Our Patrons."

5. Reed, *Platform*, 97, 99; advertisement for Union Hotel, *FJ*, 13 July 1827; F. Wiles, "A Card," *FJ*, 14 September 1827; Eliza Johnson, "Boarding & Lodging," *FJ*, 27 June 1828. These advertisements also appeared in other issues.

6. Samuel E. Cornish and John B. Russwurm, "Fuel Savings Fund," *FJ*, 25 May 1827.

7. "Notice," *FJ*, 1 February 1828.

8. "Notice," *FJ*, 19 October 1827; "B. F. Hughes' School for Coloured Children of Both Sexes," *FJ*, 15 February 1828; "St. Philips Church Music School," *FJ*, 8 February 1828; "African Free School," *FJ*, 11 January 1828; Jeremiah Gloucester, "School Notice," *FJ*, 2 November 1827; William Whipper, "Address," *FJ*, 20 June 1828; "Notice," *FJ*, 13 April 1827; untitled notice, *FJ*, 28 September 1827. Notices which were also advertisements frequently appeared in multiple issues.

9. Horton, *Free People*, 61.

10. Cornish and Russwurm, "To Our Patrons." On this function of *Freedom's Journal*, see also Nordin, "In Search," 124; Lerone Bennett, *Shaping*, 128.

11. John B. Russwurm, "Travelling Scraps," *FJ*, 27 June 1828; John B. Russwurm, "Travelling Scraps," *FJ*, 11 July 1828; John B. Russwurm, "Travelling Scraps," *FJ*, 25 July 1828; John B. Russwurm, "Travelling Scraps," *FJ*, 15 August 1828; John B. Russwurm, "Travelling Scraps," *FJ*, 29 August 1828.

12. On the communal nature of the fight for freedom for African Americans, see Lincoln and Mamiya, *Black Church*, 5; Logan, "We Are Coming," 24–27, 55.

13. "For the Freedom's Journal," *FJ*, 20 July 1827; "For the Freedom's Journal," *FJ*, 13 July 1827.

14. John B. Russwurm, "Coloured Infant School," *FJ*, 9 May 1828; John B. Russwurm, "Land of Liberty," *FJ*, 5 December 1828.

15. Schudson, *Discovering*, 4–16; Berardi and Segady, "Development," 97.

16. Cornish and Russwurm, "To Our Patrons."

17. See, for example, "Coloured Children," *FJ*, 18 January 1828; "Kidnapping," *FJ*, 25 July 1828; "Kidnapping," *FJ*, 8 August 1828; "Kidnapping," *FJ*, 5 September 1828; "Case of Mr George Hamlet," *FJ*, 28 March 1829.

18. Untitled item in "Domestic News" section, *FJ*, 23 March 1827.

19. Tripp, *Origins*, 18.

20. "Horrible! Most Horrible!" *FJ*, 3 August 1827.

21. "Shocking Occurrence," *FJ*, 5 December 1828. The article stated that the incident was reported in the "L. Fall's *People's Friend*," presumably the *People's Friend*, published in Little Falls, New York.

22. A Subscriber, "Bishop Allen," *FJ*, 22 February 1828. The article was not completely accurate; the Free African Union Society of Newport, Rhode Island, which was organized in 1780, had mutual relief as one of its goals. See Cottrol, *Afro-Yankees*, 45; Wright, *African Americans*, 152; Bethel, *Roots*, 70–71; *Proceedings of the Free African Union Society*.

23. "Negro Enterprize," *FJ*, 3 August 1827; "People of Colour," *FJ*, 14 December 1827.

24. Cornish and Russwurm, "To Our Patrons"; Samuel E. Cornish and John B. Russwurm, "Prospectus," *FJ*, 16 March 1827.

25. Kwando Kinshasa makes this point about the African-American press in general (*Emigration*, 24).

26. Samuel E. Cornish and John B. Russwurm, untitled editorial (part I), *FJ*, 30 March 1827; Samuel E. Cornish and John B. Russwurm, untitled editorial (part II), *FJ*, 13 April 1827.

27. Cornish and Russwurm, untitled editorial (part II), 13 April 1827.

28. Mordecai, letter to editors, *FJ*, 17 August 1827.

29. Samuel E. Cornish and John B. Russwurm, "Major Noah's 'Negroes,'" *FJ*, 24 August 1827. On this form of signifying, see Gates, *Figures*, 17, 236; Gates, *Signifying*, 103–24.

30. John B. Russwurm, "High Life Below Stairs—Black Ball," *FJ*, 14 March 1828.

31. Russwurm, "High Life Below Stairs."

32. Samuel E. Cornish and John B. Russwurm, "Propriety of Conduct," *FJ*, 13 July 1827; F. C. Webb et al., "Philadelphia Report," *FJ*, 18 July 1828 and 25 July 1828; Russwurm, "Travelling Scraps," 25 July 1828.

33. Hinks, *To Awaken*, 193; Bruce, *Origins*, 166; see also Bryan, "Negro Journalism," 3–4; Pride and Wilson, *History*, 7.

34. [Othello], "Othello," *FJ*, 21 November 1828; James Forten, "Letters From a Man of Colour, on a Late Bill Before the Senate of Pennsylvania. Letter I," *FJ*, 22 February 1828. The other letters in this series were published in *Freedom's Journal*, 29 February 1828, 7 March 1828, 14 March 1828, and 21 March 1828. On the legislation which these letters address, see Nash, *Forging Freedom*, 181–83.

35. John B. Russwurm, headnote to James Forten's "Letters From a Man of Colour, on a Late Bill Before the Senate of Pennsylvania. Letter I," *FJ*, 22 February 1828.

36. Nathaniel Paul, "Extract from an Address, Delivered on the Celebration of the Abolition of Slavery in the State of New-York, July 5th, 1827," *FJ*, 10 August 1827.

37. David Walker, "Address, Delivered Before the [Massachusetts] General Colored Association at Boston, by David Walker," *FJ*, 20 December 1828.

38. On these points, see McHenry, "Dreaded Eloquence," 32; McHenry, *Forgotten Readers*, 23–83; Bacon and McClish, "Reinventing."

39. William Whipper, "Extract from an Address Delivered Before the Colored Reading Society of Philadelphia," *FJ*, 26 December 1828; Whipper, "Address."

40. Phillis Wheatley, "Hymn to Humanity," *FJ*, 9 November 1827; Phillis Wheatley, "Hymn to the Morning," *FJ*, 9 November 1827; George Horton, "Slavery," *FJ*, 18 July 1828; George M. Horton, "Lines. On the Evening and the Morning," *FJ*, 15 August 1828; Geo[rge] M. Horton, "On the Poetic Muse," *FJ*, 29 August 1828; G[eorge] M. Horton, "Gratitude," *FJ*, 5 September 1828.

41. Cornish and Russwurm, "To Our Patrons."

42. On the implications of the debate about Wheatley's work, see Foner, *History . . . Cotton Kingdom*, 529–30; Watson, "Classic Case"; Isani, "Contemporaneous Reception"; Frances Smith Foster, *Written by Herself*, 31–38; Gates, *Figures*, 67–79; Brooks, *American Lazarus*, 3–5.

43. Jefferson, *Notes*, 140; J., "For the Freedom's Journal," *FJ*, 23 March 1827.

44. See, for example, "Freedom," *FJ*, 7 September 1827; Arion, "To Greece," *FJ*, 12 October 1827; Amicus, "Lines on the Death of the Reverend Jeremiah Gloucester," *FJ*, 25 January 1828; Africus, "The Tears of a Slave," *FJ*, 14 March 1828; Arion, "The Crucifixion," *FJ*, 4 July 1828; Louisa, "Recollections of Childhood," *FJ*, 5 September 1828.

45. Tolendo, "Seduction," *FJ*, 23 November 1827; Niger, "The Slanderer," *FJ*, 20 June 1828.

46. The "Observer" columns were published between August 17, 1827, and November 16, 1827. I am indebted to Nordin for noting Russwurm's authorship of the columns and pointing out his eighteenth-century British models ("In Search," 126).

47. Cornish and Russwurm, "Prospectus."

48. Cornish and Russwurm, "Prospectus"; Hutton, *Early Black Press*, 26–34; Hutton, "Democratic Idealism." On the defining tension between African Americans' allegiance to American ideals and their criticisms of America, see Berry and Blassingame, *Long Memory*, 55–56; Quarles, "Antebellum Free Blacks"; Harding, *Other American Revolution*, 24; Berlin, "Revolution," 370–77; Quarles, *Black Mosaic*, 49–64; Nash, *Race*, 57–72; Clarence E. Walker, "American Negro," 138; Leonard Sweet, "Fourth of July"; Bacon, *Humblest*, 84–93.

49. On this dual identity, see Nash, *Race and Revolution*, 72; Gravely, "Dialectic"; Leonard Sweet, *Black Images*, 5–6; Horton and Horton, *In Hope*, xii, 155; Bethel, *Roots*, 5–7; Horton, *Free People*, 146.

50. "Equality," *FJ*, 10 August 1827; "The Slave Question," *FJ*, 25 January 1828. It is unclear whether the former was original to *Freedom's Journal* or borrowed from an unspecified source.

51. Cornish and Russwurm, "To Our Patrons"; "Votes in the Several States," *FJ*, 22 August 1828; "Oration, by Thomas L. Jinnings," *FJ*, 4 April 1828. It is unclear whether "Votes in the Several States" was original to *Freedom's Journal* or reprinted from an unnamed source.

52. For an extended discussion of this rhetorical phenomenon, see Bacon, *Humblest*, 84–93.

53. John B. Russwurm, "City of Washington," *FJ*, 16 November 1827.

54. See also Kachun, *Festivals*, 42–52, on this debate in *Freedom's Journal*.

55. Leo Hirsch notes that "strictly speaking slavery did not end in New York State on Independence Day, 1827," because "travelers could still bring slaves into the state for not more than nine months," a provision that was not repealed until 1841. Thus the censuses of 1830 and 1840 recorded that there were still slaves in the state ("Negro and New York," 395–96; see also McManus, *History*, 178–79).

56. Shane White, "It Was a Proud Day," 34, 39; Bethel, *Roots*, 5–6; Leonard Sweet, "Fourth of July," 263; Fabre, "African-American Commemorative Celebrations," 76; Quarles, *Black Abolitionists*, 122.

57. "Abolition of Slavery," *FJ*, 20 April 1827; untitled notice, *FJ*, 22 June 1827. On the celebration of July 5 as a protest, see also Gravely, "Dialectic," 303–4; Quarles, *Black Mosaic*, 99; Leonard Sweet, "Fourth of July," 259, 265–66; Fabre, "African-American Commemorative Celebrations," 80–81.

58. R., letter to editors, *FJ*, 29 June 1827.

59. Cornish and Russwurm, "Prospectus"; Cornish and Russwurm, "To Our Patrons"; Nordin, "In Search," 124. On the expression of diverse perspectives in *Freedom's Journal*, see also Timothy Patrick McCarthy, "To Plead," 129–30.

60. Schudson, *Discovering*, 4; Dicken-Garcia, *Journalistic Standards*, 97–106; Humphrey, *Press*, 113–14.

61. Hutton, *Early Black Press*, 36–43.

62. Samuel E. Cornish and John B. Russwurm, "Colonization Society," *FJ*, 14 September 1827; Samuel E. Cornish and John B. Russwurm, "European Colonies in America," *FJ*, 27 July 1827.

63. Civis, "Military Academies," *FJ*, 31 August 1827; Veritas, "Colonization Society," *FJ*, 22 February 1828.

64. John B. Russwurm, "Our Vindication," *FJ*, 7 March 1829; C. D. T., letter to editor, *Liberator*, 30 April 1831.

PART II

4

⁓

"Be Up and Doing": Self-Help

Cornish and Russwurm remarked in their first editorial that their paper not only would provide "useful knowledge" for African Americans but also would promote "their moral and religious improvement." "Education," "habits of industry," and "economy," they suggested, all were worthy subjects for *Freedom's Journal*.[1] In the columns of the paper, the editors and contributors promoted self-help efforts that would lead to moral improvement, advocating that African Americans seek educational advancement and economic self-sufficiency, observe decorum, serve as exemplars, and avoid vice.

The editors' emphasis on moral uplift fit with the concerns of contemporary leaders as well as those of previous decades. African-American fraternal, religious, and educational organizations of the late eighteenth and early nineteenth centuries promoted self-help—moral improvement, educational advancement, exemplary behavior, religious commitment, and economic self-sufficiency. In the laws of the African Society of Boston, founded in 1796, members were charged to "watch over each other in their spiritual concerns" and "to live soberly, righteously, and Godly in this present world." Those who joined the organization would receive aid in the case of sickness or death, with an important exception: "Any Member bringing on himself any sickness or disorder by intemperance, shall not be considered as entitled to any benefits or assistance from the Society." The New-York African Clarkson Association, established in 1825, was dedicated to "improvement in literature" as well as to raising funds to help needy community members; its constitution specified that members must be "free persons of moral character." The African Benevolent Society of

Newport, Rhode Island, formed in 1808, had as its primary purpose "the establishment and continuance of a free school, for any person of colour" that would provide "school instruction" and daily reading of Scripture. Teachers were to "pay special attention to the morals of the scholars" and were given "power to enquire into their conduct out of school."[2]

White Americans in the eighteenth and nineteenth centuries shared with African Americans a concern with self-improvement. A concern with "character," Patrick Rael remarks, was especially strong among "those seeking middle-class status." "Elevation," he explains, was a "common, though hardly fixed, vocabulary . . . through which Americans in the antebellum North of both races expressed their values and concerns."[3] At the same time, as Raymond Mohl demonstrates, early-nineteenth-century white reformers often espoused a "harsh moralism" which assumed that poverty was the result of character flaws, "differentiated between the 'deserving' and the 'undeserving' poor," and offered plans for moral improvement as the remedy to social ills. In a similar vein, many white antislavery organizations of the late eighteenth and early nineteenth centuries called for morality among African Americans, advising them to behave in an appropriate and exemplary manner. Frequently, their approach was paternalistic and condescending, suggesting that African Americans' behavior should be monitored by reform-minded whites.[4]

At a 1789 meeting of the Pennsylvania Abolition Society, for example, members adopted a *"Plan for improving the condition of free Negroes,"* which included the creation of a *"committee of Inspection,* who shall superintend the morals, general conduct and ordinary situation of the Free Negroes, and afford them advice and instruction." A 1796 broadside from the "Convention of Deputies from the Abolition Societies in the United States" counseled free African Americans to be industrious, thrifty, temperate, and well mannered in order to avoid "deserved reproach" and "every just occasion of complaint." The burden of ending prejudice as well as slavery, they suggested, lay on the shoulders of African Americans themselves: "We beseech you to reflect it is by your good conduct alone, that you can refute the objections which have been made against you as rational and moral creatures, and remove many of the difficulties, which have occurred in the general emancipation of such of your brethren as are yet in bondage."[5]

Because some aspects of nineteenth-century African Americans' rhetoric of moral uplift appear similar to those of their white counterparts, it may be tempting to see this discourse as merely mirroring the values and ideals of white society. Frequently, in fact, antebellum African-American self-help rhetoric is viewed as a discourse that is individualistic, nonconfrontational, elitist, and focused primarily on adapting to the values of white America and gaining acceptance rather than on societal change.[6]

This characterization is incomplete on two levels. Craig Steven Wilder's research on the influence of African social organizations and traditions on New York's African-American voluntary associations reveals that these groups demonstrated a "West African legacy." Their "moralism," in particular, should not be seen as an effort to gain "white approval"; indeed, Wilder argues, the "equation of morality and whiteness creates the impression that African Americans lacked an indigenous ethical culture." "Far from reflecting accommodation or subservience," he asserts, "moralism facilitated the spread of social work in the black community."[7] In addition, while some African-American writers and speakers featured a discourse of moral improvement in arguments that seemed to take a conciliatory tone, it was a flexible form that was also used by activists who promoted social change and espoused radical goals. For antebellum African Americans, moral uplift was not solely an individualistic pursuit but was closely linked to community concerns.[8]

To fully understand antebellum African-American self-help discourse, we must consider its broad range and understand that African Americans' perspectives were complex, at times seeming to embrace the views of the larger society yet also in many cases modifying or challenging them. We must also consider the ways in which values associated with self-help were fundamentally related for antebellum African Americans to issues of freedom, survival, and identity. *Freedom's Journal* allows us to explore the variety and complexity of African-American self-help discourse of the late 1820s and the myriad goals and ideals associated with moral improvement.

CONDITION OR COLOR? PREJUDICE AND MORAL UPLIFT

For antebellum African Americans, the relationship between prejudice and moral character turned on complex yet crucial questions. If free African Americans "elevated" themselves, would prejudice against them be alleviated? Or was racism an intractable force that in fact thwarted efforts toward self-improvement by keeping African Americans in poverty and denying them educational opportunities? In other words, was prejudice due to *condition* (behavior or morality) or to *color* (the fact of being black in a white racist society)?

As African Americans engaged these questions, Americans of all races considered the relationship between racism and moral behavior. As we have seen, many white reformers placed the burden for ending racism on African Americans themselves, suggesting that the "degraded" condition of many free people of color was the primary obstacle to their full participation in society. Elevate the race, many white spokesmen advised, and prejudice would cease. For example, the New York Manumission Society maintained in a communication to the American Convention for Promoting the Abolition of Slavery and Improving the Condition of the African Race, which met in Baltimore in November 1828, that "mental cultivation" was a crucial step in ending racism. "We believe it is not the *color*, abstractly considered, which causes . . . prejudice," the Society proposed, "but the *condition* in which we have been accustomed to view the unfortunate subjects of a degrading thraldom." At the same time, various white spokesmen had since the eighteenth century argued that prejudice against people of African descent was due to physical distinctions. In *Notes on the State of Virginia*, Thomas Jefferson asserted that there was a "real distinction" between whites and those of African descent based not on "their condition" but on "nature" which would likely prevent them from coexisting peacefully in the United States.[9] As we have seen, white colonizationists often espoused this view that prejudice was inevitable and that African Americans would always be in a substandard position in American society, regardless of their accomplishments. Whether they defended this view by arguing, as Jefferson did, that blacks were inherently inferior or that white racist beliefs were intractable, the conclusion—that their color prevented them from becoming full citizens in the United States—was the same.

The debate about prejudice and self-help in *Freedom's Journal* took place in the context of this larger cultural conversation. Yet, as we will see, the editors and contributors to the newspaper did not simply echo the conventional wisdom of white Americans. They engaged the issue in a variety of ways, creating unique perspectives and challenging prevailing ideas.[10] The notion that prejudice was primarily the result of condition rather than color, for example, was adopted by some contributors to *Freedom's Journal*, yet they drew unique implications from this premise. In an article published in December 1827, contributor S. entreated African Americans to consider their moral improvement as Christmas and the dawn of the New Year approached and, in particular, to focus on education. S. declared, "The most powerful tyrant, by which the African has been degraded . . . is ignorance. Tell the Nubian . . . he is not contemned for his jetty complexion, but for the too easy compliance, with which his race have bowed at the execrable shrine of ignorance. Tell him, that this is what has rendered him an object of contempt, and his nation a people exposed to derision." S. adopted the view that prejudice was due to behavior rather than physical characteristics, yet S.'s position differed in subtle yet important ways from the common perspective of many white reformers. African Americans must convince every young person of color, S. asserted, that all that "the *white man*" can achieve is also "attainable by him." Education, then, does not serve to prove one's worth; the potential for greatness is already inherent within and must only be realized. S. also modified a central component of the thought of many white reformers, who believed that African Americans needed education in preparation for freedom. "Lend and assist the African to ascend the hill of Science," S. maintained, "and as he advances . . . ignorance must recede, and his shackles fall. . . ."[11] Instruction does not just lay the groundwork for liberty—education *is* freedom.

Other contributors built on the notion that condition and not color was responsible for prejudice to create striking arguments for self-directed efforts and empowerment. Correspondent Muta, for example, argued in a July 1827 letter to the editors that the key to ending racism was elevation. "This foul prejudice [will not] be removed," Muta asserted, "until we are raised to that point of education which alone constitutes the superiority in man." Yet, notably, Muta did not assume that whites knew what was best for African Americans or that they should control the efforts to bring about moral reform. Arguing that blacks should focus on projects established within the community such as "Literary Associations," Muta contended that African Americans could and should be responsible for their own moral and educational welfare.[12]

A two-part article by contributor Amicus published in June 1827 titled "Kosciusko School" similarly built an empowering argument for self-directed education from the premise that elevation was the key to ending prejudice. Tadeusz Kosciusko, a Polish general who fought with the American colonists and died in 1817, willed money to free and educate slaves. Because of litigation brought by Kosciusko's relatives, however, the funds were never used for this purpose.[13] Although disappointed that African Americans would likely "be defrauded of the money" left by Kosciusko, Amicus reflected upon the importance of honoring the general's commitment to education and considered how instruction could bring about liberty and equality: "Let the People of Colour, who would call themselves their own masters, join heart and hand in the work of *education*, and suffer nothing, absolutely *nothing*, for themselves and *their* children, to rival the subject of useful knowledge and right education. . . . And *then, how much longer* will the monster, Prejudice, be seen stalking abroad . . . and denying to freemen the estimation of men?" Suggesting that prejudice could be extinguished through self-improvement, Amicus implied that racism was largely due to conduct rather than inherent prejudices. Yet the purpose of education was not to gain whites' acceptance; rather, it would allow African Americans to "call themselves their own masters." Amicus appealed to the newspaper's readers to take control of their own instruction rather than wait for others to provide them with educational opportunities. In a clever play on words, Amicus used the loss of Kosciusko's money to argue that people of color must take matters into their own hands: "Let not the WILL, which was in [Kosciusko], be wanting in *us* . . . and with the *will* we find the *way*. . . ."[14]

Freedom's Journal's editors argued, by contrast, that prejudice was a result of color and not condition. Yet they drew very different implications from this belief than did white colonizationists or those such as Jefferson, who held racist views—indeed, their conception of racism contrasted sharply with the perspectives of contemporary white Americans. In an editorial published in April 1827, Cornish and Russwurm commented on the formation of a mutual improvement society in New Haven. They "concur[red]" with the "opinion" of the editor of the *Connecticut Journal*, they remarked, that such efforts "to raise the moral and political condition of the coloured population" were valuable. Yet they noted their disagreement with a central premise of their colleague: "We must dissent from the opinion that the odium is attached to our character more than colour. Many of our people are industrious and frugal. . . . [T]here are some of our brethren, who in point of character, information and competency, may justly be compared with some of the whites, and yet their colour is made the mark of reproach."[15]

Reversing the notion that prejudice would end if people of color became virtuous and industrious, Cornish and Russwurm argued that racism in many cases impeded self-improvement. "There are some very respectable mechanics among the people of colour," they noted, "and there would be many more, were it not that prejudice deprives them of the privilege of learning trades, as well as patronage, after they have obtained them." If the "debased and vile" could see that the "virtuous and good" were "esteemed" because of their character, then there would be an incentive for them to improve themselves; yet antebellum society gave them no such encouragement. Cornish and Russwurm started from the premise of many white colonizationists and apologists for slavery that prejudice was a strong force and that elevation alone would not dispel it; yet they did not suggest that it was inevitable or that as a result African Americans must accept second-class status or leave the country. Instead, they placed the primary burden of ending racism on whites, who should judge others on the basis of "merits" rather than "complexion."[16]

Cornish and Russwurm, then, defined racism in a fundamentally different way than did many white Americans. Prejudice based on color was a real force, they suggested, but it was not due to the influence of "nature" or a divine plan that relegated African Americans to positions of servitude. It was socially created for purposes of control and oppression, and mainstream society should take responsibility for it. In a sense, they identified what George Frederickson calls "societal racism—the treatment of blacks as if they were inherently inferior for reasons of race." This consciousness was not new; as Mia Bay remarks, late-eighteenth-century

African Americans were also aware of the force of "societal racism" and argued against it. In an editorial published in June 1827, an installment of a two-part series on African Free Schools in various cities, Cornish and Russwurm called attention to the social creation of racist assumptions. Refuting the notion that "nature" made people of African descent inferior, they challenged those who espoused this view to "point us to one individual who has enjoyed to the full extent all the privileges of his fairer brethren." The editors minced no words as they explained the effects of this prejudice:

> Conscious of the unequal advantages enjoyed by our children, we feel indignant against those who are continually vituperating us for the ignorance and degradation of our people. Let the most intelligent people upon earth be enslaved for ages—let them be deprived of all means of acquiring knowledge—let their very name be considered a byword through the land—and we venture to assert, that we should behold beings, as ignorant, degraded, and dead to every noble feeling, as our brethren.[17]

African Americans were not oppressed because of their moral deficiencies; on the contrary, racism kept them in an "ignorant" and "degraded" position. Expressing their anger at those who argued otherwise, the editors indicted the racism of American society.

Yet Cornish and Russwurm were practical men. Even if they believed that prejudice was due to color and not to condition and that white Americans were responsible for the racist system that they had created, the editors of *Freedom's Journal* often argued that African Americans nonetheless should behave as virtuous exemplars to disprove stereotypes that were used against them. While this advice may seem to contradict their view that whites' prejudices rather than African Americans' character were primarily responsible for oppression, we must understand it as a pragmatic strategy. Even if they were not accountable for the racist assumptions that were used to judge them—and even if upright behavior could not alone end prejudice—there were good reasons for African Americans to take away the ammunition from potential detractors by living morally upright lives.[18]

In the newspaper's second issue, for example, Cornish and Russwurm maintained that African Americans must "convince the world by uniform propriety of conduct, industry and economy, that [they] are worthy of esteem" in order to "disarm prejudice of the weapons it has too successfully used against [them]." In an editorial published in July 1827, they more fully articulated their position:

> Daily facts convince us, that we stand in daily need of [propriety of conduct]. . . . We know not why in judging of us, no distinction is ever made between the good and the bad—the virtuous and the vicious. Can we impute

it to aught but prejudice? . . . We wish not to hide the faults of our
brethren—but to correct them—to render our whole body more respectable . . . to be a "wall of fire" around them against the envenomed
darts of pretended friends—to be champions in their defence against the
attacks of open and manly foes. Constituted as the present state of society is,
with many who feel towards our whole body, the most violent prejudice . . .
it becomes our imperative duty to do nothing which shall have the least tendency to excite these prejudices; but rather to strive as much as we can, to al-
lay them.[19]

Cornish and Russwurm did not deny the power of racism, nor did they
assume that it would vanish if African Americans act virtuously. But if
their readers tried to lessen its force through exemplary behavior, the
"wall of fire" they created could offer at least some protection.

Russwurm continued to promote this perspective when he became the
newspaper's sole editor. In particular, he explained to readers the practical importance of moral cultivation. The "evil actions" of some African
Americans, Russwurm lamented in a May 1828 editorial, brought the
"whole body into disgrace" because white Americans passed judgment
on the race based on the actions of a few. Russwurm also argued that immoral conduct would tend to discourage the efforts of white reformers,
who might be inclined to help African Americans. Commenting on the
low attendance of African-American children at New York's Free
Schools—he asserts that only 600 of 2,500 children were enrolled—Russwurm admonished, "Is not such a statement discreditable to our community at large? is it not enough to discourage the most zealous of our
friends?" "Every one knows, that this is not a time to sit with folded
arms," he remarked in an editorial on the work of the Manumission Society of Stark County, Ohio, "we must be up & doing: strengthening by the
uprightness of our conduct the hands of those who are hourly labouring
in our behalf. . . ."[20]

Closely related to the practical issue of how African Americans were
judged by the larger society was the question of what constituted virtuous and decorous public behavior. Cornish and Russwurm may have
been highly critical of the prejudices of whites, but they understood all too
well the harsh standards their society imposed on African Americans in
public. As we have seen, racist Americans were often quite malicious in
their censure of African Americans' public behavior, particularly targeting
celebrations and social gatherings.[21] As a result, the editors and many
contributors often took a conservative approach, counseling readers to
pay close attention to decorum. In an essay appearing in the paper in late
June 1827, Libertinus warned readers about their behavior at the following month's celebrations of the abolition of slavery in New York: "The
eyes of the world are upon us, our enemies watch us narrowly, to catch

each little failing. Let us show them, that we are men, as well as they . . . which we shall best do, by abstaining from all riotous indulgence, from unbecoming mirth and extravagance." Libertinus was not specific, but contributor R. explicitly counseled African Americans to avoid processions, both because they "excite[d] prejudice" and gave the impression that people of color "care for nothing so much as show."[22]

As readers prepared for the anniversary of New York emancipation a year later, Russwurm gave similar advice. In a headnote to an announcement of a procession in New York, he remarked, "We hope every thing will be done with the greatest decorum, leaving it out of the power of any set of men to speak disrespectfully of us, from what they may witness on that day." In his comments after the event, he praised the gathering for celebrating "in a manner highly creditable to all concerned." He was less pleased, however, with an event in Brooklyn on the same day, in which, he claimed, "officers high in authority [were] scarcely able to hold their standards," "certain Coloured females" were "insolen[t]," and participants engaged in "debasing excesses." "On the subject of public parades," he noted, "we have never concealed our sentiments, and the recent one at Brooklyn compels us once more to denounce them. If we except the commission of crime, nothing serves more to keep us in our present condition than these foolish exhibitions of ourselves. . . ."[23]

Yet even as they held African Americans to particular moral standards when in the public eye, Cornish and Russwurm made it clear that the opinions of whites must not be accepted uncritically. When African Americans' behavior was misrepresented by whites, the editors challenged their detractors. In June 1827, for example, they responded to a particularly vicious account from the New York *Morning Chronicle* that attacked plans for a "grand coloured Jubilee," including a parade, to celebrate the day of emancipation, which, the *Chronicle* noted, would likely promote "excess, extravagance, and riot of every sort." The editors criticized these judgments and defended those who wished to celebrate. "We are no friends to public parades," they asserted, "and have long since entered our *protest against them*. Yet we hold, that our brethren (when they see proper) in common with the rest of the community, have a right to indulge in them." It was "exceedingly base," they contended, for "the inferior class of . . . editors, and newspaper writers, to indulge in low, mean, and vulgar abuse of their persons and characters on such occasions."[24] The editors may have defined decorum narrowly, but they were not conciliatory toward white society and its imposition of hypocritical and unfair standards on people of color.

By the end of his tenure as editor, as we have seen, Russwurm had given up on the notion that African Americans could enjoy true freedom and equality in the United States, regardless of their behavior or virtue. In an editorial published the week after his announcement of support for the American Colonization Society, Russwurm proposed that if African Americans removed themselves from the racist atmosphere of the United States, they could truly improve themselves. Liberia, he asserted, was "a state, where the man of colour may not only act and feel as other responsible beings, but where all the energies of his mind, impelled by the most powerful motives, will put forth their best, and astonish the most prejudiced."[25] Still endorsing the notion that, in the United States, whites' antipathy toward people of color was the primary cause of oppression—and still a practical man—Russwurm had determined that this racism could not be alleviated. Although many disagreed with him, as we have seen, believing that he had sold out, his view was a response to the question of how racism, oppression, and morality affected one another, an issue with which antebellum African-American leaders wrestled. Ultimately, Russwurm found a clear, if extreme, answer. Only when they became truly free by leaving the United States, he believed, could African Americans realize their full moral potential.

SELF-IMPROVEMENT, SELF-DETERMINATION, AND COMMUNITY

Even though they understood the practical implications of the larger society's judgments of them, antebellum African Americans believed that the power of self-help went beyond disarming their enemies and aiding their friends. Many nineteenth-century African Americans, Samuel Roberts argues, believed that "virtue" was the key to avoiding dependence on a racist society and to "construct[ing] a degree of order . . . in the precarious and unstable situation that racist America sought to impose upon blacks." The "pursuit of virtue," he remarks, allowed them to "maintain a credible identity despite racist attempts to trivialize, demean, and deny the full humanity of black people." Similarly, Martin Dann observes that for antebellum African Americans, "racial self-respect and self-help were interdependent; one without the other was meaningless." In other words, self-help for antebellum African Americans was fundamentally connected to self-determination. It also was associated with the spirit of black nationalism that, Sterling Stuckey argues, was strengthened during the early decades of the nineteenth century. The call for "a transformation of values and the creation of institutions designed to enable black people to move from oppression and dependency to liberation and autonomy," he asserts, was a central component of black nationalism.[26]

Contributors to *Freedom's Journal* proposed that African Americans should avail themselves of the spirit of moral reform present in antebellum society at large, but they emphasized that the most meaningful and effective self-help efforts were those directed by blacks themselves. In a letter to editors Cornish and Russwurm published in June 1827, correspondent R. rejoiced that "the People of Colour [are] treading in the steps of the enlightened part of the whole community, by forming themselves into Societies for the promotion of religion, the education of their children, and the relief of the needy." After noting the advancement of many African Americans, R. remarked, "Without detracting from the merits of their white friends, (to whom they are under an eternal debt of gratitude) much of this improvement (it must be allowed) has arisen from the societies formed among themselves, and on these more than ever, must their future advancement depend."[27]

Russwurm similarly built on the larger society's dedication to moral uplift to stress the importance of independent, self-directed efforts. In a November 1827 editorial on evening schools, Russwurm asserted, "Improvement is now the general cry through the land; and shall not we, whose condition stands in so much need of improvement in every particular, join heart and hand with the great master-spirits of the present age, whose great aim is to improve the condition of man at large in every corner of the globe?" He encouraged his "brethren" who "have always thought it impossible for them to learn to read and write" to attend a school run by the African Mutual Instruction Society, suggesting that education would allow African Americans to attain independence: "What knowledge a man acquires is emphatically his own; it will stand by, when riches shall take wings and fly away, and disinterested friends forsake." In an editorial on libraries, he more explicitly called upon African Americans to initiate and direct their own self-improvement. Although all who are the "real friends" of African Americans could contribute by donating books, Russwurm noted his "hope that a commencement [would] be made by [his] brethren in the different cities."[28]

In an address given in Rochester, New York, on July 5, 1827, to celebrate the end of slavery in New York, published in *Freedom's Journal* a few weeks later, businessman and reformer Austin Steward argued that self-help could allow African Americans to determine the course of their own lives in very practical ways. Advocating "INDUSTRY, PRUDENCE, and ECONOMY," Steward suggested that neglecting these virtues could have serious consequences: "Fly then, fly from idleness as from imminent and inevitable destruction: but in vain will you labor unless prudence and economy preside over and direct all your exertions." Conversely, if African Americans gained economic independence, they could control not only their futures but also those of others: "Remember at all times, that money, even in *your* hands, is power: with it you may direct as you will the actions of your proud brethren—the pale population of the country! Seek after and amass it, then, by every just and honourable means; and once in hand, never part with it but for a full and fair equivalent. . . ." Self-improvement, Steward argued, was a path to power, allowing one to determine one's own destiny and even direct the actions of others. Russwurm echoed this sentiment in an 1829 editorial about economy. He suggested that if African Americans lived economically, it "would add much to [their] respectability in the public estimation." Yet he also argued that those who were prudent in financial affairs did not merely enhance their reputation (and the public image of African Americans); they also "enjoy[ed] competency and independence" and avoided becoming "beggar[s]" who must depend upon others for help.[29]

For antebellum African Americans, whose daily lives were frequently restricted by an oppressive society, the message that economy would allow one to direct one's own life could be empowering. The emancipatory potential of financial prudence, though, went beyond mundane concerns. Steward advised his audience that diligence and thrift would help them to "rise to a respectable rank and standing in this, so late and so long the land of [their] captivity."[30] The implication that elevation was a form of resistance to slaveholding society would have resonated for his audience, not only for those who—like Steward himself—had been enslaved, but also for free-born African Americans, who were not granted full liberty or equality by a racist nation. In this context, self-help was a way of asserting one's freedom, affirming one's fundamental integrity as a human being, and countering the oppression of American society. Slavery "was a life devoid of self-possession," Roberts argues, while "virtue, on the other hand, held out the promise of a life of self-possession, a life lived in pursuit of actions consistent with a free person's conceived good end or purpose in life." Roberts explains that by cultivating virtue, antebellum African Americans affirmed that they could "determine right actions and fashion a vision of life as a powerful rebuke to the system that sought to deny them full humanity." Steward offered advice to his audience from this perspective: "Let us, my countrymen, henceforth remember that WE ARE MEN. . . . So shall every good that can be the portion of man, be ours—this life shall be HAPPY, and the life to come GLORIOUS."[31]

The emphasis on personal advancement in these arguments for moral and educational improvement should not be misunderstood as narrowly individualistic. *Freedom's Journal*'s editors emphasized that self-help was vitally connected to community development and racial advancement for antebellum African Americans. "We confess," Cornish and Russwurm maintained, "that we are so zealous for the future welfare of our race, that we cannot bear the idea, that our children should advance no further than we have, in the acquirement of knowledge, or in the acquisition of the mechanic arts." In his editorial in which he appealed to readers to "be up & doing," Russwurm made it clear that this effort was not merely an adjunct to the work of whites. African Americans must promote and direct self-help efforts themselves, he suggested, lamenting that "while our friends are making more strenuous efforts than ever to ameliorate our condition; our own endeavours, every succeeding generation, grow fainter."[32] Self-help was a crucial tool for community building; as African Americans organized to advocate moral improvement, they promoted racial advancement as well.

In a sermon delivered at New York's St. Philip's Church on April 27, 1828, which Russwurm reprinted in two parts in *Freedom's Journal*, the Reverend Peter Williams elucidated the links among self-help, community benefit, and racial progress. Preaching on Proverbs 29:15—"A child left to himself bringeth his mother to Shame"—Williams gave conventional advice: teach children "to love and fear God," discipline them strictly, and train them to be honest and industrious. But he specifically connected these efforts to the advancement of the race. "The great mass" of "parents of colour" demonstrated "criminal remissness," he lamented, not taking advantage of "all the means of literary and moral instruction which our city boasts." These were strong words, and Williams meant them to be, because so much was at stake: "The future prosperity of our race depends upon the proper rearing and education of our children, more than upon any other earthly thing. . . ." The community must work to dispel a prevalent "apathy" about education, Williams maintained. He advised anyone who knew children who did not attend school to "use [their] influence with their parents, to have them sent to these fountains of wisdom," adding, "By so doing you will serve the interests of the community at large, and the interests of your immortal souls."[33]

Similarly, in a speech to the Colored Reading Society of Philadelphia, which Russwurm reprinted in the paper in December 1828, William Whipper affirmed the effects of self-help on racial progress. "It is time," Whipper remarked, for African Americans "to be up and a-doing." Yet he stressed that personal achievement and community advancement were inextricably fused. "It shall be our whole duty," he asserted of the Colored Reading Society, "to instruct and assist each other in the improvement of our minds, as we wish to see the flame of improvement spreading amongst our brethren, and friends. . . ." Education, he emphasized, improved society because of what it allowed individuals to do for those around them: "We find those men who have ever been instrumental in raising a community into respectability, have devoted their best and happiest years to [education]; have lived laborious days, and restless nights, made a sacrifice of ease, health and social joys . . . with the only consoling hope that they had done justice to their fellow-men. . . ."[34]

Just as Peter Williams assumed a harsh tone, chastising those who did not educate their children and accusing them of "criminal remissness," so too Whipper strongly criticized those who neglected moral improvement: "There is an indifference in ourselves relative to emancipating our brethren from universal thraldom; and if this had, and would at the present be attended to, might be the means of ameliorating our condition much, and that is by a strict attention to education." It was not only those who disregarded education that Whipper decried, but also those who frequented "public house[s]." Whipper's rather severe tone was not unique; the editors and other contributors similarly rebuked African Americans—often sharply—as they advocated self-help. Cornish and Russwurm, for example, asserted, "Though it is our duty to assist to the utmost our fellows in distress; when a greater portion of it has been brought on through their imprudence, by a neglect of those maxims and rules of conduct, so necessary for every one to follow . . . our hearts feel but half that pity which distress ever elicits from the sympathetic bosom; and our hands give but half what they otherwise would." Correspondent Muta similarly denounced the moral condition of members of the community, noting that many who have "the means to improve their minds . . . have degenerated into such insignificance, that their very existence has been a matter of no great concern." Muta blamed in part "the want of literary institutions" but also cited many African Americans' "indifference" and "languid dispositions" that "curb every feeble effort [they] make to obtain [education]." "Not until we make a more strenuous effort," Muta argued, "will we ever be able to rid ourselves of this debasing lassitude: nor will this foul prejudice be removed until we are raised to that point of education which alone constitutes the superiority in man."[35]

Although these statements are severe, it is important to understand their rhetorical function. As John Waite Bowers and Donovan Ochs argue, writers and speakers from marginalized groups may use harsh language to appeal emotionally to other members. Because solidarity on certain fundamental questions is important for those who are disenfranchised in society, sharp rhetoric—even criticism and rebuke—functions strategically, appealing to group members to identify with and commit to certain goals. We must also consider the very serious implications for antebellum African Americans of choosing to live virtuously. Survival, Roberts notes, depended upon "racial unity and integrity." Immoral behavior would "dissipate the energies of the race" and "destroy the social bond between oppressed blacks."[36]

A speech given in 1828 to New York's African Society for Mutual Relief by Thomas Jennings, which was reprinted in *Freedom's Journal*, illustrates the way censorious self-help rhetoric connected individual advancement to racial unity and survival. Jennings exhorted,

> It is a lamentable fact, that many of our young men after acquiring a knowledge of letters and figures, born of free parents, bury their talents in the earth,

and are lost to society; they sorrow for themselves, the selfish soul deserves the pain it feels.

My Young Friends, be animated, be awake to your interest. Come forward and help us; we want you to display your talents as men, and co-workers with us.

Similarly, David Walker chided those who were selfish or indifferent to the communal responsibilities that went with self-improvement. In his speech before the MGCA reprinted in *Freedom's Journal*, Walker condemned apathy and urged his audience to see the critical connection between self-help and racial unity. After remarking on the importance of education, he asked, "Do not two hundred and eight years [of] very intolerable sufferings teach us the actual necessity of a general union among us? . . . Shall we keep slumbering on, with our arms completely folded up, exclaiming every now and then, against our miseries, yet never do the least thing to ameliorate our condition, or that of posterity?"[37] Strong language was fitting, given what was at stake, and could spur audiences to commit themselves to self-help and to understand the corporate implications of their own moral and educational advancement.

"KNOWLEDGE IS POWER": ELEVATION AND RADICALISM

In the first installment of their 1827 editorial on African Free Schools, Cornish and Russwurm noted the importance of education on "the future 'pride and glory' of [the] race." Considering existing opportunities for African Americans, they remarked,

We believe, that it is time for us to be dissatisfied with our former irregular mode of education. The day has been, when if any of us could read it was considered 'passing strange;' and we believe this has been unfavourable towards our improvement. . . . We feel that we cannot reprobate too highly this custom of lauding the most simple actions performed by a person of colour. Can he read and write a little? Can he cypher and transact the common affairs of life. . . ? He is praised and flattered—he is considered a prodigy of learning. . . .

Two weeks later, the editors built on this theme. After noting that "committees or trustees" at schools for African-American children had much lower expectations than their counterparts at white institutions, they asserted, "Let our children and youth be but once convinced, that as much is expected from them as from other boys of the same standing . . . and then shall we be convinced that really we are of a *different species* and not variety, and that the Creator has, in his providence, designed us for 'hewers of wood' and 'drawers of water," and 'beasts of burden,' for our fairer brethren[?]"[38]

The radical implications of these statements resonated on two levels. By urging readers to work for improved educational opportunities, the editors aimed to create activists who would fight societal limitations. They also suggested that for African Americans to seek a rigorous and complete education was itself a form of resistance, an act of defiance against the condescension and control of a society that expected them to rise no higher than was needed for them to serve whites. There was an implicit corollary to Cornish and Russwurm's assertions—white Americans actively denied African Americans educational opportunities in order to keep them oppressed. In his speech to the MGCA, David Walker made this point explicit, asserting that there were those who "delight in" the "degradation" of African Americans and "glory in keeping [them] ignorant and miserable, that [they] might be the better and longer slaves." He illustrated his point with a striking narrative: "I was credibly informed by a gentleman of unquestionable veracity, that a slaveholder upon finding one of his young slaves with a small spelling book in his hand (not opened) fell upon and beat him almost to death, exclaiming, at the same time, to the child, you will acquire better learning than I or any of my family." "Educating was a highly political task" for reformers such as Walker, Peter Hinks maintains, because they knew that literacy was "such a potent tool that such skills in African Americans were stamped subversive." Moral improvement in general, Hinks argues, was seen by Walker and other African-American reformers as "an act of empowerment and even resistance" because "an integral part of white America's oppression of blacks was to deprive them of the opportunity to acquire knowledge and to discourage habits that did not generate individual and collective respect."[39]

Education could also foster resistance by creating leaders who would argue and agitate on subjects concerning African Americans. "Let us endeavour to increase our store of knowledge," Thomas Jennings asserted, "ever recollecting that knowledge is power." Jennings maintained that learning would enable African Americans "to be awake to their political interest," to "convince [their] detractors that [they] disdain to praise that hand that oppresses [them]," and to avoid "submitting [themselves] to low dishonourable treatment" that was "beneath the dignity of man." Russwurm specifically suggested that instruction in rhetoric would give African Americans authority and empower them to argue for their rights. Russwurm described the effects of rhetorical education in one of his "Observer" columns, written in the form of letters to "Mr. Observer" and his responses. In this installment, "A Young Man" maintained that African Americans in New York should form "a Debating Society":

Eloquence . . . added force to the words of Paul, and made a monarch tremble upon his throne. In all ages of the world, it has wielded a tremendous
power over the affairs of men. Need I mention how a Demosthenes, tried to
rouse the dormant spirit of his countrymen from their long sleep of inaction,
and oppose the progress of the invaders of his country. . . . What caused the
Abolition of the Slave trade, but the glowing language and vivid colouring
given to its abominations? . . . [A] Debating Society will . . . enlarge our powers of reasoning by teaching us to express our thoughts as brief as possible,
and to the best advantage. It will also enable us to detect at a glance whatever sophistry is contained in the arguments of an opponent.[40]

As we have seen, African Americans of the 1820s realized the tremendous
power of literacy and rhetoric; self-help, Russwurm proposed, could enable them to marshal this influence.

In an article published in the newspaper in April 1827, contributor Philanthropos suggested another potentially radical result of education. "We
have this, among other considerations to incite us to action," Philanthropos maintained, "that it will be grateful to our posterity to be enabled to
say,—We honour and revere the memory of our fathers who have for generations slept and mouldered into dust, as the instruments of producing
this general emancipation among men." The notion that education would
allow African Americans to preserve their histories is noteworthy. The
"main function" of history for antebellum African Americans, Benjamin
Quarles explains, "was to furnish them with a more positive self-percep-
tion." Antebellum African Americans also believed that taking control of
their history would "prepar[e]" African Americans "for the responsibilities of full citizenship," Quarles asserts, by giving them knowledge of
their heroes, achievers, and contributors to America's greatness.[41] Because
of the centrality of history to their identity and their claim to equality and
civil rights, preserving the past was a potentially revolutionary act. If
white society sought to control their history, either through negative de-
pictions or omission, educated African Americans must counter these
portrayals. To write their own history was an act of resistance, allowing
them to determine how they were to be represented and to challenge the
narrow identities white society provided for them.

Education could also allow African Americans to resist common misperceptions about African history. Contributors to *Freedom's Journal* explicitly maintained that for African Americans to gain education was not
to reject their African past but, by contrast, to embrace it. As we shall explore further in chapter 6, *Freedom's Journal*'s readers and contributors
took a strong interest in the history of African nations, particularly in re-
claiming an honorable past in Africa. Correspondent Muta connected the
education African Americans could gain through organizations such as
"Literary Associations" to this former glory: "We should endeavour to

show to all, that there exists in Afric's injured race, a gem, that once gave light to all the world; whose lustre has been tarnished by oppression, but whose resplendent gleams are not extinct." Similarly, in a short letter to Russwurm—sent with an essay titled "Observations on the Early History of the Negro Race" from the *African Repository and Colonial Journal*—a reader asserted that self-help was linked to respect for African origins and traditions. Commenting on the *African Repository* article, the reader declared,

> You will find that our origin is such, that no one, however exalted his situation in life, need be ashamed of having descended from black parentage. We may be a very degenerated people, so are the Greeks, but this is the result of circumstances not within our control, but that our origin is a reproach to us, I most positively deny. We ought to cultivate all the social virtues, improve our intellect, and render ourselves worthy of our origin.

Moral uplift tied African Americans to their African heritage. Indeed, self-help was central to the dialectic that informed the views of many antebellum African-American leaders. Arguments for elevation, Celeste Michelle Condit and John Louis Lucaites argue, were part of a "rhetorical process" that enabled them "to fuse African and American values so as to form a unique African-American identity."[42]

In the columns of *Freedom's Journal*, we also find radical arguments for self-help that are linked to early-nineteenth-century black nationalism. As Sterling Stuckey asserts, "black nationalism was fashioned" out of "a recognition of bonds and obligations between Africans everywhere" and "an irreducible conviction that Africans in America must take responsibility for liberating themselves." Various African-American spokesmen in the 1820s—most notably Robert Alexander Young in his 1829 *Ethiopian Manifesto* and David Walker in his 1829 *Appeal to the Coloured Citizens of the World*—championed the Pan-African notion that people of African descent throughout the world were linked as a nation.[43]

Contributor Amicus created a Pan-Africanist argument for education in *Freedom's Journal*, asserting that the elevation of African Americans was important not only for their future in the United States, but as part of a global plan:

> The *African* nation needs something to be done for it, that it may be *"exalted."* . . .
>
> At the head of this great nation are the free people in America. . . . Their greatest resources are now in their own hands, and they can now avail themselves of those moral, intellectual, and spiritual treasures, which make this what Canaan was anciently, "the glory of all lands." The means of restoration, of light and knowledge, are mysteriously brought into their hands, in connexion with their wrongs and humiliations. . . . And let enterprising spir-

its . . . [be] employed in works of righteousness, and labors of love and goodwill, until all the millions of the earth shall truly be "One in Many," one *family* of "all the families of the earth."

As we shall see, the argument that moral uplift was connected to a greater
destiny for African Americans was linked to contemporary views about
Africa's present and future. Self-help, Amicus suggested, was fundamentally connected to the ultimate salvation of Africa itself. Yet Amicus
stressed that African Americans did not need to return to Africa to uplift
African peoples everywhere; America could be for them the promised
land. In the tradition of early-nineteenth-century African Americans who,
as Shirley Logan remarks, not only looked to "future political empowerment in America" but also invoked "the messianic destiny of African peoples internationally," Amicus created a foundation for self-help that incorporated American, African, and Pan-African identities.[44]

Although the potentially radical self-help arguments in *Freedom's Journal* engaged complex theoretical issues such as Africa's historical role
and the global destiny of African Americans, it is important to understand that moral reform and uplift were hardly abstract concerns for antebellum African Americans. As the editors and contributors to *Freedom's
Journal* connected a variety of important causes to virtue and morality,
they called for the principles of self-help to be translated into action. In
their two-part editorial on African Free Schools, Cornish and Russwurm
appealed to their audience: "Schools then, being so necessary to the welfare and existence of society; how can we . . . remain silent, when we behold our children neglected, and enjoying so few advantages?" They
concluded by challenging "all the friends of humanity in all quarters of
this extensive country, to come forward and use their endeavours, for the
establishment of schools" for African Americans. Philanthropos maintained that African Americans must act to promote and advance learning: "This is to us, an eventful crisis . . . because we are convinced that
something must be done in the way of education—and that it must be a
work of our own. Let us . . . gird ourselves and vigorously engage, each
one in his sphere, for the promotion of our dearest interests."[45]

These were, above all, calls for activism, for efforts that would be, as
Philanthropos made clear, "vigorous" and self-directed. Self-help—from
promoting economy and industry to taking advantage of educational opportunities—informed concrete projects through which African Americans resisted narrow definitions and took control of their destinies. In the
columns of *Freedom's Journal*, we discover the interconnectedness of independent and powerful action and moral, educational, and racial advancement for African Americans of the late 1820s, who took seriously
the mandate to be "up and doing."

NOTES

1. Samuel E. Cornish and John B. Russwurm, "To Our Patrons," *FJ*, 16 March 1827.

2. *Laws of the African Society, Instituted at Boston, Anno Domini 1796*, in Porter, *Early Negro Writing*, 11; *Constitution of the New-York African Clarkson Association*, in Porter, *Early Negro Writing*, 45; "Constitution of the African Benevolent Society of Newport, Rhode Island, 1808," in Porter, *Early Negro Writing*, 84–85. On morality as a prerequisite for membership in African-American community organizations, see Wright, *African Americans*, 153; Roberts, *In the Path*, 33–34; Carson, *Hand Up*, 11.

3. Rael, *Black Identity*, 124–25; see also Roberson, "Advice."

4. Mohl, *Poverty*, 23.

5. "A Plan for Improving the Condition of the Free Blacks," *Pennsylvania Gazette*, 25 November 1789; *To the Free Africans and other Free People of Color in the United States*, in *American Time Capsule* [electronic archival collection]. On white antislavery organizations' perspectives on the morality of African Americans, see also Rury, "Philanthropy"; Zilversmit, *First Emancipation*, 224; Ryan, *Grammar*, 171.

6. For examples of this perspective, see Cooper, "To Elevate the Race"; Fordham, *Major Themes*, 33–56; Kinshasa, *Emigration*, 45–62; Finkle, *Forum*, 20; Kessler, *Dissident Press*, 28.

7. Wilder, *In the Company*, 4, 81, 88.

8. For further discussion of the connections among self-help, activism, and community concerns for antebellum African Americans, see Quarles, *Black Abolitionists*, 91–115; Quarles, "Freedom's Black Vanguard," 176–77; Hinks, *To Awaken*, 85–86, 104–11; Horton, *Free People*, 55; Horton and Horton, *In Hope*, xii; Roberts, *In the Path*, 34–36, 47–51; Leonard Sweet, *Black Images*, 129–30; Wilder, *In the Company*, 81–97.

9. *Minutes of the Adjourned Session of the Twentieth Biennial American Convention for Promoting the Abolition of Slavery and Improving the Condition of the African Race, Held at Baltimore, Nov. 1828*, in *African American Perspectives* [electronic archival collection], 37; Jefferson, *Notes*, 138–42.

10. On this point, see also Rael, *Black Identity*, 125.

11. S., "Christmas," *FJ*, 21 December 1827.

12. Muta, letter to editors, *FJ*, 27 July 1827.

13. Foner, *History . . . Cotton Kingdom*, 573; Franklin, "Education for Colonization," 93, 96.

14. Amicus, "Kosciusko School. No. I," *FJ*, 8 June 1827.

15. Samuel E. Cornish and John B. Russwurm, untitled editorial, *FJ*, 27 April 1827.

16. Ibid.

17. Frederickson, "Toward a Social Interpretation," 251; Bay, *White Image*, 13; Samuel E. Cornish and John B. Russwurm, "African Free Schools in the United States," *FJ*, 1 June 1827.

18. See also Bacon, *Humblest*, 55–56, for further discussion of this perspective among antebellum African Americans.

19. Samuel E. Cornish and John B. Russwurm, editorial remarks, *FJ*, 23 March 1827; Samuel E. Cornish and John B. Russwurm, "Propriety of Conduct" (part I), *FJ*, 13 July 1827.

20. John B. Russwurm, "Fashion," *FJ*, 30 May 1828; John B. Russwurm, "Coloured Free Schools," *FJ*, 12 September 1828; John B. Russwurm, untitled editorial, *FJ*, 7 February 1829.

21. On antebellum whites' judgments of African Americans' public behavior, see also Susan Davis, *Parades*, 46–47; Zilversmit, *First Emancipation*, 224.

22. Libertinus, "For the Freedom's Journal," *FJ*, 29 June 1827; R., letter to editors, *FJ*, 29 June 1827.

23. John B. Russwurm, headnote to "Notice," *FJ*, 4 July 1828; John B. Russwurm, "Celebration of the Second Anniversary of the Abolition of Domestic Slavery in the State of New-York," *FJ*, 11 July 1828; John B. Russwurm, "The Brooklyn Celebration," *FJ*, 18 July 1828.

24. Samuel E. Cornish and John B. Russwurm, editorial, *FJ*, 29 June 1827.

25. John B. Russwurm, "Liberia," *FJ*, 21 February 1829.

26. Roberts, *In the Path*, 15–18; Dann, *Black Press*, 333; Stuckey, *Ideological Origins*, 5. On this connection between self-help and self-determination, see also McKeen, "Whose Rights?" 422.

27. R., letter to editors, *FJ*, 1 June 1827. Although R. often referred to African Americans as "they," he also used "we" and "us," identifying himself as a man of color.

28. John B. Russwurm, "Evening Schools," *FJ*, 23 November 1827; John B. Russwurm, "Libraries," *FJ*, 5 October 1827.

29. Austin Steward, "Extract from Mr. A. Steward's Address, To his Brethren on their Emancipation from Slavery," *FJ*, 27 July 1827; John B. Russwurm, "Economy," *FJ*, 21 March 1829.

30. Steward, "Extract."

31. Roberts, *In the Path*, 3–4; Steward, "Extract." On the connection between elevation and freedom, see also R. J. Young, *Antebellum Black Activists*, 110. On self-help rhetoric as antislavery persuasion, see also Bacon, *Humblest*, 53–60.

32. Samuel E. Cornish and John B. Russwurm, "African Free Schools in the United States," *FJ*, 18 May 1827; John B. Russwurm, untitled editorial, *FJ*, 7 February 1829.

33. Peter Williams, "Education" (part I), *FJ*, 6 June 1828; Peter Williams, "Education" (part II), *FJ*, 13 June 1828.

34. William Whipper, "Extract. From An Address Delivered before the Colored Reading Society of Philadelphia," *FJ*, 26 December 1828.

35. William Whipper, "Extract"; Samuel E. Cornish and John B. Russwurm, "Propriety of Conduct" (part II), *FJ*, 20 July 1827; Muta, letter to editors.

36. Bowers and Ochs, *Rhetoric of Agitation*, 26; Roberts, *In the Path*, 78–79. On the rhetorical functions of African-American self-help rhetoric that takes a harsh, censorious tone, see Bacon, *Humblest*, 56–58.

37. "Oration, by Thomas L. Jinnings," *FJ*, 4 April 1828; David Walker, "Address, Delivered Before the [Massachusetts] General Colored Association at Boston, by David Walker," *FJ*, 20 December 1828.

38. Cornish and Russwurm, "African Free Schools," *FJ*, 18 May 1827; Cornish and Russwurm, "African Free Schools," *FJ*, 1 June 1827.

39. Walker, "Address"; Hinks, *To Awaken*, 106–7, 111.

40. Jinnings, "Oration"; John B. Russwurm, "Observer—No. III," *FJ*, 7 September 1827. On the radical potential of rhetorical education, see also Bacon and McClish, "Reinventing."

41. Philanthropos, "Education. No. III," *FJ*, 13 April 1827; Quarles, *Black Mosaic*, 113–14.

42. Muta, letter to editors; A Constant-Reader, letter to editor, *FJ*, 5 December 1828; Condit and Lucaites, *Crafting Equality*, 76.

43. Stuckey, *Ideological Origins*, 6–12; see also Moses, *Classical Black Nationalism*, 7–17.

44. Amicus, "Kosciusko School. No. II," *FJ*, 15 June 1827; Logan, "*We Are Coming*," 27.

45. Cornish and Russwurm, "African Free Schools," *FJ*, 18 May 1827; Cornish and Russwurm, "African Free Schools," *FJ*, 1 June 1827; Philanthropos, "Education. No. III."

5

❧

Men and Women, Private and Public

In August 1827, Cornish and Russwurm published a letter signed with the name Matilda that began with a request: "Will you allow a female to offer a few remarks upon a subject that you must allow to be all-important[?]"[1] It is not surprising that Matilda adopted a traditionally deferent ethos at the start of this epistle on the topic of women's education; antebellum women often did so in response to cultural unease about women's public communication.[2] Yet the form of her question also highlights a central feature of the periodical. Although occasional pieces in *Freedom's Journal* were specifically identified as the work of women, they were relatively rare.

Given that many articles in the newspaper were published under pseudonyms and initials, we often cannot determine with certainty the gender of their authors. It is possible that articles signed with men's names were written by women adopting male personae; it is likewise conceivable, as Judith Sealander points out, that editorials signed with women's names were "written by males using pen names."[3] There is no way around these uncertainties; we must always keep them in mind as we examine articles in *Freedom's Journal*. With the exception of editorials and material written by known figures such as James Forten or Maria Edgeworth, we can conclude definitively only that they were written either by women or men adopting a female or male persona.

There are reasons, though, to conclude that male voices predominated in the periodical. Cornish and Russwurm, of course, wrote numerous editorials, but most of the material supplied by others also was probably written by men. The "culture of black Manhattan" in the antebellum period, Craig Steven Wilder asserts, was "patriarchal and man-centered," and "the black public sphere had a masculine idiom."[4] *Freedom's Journal*, as we shall see, fit this description in many ways. Yet even given the masculine nature of much of the discourse in the periodical, *Freedom's Journal* is nonetheless a rich source for understanding the way femininity as well as masculinity influenced the perceptions and life experiences of African Americans in the late 1820s. For the purposes of analyzing the rhetoric about gender in the periodical, what is said *about* gender is, in most cases, more relevant than the actual sex of the author, although female voices, as we shall see—whether of actual women or female personae—enacted womanhood in important ways. In addition, although rarely identified as women's writing, the periodical contains numerous articles about them as well as many pieces exploring relationships between the sexes.

Scholars have noted that to fully explore gender, we need to examine manhood as well as womanhood and to see each in relation to the other. Bruce Dorsey explains that "recent scholarly initiatives have encouraged historians to pursue histories that view gender as a whole, recognizing men and masculinity, as well as how gender has signified power relationships throughout human history, as indispensable subjects for historical inquiry." Just as those who study women's roles have considered both their private and public manifestations, Darlene Clark Hine and Earnestine Jenkins note that historians have begun to consider the role that "the private sphere—the realm of courtship and marriage, the home and family, men's relationship to women and to each other, sexuality, religious beliefs, and cultural expression—plays . . . in creating masculinities."[5] We shall follow this lead as we examine rhetoric about men, women, and their roles and relationships in *Freedom's Journal*.

In some respects, scholars have noted, antebellum African Americans endorsed gendered language, behavior, and roles characteristic of their society. Masculinity depended upon power, achievement, economic self-sufficiency, and the ability to support and protect wives and children.[6] Women were, to a certain extent, expected to conform to some aspects of the ideal of "true womanhood" that has come to be associated with traditional gender roles of the early nineteenth century. They were to nurture and care for husbands and children, to perform their domestic duties appropriately, and to defer to male authority.[7] Of course, economic and practical considerations rendered these ideals unattainable for many men and women—not only for many African Americans, but also for others in antebellum America who were not middle class—yet they exerted a strong influence. Many articles in *Freedom's Journal*, especially those reprinted from popular periodicals of the day, presented conventional wisdom about the relationships between the sexes and the proper duties for men and women.[8]

It is reductive and inaccurate, however, to see African Americans' views of gender as either derivative of the attitudes of whites or adopted in order to gain acceptance from a white-dominated society. The construction of masculine and feminine roles and ideals for antebellum African Americans differed in important respects from those of many white Americans. Gender roles and expectations had significant functions in community life for African Americans of the late 1820s and must be considered on their own terms. Men's and women's public and private responsibilities were not merely individual matters; manhood and womanhood were related to larger questions about the African-American community and about the roles of men and women of color in American society. We must also appreciate that African Americans' perspectives and experiences were not monolithic. For African Americans of the late 1820s, expectations about gender were complex and controversial. As women and men negotiated the experiences of everyday life and interacted with each other, they discussed and debated issues relating to gender in a variety of ways, on both practical and theoretical levels. The columns of *Freedom's Journal* reveal how this richness and diversity manifested itself in community discourse.

"WE ARE MEN": MANHOOD, FREEDOM, AND COMMUNITY

African-American men did not simply adopt the masculine ideals valued by their white counterparts. Although they, like all antebellum men, would have felt the influence of dominant notions of masculinity, other factors played a role in determining how they viewed manhood and men's roles. "In spite of their status as an oppressed group," Hine and Jenkins assert, "the first generations of African men and women arrived on these shores with certain established notions about gender roles and identity. These values and beliefs were the basis for constructing models of manhood that echoed hegemonic masculinities in America but were unique to the experiences of African Americans." Hine and Jenkins explain that "by the early nineteenth century, [African-American men] were selectively blending certain African, Euro-American, and Native American ideas into their own complex socialization into adult men."[9] In addition, masculinity for antebellum African-American men was not merely a matter of personal behavior; it had political and communal implications. Resistance to white oppression, for example, was a key component of self-determination, just as political participation was a central aspect of full citizenship. These traditionally masculine ideals were linked, then, to freedom and equality. For men to assert themselves and to achieve power was also a way of serving the community, of gaining respect and freedom for the race as a whole.[10]

Thus, even those articles in *Freedom's Journal* reprinted from sources aimed primarily at white men took on a new significance in the context of the concerns and experiences of African-American men. In July 1828, for example, Russwurm offered readers a piece titled "A Self Made Man," an excerpt from a speech by Samuel P. Newman to the Benevolent Society of Bowdoin College. Newman's central theme that a man of humble station can rise if he combines talent with good sense, hard work, and persever-ance—illustrated by the example of American politician and jurist Roger Sherman—was in keeping with the model of manhood described by historian Michael Kimmel. Self-made men, Kimmel explains, earned their success, "create[d] their own destinies," and "proved" their manhood in the workplace.[11] Newman's description of Sherman's rise evoked these qualities; with the "advantages of education" out of "his reach," he real-ized that "all his resources were in himself"; and, "in the strength of this resolution" he was able to rise "from the bench of the shoemaker" to the "Halls of our Congress."[12] The democratic overtones of this story would naturally have appealed to many African-American male readers who, like Sherman, would not have had the opportunities available to many privileged white men and who would have been empowered by the no-tion that they could control their futures.

Yet there is another implication of Russwurm's insertion of this story into *Freedom's Journal*'s columns. As Kimmel explains, although demo-cratic in theory, in practice the ideal of the self-made man depended upon the restriction of true manhood to native-born white men through vio-lence and the exclusion of others from the workplace.[13] In the context of *Freedom's Journal*, Newman's speech invited readers to challenge society's definition of the self-made man as white and to claim a model of mas-culinity that would allow them to gain success and independence. African-American men could redefine what it meant to be "manly" in an-tebellum America, using the very ideals of a racist and oppressive society to resist it.

Other reprinted essays similarly suggested both the relevance of tradi-tional ideals and their unique implications for the lives of antebellum African-American men. "Good Advice to Young Men," from a source Russwurm identified as the "St. Johnsbury Herald"—apparently the *Farmer's Herald*, published in St. Johnsbury, Vermont—counseled young men who were "mechanics and apprentices" to spend their evenings "im-prov[ing] [their] minds." History, geography, and the Bible, the author re-marked, deserved their study. For antebellum African Americans, as we have seen, to gain knowledge was an empowering, even potentially mili-tant, act, allowing them to resist stereotypes and oppression. If, as Hine and Jenkins maintain, resistance to oppression was a key component of manhood for antebellum African Americans, the inherent power of education had both racial and gendered dimensions. An essay titled "The Modest Man" described the pitfalls faced by a man who is "difident [*sic*] of his own abilities" and "can hardly be made to believe he possesses the merit he is praised for." Such a man would be "soon neglected and forgotten." In contrast, a man "ought to be too modest to take to himself any undue praise, but he ought to accept what he knows he is deserving of without arrogance" and welcome "that respect which is due to himself."[14] This advice would no doubt have resonated for most antebellum American men, for whom manhood depended upon a (good natured and polite) spirit of competition and assertiveness.[15] For African-American men, these qualities could also have signified a confidence in their equality with white men and their ability to succeed in spite of the obstacles posed by a racist society. If excessive modesty was conflated with subservience, deference to whites, or a lack of confidence in one's right to equality, it could hinder one's advancement.

In contrast to these reprinted pieces, which engaged the racial dimensions of manhood implicitly, reprinted articles and speeches by black authors and original essays written for *Freedom's Journal* more directly confronted the intersections of race and gender for African-American men. In particular, these works addressed a central aspect of African-American masculinity: the relationships among slavery and other forms of racial oppression, freedom, and manhood. Consider, for example, an installment from James Forten's *Series of Letters by a Man of Color*, originally published as a pamphlet in 1813, which Russwurm reprinted in 1828. Responding to a proposed law that would have forbidden free African Americans from entering Pennsylvania and placed restrictions on those already living there, Forten referred to the affirmation of the Constitution "that all men are born equally free and independent." Either Pennsylvania lawmakers "do not consider us as men," Forten remarked, or those who framed the Constitution did not intend for its promises to extend to African Americans. He dismissed the latter: "The authors of our Constitution . . . acknowledged us as men. . . . [D]eclaring 'all men' free, they did not particularize white and black, because they never supposed it would be made a question whether *we were men or not*." Of course, the phrasing Forten invoked was part of the American lexicon, but it was also highly gendered; in post-Revolutionary America, as James Oliver Horton remarks, "the language of independence, of civil rights and of citizenship was the language of masculinity." Freedom was a central component of what it meant to be a man, and the struggle for liberty was often framed in terms of manhood. Forten's language invoked the particular implications of manhood for African Americans; as R. J. Young notes, the phrase "we are men" and "variations of it" were often used by antebellum black men in their arguments for civil rights and against slavery.[16]

The masculine language of freedom was similarly invoked in an article by (the aptly named) Libertinus published in *Freedom's Journal* in June 1827. Discussing the upcoming abolition of slavery in New York, Libertinus remarked, "This event . . . affords a lively and convincing proof that the spirit of the age is hostile to the doctrine, that all men are not born free and equal. . . ." Like Forten, Libertinus drew on the gendered American vocabulary of liberty and equality. But Libertinus took this language in a unique direction, explicitly considering how slavery and resistance shaped African-American masculinity. "I would," Libertinus affirmed, "give vent to the feelings of a heart, that feels deeply for those of his brethren, who are unrighteously debarred of man's dearest privileges." Opposing bondage and manhood, he highlighted the central role of slavery in conceptions of African-American masculinity.[17] As Aldon Morris asserts, "An important goal of slavery was to prevent the emergence of a sense of Black manhood. The slaveholders realized that the solidification of a robust Black masculinity could prove detrimental to the institution of slavery."[18]

As Morris indicates, slavery and manhood were antithetical in two senses. If a slave was prevented from truly being a man, manhood also meant one would be unwilling to submit to slavery and would struggle for freedom. More generally, as Hine and Jenkins maintain, resistance to oppression was a key component of manhood for antebellum African Americans.[19] Libertinus's reflections on slavery drew heavily on the notion that true men would fight enslavement. Noting that the "abettors" of slavery "may talk of the happy situation of slaves, of their comfort and contentment," Libertinus asserted, "Their own hearts give the lie to what their tongues utter. . . . They know full well, that so far from being satisfied and contented with their situation, the poor beings, in their despair, have often lighted the torch of conflagration, and drawn forth the dagger, to rid themselves of their oppressors. This is their contentment! Talk of the happiness of men in a state of thraldom!"[20] In Libertinus's vivid affirmation, manhood meant fighting one's oppressors, even with physical force.

Just as Libertinus suggested that slaves might affirm their manhood through insurrection, so too Thomas Jinnings argued more generally in his speech to New York's African Society for Mutual Relief, printed in *Freedom's Journal* in April 1828, that to be a man may involve, in certain cases, physical resistance to oppression. The object of this male organization,[21] he maintained, was to create men who would fully assert their manhood: "As the constant dropping of water, will make impression on the hardest stone, so will our feeble efforts in time, rear a fearless front of men, zealous of their rights not to be trampled on with impunity." Jinnings did not explicitly advocate any form of violence; in contrast, as we have seen, he elevated rhetorical means as the preferred method of asserting men's rights. Yet his image of a "fearless front of men" who would not be "trampled on" implied that physical confrontation was not out of the question. And even as he endorsed political persuasion, his language did not rule out the possibility of violence: "We have a just right to enter our claim to justice . . . and thereby convince our detractors that we disdain to praise the hand that oppresses us: no man is respected for submitting himself to low dishonourable treatment, it is beneath the dignity of man."[22] A true man would not submit, whatever the consequences.

Libertinus's implicit endorsement of slave revolt and the undertones of violence in Jinnings's language were connected to a central debate among antebellum African-American reformers: whether violent means were justified in the struggle for freedom and manhood. Various leaders, often inspired by the Haitian Revolution, frequently reflected on the role of violence as an antislavery tactic, and even those who may have supported nonviolence in theory often were ambivalent about the use of force when confronted with specific instances of oppression. For many, as James Oliver Horton and Lois E. Horton assert, physical resistance was justified in certain cases and was framed in masculine terms. Those who formed vigilance committees "to protect the safety of fugitives" and "publicly vow[ed] that no slave would be taken," for example, were engaged in "a manly pursuit." Hine and Jenkins similarly note that "the call to 'be a man' was often used to counter arguments about the dangers of open rebellion for those still enslaved." Although the "emotional appeal of this position" was "powerful," Hine and Jenkins caution against categorically "equating manhood with violence" for antebellum African Americans. While some viewed physical resistance as inherent to masculinity, others found "alternative definition[s]" that were empowering.[23]

In particular, we need to look not only at how definitions of manhood addressed the oppression of the larger society but also at the functions of masculinity within the African-American community. A "discourse about masculinity," Wilder explains, was fostered through community organizations, and the "masculine idiom" of the antebellum African-American public sphere was "sustained through the constant production of young intellectuals in community institutions." In particular, he notes that "performances of black masculinity" were often part of speeches, ceremonies, and rituals that allowed African-American men to assert "their right to exercise the privileges of manhood" and "to express social obligations." Because reports of the activities of male societies were a part of *Freedom's Journal*'s offerings, the language of manhood and community became part of the discourse of the newspaper as well. In 1828, for example, Russwurm printed an account of a celebration by New York African Americans on the second anniversary of the abolition of slavery in the state. Offering a brief toast, attendee H. M. Goodman proclaimed, "May every man, a man be, / And unite in Liberty."[24] A central component of manhood,

Goodman implied, was racial unity and commitment to the freedom and good of the community.

The communal aspects of manhood were often expressed in the language of moralism. As we have explored in chapter 4, moral uplift was a central concern of antebellum African Americans of both sexes; frequently, men's moral obligations (and women's, as we shall see) were tied to gender-specific roles.[25] In "Major Noah's 'Negroes,'" their August 1827 editorial responding to Mordecai Noah's characterizations of free African Americans in New York as a "nuisance incomparably greater than a million of slaves," Cornish and Russwurm linked manhood to morality and community. The editors expanded the traditional requirement that a man protect women and children in his care into a community role. Chastising Noah for emphasizing the immoral behavior of "a very small portion of the people of colour" and for ignoring the "baseness of character and conduct" of many whites, the editors noted that many African-American men "as deeply regret the conduct of the vile" as Noah did. In fact, they had a stake in seeing this behavior prevented: "Many of us have wives and daughters, whose character and interests to us, are sacred and dear; and therefore we feel as much interested in the removal of the nuisance, and the good morals of the city, as any of the citizens."[26]

Cornish and Russwurm made it clear their opposition to Noah's slanders had little to do with impressing whites. Rather, as men, they had a responsibility to protect the community, which was threatened by Noah's misrepresentations: "Major Noah's efforts to increase the prejudice of the lower orders of society, against our brethren, is [sic] exceedingly unkind. . . . Blackguards among the whites, are sufficiently ready to insult decent people of colour. The Major ought to have gained experience from the situation of his brethren in other countries, and learned to be more cautious." Indeed, Noah's attacks were "unmanly," the editors asserted. As a Jew and thus a marginalized person in the United States, proper masculine behavior required Noah to protect those often abused by society: "We should think, if Major Noah were a man of reflection, he would be the last, to aggravate the wrongs of the oppressed. Has he forgotten, that this is the only country, in which the *descendants of Abraham*, sustain a standing equal to that of the *African*? . . . We should expect him to sympathize with the oppressed of every hue."[27]

In addition to protecting others from those who are immoral, a true man should himself have certain exemplary qualities and behave morally. Libertinus, for example, advised African Americans to behave in an appropriate and manly fashion at the celebration of abolition in New York:

> Let no act be done to sully the sacred character of the day. The eyes of the world are upon us, our enemies watch us narrowly, to catch each little falling. Let us

show them, that we are men, as well as they—let us show them, we have hearts capable of feeling gratitude for those, who have spent their lives and their fortunes in the promotion of our welfare, which we shall best do, by abstaining from all riotous indulgence, from unbecoming mirth and extravagance.

Libertinus was clearly concerned that African Americans should avoid behaving in ways that would cast reproach on the community, but in the context of his article—which, as we have seen, was hardly accommodationist—we cannot conclude that he believed masculinity depended upon whites' moral approval. "We are men," Libertinus asserted; although he wished his brethren to "show" proper masculine behavior, their manhood was granted. In his conception, avoiding "indulgence" and "unbecoming mirth and extravagance" constituted the appropriate manly response to a "sacred" event. Manhood was often connected to proper moral behavior, Wilder asserts, not because African Americans privileged the judgments of whites but because they felt the weight of their actions and the "responsibility" that "being free, black, and men" brought with it to "demonstrate that the subjection of Africans was immoral and unnatural."[28]

As Libertinus's comments suggest, masculinity—like the morality with which it was connected—transcended one's individual achievements and character. Personal manhood had communal and social implications. In the terms of the "common rhetoric," James Oliver Horton explains, "the fate of the race was directly connected to the standing of black men" and the "burden of racial progress" was principally "in [their] hands." As we have seen, the language of morality and self-improvement that fostered community solidarity was often combined with masculine terms that suggested that individual masculine behavior had an impact on all African Americans. Austin Steward's speech in Rochester on July 5, 1827, for example—which, as we have discussed, advocated various forms of self-help, including industry and economic advancement—suggested that morality produces true men, which in turn leads to community advancement. The moral principles he endorsed, Steward suggested, were emblematic of manhood and of a masculine responsibility to the community: "Let us, my countrymen, henceforth remember that WE ARE MEN: let us as one man, on this day resolve that henceforth, by continual endeavours do good to each other and to all mankind, to claim for ourselves the attention and respect which as men we ought to possess."[29] Like Libertinus, Steward asserted the manhood of his brethren unequivocally, and his suggestion that they "claim" the "attention and respect" they deserved equated their morality with masculine strength and agency.

Given the links among manhood, freedom, and community, it is not surprising that both supporters and foes of colonization marshaled gendered language to defend their positions. As Bruce Dorsey maintains, because any form of political exclusion was considered by African Americans to be "an assault on their own manhood," those who opposed colonization often expressed their objections in masculine terms. Such was the case with *Freedom's Journal* correspondent Investigator, who wrote in September 1827 to criticize the ACS. By "pushing" colonization with "all the zeal and influence they can possibly command," members of the ACS challenged the rights of African-American men: "The Colonization Society trifle[s] with the liberties of five hundred thousand freemen of colour, whose rights to the country are equally as good as theirs . . . and many of whose fathers fought and bled for the liberty we enjoy. . . . I know that I speak the sentiments of nearly all my brethren."[30] Of course, Investigator was aware that colonizationists did not intend for only men to emigrate, yet his language reveals that the struggle against colonization was gendered, evoking concerns about who was truly a man and what that meant. Indeed, he combined the language of manhood with references to military service to the country, an activity at once quintessentially masculine and fundamentally American. Colonization was a dual affront to African-American men, who had proved their citizenship as well as their manhood.

At the same time, Dorsey maintains, among those African-American men who favored colonization, manhood also was connected to their opinions. In particular, he notes, they argued that "racial prejudice was so unalterable in America that Africa offered a place of true freedom and manhood." Such were the views of Russwurm himself in 1829. Elaborating in his final editorials on his reasons for favoring colonization, Russwurm explained that any African-American man with "the feelings a man . . . must be sensible of the degraded station he holds in society; and from which it is impossible to rise." He described his desire to find "some other portion of the globe . . . where the Man of Colour freed from the fetters and prejudice, and degradation, under which he labour in this land, may walk forth in all the majesty of his creation—a new born creature—a *Free Man!*"[31] Russwurm's disillusionment with the United States, as we have seen, was the central reason *Freedom's Journal* ceased to exist. If the quest to be a truly free man was part of Russwurm's motivation for supporting colonization and giving up the editorship of *Freedom's Journal*, it seems that manhood not only influenced the material published in the newspaper's columns but also was a factor in its demise.

WOMANHOOD: IDEALS AND REALITY

African-American womanhood, too, was neither monolithic nor dependent upon whites' ideals. Unique factors shaped perceptions of femininity and views about women's proper roles, and there were notable differences between white women's and African-American women's experiences of womanhood. Like other Americans, African Americans held opinions about women's proper roles that conformed in some ways to traditional antebellum "true womanhood." African-American women were expected, for example, to defer to male authority and to take secondary roles in organizations composed of men and women. Yet just as notions of manhood developed from and in response to a variety of cultural influences, so too did perceptions of womanhood. Factors within the black community were at least as important in shaping notions of femininity as the values of the larger society; as with men, African-American women felt the communal and social implications of their gender roles.[32]

African-American women were aware of the fact that antebellum ideals of womanhood were based on the experiences of white women—indeed, of a small segment of upper-middle-class white women with the financial resources to avoid work outside the home and maintain a privileged lifestyle. In many cases, other women were excluded from "true womanhood," and it was often used against them.[33] Even, then, as African-American women accepted some of the facets of conventional femininity—such as the emphases on domesticity, motherhood, and piety—in many cases they also were able to resist these constraints, defying expectations, challenging the tenets of "true womanhood," and creating alternative roles. In addition, African-American male leaders were, for the most part, more open to female leadership and participation in community affairs than were many of their white counterparts. Women's contributions were considered crucial to realizing various collective goals, such as fostering economic self-sufficiency and expanding educational opportunities. Because many African-American women worked outside the home, both to earn money and to advocate for education, religion, and reform, their activities were not limited to the domestic sphere. Nor did they always accept the societal assumptions that constrained their white counterparts, such as the notion that a proper regard for domestic concerns excluded political activity.[34]

Because, with a few notable exceptions, material about women in *Freedom's Journal* appears to have been written by men, it was frequently more representative of men's views of women than women's own articulations of their concerns or experiences. We must keep in mind that we are most often reading male advice and commentary and that women's voices appear, for the most part, to have been absent from the periodical. Yet, despite these limitations, the periodical still provides some sense of the range and complexity of both the ideals and realities of African-American womanhood. We also can explore the views of African-American male leaders about women's roles.

Frequently, traditional notions about womanhood were endorsed in *Freedom's Journal*. Various reprinted articles proposed that women should keep well-ordered homes, care for their families, and be generous and good-tempered.[35] Other pieces emphasized the virtue and morality of the ideal woman. An 1828 piece titled "Woman," for example, declared, "The female sex is greatly superior to the male in mildness, patience, benevolence, affection and attachment. . . . [Women's] virtues . . . constitute in its rude or civilized state, the solace, the cement, and the ornament of life." In an 1829 essay of the same title, readers were advised that "she who makes her husband, and her children happy, who reclaims the one from vice, and trains up the other to virtue, is a much greater character, than ladies described in romance."[36]

Such advice was traditional, to be sure;[37] but, as with masculine imagery, conventional aspects of womanhood often took on a new meaning in the context of a newspaper aimed primarily at African-American readers. Frankie Hutton suggests that we must consider African-American male editors' concerns with representing black women as moral exemplars: "The overriding concern of editors in their coverage of women appears to have been to dispel unsavory images about them. . . . The image of the immoral black female was quite pervasive during the mid nineteenth century; it required the astute mutualism of the editors and women working together to wage war against it." Traditionally moralistic representations, Hutton argues, often functioned "not to oppress women, but to dispel" negative images of them.[38] Applying Hutton's assertions to *Freedom's Journal*, we can speculate that many readers would have appreciated the endorsement of proper and virtuous behavior for African-American women. Morality, these articles implied, was not the sole province of white women; black women, too, were worthy of being uplifted rather than demoralized.

While these articles did not mention race explicitly, various original essays for *Freedom's Journal* explored the racial implications of womanhood. In these contributions, notions that might seem to conform to antebellum conventions assumed a new significance. In "Female Tenderness," for example, contributor S. attached a particular meaning to women's traditional role for African Americans:

> When my sufferings had destroyed all the energy and vigour of my soul . . when prejudice had barred the door of every honourable employment against me, and slander too held up her hideous finger . . . when I wished . . . that I could end my days far from the white man's scorn; the kind attentions of a woman, were capable of conveying a secret charm, a silent consolation to my mind. Oh! nothing can . . . so sweetly soften all our woes, as a conviction that woman is not indifferent to our fate.

If traditional antebellum rhetoric proposed that, in Christopher Lasch's description, the home should be for a white man "a refuge from the highly competitive and often brutal world of commerce and industry," S. suggested that African-American women could create in the domestic realm a haven in an environment of racism.[39] Femininity here was related to and constitutive of masculinity; the African-American woman's duty to provide the men in her life with solace and support in the face of prejudice and injustice enabled them to gain confidence in their worth and dignity.

An 1828 letter to Russwurm by Ophelia—one of the few contributions signed with a woman's name—similarly suggested that African-American women could offer the men in their lives an antidote to the oppressions they faced in society: "In adversity [woman] is a ministering angel . . . whose inspiring and consoling tenderness, wipes away the tear of misery . . . and smooths the ruffled brow of misfortune. . . . If [her husband] be overcast with the gloomy shadow of adversity she will console him." In another article signed with the initial S., a contributor explicitly connected womanly sympathy and encouragement to a man's ability to confront and try to overcome the obstacles posed by a racist society. S. described Medillia, a virtuous and beautiful woman whose generous and unselfish influence on Manlius was cut short only by her death. While Medillia urged Manlius to look toward happiness in a "future world," she also impelled him to take manly action to gain the respect he deserved: "She pointed him to the place where there is no prejudice, and where injustice is known; while, she as kindly aided Manlius to ascend the highest summit in fame's temporal empire."[40] Woman's power here may have been indirect—she could inspire a man to achieve, to resist oppression, and thus to assert his masculinity—but it had significant implications for the community. Encouraging African-American men to challenge the limitations of society, women bore central responsibility in advancing racial causes.

Thus even as they at times affirmed somewhat traditional conceptions of femininity, contributors to *Freedom's Journal* gave these notions particular meaning. In some cases, they also recast antebellum perceptions of womanhood. Antebellum society's judgments of African-American women were hypocritical, measuring them in terms of standards based on the experiences of upper-class white women. These criteria led to the further subjection of African-American women, who were not considered "true women" and were thus denied protection and respect. Women who were enslaved presented the most striking example of the hypocrisy of a society that abused and exploited some women while professing honor for womanhood. Many free women were also considered to be less than feminine; required in many cases to work outside the home, these women assumed roles that fell outside the narrow confines of what the larger society considered appropriate for women. In *Freedom's Journal*, contributors described the very real circumstances of poor women, particularly those of African descent. In effect, they told stories that provided an antidote to the idealism inherent in antebellum rhetoric about gender, exposed the hypocrisy of their society's views of womanhood, and expanded the definitions of what it meant to be feminine in ways that were often empowering.

A dialogue published in the newspaper in August 1827, for example, explored the abuse of female slaves, explicitly calling attention to the limitations of antebellum society's professed respect for women. The piece—titled "What Does Your Sugar Cost?"—was apparently reprinted from a British periodical (although the source is not specified) and referred to slavery in the West Indies, but the parallels to American slavery were clear. A woman and her daughter entertained a female guest who informed them that by consuming West Indian sugar, they "help to keep a poor black negro in slavery." The guest bolstered her case with an example from testimony before the House of Commons about the cruelty of a particular plantation manager, who ordered a pregnant slave named Rosa to be flogged, causing the death of her child. The woman of the house asked her guest, "Why, Madam, is a black woman to be used worse than a white one?" Her daughter answered that it is because "*she has no one to stand up for her*," but their guest corrected her: "If the father of Rosa's seven children had raised his arm to defend her, he would have been put to death."[41] By publishing this article in *Freedom's Journal*, the editors called attention to the hypocritical and unfair treatment of women in antebellum society. Notably, too, the story contained an implicit reference to the demoralizing effects of slavery on manhood. The father of Rosa's children, like other male slaves, could not fulfill his masculine role of protecting his family.

The narrative of Mary Davis similarly called attention to a woman who did not fit narrow standards of womanhood. In her case, though, she challenged an oppressive society while demonstrating strength and femininity. A poor British woman, Mary Davis was forced when her husband went to war to leave her seven-year-old son "to the care of strangers, whilst she went out to wash for his maintenance and her own." When "the woman (if she deserves that name) in whose care she had left her darling boy" kidnapped her son, Mary set out to find him with her five-week-old infant. Discovering him at an inn, she learned that he was sold to a master and put to work sweeping chimneys. Cornish and Russwurm's inclusion of this narrative would have resonated on a variety of levels for their readers. Mary Davis was described in terms of traditional qualities associated with the ideal antebellum woman. She had true maternal affection; she was pious, teaching her son "to know, to fear, and to love his God"; and she unselfishly put the needs of her family before her own comfort.[42] Yet circumstances placed her in a situation that required her to forgo a narrowly conceived model of womanhood. This heroine, who did not conform to traditional antebellum roles but who was nonetheless virtuous and morally upright, demonstrated that true femininity should not be limited only to women with privilege and leisure. For African-American female readers, we might expect that this narrative would have been empowering, validating their experiences and granting them respect as women.

Another feature of the story would also have had particular relevance for readers of *Freedom's Journal*. As frequent reports in the newspaper demonstrated, the kidnapping and sale of children was a constant and real fear for free African Americans in the late 1820s. Russwurm and Cornish, in fact, declared in their headnote to the piece, "We insert the following narrative, hoping that it may meet the eye of Woolfolk, or some other slave dealer or betrayer, who has accustomed himself to severing the tenderest ties and inflicting the deepest wounds with brutal insensibility."[43] The reference to Austin Woolfolk, a notorious Baltimore slave dealer, explicitly linked Mary Davis and her experiences to the concerns of African-American women of the late 1820s. The editors suggested the hypocrisy of a society that professed respect for women's "tenderest ties" while exploiting some women and their children for material gain.

An original piece written for *Freedom's Journal* titled "Seduction" suggested another danger faced by African-American women—their sexual exploitation. The author, Tolendo, related the tale of "Julia B.," "victim to the seductive arts of a villain" who was "expelled [from] her parental roof" and gave birth to a child after arriving, disheveled and distraught, at Tolendo's door. Tolendo's story was conventional and sentimental, with the requisite ironic twist—Julia B.'s seducer was the new husband of Tolendo's niece Ann. Yet while it did not specifically refer to race, the narrative presented a circumstance with connections to women's experiences and fears. As Paula Giddings explains, because working-class women— and particularly African-American women—were considered to be "outside the realm of 'womanhood' and its prerogatives," they were often exploited sexually. Julia B.'s story was, of course, about seduction, a murkier realm than that involving explicit domination and control, but the results were the same. She was left powerless and vulnerable and, ultimately, died along with her infant.[44]

The four-part "Theresa,—A Haytien Tale," another narrative written for the newspaper, presented more racially identified female protagonists. Madame Paulina, "left a widow" during the Haitian Revolution, could not afford to be passive or retiring; she had to protect her daughters from the approaching French troops and a "cruel and ignominous [sic] death." Paulina was clever and resourceful, the author S. recounted, disguising herself as "a captain of the French army" and her daughters as prisoners, but it was Mademoiselle Theresa, her younger daughter, who carried the day. Pretending "to be inattentive," she listened when a military officer related to her mother "many military schemes, which were about being executed, and if successful, would, in all probability, terminate in the destruction of the Revolutionists, and, in the final success of the French power." Theresa then traveled to the military camp of Toussaint L'Ouverture to relate this valuable intelligence.[45]

S. was clearly conscious both of what would have been considered appropriate for these heroines and of the ways they pushed the boundaries of traditional femininity. S. described Paulina's "maternal affection" and her unselfish devotion to her daughters which caused her to ignore "her own danger." Theresa, in turn, weighed her duty to her mother and sister, who would be alarmed by her plans to leave them to journey to the military camp. But although Theresa's actions were unconventional, S. made it clear that they were justified. "Recollecting again the important services, she had rendered her aggrieved country and to the Haytien people— the objects which prompted her to disobedience, which induced her to overstep the bounds of modesty, and expose to immediate dangers her life and sex," Theresa concluded "that her conduct was exculpated, and self-reproach was lost in the consciousness of her laudable efforts to save St. Domingo." Theresa was a true woman, a loyal patriot, and a racial exemplar; her actions, however bold, were to be celebrated.[46]

PUBLIC WOMEN AND WOMEN IN PUBLIC

Many nineteenth-century African-American women did not face the extreme circumstances of Theresa, yet they often could not shield themselves from the public world by remaining in a private, domestic sphere. Nor did they necessarily want to; frequently they were called upon to contribute to the community. As we have seen, to improve oneself was considered a duty and a service to the race, and women as well as men were expected to work for intellectual and moral advancement. Women also played important roles in organizations that took up causes to benefit the community and to reform society. Thus they were, in a sense, "public women" in ways that white women of their time often were not. Yet just what women should be and do in public was a source of discussion among African Americans. There were restrictions and conventions that suggested certain boundaries that women in public should not cross. The editors and contributors to *Freedom's Journal* engaged questions about how rigid these limits should be and when and how it was appropriate for women to challenge them.

For nineteenth-century women, education—both in formal settings and through reading and individual study—was frequently advocated as preparation for women's domestic roles, particularly teaching and overseeing the instruction of children.[47] This perspective was reflected in various articles in *Freedom's Journal*. A reprinted article published in the newspaper in 1829 advised women to avoid overemphasizing "their appearance" and to instead take the time "to make their bodies strong and active by exercise" and "their minds rational by reading." This article explicitly linked these pursuits to the "domestic economy of a family," which was "entirely a woman's province." Correspondent E. remarked to editor Russwurm that a man should seek not a woman who is beautiful but one who "applies herself to the enlargement and refinement of her mind, by reading such books as are best calculated to afford instruction, and by conversing with persons whose experience gives weight to their precepts." "That such a woman is better qualified to render a man happy than the illiterate beauty," E. declared, "is a truth which must be admitted by the most limited capacity."[48]

These articles had a conventional message, yet they would have taken on a particular significance for an African-American audience. Education for African Americans, as we have seen, was an avenue to community empowerment and self-determination. Women's education, then, was not just a private, domestic matter but was often tied to public roles and to a civic commitment to the welfare of the race.[49] Matilda's aforementioned letter to the editors of *Freedom's Journal* provided a striking example of this perspective as she gently but firmly criticized Cornish and Russwurm:

> I don't know that in any of your papers, you have said sufficient upon the education of females. I hope you are not to be classed with those, who think that our mathematical knowledge should be limited to "fathoming the dish-kettle," and that we have acquired enough of history, if we know that our grandfather's father lived and died. 'Tis true the time has been, when to darn a stocking, and cook a pudding well, was considered the end and aim of a woman's being. But those were days when ignorance blinded mens' [*sic*] eyes. The diffusion of knowledge has destroyed those degrading opinions, and men of the present age, allow, that we have minds that are capable and deserving of culture.[50]

Matilda referred to the traditional rationale for female education in her letter—women must "form the minds" of their children—but she did not limit the value of their education. Women's influence on others may begin in the home, but it need not end there. For African-American women in particular, Matilda implied, gaining knowledge in order to educate others was a duty to the community: "Ignorant ourselves, how can we be expected to form the minds of our youth, and conduct them in the paths of knowledge? how can we 'teach the young *idea* how to shoot,' if we have none ourselves? There is a great responsibility resting somewhere, and it is time for us to be up and doing." In addition, Matilda suggested that women should be educated not just to serve others but because their intellectual growth empowered them and advanced the race. She remarked, for example, that women should encourage their daughters to "devote their leisure time to reading books, whence they would derive valuable information, which could never be taken from them."[51] It is notable, too, that in this letter Matilda enacted the principles she endorsed. Whether Matilda was truly a woman writing to male editors or a man adopting a female persona, she did not confine herself to a limited domestic sphere; she used her literary skills to take male leaders—in this case, Cornish and Russwurm—to task in a public forum on an issue that was vital to the community's future.

Cornish and Russwurm's inclusion of Matilda's letter is noteworthy, demonstrating that they did not believe women's voices should be excluded from public discussion and even disagreement with men. This openness was in keeping with the views of many black male leaders of the time. Linda Perkins notes that for antebellum African Americans, the "perception of a woman's 'place' and role within the black community" differed from the views "of the larger American society." Many African-American women worked with men in reform organizations, and they were frequently praised for their efforts on behalf of various causes. As Carla Peterson suggests, African-American men endorsed such work by women "as necessary to the success of racial uplift."[52]

Various reprinted articles about British reformer Frances Wright suggested this support for women's activism, even when society deemed it controversial. In 1825, Wright created a settlement in Tennessee called Nashoba, where slaves whom she had purchased worked to buy their freedom.[53] Although some reformers supported her, her efforts were criticized by many. In May 1827, Cornish and Russwurm reprinted an article about Wright's work from the Philadelphia *Ariel*. Although, as we have seen, this periodical frequently denigrated African-American Philadelphians, at least in this case its message appears to have coincided with the views of Cornish and Russwurm, who republished the article without additional editorial comment. The author lauded Wright's attempts to go beyond "the emancipation of the mere body of the slave" by "inform[ing] the mind; to prepare them for the enjoyment of liberty" and declared that she "has already made herself a valuable citizen of America; and her career of usefulness seems, also, to be progressive." Russwurm similarly reprinted a positive piece from the Pottersville, South Carolina, newspaper the *Edgefield Hive* about Wright's efforts in June 1828. Responding to criticisms of Wright in a Philadelphia periodical, the *Hive* article defended her: "She is rather entitled to sympathy and praise, than ridicule and censure. . . . If an unmarried lady has the boldness to exchange a life of blushing and smiling behind her fan for one which contemplates a solid good, the giving of Liberty to her fellow creatures, she must be told, forsooth, by a Philadelphia editor, 'that she is past eighteen and without a husband!'"[54] Russwurm's inclusion of this commentary suggested that he agreed with its author about the importance of women's civic efforts. Women should not be confined by society's narrow expectations or dismissed with trivializing criticisms when they aimed to do "solid good," particularly to relieve those who were oppressed or to improve society.

Original material written for the newspaper was similarly approving of the work of women in reform organizations. Indeed, in various African-American groups (unlike in many white organizations), men and women cooperated. Often, as Carla Peterson notes, women's "benevolent activities" took place in a "community sphere" that "functioned as an intermediate sphere situated somewhere between the domestic/private and the public." This arena was "public," Peterson notes, in that it was "located outside the 'home,'" yet it was "also 'domestic' in that it represent[ed] an extension of the values of 'home' into the community." *Freedom's Journal*'s coverage of the African Dorcas Association, a organization of African-American women formed to collect donations of clothing for children who otherwise would have had no proper attire for school, illustrated both how women's work in this "community sphere" functioned and the gendered rhetoric that supported it. Because religion, as various scholars have demonstrated, could empower African-American women to speak and act publicly,[55] spiritual duty was often invoked in connection with the Dorcas Association's selfless and charitable work. Various articles described the society's efforts in terms of religious duty, quoting scriptural references that mandated good works on behalf of others. Since the focus of the Dorcas Association was on aiding children, it also could be defended in terms of women's devotion to them. Contributor A. praised the society's efforts in maternal terms: "How *pleasant*, and how *profitable* must it be to our females to spend their leisure evenings, in clothing and making comfortable, & thus keeping in school (where they may learn wisdom and virtue) many little children, who would be otherwise running the streets at this inclement season, suffering for the want of clothing, and learning nothing but wickedness!"[56]

Yet the editors did not always confine women even to this "intermediate sphere" between the domestic and civic realms. Although they did not specifically address when and on what topics women should be able to speak, the editors rejected the notion that women need always remain silent when in public. In 1827, Cornish and Russwurm included an item in the "Varieties" section—whether original or reprinted is unclear— questioning the Roman king Numa's "severe" laws "against the prattle of the ladies, whom he prohibited from speaking, but in the presence of their husbands." The piece noted that if, as Sophocles said, *"Silence is the female ornament,"* this aphorism may be misapplied: "It is indeed an ornament expressive of modesty at times—but ornaments are not to be used at all times. What is more graceful, or even forcible, than good sense, from the lips of an intelligent female?"[57]

In some cases, specific women who took on public roles were lauded in *Freedom's Journal*. In a series of letters written while he was traveling in July 1827, Russwurm reported on the active participation of women in an important public meeting in New Haven, Connecticut. The gathering was called to "further the object of [Russwurm's] visit," which, his letters suggested, was to foster support for *Freedom's Journal*. Although he noted his disappointment "that the number assembled was very few," he added that "females, be it written to their credit, composed a large majority." This public work on behalf of the community was not unusual, he indicated: "The spirit of enquiry among [females], whether derived from their mother Eve or not, is always greater than among an equal number of males. Hence we find so many more of them engaged in the active duties of Societies, which have not only the moral improvement of man in view, but whose aim is also, to disseminate the charities and necessities of life among the poor and sick."[58] The women at the New Haven meeting gathered publicly with men to consider an important public question—the future of the newspaper that served as a forum for African Americans to debate and discuss issues and concerns. Notably, too, "mother Eve" here was not invoked as a reason to silence women—an interpretation proposed by various nineteenth-century commentators[59]—but to explain their "spirit of enquiry."

Because Russwurm did not give details about the meeting, we have no way of knowing if women spoke publicly on this occasion. Yet his praise for their attendance and for women's "spirit of enquiry" suggested that he was not opposed to women's contributions to public discussions. Given common opinions in antebellum society about women's public speech, this openness is noteworthy. Commentators conventionally called upon domestic ideology and religious doctrine—particularly the Pauline admonitions that women should remain silent in church, often interpreted to forbid women's public speaking—to argue that it was inappropriate and unfeminine for women to take public rhetorical roles.[60] Not all references to women's speech in *Freedom's Journal* were positive; in the context of the domestic sphere, particularly, contributors often endorsed the conventional notion that women's speech was annoying at best and destructive of domestic harmony at worst.[61] It is significant, though, that, in various cases, women's *public* discourse was portrayed positively in the newspaper, suggesting that just as African-American women were given more opportunities than many of their white counterparts when it came to the struggle for civil rights, so too their public speech was, in some cases, acceptable.

Yet even given the greater latitude African-American women may have had in public, there were still boundaries that women were expected to respect. Contributions to *Freedom's Journal* demonstrated leaders' concerns with how prominent a role women should take in working for reform, how visible their activism should be, and how they should appear in public. On the one hand, the positive coverage of women's activism indicates that, unlike many of their white counterparts, African-American women of the late 1820s did not see political involvement as inherently contradicting women's proper domestic roles.[62] On the other hand, as James Oliver Horton notes, many antebellum African-American male leaders felt that "even though black women might shoulder activist obligations far beyond those expected of white women, black men should represent and defend the race." Women should "participate in the political action of racial protest," he explains, but they should also "affirm black manhood." Public works, then, were valuable, but a woman might go too far if she could no longer create an environment suitable for the men in her life. A reprinted item published in the newspaper in June 1828 suggested this potential dilemma: "An editor in one of the country towns in the Western States, makes a most strange apology for the non-appearance of his paper on the regular day of publication. . . . 'I feel ashamed to own the fact, but . . . my wife said *I must stay at home and take care of the children, while she went to a Camp Meeting. . . .'*"[63] Although whimsical, this contribution sounded a cautionary note to women in public. They may be valuable contributors to society, but they must take care that their activism did not threaten their duties at home and especially the masculinity of their husbands.

Similarly, the newspaper suggested that women should avoid activism that was too self-consciously public. In an 1828 article, Russwurm criticized the Daughters of Israel, a women's organization. Although he declared himself "very much in favour of all associations, whose immediate objects are to afford assistance to the sick and distressed—to feed the hungry and clothe the naked," his "duty to the community compel[led] [him] . . . to denounce such an uncommon sight as a female procession, dressed in the full costume of their order." As we have seen, many antebellum African Americans were opposed to overly public celebrations for various reasons, and Russwurm noted that he had "said much against public processions lately." But he suggested that such behavior by women was particularly troublesome, remarking that "little did [he] dream an opportunity would be afforded [him] so soon, of writing aught against *female evening processions.*" It is instructive to compare Russwurm's distress in this case with his praise for the decidedly unassuming ethos of the African Dorcas Association, who "conduct their affairs" in a "business like manner" and whose members "have no annual processions . . . no blazing banners; pharisee-like to proclaim to the world the nature of their work."[64] It might have been acceptable for women to work in public, but Russwurm implied that they should take particular care to be modest and to resist calling attention to themselves.

Women's activism also should be focused on appropriate issues. Frances Wright, as we have seen, was supported by the editors for confronting the system of slavery. Yet she was also known as an advocate of sexual freedom and a freethinker, problematic enough for a man in antebellum America but shocking for a woman.[65] An announcement in *Freedom's Journal* in December 1828 asserted, "Miss Frances Wright advertises for sale a few copies of Paine's Age of Reason, and another book equally vile. This woman ought to get into pantaloons immediately, she is a disgrace to the fairer part of creation." Whether the words were Russwurm's or borrowed from another publication, it appears that he agreed with the sentiment; if it was reprinted, he added no editorial comment contradicting it. It was one thing for a woman to attack slavery; it was quite another to endorse Thomas Paine's infamous attack on religion. The language of the criticism called not only her piety but also her womanhood into question. As Barbara Welter notes, religious devotion was considered a vital attribute of the antebellum woman, and Wright was often attacked for her impiety.[66] African-American leaders may have given women more latitude in public to persuade, to work for the community's benefit, and to fight for freedom and civil rights, but they still, like their white counterparts, expected women to be reverent and faithful.

Although Matilda's letter to the editors suggested that it was acceptable for women to persuade publicly through writing, these opportunities were also limited. As Elizabeth McHenry demonstrates, African-American women wrote and critiqued others' writing in literary societies, creating texts that argued for freedom. McHenry aptly notes that these literary activities reveal that the public/private dichotomy often applied to men's and women's work in nineteenth-century America is "an inadequate framework for understanding the importance of literary societies for African American women." Yet even as they connected their writing to public causes, McHenry maintains, these women often encountered expectations that they be "amiable and meek."[67] The fact that articles specifically identified as women's writing were rare in *Freedom's Journal* suggests that this was a difficult tension for potential female contributors to negotiate. In addition, the limits on women's contributions to *Freedom's Journal* were not merely self-imposed. In October 1828, Russwurm inserted a note in the newspaper suggesting that he had received a contribution from a female reader calling herself the "City 'Peasant'" which he chose not to publish. Peasant was apparently responding to a letter from Dick Dashall, who expressed frustration at his falling in love with a woman who was engaged and offered women "hints for their conduct in courtship" so that men would be able to determine whether they were interested in finding a mate or already spoken for. Russwurm remarked that Peasant is "rather severe in her kind epistle," noting that he was "sure it was not the object of D. D. to wound the feelings of any of our fair readers."[68] It is significant that Russwurm chose not to publish this letter because of both its "severe" tone and its content. As McHenry remarks, African-American women were expected to avoid attacks on male leaders' "authority, their manhood, and their sense of a woman's place."[69]

Given Russwurm's rejection of Peasant's contribution, the publication of Matilda's criticisms of the editors is all the more notable. It also is, perhaps, a bit surprising. Russwurm rejected a woman's critique of Dick Dashall's seemingly lighthearted piece, yet he and Cornish were open to publishing a more serious challenge to their own authority that was signed with a woman's name. The discrepancy points to the complex and often contradictory views of manhood and womanhood among antebellum African Americans. There were many demands that they had to negotiate, in public and in private, as they debated what it meant to be men and women, both individually and in relation to one another, as well as participants in the struggle for racial equality. These questions cannot be resolved. Indeed, the diversity of perspectives represented in *Freedom's Journal* reveals that these significant and defining tensions were at the heart of questions about gender, as readers were invited by turns to affirm, re-create, test, and challenge the norms and limits of manhood and womanhood.

NOTES

1. Matilda, letter to editors, *FJ*, 10 August 1827.
2. See Bacon, *Humblest*, 117, 137–39.
3. Sealander, "Antebellum Black Images," 10.
4. Wilder, *In the Company*, 129, 123; see also Booker, *I Will Wear*, 57; Horton, "Freedom's Yoke," 53–55.
5. Dorsey, "Gendered History," 77; Hine and Jenkins, "Introduction," 1.
6. Hine and Jenkins, "Introduction," 2, 13–14; Booker, *I Will Wear*, 58; Horton and Horton, "Violence," 382; 389–90.
7. Sealander, "Antebellum Black Images," 2–8; Horton, "Freedom's Yoke," 56–60; Yee, "Organizing," 40–41; Yee, *Black Women Abolitionists*, 4–5; Bacon, *Humblest*, 45–47, 165–66.
8. See, for example, "Thoughts," *FJ*, 13 April 1827; John B. Russwurm, "Observer, No. II," *FJ*, 24 August 1827; John B. Russwurm, "Observer.—No. IX," *FJ*, 16 November 1827; [Oliver] Goldsmith, "Old Maids," *FJ*, 16 May 1828; "Recollections of Thomas Tompkins," *FJ*, 6 June 1828.
9. Hine and Jenkins, "Introduction," 2, 14; see also Booker, *I Will Wear*, 57.

10. Hine and Jenkins, "Introduction," 2–3, 30–31; Horton and Horton, "Violence," 387, 391; Dorsey, "Gendered History," 87–88; Booker, *I Will Wear*, 58; Wilder, *In the Company*, 123–27, 131–41; Horton, "Manhood," 2–6, 15; Horton, "Freedom's Yoke," 57; Dixon, "True Manly Life," 214–15.

11. Kimmel, *Manhood*, 17–26; see also Roberson, "Advice"; Harrold, *Rise*, 12.

12. [Samuel P. Newman], "A Self Made Man," *FJ*, 25 July 1828. Notably, the date of Newman's address was the evening before Russwurm's graduation from Bowdoin, and it was published in pamphlet form (Newman, *Address*). Possibly, Russwurm was in attendance; at least, he was likely familiar with the speech as a member of the Bowdoin community at the time.

13. Kimmel, *Manhood*, 32–33; see also Hine and Jenkins, "Introduction," 13–14.

14. "Good Advice to Young Men," *FJ*, 9 January 1829; Hine and Jenkins, "Introduction," 2, 57; "The Modest Man," *FJ*, 22 August 1828. Whether "The Modest Man" was original to *Freedom's Journal* or reprinted from an unspecified source is unclear, although its placement in the paper—between articles from other sources—and the lack of any references in or introducing it to *Freedom's Journal* suggest the latter.

15. Kimmel, *Manhood*, 26–27.

16. James Forten, "Letters from a Man of Colour, on a Late Bill before the Senate of Pennsylvania. Letter II," *FJ*, 29 February 1828; Horton, "Manhood," www.law.yale.edu/outside/pdf/centers/sc/Horton-Manhood.pdf, 9; R. J. Young, *Antebellum Black Activists*, 67. For further discussion of the connections between manhood and freedom, see Hine and Jenkins, "Introduction," 30; Horton and Horton, "Violence," 382.

17. Libertinus, "For the Freedom's Journal," *FJ*, 29 June 1827. I use the pronoun "he" here because wording of the article indicates that Libertinus was a man (or possibly, although not likely, a woman adopting a male persona), just as Matilda was a woman or a man writing in a woman's voice. In most cases of pseudonyms or initials throughout this chapter as well as the book as a whole, I have avoided using pronouns unless textual clues indicated the gender of a writer or a writer's persona.

18. Aldon Morris, foreword to *Question of Manhood*, xiii. On the relationships between African-American masculinity and slavery, see also Horton and Horton, "Violence," 384; Horton, "Manhood," 14–15; Horton, "Freedom's Yoke," 53.

19. Hine and Jenkins, "Introduction," 2, 57; see also Harrold, *Rise*, 12.

20. Libertinus, "For the Freedom's Journal."

21. Wilder indicates that this organization had an exclusively male membership (*In the Company*, 74).

22. "Oration, by Thomas L. Jinnings," *FJ*, 4 April 1828.

23. Horton and Horton, "Violence," 391; Hine and Jenkins, "Introduction," 30–31.

24. Wilder, *In the Company*, 121–24; "Celebration," *FJ*, 11 July 1828.

25. Wilder, *In the Company*, 133.

26. Samuel E. Cornish and John B. Russwurm, "Major Noah's 'Negroes,'" *FJ*, 24 August 1827.

27. Ibid.

28. Libertinus, "For the Freedom's Journal"; Wilder, *In the Company*, 94.

29. Horton, "Manhood," 2; Austin Steward, "Extract from Mr. A. Steward's Address, To his Brethren on their Emancipation from Slavery," *FJ*, 27 July 1827.

30. Dorsey, "Gendered History," 87; Investigator, "Colonization Society. No. I," *FJ*, 7 September 1827.

31. Dorsey, "Gendered History," 91–92; John B. Russwurm, "Our Vindication," *FJ*, 14 March 1829; John B. Russwurm, "Colonization," *FJ*, 14 March 1829. It appears that here Russwurm ironically reversed (thus signified on) the definition of an American as a "free man" and the association of Americanization with rebirth famously expressed by J. Hector St. John de Crèvecoeur in his 1782 *Letters from an American Farmer*: "Here man is free; as he ought to be. . . . The American is a new man. . . . An European, when he first arrives . . . no sooner breathes our air than he . . . begins to feel the effects of a sort of resurrection . . . he now feels himself a man. . . . From nothing to start into being; from a servant to the rank of a master; from being the slave of some despotic prince, to become a free man. . . ." (50–79). I am indebted to Glen McClish for suggesting this connection.

32. Perkins, "Black Women," 317; Perkins, "Impact," 18–19; Peterson, *"Doers of the Word,"* 15–17; Bacon, *Humblest*, 47–50; Dabel, "I Have Gone," 13–20.

33. Giddings, *When and Where I Enter*, 47–49; Carby, *Reconstructing Womanhood*, 6, 32; Bacon, *Humblest*, 175–96; Tate, *Unknown Tongues*, 16.

34. Booker, *I Will Wear*, 44, 57–58; Horton and Horton, "Violence," 393–95; Horton, "Manhood," 3–5; Horton, "Freedom's Yoke"; Terborg-Penn, "Black Male Perspectives"; Judith Sealander, "Antebellum Black Press"; bell hooks, *Ain't I A Woman*, 88–92; Perkins, "Black Women," 321; Yee, *Black Women Abolitionists*, 3, 46, 56–58; Horton and Horton, *Black Bostonians*, 19–21; Boylan, "Benevolence," 125–28; Giddings, *When and Where I Enter*, 52; Loewenberg and Bogin, *Black Women*, 28–29; Bacon, *Humblest*, 43–50; 175–86; Bacon, *"Liberator's* 'Ladies' Department,'" 14–16; Tate, "Political Consciousness"; Armstrong, "Mental and Moral Feast," 78–79; Tate, *Unknown Tongues*, 12–19; Dabel, "I Have Gone."

35. See, for example, Edmund Burke, "The Idea of a Perfect Wife," *FJ*, 20 June 1828; Maria Edgeworth and Richard Lovell Edgeworth, "A Hint to House Wives," *FJ*, 7 December 1827.

36. "Woman," *FJ*, 11 April 1828; "Woman," *FJ*, 14 February 1829. It is not clear whether these articles were written by Russwurm or reprinted from an unspecified source.

37. See Welter, *Dimity Convictions*, 21–26.

38. Hutton, *Early Black Press*, 58.

39. S., "Female Tenderness," *FJ*, 27 July 1827; Lasch, *Haven*, 5.

40. Ophelia, letter to editor, *FJ*, 22 August 1828; S., "For the Freedom's Journal," *FJ*, 10 August 1827.

41. "What Does Your Sugar Cost?" (part I), *FJ*, 17 August 1827; "What Does Your Sugar Cost?" (part II), *FJ*, 24 August 1827.

42. "Mary Davis," *FJ*, 16 March 1827.

43. Samuel E. Cornish and John B. Russwurm, "Kidnapping," *FJ*, 16 March 1827.

44. Tolendo, "Seduction," *FJ*, 23 November 1827; Giddings, *When and Where I Enter*, 49.

45. S., "Theresa,—A Haytien Tale," *FJ*, 18 January 1828; S., "Theresa,—A Haytien Tale," *FJ*, 25 January 1828; S., "Theresa,—A Haytien Tale," *FJ*, 8 February 1828;

S., "Theresa,—A Haytien Tale," *FJ*, 15 February 1828. Dickson Bruce notes that "Theresa" was "one of the first lengthy pieces of fiction by a black American writer" and "perhaps the first attempt by an African American writer to create a black romantic heroine" (*Origins*, 172–73).

46. S., "Theresa," 18 January 1828; S., "Theresa," 8 February 1828. See also Bruce, *Origins*, 173, on conventions of femininity in "Theresa."

47. Rouse, "Cultural Models"; Welter, *Dimity Convictions*, 15, 34–35.

48. "Female Education," *FJ*, 9 January 1829; E., letter to editor, *FJ*, 11 January 1828.

49. Terborg-Penn, "Black Male Perspectives," 30; Loewenberg and Bogin, *Black Women*, 20–21; Perkins, "Black Women," 323–30; Perkins, "Impact," 18–21; Bacon, *Humblest*, 49.

50. Matilda, letter.

51. Ibid.

52. Perkins, "Black Women," 317; Peterson, *"Doers of the Word,"* 16. On African-American women's public participation in reform, see also Giddings, *When and Where I Enter*, 7; Terborg-Penn, "Black Male Perspectives," 28–29.

53. Ginzberg, "Hearts," 201.

54. "Philanthropy of Miss Wright," *FJ*, 11 May 1827; "Philanthropy," *FJ*, 6 June 1828.

55. Loewenberg and Bogin, *Black Women*, 9–12; Bacon, *Humblest*, 50, 196–209.

56. Peterson, *"Doers of the Word,"* 16; A Member, "Female Dorcas Society," *FJ*, 26 September 1828; Cato, "Dorcas Association," *FJ*, 21 November 1828; A., "Dorcas Association," *FJ*, 7 February 1829.

57. Untitled item in "Varieties" section, *FJ*, 15 June 1827.

58. [John B. Russwurm], "To the Senior Editor—No. II," *FJ*, 10 August 1827; [John B. Russwurm], "To the Senior Editor—No. III," *FJ*, 17 August 1827. Although these letters were unsigned, a comment in a September editorial specified that they were written by "the Junior Editor" Russwurm (Junior Editor, "Wilberforce," *FJ*, 7 September 1827).

59. Bacon, *Humblest*, 35–36.

60. Ibid., 34–41.

61. See, for example, "Female Temper," *FJ*, 20 April 1827; Ned, "For the Freedom's Journal," *FJ*, 11 May 1827; Russwurm, "Observer, No. II"; John B. Russwurm, "Observer.—No. V," *FJ*, 5 October 1827; Maria, "Female Scandal," *FJ*, 4 April 1828; Job, "A Husband's Complaint," *FJ*, 5 September 1828.

62. See Giddings, *When and Where I Enter*, 52; Bacon, *Humblest*, 48–49.

63. Horton, "Manhood," 5–6; untitled item in "Varieties" section, *FJ*, 13 June 1828.

64. John B. Russwurm, "Another Celebration! ! !" *FJ*, 15 August 1828; John B. Russwurm, "Our Dorcas Association," *FJ*, 9 January 1829.

65. See Ginzberg, "Hearts."

66. Untitled item in "Summary" section, *FJ*, 12 December 1828; Welter, *Dimity Convictions*.

67. McHenry, *Forgotten Readers*, 57–79.

68. Dick Dashall, "Girls 'Have At Ye All,'" *FJ*, 10 October 1828; John B. Russwurm, "To Correspondents," *FJ*, 24 October 1828.

69. McHenry, *Forgotten Readers*, 72; see also Horton, "Manhood," 5–6.

6

$\sim$

Redemption, Regeneration, Revolution: Africa and Haiti

In the first issue of *Freedom's Journal*, Cornish and Russwurm pledged to their readers that "every thing that relates to Africa, shall find a ready admission into [their] columns." They emphasized that they would not merely accept conventional wisdom about the continent but would in fact seek to correct common misperceptions: "As that vast continent becomes daily more known, we trust that many things will come to light, proving that the natives of it are neither so ignorant nor stupid as they have generally been supposed to be." More broadly, the editors suggested that they were interested in Africa as well as in Haiti because these regions raised questions about history, religion, and the destiny of people of African descent throughout the world. They asked readers,

> If ignorance, poverty and degradation have hitherto been our unhappy lot, has the Eternal decree gone forth, that our race alone, are to remain in this state, while knowledge and civilization are shedding their enlivening rays over the rest of the human family? The recent travels of Denham and Clapperton in the interior of Africa, and the interesting narrative which they have published; the establishment of the republic of Hayti after years of sanguinary warfare; its subsequent progress in all the arts of civilization . . . prove the contrary.[1]

The attention given to the past, present, and future of Africa and Haiti in *Freedom's Journal* did not, in most cases, signify emigrationist sentiment or support for colonization. Indeed, as we have seen, the editorial position of *Freedom's Journal* for most of its run was in opposition to African colonization, and this sentiment would have been shared by many of its readers. As we shall examine in detail in the next chapter, African Americans discussed and debated colonization and emigration extensively in *Freedom's Journal*. In this chapter, though, we will explore coverage of Africa and Haiti that did not specifically feature the controversy surrounding colonization. The articles and editorials that we shall examine in this chapter focused broadly on the implications of the histories, representations, and destinies of these regions for African Americans.

As various scholars have noted, there was a strong interest among African Americans in the late 1820s in the history of African peoples and their destiny.[2] In the midst of oppression, St. Clair Drake asserts, antebellum African Americans were confronted with the questions "Who are we?" and "Why have we suffered this fate?" A third question naturally arose as well: What does the future hold for us? They looked to Africa and Haiti for answers, seeking self-respect, self-definition, and hope. For African Americans in New York in the early nineteenth century, Craig Steven Wilder notes, "Africa was not a destination but a heritage," "a balance to Europe," and "the physical source of their humanity and equality," while Haiti represented "the culmination of God's plan for African freedom."[3] As we have seen in our exploration of self-help, African Americans in the early nineteenth century were also guided by a sense of the connections between Africans throughout the globe and the unique destiny of the African race. In the columns of *Freedom's Journal*, we discover the complex and often contradictory ways that Africa and Haiti informed the views of African Americans in the late 1820s about their heritage, sufferings, responsibilities, and roles in the world.

Cornish and Russwurm's remark in their opening editorial about common stereotypes and misperceptions suggests the context in which they and their contributors wrote. Even as European contact with Africa increased in the eighteenth and nineteenth centuries, information about the continent that reached Americans was based on and perpetuated Western prejudices and cultural biases. Reports of Africa generally alleged, implicitly or explicitly, that Africa was an "uncivilized" continent, populated by people who were intellectually backward, lazy, and barbaric. Throughout history, eighteenth and nineteenth-century European and American thinkers proposed, Africans had failed to develop great "civilizations" or to "advance" socially or economically.[4] Many whites believed, Benjamin Quarles explains, that African Americans could claim no honorable past, "whether in Africa or the United States . . . because their historical record—their achievements and contributions to civilization—had been so negligible, so abysmally low."[5] Moreover, many white Americans viewed the Haitian Revolution as an example of the barbarism they associated with people of African descent.[6]

The editors of and contributors to *Freedom's Journal* naturally looked to sources other than traditional Western histories and conventional, distorted reports about Haiti or Africa for information relevant to their history and destiny. As we shall see, they marshaled ancient historical writings, including biblical texts, to create an empowering history with an honorable past and a hopeful future. Cornish and Russwurm's reference to Dixon Denham, Hugh Clapperton, and Walter Oudney's 1826 *Narrative of Travels and Discoveries in Northern and Central Africa* suggests that they also turned to various contemporary accounts that provided positive information about Africa and its inhabitants. In addition, encouraging information about Africa came from what might be considered an unexpected source—the writings of colonizationists. As George Frederickson notes, although colonizationists argued that those of African descent would inevitably be in a "'degraded' condition in America," their rhetoric was often "respectful, even complimentary," when describing Africans' "innate racial character and capacity."[7]

Even as they rejected many of the claims of white America, African Americans shared some prejudices and predispositions that shaped many early-nineteenth-century treatments of Africa and Haiti. Yet they also questioned fundamental aspects of dominant portrayals of black nations and revised traditional beliefs. The complex combination of conventional assumptions and empowering challenges to them as well as the desire to create positive images of Africa and Haiti, past and present, shaped the coverage of these regions in *Freedom's Journal*.

A "NOBLE AND VIRTUOUS" PAST: EGYPT AND ETHIOPIA

Doubts about colonization and contemporary Africa among early-nineteenth-century African Americans, Quarles asserts, "did not deter the majority of articulate blacks from identifying with an Africa of antiquity."[8] Their focus was not on West Africa or sub-Saharan societies, but rather on two regions: Egypt and Ethiopia. "Egyptocentrism," to use Wilson Moses's term, was founded on the notions "that Egypt is geographically and culturally part of Africa" and that African Americans could thus "claim ancient Egyptian ancestry." Antebellum Egyptocentrists, as Moses explains, were not cultural relativists: "From their perspective of cultural absolutism, the Nile valley was the only region of Africa that could claim a true 'civilization.'" Civilized cultures were those that built great monuments and cities and contributed to "the development of literature, the arts, and the sciences." Nineteenth-century African Americans, then, turned to Egypt to claim an honorable past in Africa—to create, in Drake's terms, "vindicationist" histories that could "serve as a corrective to biases" and challenge traditional narratives "from a black perspective"—and to demonstrate that Africans played a central role in the ancient world, influencing the cultures of Greece and Rome.[9]

As they sought to connect African Americans to Egypt's proud history, commentators in *Freedom's Journal* had first to establish that the ancient Egyptians were indeed Africans, racially and culturally. Thus they directly engaged contemporary controversies about human origins and the histories of ancient peoples, debates which were inextricably tied to religious beliefs and interpretations of historical narratives in the Bible. Contributors to the newspaper marshaled both sacred and secular sources to create detailed arguments. In a three-part article published in the newspaper in August 1827, contributor S. proposed to create an "African Genealogy" to give African-American readers "a particular account of their origin, and . . . to acquaint them with what nations, people, and family they stand connected." "It is certain," S. argued, that "the original name of Egypt was Misraim," implying that the offspring of Mizriam, the second son of Noah's son Ham, "first peopled Egypt." Because biblical scholars regarded Ham as the progenitor of the black race, this name suggested that the inhabitants of ancient Egypt were racially Africans. S. supported this claim by drawing on classical and sacred texts (the ancient writer Eupolemus and the seventeenth-century French scholar and divine Samuel Bochart), concluding, "It being, thus, satisfactorily proved, that the Africans are the descendents of Ham, the son of Noah, the smallest doubt cannot exist, that these degraded, and too long oppressed people are the same, with the once noble and virtuous inhabitants of the empire of the great Sesostris, and enterprizing Mœris."[10]

An early three-part editorial in the newspaper titled "Mutability of Human Affairs" similarly combined biblical history with a classical source, in this case a passage from the Greek geographer Herodotus. The editors declared:

> History informs us that Cush and Menes (the Misriam of scripture) were the sons of Ham. The former is supposed to have settled in the Arabic Nome, near the Red Sea, in Lower Egypt; whence his descendants spread over the southern regions of Asia, along the Persian Gulph, and the easterly parts of Africa, on the western borders of the Red Sea; and the latter, the Northerly parts of Africa, including Upper and Lower Egypt and Barbary. . . . Herodotus, "the father of history," expressly declares that the "Egyptians had black skins and frizzled hair."

An excerpt from the white diplomat Alexander Hill Everett's 1827 *America: Or, A General Survey of the Political Situation of the Several Powers of the Western Continent, with Conjectures on Their Future Prospects*, which the editors printed in the newspaper in 1827, also referred to Herodotus's claim that classical Egypt "was peopled . . . by a black race with woolly hair."[11]

Whatever sources they drew on to link African Americans to Egypt, these arguments shared a single purpose: to allow black readers to claim Egypt's greatness as part of their heritage. "All ancient authors agree," S., the explicator of the "African Genealogy," asserted,

> that Egypt was once the richest and happiest country in the world. . . . Trip-
> tolemus, the founder of agriculture, came out of Egypt; Bacchus, the first
> who taught man to convert the juice of the grape into wine, came also out of
> Egypt, or Lybia, which borders on it. . . . It is also a well known fact, that with
> the Romans, and Grecians, their great mens' education was not considered
> complete, until they had made the tour of Egypt.

Cornish and Russwurm similarly cited the Egyptians' "obelisks and pyr-amids" and their "introduction of the arts and sciences" to the world. In the excerpt of *America* reprinted by the editors, Everett declared, "It is to Egypt, if to any nation, that we must look as the real *antiqua mater* of the ancient and modern refinement of Europe."[12]

The references here to monuments, agriculture, arts, sciences, and Euro-pean "refinement" suggest that the editors and contributors to *Freedom's Journal*, like other Americans of the time, judged civilizations by compari-son to European standards. Wilson Moses stresses, though, that we should not be quick to judge those nineteenth-century African Americans who em-phasized a glorious past in ancient Egypt as "uncritical" or "naïve emula-tors of European racialism." Indeed, he notes, the "contradictions" in their views "reflected the complexity of the situation they encountered," in which they were continually confronted with "the demeaning characteri-zation of African Americans in popular culture" and the need to use history to bolster self-esteem and offer alternatives to "degrading stereotypes."[13]

In addition, their emphasis on African influences on Greek and Roman culture is significant. Although antebellum vindicationists often mea-sured culture in ways that we might deem Eurocentric, this assessment is an oversimplification. Because they claimed that Western cultures were built on African foundations, they asserted that the standards used to measure civilizations—criteria associated with European knowledge and advancement—could be traced to Africa. In other words, they argued that the very hallmarks of civilization that many associated with Europe and the West were actually African in origin; those who did not acknowledge this fact were ignoring history. In 1828 and 1829, Russwurm reprinted ex-cerpts from the writings of Pompée Valentin, Baron de Vastey, a Haitian scholar whose works included defenses of the Revolution and historical treatments of Africa.[14] De Vastey explicitly highlighted the African origins of those qualities associated with high culture:

> Every body knows that the Greeks, so celebrated for the polish of their man-
> ners, and the refinement of their taste, were in a state of the grossest ignorance

and barbarity, living like the beasts, upon herbs and acorns, till civilized by colonies from Egypt; while the rest of Europe was yet unknown, and its inhabitants were certainly as barbarous, as ignorant, and as brutal as those of Benin, of Zanguebar, and of Monomotapa can possibly be at this day.

The very standards that were used to declare those of African descent inferior, Everett noted in the excerpt of *America* reprinted by the editors, could, when a proper historical view was taken, give them "some plausible pretensions to a claim of superiority." Looking back to Africa, Everett argued, we find those who "must be regarded as the real authors of most of the arts and sciences which give us at present the advantage over them."[15]

Even Christianity, considered to be a necessary component of civilization by antebellum American standards,[16] could be traced to Egypt. A two-part article titled "Africa," originally published in the *African Repository and Colonial Journal* and reprinted in *Freedom's Journal* in February 1829, made the case: "Moses, we are told, was skilled in all the learning of the Egyptians: and we find in him, aside from his functions as an inspired prophet, at that early period when written language was scarcely known at all, and [*sic*] eminent example of learning and acquired abilities: a striking and decisive proof of the greatness at that time of African attainments." Everett similarly referred to the fact that the development of the Israelite nation took place in Egypt, noting that "as far as human agency was concerned . . . we must look to Egypt as the original foundation of our faith, which, though developed and completed in the new Testament, reposes on the basis of the old."[17]

Thus the vindicationist, Egyptocentric histories in *Freedom's Journal* fulfilled complex rhetorical purposes, promoting positive identities, countering conventional wisdom, and encouraging African Americans to claim the proud cultural heritage they were frequently denied. The editors and contributors to *Freedom's Journal* made no secret of these goals. S. noted explicitly the desires to correct and counter racist stereotypes and to set the record straight about African influences on European cultures:

I am thus profuse in my observations, because, in the first place, I would let my brethren know, that though ages have witnessed their truly lamentable degradation, they are no other than the descendants of this once illustrious people, to whom, even the literati, of the day, while they use in contempt, the epithet "Negro," are indebted for much of their intelligence. . . . [T]he African, of the present day, who is so generally accused of every species of infidelity, and who the vile Calumniator represents as dead to every ennobling quality; stupid, and incapable of moral improvement, is no other than the unfortunate descendant of the Egyptians, whose learning the ancients vainly emulated, and to whose eminence in the sciences, the moderns have not attained.[18]

S. suggested only implicitly that there might be ideological reasons that traditional histories ignored the contributions of people of color, but Cornish and Russwurm were more forthright. "Mankind generally allow," they remarked, "that all nations are indebted to the Egyptians for the introduction of the arts and sciences; but they are not willing to acknowledge that the Egyptians bore any resemblance to the present race of Africans."[19] Through their choice of words—"not willing to acknowledge"—they proposed that history is inherently rhetorical, even when those who write it maintain the pretense that it is neutral or value-free. And the purpose of traditional histories is often to maintain the status quo, denying the contributions of people of color in order to further oppression.

An even more potentially radical idea was suggested by Cornish and Russwurm's reference to the "indebtedness" of "all nations" to the Egyptians. S. likewise declared that Western civilization was obliged to ancient Egypt for the knowledge they "diffused . . . among the Greeks, who afterwards civilized the Romans, and the Romans extending civilization with their arms, civilized the world." Not only have Europeans (and their American descendants) not acknowledged their debt; they have oppressed the descendants of those to whom they owe their greatness:

> How ungrateful is man! How flagrant, has been the ingratitude of the Europeans, that to the descendants of their kindest benefactors, they have been most unjust and cruel. Their learning and their intelligence, and the basis of those very Sciences, by the improving of which, they have held a rank superior to the inhabitants of the other continents, came originally from the forefathers of the Africans, towards whom they have ever dealt with injustice and with disgrace to themselves.[20]

Western "superiority," S. proposed, was built on African foundations, and Europeans have gone beyond ingratitude by using the advantage gained from the very knowledge that originated in Africa to oppress that continent's descendants. While not specifically calling for any particular plan to remedy the resulting imbalances of power between Western cultures and people of African descent, S. nonetheless raised the notion that a debt is owed, a statement that brings to mind later calls for reparations.

There was, however, a potential dilemma that vindicationists faced when connecting Arican Americans to the ancient Egyptians. African Americans also identified with the Hebrews of Scripture, oppressed and in slavery in Egypt, whom God set free.[21] An 1827 article in *Freedom's Journal* opposing the ACS, for example, described colonizationists as modern-day Pharaohs, worried about the potential power of those whom they oppressed within their borders and seeking a way "to get rid of them." A seeming contradiction arose, as Moses explains: "How could they simultaneously nurture the belief that they bore a special historical relationship to . . . those same pharaohs who had oppressed the biblical Hebrews?"[22]

Two multipart commentaries published in *Freedom's Journal* in 1827 offered a potential resolution to this rhetorical difficulty. The four-part "History of Slavery," which was reprinted from the *African Observer*—a monthly periodical edited by the Quaker Enoch Lewis—drew a distinction between Egyptian servitude and slavery in later periods. "The servitude to which the descendants of Jacob were subjected during their residence in Egypt," the article noted, although "severe and degrading," was "of a national, rather than a personal character," allowing the "right of private property and the maintenance of their religion and laws." As a result, "we should naturally conclude that the Egyptian bondage, though severely and justly reprobated by the sacred historian, was clear of most of those accompaniments which give to the personal slavery of subsequent ages its most repulsive character." It is important to note here that the original author of the "History of Slavery" was not attempting to argue in an Egyptocentric mode but rather to distinguish biblical slavery and Southern slavery; the article declared that *"slavery,* as it existed among the nations of antiquity" was an essentially different system that that of the antebellum United States.[23] (As we shall explore further in chapter 8, such distinctions were important in antislavery argumentation.) Yet the piece took on an additional significance when reprinted in the columns of *Freedom's Journal* along with various Egyptocentric articles, suggesting at least a potential solution to the dilemma posed by the desire to identify with the slaveholding nation Egypt.

The 1827 article "An Apology for Pharaoh," which was signed with the name Interpreter and which was originally published in the *New-York Observer*, similarly argued that Hebrew slavery in Egypt "was rather political than personal" and that the enslaved were "held as public, not as private property." Interpreter noted particular features of the Hebrews' enslavement in Egypt—they could "retain their own manners, customs and religion"; their "family connexions . . . were not broken in upon" by sale; they were not "shut out from any of the common modes of improvement and education"—that demonstrated that "Egyptian slavery was much milder than has often been practiced since, and is now practiced by a good many who profess Christianity." "I fully believe that Pharaoh did wrong in enslaving Israel," Interpreter insisted; yet, true to the article's title, Interpreter offered many detailed reasons why Pharaoh might have felt justified in acting as he did, concluding, "Pharaoh's excuses are, I think, better than what have satisfied, and now satisfy, many."[24] As with the "History of Slavery," "An Apology for Pharaoh" was originally written and published not to create an identification between

African Americans and Egypt but to dissociate Egyptian and American slavery. Again, though, the reprinting of the article in *Freedom's Journal* gave it a new meaning for readers exploring ancient Egypt and its implications for their history.

Egypt was not the only great ancient civilization to which *Freedom's Journal*'s editors and contributors connected African Americans. S. argued that "the people of Colchos and the Sidonians and Carthagenians" were "originally Egyptians, and descendents of the illustrious Misraim." Everett, in the section of *America* reprinted by the editors, asserted, "It appears in fact, that the whole south of Asia and north of Africa were [in classical times] possessed by a number of powerful, polished, and civilized communities of kindred origin, differing among themselves in some points of their outward conformation, but all black." The link to Carthage was particularly empowering because of the military greatness of Hannibal. In his 1828 speech to New York's African Society for Mutual Relief, reprinted in *Freedom's Journal*, Thomas Jinnings noted the greatness of "the country of our forefathers . . . as she was when Hannibal crossed the mountains of the Alps with his African soldiers, who were the terror of Rome." The radical implications of this association were suggested by Jinnings, who argued in his address that African Americans would eventually "rear a fearless front of men, zealous of their rights not to be trampled on with impunity."[25]

Although the histories of various regions of Africa were explored in *Freedom's Journal*, one nation was featured nearly as prominently as was Egypt: Ethiopia. As we shall see, in the rhetoric of the time, Ethiopia was often used to symbolize all of Africa; yet in the pages of *Freedom's Journal* we also find specific explorations of the history of the Abyssinian region itself. Building on their argument about the greatness of Egypt in their "Mutability of Human Affairs," Cornish and Russwurm asserted that African Americans could also claim a noble past in Ethiopia. Drawing on the findings of various historians and travelers, the editors demonstrated that Ethiopia "was early inhabited by a people, whose manners and customs nearly resembled those of the Egyptians" and that "there could not possibly have been any great difference as to the state of the arts and sciences in the two kingdoms." This people, the editors maintained, was also descended from Ham, the biblical progenitor of the black race (through his son Cush); indeed, "the Egyptians and Ethiopians were of one colour, and possessed a striking similarity of features."[26]

An article reprinted in *Freedom's Journal* in December 1828, which originally appeared in the *African Repository and Colonial Journal* and was sent to Russwurm by "A Constant-Reader," related that the "Cushites, or Ethiopians, established the first government, and the first regular Police, which history records. The first great city which we have described in history was "arts and sciences" and "classic built by them. . . . Thus at a time when the rest of the world was in a state of barbarism, the Ethiopian family were exhibiting prodigies of human genius, at which mankind have not yet ceased to wonder and which they have never so much dreamed of being able to transcend." It was to the Ethiopians, in fact, that the Egyptians owed their great civilization when the Ethiopians colonized "upper Egypt," they "found that country in a state of barbarism" and "left it the monther [*sic*] of Science." Since Greek mythology" were in turn "borrowed" from Egypt, classical civilization was indebted for its eminence to Ethiopia.[27]

Yet many antebellum vindicationists were less enthusiastic about other regions in Africa whose histories were less familiar.[28] The reprinted 1829 article "Africa" from the *African Repository and Colonial Journal* which affirmed the greatness of classical Egypt declared that although little was known about the history of "the interior" of Africa, the "decided though confused impression" was one "of depravity and cruelty in the extreme; of vice and disorder; of mental and moral imbecility; of ignorance and barbarism; of degradation and wretchedness." The piece drew on the history of Africa written by the sixteenth-century diplomat Joannes Leo Africanus, a Moor from Spain. As Kim Hall notes, Leo Africanus "seemingly share[d] with his European audience a disdain for the darkest African peoples, and he introduce[d] judgments that juxtapose[d] negative assessments of their appearance with disapproval of cultural practices." The author of "Africa" echoed this uneasiness, declaring that in Timbuktu at the time of Leo Africanus's exploration, "hardly any characteristics were then to be found, but those of barbarism and rudeness."[29] *Freedom's Journal*'s editors and contributors clearly believed that contemporary African Americans could claim a great history in Africa; yet they suggested that this history did not include its sub-Saharan cultures.

HISTORIES OF DECLINE

If ancient Egypt and Ethiopia were considered by *Freedom's Journal*'s editors and contributors to be exemplars of civilization, they believed that present-day Africa could no longer claim such glory. At times, as we shall see, articles in the newspaper countered certain negative representations of contemporary Africa and pointed to admirable aspects of its cultures. Yet *Freedom's Journal*'s vindicationists, like other antebellum African Americans, accepted to a great extent the view of Africa as a continent greatly in need of redemption, regeneration, and elevation.[30] They were left, then, with two difficult questions to answer. If Africa had an illustrious past—if it was, as the aforementioned article "Africa" reprinted from the *African Repository and Colonial Journal* described, "the birthplace and cradle of civilization"[31]—why were its civilizations no longer dominant? And would Africa eventually rise again? Just as they looked to the Bible for historical evidence of Africa's former glory, so too did antebellum African Americans seek scriptural guidance about its present and future. Contributors to *Freedom's Journal* took a variety of approaches to the complex question of Africa's decline, combining biblical references, a belief in God's intervention in human affairs, and a close attention to humans' uses and misuses of power in global history.

Various scholars have noted that some African-American vindicationists of the eighteenth and early nineteenth centuries maintained that Africa had fallen from its former glory because of the sins of paganism and polytheism.[32] Yet this aspect of vindicationist thinking has been overemphasized. It is true that contributors to *Freedom's Journal* described present-day Africa as spiritually impoverished, as we shall see, and believed that bringing Christianity to the continent was an important component of its regeneration and redemption. Yet they did not generally denigrate the religions of the ancient Africans, nor did they in most cases assert that they brought their decline upon themselves by rejecting God. Cornish and Russwurm noted, in fact, that the "ancient Ethiopians were considered as a blameless race, worshipping the Gods, doing no evil, exercising fortitude, and despising death."[33]

Why, then, had the glory of ancient Egypt and Ethiopia faded? The answer was suggested by the title of Cornish and Russwurm's editorial "Mutability of Human Affairs." The decline of these nations, the editors remarked, did not represent historical anomalies; rather, they illustrated history's eternal laws:

> Egypt and Ethiopia are not the only kingdoms where we behold the effects of the mutability of human affairs. The extensive empire of Macedon's proud king, has passed into other hands and even Greece, herself, bows before the proud scepter of the Moslem. . . . Time has not spared even imperial Rome, but she and her conquests, which comprehended the greater part of the civilized world at that period have changed masters.

The reprinted article from the *African Repository and Colonial Journal* sent to Russwurm by "A Constant-Reader" similarly noted the movement of "civilization" from Egypt to Greece to Italy to Europe. The fact that Africa was "now in barbarism," the article maintained, was due to the "transitory" nature of the "civilization" she once claimed, which "has often been exhausted in one country as it was awakened in another." "Each great division of the species has had in its turn the advantage of civilization, that is in industry, wealth, and knowledge, and the power they confer," Everett noted in the portion of *America* reprinted in *Freedom's Journal*. "But on reviewing the course of history, we find . . . the sceptre of civilization passing from the hands of the supposed superior race into those of some other, before inferior, which claims in its turn, for a while, a similar distinction."[34]

The fact that Everett's comments were similar to those found in original contributions to *Freedom's Journal* demonstrates that the model of history invoked in the vindicationists' narratives was not unique to African Americans. As Moses explains, various American historians by the end of the eighteenth century suggested that there were "cycles of history" in which "civilizations . . . must unfold, blossom, and decay." Frequently linked to this view was "a theological historicism that postulated the direct intervention of the hand of God in history." African-American historians of the early nineteenth century combined these elements to create a worldview that held out "the optimistic hope of racial redemption" and "offered reassurances of progress."[35] Cyclical history meant that cultures that had once been "barbaric" had risen to greatness—indeed, as readers were reminded in the excerpt from De Vastey's work published in the newspaper, Europe was once in the "state of the grossest ignorance and barbarity"—and thus Africa, too, could rise again. As Cornish and Russwurm explained in "Mutability of Human Affairs," "As human affairs are continually revolving, who will predict that the day may not come when our people shall be duly considered in the scale of nations, and respected accordingly. We are no enthusiasts, but it must certainly be considered uncommonly miraculous that mutability should attend all other nations."[36]

If one way of explaining the historical decline of Africa was in terms of "mutability" and God's guiding role in history, there was also another approach that emphasized not divine but human intervention in historical affairs. In particular, various contributors to *Freedom's Journal* did not shy away from examining carefully and critically the role of the West's exploitation and oppression of African nations and peoples, arguing boldly that human agents could and should be held responsible for Africa's fall from its former glory. Consider, for example, Thomas Jinnings's commentary on the history of relations between Africa and the West: "O! unhappy country [Africa], how hast thou been harassed: thou hast been made to groan from thy sea line to thy centre—thy sons and daughters have been dispersed throughout the globe, and the white man has taken advantage of thy misfortunes to increase his treasures."[37]

Baron de Vastey, in the excerpt which Russwurm reprinted in *Freedom's Journal*, similarly called attention to human intervention in history. He noted the treatment of the then-barbaric Greeks by their Egyptian conquerors: "Instead of enslaving the Whites, and instructing the Greeks in burning, pillaging and defrauding; instead of furnishing them with arms . . . or strong liquors to derange their intellects, and induce them to sell one another; instead, I say, of promoting an inhuman traffic, [the Egyptians] introduced corn and instructed them in Egyptian agriculture and learning." De Vastey's implications were clear. Unlike the honorable Egyptians in Greece, white colonizers in Africa did, in fact, instigate, encourage, and support the slave trade and the destruction of African society. De Vastey noted the effect of many developments on Africa's degeneration, such as the "destruction of Carthage by the Romans, together with the irruption of the Northern Barbarians" and the "establishment of Mahometanism." He asserted, though, that it was "the introduction of the Slave Trade" that "put a finishing stroke to the calamities of this unhappy country"—and his comparison to the Egyptians made it clear that he held the West responsible for it.[38]

EXPLORATION AND ETHIOPIANISM

Even though they believed that Africa had declined and was in need of uplift, spiritually and culturally, Cornish and Russwurm, as we have noted, considered current news and information about the continent relevant and necessary for their readers. Often this coverage took the form of references to or excerpts from contemporary travel accounts or news of African explorers, including Denham, Clapperton, and Oudney; the British Major Alexander Gordon Laing; and the French explorer René-Auguste Caillié, the first European to reach Timbuktu and return.[39] These articles were not necessarily positive. An article describing the gruesome murder of Major Laing after he had reached Timbuktu, for example, gave far from a favorable impression of the natives of Africa. An account from a Paris newspaper of Caillié's travels to Timbuktu described it as less than the fabled city of the Western imagination; "the town is poor," the report noted, "and the surrounding country barren." Neither were the residents necessarily disposed to treat Caillié well; the article related that "he was obliged to represent himself as persecuted by Europeans, to obtain protection from the inhabitants of Tombuctoo." The 1829 article "Africa" reprinted from the *African Repository and Colonial Journal* remarked that the "richness and fertility of [Africa's] soil," and the resulting "comparative ease with which life and even luxury may be supported" had helped "lower the character of the African race." Without "a wise and rigid government" and "sufficient moral influence," Africa's "resources" were "wasted in dissipation, and consumed in comparative idleness," and its inhabitants were "degrade[d]."[40]

Yet in various cases, accounts the editors published countered conventional perceptions of Africa's barbarism and lack of civilization. In their opening editorial, as we have seen, Cornish and Russwurm referred to Denham, Clapperton, and Oudney's 1826 *Narrative of Travels and Discoveries in Northern and Central Africa* as proof that "ignorance, poverty and degradation" were not always to be the "unhappy lot" of the African race. In the excerpt of *America* published in *Freedom's Journal*, Everett cited this text more specifically. "Notwithstanding the present general inferiority of the Africans," Everett commented, "we find even now, that the high intellectual spirit that once flashed out so finely in their sunburnt climates is not yet wholly quenched. Major Denham, in his late volume of travels, has presented us with several specimens of contemporary African poetry, which are hardly inferior to the sweet and lofty strains of the ancient Monarch Minstrel." Everett described various poems, which were published as an appendix to Denham, Clapperton, and Oudney's *Narrative*, asserting, for example, that "an extempore love song . . . unites the tenderness and purity of the Canticles with something of the delicacy of imagery that distinguished the poetry of Moore," and that "the triumphal ode of the Sheik of Bornou . . . may fairly be considered as poetry of the first order." He also provided an extensive excerpt from the "dirge of the Fezzauners in honour of their chief Boo-Khaloom," which, he maintained, "will bear a comparison with the lamentation of David over Saul and Jonathan."[41]

In April 1827, the editors reprinted a selection from Mungo Park's 1799 *Travels in the Interior Districts of Africa*. The excerpt described the honorable treatment of Abdulkader, king of Foota Torra, by Damel, ruler of the Jaloffs, after the former's defeat in battle by the latter.[42] Indeed, as scholars have observed, although Park's complex text was rooted in many ways in European assumptions, it is notable for its emphasis on the humanity of the Africans.[43] The selection from Everett's work reprinted by the editors was distinguished also by its frank admission that cultural biases and imperial interests tainted current information about Africa. Before Denham's expeditions, Everett remarked, "little or nothing" was known of most of Africa,

> excepting that we civilized Christians had purchased and made slaves of a considerable number of persons belonging to them, and that these persons thus kidnapped and reduced to slavery, appeared to us who did not understand their languages, and could not of course converse with them, as a degraded and stupid race of men, incapable of writing epic poems, commanding armies, enlarging the limits of science, or superintending the government of a country.

Everett emphasized that "this reasoning proved the stupidity and degradation of those who thought it satisfactory, and not the Africans."[44]

The excerpt from the work of Baron de Vastey published in *Freedom's Journal* featured testimony from numerous travelers to counter traditional monstrous images of Africans: "Bosman extols the beauty of the Negresses of Juida; Ledyard and Lucas that of the Jalof Negroes; Lobo that of the Abyssinian. Those of Senegal says Adanson, 'are the handsomest men of Nigritia; their form is without blemish, and I never observed an ill made person among them.'" Some of these assessments revealed a Western bias; he related, for example, that "Cossigny saw at Goree Negresses of great beauty . . . and with Roman features." Yet it is significant not only that de Vastey provided examples of travelers who admired African beauty but also that he suggested the ways culture informs such judgments. He noted that the eighteenth-century Scottish explorer James Bruce, for example, was struck with the beauty of "a young girl of Abyssinia"; by contrast, the Abyssinian women found Bruce's white skin and sharp nose unattractive.[45]

Just as colonizationist texts about Africa's history were often positive, so too were contemporary portrayals of Africa in various accounts by members of the ACS, who naturally had an interest in recruiting potential emigrants. Although the editorial position of *Freedom's Journal* was against colonization for most of its tenure, news from Liberia appeared in the paper from the outset, usually gathered from colonizationist sources. As we have seen, this tendency on Russwurm's part became more pronounced late in 1828—suggesting his increasing personal interest in the Liberian venture—yet his earlier inclusion of reports from ACS sources does not necessarily suggest that he already favored colonization or that his readers would have viewed such pieces as indicative of a procolonizationist view. Indeed, it seems likely that even when Russwurm was opposed to the ACS (or at least professed to be in his official editorial statements), he wanted to provide news from Liberia, like the rest of Africa, particularly when it demonstrated that Africa was not the backward or uncivilized continent it was often thought to be. In September 1827, for example, Russwurm reprinted part of a letter from Jehudi Ashmun, the ACS agent in Liberia. The letter noted that an "excursion of one of our people in the interior to the distance of about 140 miles, has led to a discovery of the populousness and comparative civilization of this District of Africa." This previously unknown region, Ashmun related, boasted "a highly improved agriculture," domesticated horses, "large tracts of land" that were "cleared and enclosed," a "written language" (Arabic) "used . . . in the ordinary commerce of life," and inhabitants of "a degree of intelligence and partial refinement" that belied "current notions . . . of the people of Guinea."[46]

In 1828, news in *Freedom's Journal* about the case of Abduhl Rahahman served to bring readers further positive information about Africa. Born in Futa Jallon, Rahahman was the son of a ruler and was educated in various cities, including Timbuktu. He was captured in 1788 after a military campaign and sold, first to British traders and then, in the United States, to a Natchez, Mississippi, planter named Thomas Foster. Named Prince by Foster because of his background, Rahahman became a valued slave.

In the 1820s, he gained notoriety when his desire to return to Africa was publicized by a newspaper editor and various prominent people became involved, including ACS members such as Secretary of State Henry Clay. Rahahman's master—now the son of Thomas Foster—agreed to release him on the condition that he emigrate, and in 1828 he became a free man. Yet his repatriation was complicated by the fact that he now had a wife, Isabella, and children whom he obviously wished to go with him. Although Isabella was purchased with money raised in Natchez, funds for his children's freedom were still lacking. During 1828, he toured cities in the North, seeking to raise the money needed. He and Isabella sailed to Africa in 1829; at least some of their children were eventually freed and reunited with them.[47]

Despite their opposition to the ACS, northern African Americans were supportive of Rahahman's desire to return to Africa. News of his cause was publicized in *Freedom's Journal*, as were reports of gatherings held by African Americans in various cities to raise money for his children's freedom. Because of Rahahman's background, these articles also were sources of information about Africa. An April 1828 letter "from a gentleman of Natchez to a Lady of Cincinnati" published in *Freedom's Journal* described "Prince" as "really a most extraordinary man—born to a kingdom—well educated, for he now writes Arabic in a most elegant style—brought a slave in a foreign country, he has sustained a character for honesty and integrity which is almost beyond parallel." Rahahman's high education and connections suggested that the region of his upbringing was civilized, in antebellum American terms; his unassailable character belied stereotypes of cruel or barbaric Africans.[48]

An October 1828 article reprinted from the *New York Journal of Commerce* noted the details Rahahman had revealed about the fabled city of Timbuktu:

> He describes it as a large walled city . . . and a place of great business. . . .
> Timbuctoo is further described as a place not only of business and power, but as having at least a shadow of civilization. Here is a Prince who for years attended a school where 200 scholars were taught. There he learned some rude notions of Geography and Astronomy, and a little of Arithmetic. . . . He also describes Timbuctoo as having various other institutions, never existing in savage and barbarous countries.

There was a particular agenda here; with "a little management," the author noted, enterprising Americans could make use of Rahahman's return to Africa to gain entry into a potentially "thriving commerce" with "the whole of [Africa's] vast interior." Regardless of its goals, however, the article countered common perceptions of Africa and Africans as uniformly "savage and barbarous." Indeed, according to Rahahman, Timbuktu was not an anomaly. Although, as Russwurm noted, "it has ever been the current belief that Timbuctoo was the only city of size in the interior [of Africa] . . . the Prince assures us that there are two others nearly as large near the banks of the Niger."[49]

Rahahman was an important figure in the late 1820s not only because of his link to present-day Africa. Because he wished to return there, his case was connected for his supporters to questions about Africa's future, specifically God's plans for the continent. The reprinted *New York Journal of Commerce* article noted that, in addition to facilitating trade, Rahahman's return to Africa could bring "charity and the christian religion" to the continent. Coverage of Rahahman's fund-raising tour in the North in *Freedom's Journal* also specifically engaged the religious dimension of Africa's destiny. Consider, for example, two toasts offered at a public dinner given for Rahahman by African Americans in Boston, a report of which was published in the newspaper. James Barbadoes proclaimed, "May the sons and daughters of Africa soon become a civilized and charistian-like [*sic*] people, and shine forth to the world as conspicuous as their more highly favored neighbours." Another toast declared, "May the happy Era be not far distant when Africa universally shall stretch forth her hands unto God."[50]

These pronouncements point to an important aspect of antebellum African Americans' views of the present and future of Africa. Psalms 68:31, to which the latter toast referred, promised that Africa would ultimately be regenerated: "Princes shall come out of Egypt; Ethiopia shall soon stretch out her hands unto God."[51] This verse informed a perspective which Moses terms "Ethiopianism." Ethiopia was seen as symbolic of all of Africa; God's promise, then, was that Africa would ultimately be redeemed from its present state.[52] S. assured readers of the "African Genealogy," for example, that even though Africa's "former greatness is buried with time in forgetfulness," God had plans for a promising future: "There is a Providence, who never sleeps; and who has promised, that a period should arrive, in the which Ethiopia shall stretch forth her arms."[53]

For Africa to be truly redeemed from its fallen state, though, as James Barbadoes's toast implied, it had to embrace Christianity. Even though most African Americans of the late 1820s did not wish to emigrate and opposed colonization, they had a strong interest in the spiritual future of Africa and frequently supported missionary activity there.[54] In the first issue of *Freedom's Journal*, for example, the editors reprinted a letter from the Church Missionary Society in London to Bishop White of Philadelphia calling for African Americans to volunteer to provide "religious instruction [to] the liberated Africans congregated in Sierra Leone, from all parts of Africa."[55] Rahahman's case is worthy of note in this regard; a Muslim, he nonetheless expressed an interest in Christianity and in promoting the

Gospel upon his return to Africa. It appears that he was perhaps motivated pragmatically; as Allan Austin notes, he "reverted to Islam immediately upon his ship's dropping anchor," was critical of Christianity, and
no doubt sensed that promises to evangelize in Africa would help win
supporters for his battle to free his children.[56]

Whatever Rahahman's true motives were, contributions to *Freedom's
Journal* frequently noted his attraction to Christianity and connected his
case to the larger goal of the Christianization of Africa. The aforementioned letter "from a gentleman of Natchez to a Lady of Cincinnati" remarked, for example, that "although [Rahahman] adheres strictly to the
religion of his country (Mahometism) he expresses the greatest respect for
the Christian religion, and is very anxious to obtain a Testament in his
own language, that he may read the history of Jesus Christ." An article
from the *Connecticut Observer*, which Russwurm reprinted in the newspaper in 1828, included the text of a letter Rahahman wrote as a response to
a gift from the Reverend Thomas Hopkins Gallaudet, educator of the
deaf, colonization supporter, and the author of an 1828 tract supporting
Rahahman. Gallaudet—who asserted in this pamphlet that Rahahman
wished upon his return to Africa "to lend his aid . . . in introducing commerce, and civilization, and freedom, and intelligence, and Christianity, in
to the heart of Africa"—had provided Rahahman with "an Arabic Tract on
the Truth of Christianity." In his letter, Rahahman proclaimed, "After I
take this book home, I hope I shall get many to become Christians. . . . I
go to give them light. I will show them the way of the Christian religion."[57]

A reprinted poem from the *Connecticut Mirror* went even farther, suggesting that Rahahman's enslavement in the United States could be prov-
idential both for himself and for his native land: "He hath gathered, in the
land of slaves, / Far nobler aspirations, and hath built / His hope of future bliss above the waves / That dash'd the Moslem heaven and Moorish guilt." The underlying notion here recalls what Moses deems "the
doctrine of the 'Fortunate Fall,'" the notion that "slavery, although a ter-
rible affliction on the African people, would become . . . a blessing in the
fullness of time." Certain African-American writers of the eighteenth and
nineteenth centuries, Moses explains, who "condemned slavery unequivocally" nonetheless believed that Africa could "draw good out of evil" by
"capitalizing on the effects of the slave trade" to bring "Christianity, commerce and civilization into the black world."[58] It is notable that this justification did not appear elsewhere in the coverage of Abduhl Rahahman;
and because this poem was reprinted from a white newspaper, it seems
likely that its author was not an African American. That Russwurm
reprinted it does not, of course, demonstrate that he or any readers necessarily subscribed to the doctrine of the "Fortunate Fall"; yet it reveals

one more facet of the complex connection of Christianity to Africa's redemption in antebellum American thought.

Other news items also emphasized the potential influence of Christianity on Africa. An article about South Africa, for example, related that a Wesleyan Missionary Station at Lily Fountain "has had a powerful influence" in stopping wars, theft, and "bloodshed." An unsigned response to a letter from correspondent F. A. on the importance of education for African Americans in the United States similarly emphasized the value of missionary activity in Africa. Although the author agreed with F. A. that African Americans should be educated to be citizens, "true Americans," whose "interests are inseparably connected with the interests of the country," rather than to prepare them to emigrate, Africa would nonetheless ultimately benefit from such instruction: "If this object could be obtained, there would be no want of Pioneers to go forth with the instruments of civilization and christianity to our benighted brethren in Africa, and throughout the world."[59]

Russwurm's comments here suggest another aspect of the complex relationship between African Americans and Africa. Although missionary activity in Africa was valued by antebellum African Americans, it was not necessary to leave the United States in order to uplift Africa. By improving themselves and living virtuous and Christian lives in the United States, they would become part of God's plan for the world, which would lead to Africa's eventual salvation. In a June 1827 article about money bequeathed by Tadeusz Kosciusko to free and educate slaves —which, as we have seen, was never used for the purpose—contributor Amicus noted that African Americans could help all "coloured nations" by "provid[ing] for [their] own house" through promoting the "cause of education." Through these efforts, the "African nation" could be "exalted." Amicus clearly defined the "African nation" in a global, Pan-African sense, as peoples of African descent throughout the world, and he noted that African Americans had a special role to play in its uplift: "The means of restoration, of light and knowledge, are mysteriously brought into their hands, in connexion with their wrong and humiliations." Indeed, "the free people in America" stood "at the head of this great nation." In the United States as well as "in their own infantine republics," people of African descent could play a messianic role in history; on their achievements, the future destiny of Africans throughout the world depended.[60]

"THE CRADLE OF HOPE": HAITI

For readers of *Freedom's Journal*, the fate of one "infantine republic" had a particular significance. Haiti was an important source of pride for African

Americans; and, in the late 1820s, they connected its destiny to the global vision that linked them to people of African descent throughout the world. As we have seen, Cornish and Russwurm noted in their opening editorial that the establishment of Haiti demonstrated that Africans throughout the world would not be left behind as the rest of the world advanced in civilization and enlightenment. Haiti also illustrated vividly that the destiny of Africans could very much be in their hands. If an oppressed nation could rise through redemption and regeneration, so too could it take another, more militant, path—that of revolution.[61]

In contrast to the glories of Egypt and Ethiopia, which lay in the far distant past, the history of Haiti provided for readers of *Freedom's Journal* a recent example of African ingenuity, courage, and determination. As we have seen, African Americans of the early nineteenth century took pride in the creation of the independent black republic of Haiti in 1804, a victory brought about by the successful rebellion of the slaves against their French colonial masters. Articles in *Freedom's Journal* about the history of the island and the revolution were explicit about their rhetorical purpose. Haiti's history, they emphasized, proved that those of African descent were not destined to be oppressed forever. Not only could they rise to greatness; they could be active and courageous participants in history, demonstrating the power of subjugated Africans to fight for and win the right to determine their own futures.

Consider, for example, a detailed six-part series of articles about the history and present condition of Haiti, which appeared in *Freedom's Journal* in 1827.[62] The author began, "As many of our New England friends believe and practise the self-evident truths, that all men are created equal, that they are endowed by their Creator, with certain inalienable rights . . . perhaps a few lines on the past and present condition of a people, who have bravely burst asunder the galling chains of slavery, may be interesting to some of your readers." The series described the island from its "discovery" by Columbus, through its colonization by the Spanish and the French, to the slaves' rebellion. The oppression of the slaves of Saint Domingue was emblematic of the plight of Africa and the peoples of the Diaspora throughout the world: "When I reflect on the many cruelties inflicted by man on his African brother, my indignation is roused—my mind becomes confused—my hand trembles, and refuses to record my passing thoughts. Africa! Africa! ill fated country! What mind can conceive—what tongue express—what pen pourtray [*sic*] thy bleeding wrongs?"[63]

But if the cruelty perpetrated against the slaves of Saint Domingue represented the subjugation of Africa's peoples, their victory over their oppressors demonstrated that Africans could bravely, directly, and forcefully throw off their chains. Noting the first attempt at gaining freedom through rebellion—an aborted effort by Jacques Vincent Ogé in 1790 to lead the mulattoes to revolt—the author declared, "Thus were the first seeds of a revolution unexampled in the history of man sown . . . I conceive, that many who then took up arms in the defence of all that is dear to every one *who thinks himself a man*, never laid them down until the recent and partial acknowledgment of the island."[64] Discourses of manhood and freedom, as we have seen, were often linked in antebellum African-American discourse; here, the drive for liberty that inspires true men made the slaves of Saint Domingue subjects and not objects in history. The four-part "Theresa,—A Haytien Tale," also built on this connection. The brother of the widowed Madame Paulina, author S. described, was "at the head of a party of his patriot brethren, who like him, disdained slavery, and were determined to live free men, or expire in their attempts for liberty and independence."[65] As we have seen in the previous chapter, it was not just men in this narrative who participated dynamically in the struggle for freedom; the heroine Theresa bravely and shrewdly acted as a spy for the revolutionists. Haiti's history demonstrated what African men and women could do to gain the freedom and dignity which had been promised to them.

The emphasis in *Freedom's Journal* on the active role of the black revolutionists in fighting for their own freedom deepens our understanding of the ways African Americans linked theology and history in the early nineteenth century. Their "theological historicism" and belief in "the direct intervention of the hand of God in history," to return to Wilson Moses's terms, did not preclude direct, militant action on the part of the oppressed. In other words, God's control over history did not mean that humans should passively wait for divine deliverance from subjugation; by contrast, they could actively become part of God's plan for liberation. An early article in *Freedom's Journal* about the Haitian Revolution stressed this interaction of human agency and God's design for history. The author J. declared, "There is something in the firm establishment of a free government by those who but lately were in the bonds of slavery that strikes us as manifesting in a peculiar degree the interposition of Divine Providence." The Haitians fought bravely, discovering in themselves "hidden powers" that were previously "unknown," and they were aided by "the arm of HIM who is ever ready to protect the oppressed."[66]

One figure, in particular, demonstrated strikingly the determination, capabilities, and accomplishments of people of African descent. Toussaint L'Ouverture, the powerful leader of the slaves during the revolution and subsequent governor of the island as a French colony after their emancipation, was celebrated in *Freedom's Journal* for his courage and military leadership. In a three-part biographical account of Toussaint reprinted in the newspaper in May 1827—which was first published in the British periodical the *Quarterly Review*[67]—Toussaint was presented as a skilled commander who successfully led his troops against the Spanish and British forces and who subsequently ruled the colony confidently and competently as governor. Notably, Toussaint demonstrated not only physical strength and heroism, but the intellectual acumen and morality necessary for effective leadership. Toussaint's discipline, fairness, and "the integrity of his character" earned him the respect and favor of those whom he governed. Toussaint was viewed as a "guardian angel" by the black residents of the colony, the author related, and was a "favourite of the whites" as well, "whose confidence he studied to gain, and who were always invited to his private parties." (These events, the author described, were respectable affairs that "might vie with the best regulated societies in Paris.") His skills were not only political but interpersonal: "It is said that no one left his presence dissatisfied, though his request was not granted."[68]

Under Toussaint's governance, the author of this biographical sketch maintained, "the colony advanced as if by enchantment towards its ancient splendour." Although the island was a French protectorate during Toussaint's rule, the article made it clear that this success was due to his leadership. "The order and regularity established in the island among all ranks," the author asserted, was due to "the influence and example of this singular man; the duties of morality and religion were strictly enforced, and the decencies of civilized life sedulously studied." Toussaint was "particularly attentive to the means of reforming the loose and licentious manners of the females; and would suffer none of the white ladies to come to his court with the neck uncovered."[69] On both a political and ethical level, Haiti was an example of successful black self-rule.

Coverage not only of Haiti's recent past but also of its present state in *Freedom's Journal* highlighted the capacities of Africans to effectively lead and govern themselves. This emphasis constituted more than a counter to the proslavery contention that those of African descent must always remain a dependent people; it also provided an empowering example of self-determination and, as Alfred Hunt maintains, was a strong "symbol of black nationalism." Cornish and Russwurm suggested the pride that African Americans should take in Haiti's devotion to its hard-won freedom. "The Haytiens, in declaring their independence, and their determination to maintain it, have done so in the face of the universe," they asserted in an editorial in the newspaper's first issue. "Though desirous of conciliating all nations, yet they fear none; and . . . never were all parties more united and determined to support their hard-earned liberty."[70]

In the fifth installment of the aforementioned six-part series on the past and present of the island, which outlined the "present Government of Hayti," the author underscored the central role of the Haitians in their own destiny. A "decidedly Republican" system, the government was elected and accountable, allowing Haitians to rule themselves. They also held their own in a global sense, the article suggested, remarking that

Haiti's "present foreign trade is considerable, giving in exchange for the manufactured goods of Europe and [American] produce, the natural productions of the soil." If these affairs were managed correctly, Haiti and its supporters throughout the world could "indulge the pleasing hope" that "its trade will again revive, equal and even surpass its former prosperity." The author ended the series by explicitly noting what the past and present of Haiti exhibited to the world: "It is now demonstrated, that the descendents of Africa are capable of self-government: the plea so often urged by the adherents of slavery, 'the poor creatures, should we free them, will starve to death,' will now be but 'sounding brass' in the opinion of every reasonable man."[71]

Current news about Haiti was "highly important" to their readers, Cornish and Russwurm maintained. Yet they expressed their anger at those who, for base reasons, were less than truthful: "We caution the dissatisfied and envious in this country, who are continually forging 'News from Hayti,' to desist from their unmanly attacks upon a brave and hospitable people. Were our readers as well acquainted with their motives for venting their spleen as we are, they would give as little credit to their fabrications." Because they would never publish "any news whatever, of a doubtful nature, concerning that island," readers could "depend on" the coverage of Haiti in *Freedom's Journal*. The "doubtful" reports and "unmanly attacks" to which Cornish and Russwurm referred were not just slanders of the Haitian people; they maligned all people of African descent as they reinforced white supremacist beliefs. Various proslavery commentators in antebellum America cited the island as ostensible proof that emancipation could only lead to disaster and that those of African descent needed to be governed by a strong hand.[72] Articles in *Freedom's Journal* countered these assumptions and provided an empowering alternative to traditional perceptions of black leadership.

The "Foreign News" column of August 3, 1827, for example, contained a report about the "detection of a band of conspirators," led by a Haitian lieutenant against President Jean-Pierre Boyer, and the successful disruption of their planned coup. Boyer's proclamation on the event, which was printed in full, portrayed the aborted attempt not as evidence of Haiti's instability but of its strength, pride, and efficiency. Boyer assured the island's soldiers, "The crime of a few officers and subalterns, unworthy of marching by your side ought not to tarnish the honor of an army which deserve the gratitude of the nation, and which possess my entire confidence. Faithful to your duty, you will continue to sustain, in the opinion of the world, the immortal glory which you have acquired." An article in the April 11, 1828, issue informed readers that news of a recent "reported insurrection at Aux Cayes . . . has been much exaggerated [*sic*]." The response of the Haitian government to the "evil disposed persons" who attempted to "disturb the tranquility of the community" was swift and effective; a translation of an account from the Port-au-Prince newspaper the *Feuille du Commerce* declared, "As it is difficult to seduce Haytiens from the paths of honour . . . every one knows that our political existence depends upon our union,— these deluded men . . . could persuade no influential citizen to join their designs. A few hours were sufficient to disperse the assembly. . . . [O]rder and tranquility have been perfectly restored." The implications of these accounts were made explicit in a article reprinted from the *Baltimore American*, which reported on a visit by two New York Quakers to Port-au-Prince: "It is said that they were much pleased with their reception, and are convinced that Hayti is not different from any other civilized country, and that those persons who have defamed her, had their interest in so doing."[73]

Just as masculinity and freedom were connected in history of the revolution, these military and governmental exemplars provided positive contemporary images of African manhood and countered demeaning images. African womanhood, too, was defended through the coverage of current affairs in Haiti. In particular, various articles described Madame Christophe, wife of the former King of Haiti Henri Christophe. One of the leaders of the revolution in Haiti, Henri Christophe became president in 1806; declared himself king in northern Haiti in 1811 after a civil war against the mulatto forces of the south; and, facing revolts and having suffered a stroke, committed suicide in 1820. Jean-Pierre Boyer, who had become president of the south in 1818, took over the nation at this point; and Madame Christophe left Haiti for England, subsequently settling in Italy.[74] In May 1827, *Freedom's Journal's* editors reprinted an article from the Boston newspaper the *Columbian Centinel* which countered the coverage of Madame Christophe by the notoriously racist editor Mordecai Manuel Noah in his *New-York Enquirer*. After citing Noah's description of Madame Christophe as "a fat, greasy wench, as black as the ace of spades, and one who would find it difficult to get a place as a Cook in this country," the article's author D. defended her: "We are induced, from a personal acquaintance with Madame Christophe . . . to bear testimony against the above illiberal and unjust representation." In fact, D. asserted, "the Ex-Queen" was "a good and virtuous wife, an affectionate mother, and an amiable friend," who was "neat in her person," and, during her reign, "when not compelled by *etiquette* to appear in regal attire, was very modest in her dress and deportment."[75]

A series of articles reprinted from the New York newspaper the *Albion* in 1828 similarly portrayed the former queen in terms that suggest she was, by antebellum standards, a proper woman. Describing a chance meeting with Madame Christophe in Florence, the author noted that even though she had seen "happier times," she exuded "an air of suppressed dignity . . . which seemed to say, that she had made up her mind to forget her former situation, and bear with her present, if not with cheerfulness at least with resignation." Proper, religious, and unassuming, Madame Christophe performed the offices of a good hostess to the author during his visit. Remarking that "there was nothing selfish about her," the author maintained that she "seemed to regret more those she had lost"—her husband and children—"than the worldly advantages she had once enjoyed, and the high estate from which she had fallen."[76] Antebellum African Americans, as we have seen, had an interest in positive portrayals of black femininity. These articles assured *Freedom's Journal's* readers that Madame Christophe should be honored not only as a former queen, but as an exemplar of African womanhood.

For readers of *Freedom's Journal*, then, Haiti illustrated God's promise of a glorious future for Africans throughout the world. "The Haytiens . . . have fought the good fight of *Liberty* and conquered," Russwurm maintained in a December 1828 editorial, "and all that is . . . required of them, is, to enjoy this invaluable blessing, as accountable beings, who look forward to what man, even the descendant of Africa, may be, when blessed with Liberty and Equality and their concomitants."[77] Haiti, a nation built by revolution and sustained through pride and self-rule, linked the African past to the present and future. The association between Africa's glorious history and Haiti's promising future was highlighted by the language used to describe each nation. At the public dinner given for Rahahman by African Americans in Boston, in addition to the toasts that evoked Africa's divine destiny, Oliver Nash lauded the "Island of Hayti, the only country on earth where the man of color walks in all the plentitude of his rights . . . the cradle of hope to future generations." Nash's language complemented the aforementioned description of Africa in the newspaper as "the birthplace and cradle of civilization."[78] Africa's history demonstrated what Africans had been; Haiti symbolized what they could become: free, proud, and self-determining.

NOTES

1. Samuel E. Cornish and John B. Russwurm, "To Our Patrons," *FJ*, 16 March 1827.

2. Quarles, *Black Mosaic*, 117–23; Stuckey, *Ideological Origins*, 10; Wilder, *In the Company*, 76–78.

3. Drake, *Redemption*, 10; Wilder, *In the Company*, 76–77, 150.

4. Michael McCarthy, *Dark Continent*, 14–15, 28; Jordan, *White Over Black*, 305; Frederickson, *Black Image*, 49.

5. Quarles, *Black Mosaic*, 109.

6. Wilder, *In the Company*, 150–51; David Brion Davis, "Impact," 4–5.

7. Frederickson, *Black Image*, 12–13.

8. Quarles, *Black Mosaic*, 118.

9. Moses, *Afrotopia*, 1, 24, 229; Drake, *Black Folk*, vol. 1, 1–4. For further discussion of nineteenth-century African Americans' perspectives about ancient Egypt, see Bay, *White Image*, 21; Drake, *Black Folk*, vol. 1, 130–34; Drake, *Redemption*, 11; Quarles, *Black Mosaic*, 116–20; Moses, *Classical Black Nationalism*, 3; Kachun, *Festivals*, 31–33.

10. S., "For the Freedom's Journal," *FJ*, 24 August 1827; S., "For the Freedom's Journal," *FJ*, 17 August 1827. On Ham as the father of black peoples, see Moses, *Afrotopia*, 49–50; Copher, "Black Presence," 148; Sanders, "Hamitic Hypothesis," 521–22; Haynes, *Noah's Curse*; Goldenberg, *Curse of Ham*, 105–6; Johnson, *Myth of Ham*; Gomez, *Reversing Sail*, 20–22.

11. Samuel E. Cornish and John B. Russwurm, "Mutability of Human Affairs," *FJ*, 6 April 1827; [Alexander Hill Everett], "European Colonies in America," *FJ*, 13 July 1827. Herodotus's description appeared in his *Histories*, vol. 1, 164. On Cornish and Russwurm's reprinting of Everett's text, see also Ernest, *Liberation*, 289–90; Dain, *Hideous Monster*, 124–25.

12. S., "For the Freedom's Journal," 17 August 1827; Cornish and Russwurm, "Mutability," 6 April 1827. See also Bruce, *Origins*, 167–68, on the treatment of Africa's historical significance.

13. Moses, *Afrotopia*, 229; Moses, *Wings of Ethiopia*, 84.

14. On de Vastey, see Nicholls, *From Dessalines*, 43–46; Lewis, *Main Currents*, 254–56; Francis, "Nineteenth," 123–29.

15. [Pompée Valentin, Baron de Vastey], "Africa," *FJ*, 7 February 1829; Everett, "European Colonies," 13 July 1827. On the publication of de Vastey's text in *Freedom's Journal*, see also Dain, *Hideous Monster*, 125–26.

16. Moses, *Wings of Ethiopia*, 146; Moses, *Afrotopia*, 27; Adefila, "Black Press," 34.

17. "Africa," *FJ*, 21 February 1829; Everett, "European Colonies," 13 July 1827.

18. S., "For the Freedom's Journal," 17 August 1827.

19. Cornish and Russwurm, "Mutability," 6 April 1827.

20. S., "For the Freedom's Journal," *FJ*, 31 August 1827.

21. Moses, *Afrotopia*, 47; Bacon, *Humblest*, 81–82; Raboteau, "African-Americans"; Coleman, *Tribal Talk*, 128.

22. S**** B—, "Colonization Society," *FJ*, 9 November 1827; Moses, *Afrotopia*, 47.

23. "History of Slavery," *FJ*, 13 July 1827.

24. Interpreter, "An Apology for Pharaoh," *FJ*, 29 June 1827; Interpreter, "An Apology for Pharaoh," *FJ*, 6 July 1827. For commentary on these articles, see also Dain, "Haiti and Egypt," 149–50.

25. S., "For the Freedom's Journal," 31 August 1827; Everett, "European Colonies," 13 July 1827; "Oration, by Thomas L. Jinnings," *FJ*, 4 April 1828. Hannibal was also mentioned in a reprinted article from the *Abolition Intelligencer*, "The Surprising Influence of Prejudice," *FJ*, 18 May 1827.

26. Cornish and Russwurm, "Mutability," 6 April 1827; Samuel E. Cornish and John B. Russwurm, "Mutability of Human Affairs," *FJ*, 13 April 1827; Samuel E. Cornish and John B. Russwurm, "Mutability of Human Affairs," *FJ*, 20 April 1827.

27. "Observations on the Early History of the Negro Race," *FJ*, 5 December 1828.

28. See Moses, *Afrotopia*, 24.

29. "Africa," 21 February 1829; Kim Hall, *Things of Darkness*, 30. On Leo Africanus's attitude toward Africa, see also Christopher Miller, *Blank Darkness*, 16; Vaughan and Vaughan, "Before Othello," 41.

30. Sylvia M. Jacobs, "Historical Role," 17; Moses, *Afrotopia*, 16; Gomez, *Exchanging*, 214–16; Meier and Rudwick, *From Plantation*, 5.

31. "Africa," 21 February 1829.

32. Moses, *Afrotopia*, 26; Drake, *Redemption*, 49–50; Quarles, *Black Mosaic*, 120.

33. Cornish and Russwurm, "Mutability," 20 April 1827.

34. Cornish and Russwurm, "Mutability," 20 April 1827; "Observations on the History of the Negro-Race," *FJ*, 12 December 1828; Everett, "European Colonies," 13 July 1827.

35. Moses, *Afrotopia*, 53–55; see also Bay, *White Image*, 26–30.

36. De Vastey, "Africa," 7 February 1829; Cornish and Russwurm, "Mutability," 20 April 1827. See also Dain, "Haiti and Egypt," 147–149, on the "Mutability" series.

37. Jinnings, "Oration."

38. De Vastey, "Africa," 7 February 1829.

39. See, for example, untitled report of the death of Major Laing, *FJ*, 22 June 1827; "Death of Capt. Clapperton," *FJ*, 13 June 1828; "Africa," *FJ*, 10 October 1828; "Timbuctoo," *FJ*, 28 December 1828; "Africa. Physical Geography," *FJ*, 14 March 1829; "Africa," *FJ*, 21 March 1829.

40. "Africa," *FJ*, 28 March 1829; "Timbuctoo," *FJ*, 28 February 1829; "Africa," 21 March 1829.

41. Cornish and Russwurm, "To Our Patrons"; [Alexander Hill Everett], "European Colonies in America," *FJ*, 20 July 1827. For the poetry referred to by Everett, see Denham, Clapperton, and Oudney, *Narrative*, vol. 2, 409–13.

42. [Mungo Park], "African Magnanimity," *FJ*, 20 April 1827.

43. Pratt, *Imperial Eyes*, 84; Shepperson, "Mungo Park," 278; Nichols, "Mumbo Jumbo."

44. Everett, "European Colonies," 20 July 1827.

45. [Pompée Valentin, Baron de Vastey], "Africa," *FJ*, 14 February 1829.

46. "Discovery in Africa," *FJ*, 28 September 1827.

47. This account of Rahahman draws on Gomez, "Muslims," 689–91; Horton and Horton, *In Hope of Liberty*, 189–91; Alford, *Prince among Slaves*; Austin, *African Muslims . . . Struggles*, 65–82; Gallaudet, *Statement*. Rahahman was called in various histories Ibrahim, Ibrahima, Abd ar-Rahman, Abd al-Rahman, or Abd al-Rahman Ibrahima. Although he was called Abduhl Rahahman in *Freedom's Journal*, the spelling in different accounts varied.

48. "The Captive African Restored to Liberty," *FJ*, 16 May 1828.

49. "Abduhl Rahahman," *FJ*, 31 October 1828; Russwurm, "Travelling Scraps," 29 August 1828.

50. "Abduhl Rahahman," 31 October 1828; "Public Dinner in Boston," *FJ*, 24 October 1828.

51. Quotations from the Bible, here and elsewhere in this book, are from the King James Version, the standard antebellum translation (Cmiel, *Democratic Eloquence*, 121).

52. Moses, *Wings of Ethiopia*, 102–3, 143–44, 214; see also Drake, *Redemption*, 49.

53. S., "For the Freedom's Journal," 31 August 1827.

54. Drake, *Redemption*, 52–53; Moses, *Afrotopia*, 26–27; Michael McCarthy, *Dark Continent*, 101; Sylvia M. Jacobs, "Historical Role," 17–18.

55. "Missions to Africa" [letter from Edward Bickersteth to the Right Reverend Bishop White], *FJ*, 16 March 1827.

56. Austin, *African Muslims . . . Struggles*, 68, 73–76; see also Gomez, *Exchanging*, 74.

57. "Captive African"; Gallaudet, *Statement*, 6; "Abduhl Rahhahman," *FJ*, 27 June 1828.

58. U., "Abduhl Rahaman," *FJ*, 24 October 1828; Moses, *Wings of Ethiopia*, 141–46.

59. "South Africa," *FJ*, 4 May 1827; untitled and unsigned response to F.A., letter, *FJ*, 15 February 1828.

60. Amicus, "Kosciusko School. No. II." On the notion of African Americans' messianic role, see Logan, *"We Are Coming,"* 27; Moses, *Afrotopia*, 27, 238.

61. As this section will make clear, I disagree with Bruce Dain's claims that *Freedom's Journal* demonstrates an "abandonment by African-Americans of Haiti as ideological model after the first emigration failed" and that, with a few exceptions, the coverage of Haiti in the newspaper was relatively inconsequential ("Haiti and Egypt," 142).

62. The first two installments of this series were reprinted from the *Christian Watchman*, the weekly publication of the Baptist Missionary Society of Massachusetts, on December 1, 1826, and December 8, 1826. The remaining six articles were identified as original to *Freedom's Journal*. It seems quite plausible that they were written by the same author; the third part of the series picked up where the second left off (in 1789) and continued to detail the history of the island. We might speculate that perhaps, after submitting two articles to the *Christian Watchman* in 1826, the author found *Freedom's Journal*—a venue obviously not yet existent when these first two installments were published—a more appropriate place to publish the rest of the work. (It is also possible that the author offered or planned to submit the subsequent four parts to the *Christian Watchman*, which for some reason refused to publish them or that, after the first two installments appeared, a different author decided to continue the series in *Freedom's Journal*.)

63. "Hayti, No. I," *FJ*, 20 April 1827; "Hayti, No. II," *FJ*, 27 April 1827.

64. "Hayti, No. III," *FJ*, 4 May 1827. On Ogé and the rebellion, see Alderson, "Charleston's Rumored Slave Revolt," 104; Tise, *American Counterrevolution*, 217–19.

65. S., "Theresa,—A Haytien Tale," *FJ*, 18 January 1828. The phrasing here seems to echo the "live free or die" motto created by Revolutionary War hero John Stark on the occasion of the 32nd anniversary of the 1777 Battle of Bennington (see Libbie Payne, "The Man Who Declared, 'Live Free or Die,'" *Boston Globe*, 1 September 2002). Notably, Russwurm also used a variation of the phrase to describe the Haitians—a "population which is determined to live free or die gloriously"— in his Bowdoin commencement speech ("The Condition and Prospects of Haiti,"104).

66. Moses, *Afrotopia*, 54–55; J., "Haytien Revolution," *FJ*, 6 April 1827.

67. This London quarterly was published in a New York edition as well.

68. "Toussaint L'Ouverture," *FJ*, 4 May 1827; "Toussaint L'Ouverture," *FJ*, 11 May 1827.

69. "Toussaint L'Ouverture," 11 May 1827.

70. Hunt, *Haiti's Influence*, 147; Samuel E. Cornish and John B. Russwurm, untitled editorial, *FJ*, 16 March 1827.

71. "Hayti, No. V," *FJ*, 29 June 1827; "Hayti, No. VI," *FJ*, 12 October 1827.

72. Hunt, *Haiti's Influence*, 123–27; Bellegarde-Smith, *Haiti*, 48–52.

73. "Conspiracy Against the President of Hayti," *FJ*, 3 August 1827; "Hayti," *FJ*, 11 April 1828; "Hayti," *FJ*, 14 February 1829.

74. Cole, *Christophe*; Nicholls, *From Dessalines*, 33–60.

75. D., "Madame Christophe," *FJ*, 11 May 1827.

76. "Madame Christophe," *FJ*, 27 June 1828; "Madame Christophe," *FJ*, 11 July 1828.

77. "Public Dinner in Boston"; John B. Russwurm, "Hayti," *FJ*, 12 December 1828.

78. "Public Dinner in Boston"; "Africa," 21 February 1829.

7

~

"Save Us from Our Friends": Colonization and Emigration

Although African Americans of the late 1820s were interested in the past, present, and future of Africa, they did not, in most cases, support contemporary efforts to promote colonization, particularly those of the ACS. As we have seen, protests against colonization linked African-American communities in various cities. *Freedom's Journal* played a crucial role in giving voice to the resistance of many African Americans to the ACS's plans. Recall Theodore Wright's 1837 comments to the New York State Anti-Slavery Society that prior to the periodical's founding, African Americans "could not gain access to the public mind" to express their anti-colonization sentiments because "the press" either "was silent" or explicitly advocated colonization. *Freedom's Journal*, Wright explained, "announced the facts in the case," publicizing African Americans' "opposition" to the ACS and allowing "the united views and intentions of the people of color" to be "made known."[1]

Wright emphasized the anti-colonization material published in *Freedom's Journal*; and, as we have seen, the editorial position for most of the paper's run was against colonization. As a result, the editors printed many articles that countered the ACS and its proposals. These arguments went beyond critiques of the ACS's plans, engaging the assumptions and the rhetoric of colonizationists as well as their implications for the rights and freedom of African Americans. As we have discussed, the ACS was not a monolithic organization, and its membership held varying views about slavery, abolition, and emancipation. However varied, though, their perspectives and objectives were based on underlying assumptions that were troubling and threatening to African Americans: that free people

177

of color would always be considered inferior to whites and that they could never be full participants in the civic life of the nation and its institutions. Refuting the claims of colonizationists—both those that were explicitly racist and those that were couched in reformist language—*Freedom's Journal*'s editors and contributors exposed the biases and uncovered the racist goals of many ACS supporters, including those who wished to prop up slavery. They also argued forcefully that African Americans had not only the right but the responsibility to remain in the land of their birth and fight for their own rights and for the freedom of the enslaved.

Yet for a variety of reasons, the editors also published arguments favoring emigration and/or colonization. As we have seen, in the late eighteenth and early nineteenth centuries, some African Americans expressed an interest in leaving the United States for Africa or other regions, such as Haiti. Although by the era of *Freedom's Journal*, opposition to the ACS was strong and many were disappointed by the relative lack of success of the Haitian emigration movement in the mid-1820s, some African Americans continued to seek better lives beyond the borders of the United States. In many cases, those with this view did not explicitly advocate the ACS's plans, instead focusing on ventures that would allow African Americans a more active role. Indeed, as we shall see, the distinction between plans proposed and controlled by white colonizationists and those directed by African Americans was crucial.

Even on the specific subject of the ACS, though, *Freedom's Journal*'s columns contained articles with diverse and often conflicting views. As we have seen, Cornish and Russwurm stated from the outset that one of their goals was to encourage debate on important issues. In particular, they maintained that proposals that were advocated by self-professed friends of African Americans should be scrutinized; in their opening editorial, they suggested that "plans which apparently are beneficial" should be "candidly discussed and properly weighed" to determine whether they merited "cordial approbation" or "marked disapprobation." Even though the editors' official stance was in opposition to African colonization for most of the newspaper's run, they noted that their opinions did not negate their determination to air both sides of the issue. In fact, they believed that a thorough examination was the best way to persuade others of their view. "We can assure our readers," they remarked, "that, though we have expressed our decided disapprobation of the [American Colonization] Society, we wish to see the subject fully discussed in our columns, being truly anxious to make a few converts among our friends."[2]

There was, of course, another reason for the inclusion of pro-colonization material in *Freedom's Journal*, particularly in late 1828 and 1829, namely Russwurm's increasing interest in and eventual support for the ACS. As we have explored, although Russwurm did not officially announce his endorsement of colonization until his editorial of February 14, 1829, by January of that year he had, in his words, *"materially* changed" his "views on the subject of Colonization" and decided to emigrate to Liberia and to seek employment there under the auspices of the ACS.[3] Yet because pro-colonization articles and news were always included in the columns of *Freedom's Journal*, it is important to avoid simplistic generalizations about Russwurm's motives prior to his overt advocacy of the ACS and its plans. As we shall see, the subjects of emigration and colonization were explored from various angles in the periodical. *Freedom's Journal's* coverage reveals the depth and complexity of sentiment and opinion evoked by these multifaceted issues among African Americans of the late 1820s.

EMIGRATION AND SELF-DETERMINATION

As we have seen, some African Americans in the late eighteenth and early nineteenth centuries favored leaving behind the oppression of the United States and beginning new lives in other regions. It is important to appreciate the distinction between the views of many who supported these efforts and the perspectives of colonizationists. As V. P. Franklin explains, emigration that was rooted in "black self-determination" met a very different response than did white-dominated plans such as those of the ACS. "Free blacks," Franklin asserts, "knew the difference between leaving the United States for a black nation and emigrating to a white-controlled 'colony'" where they would not achieve the goal of "freedom from white domination." Indeed, some made this distinction explicitly. When in the late 1780s a slaveholder, architect, and physician named William Thornton—who would later join the ACS—attempted to recruit African Americans to settle in Sierra Leone, even those interested in emigrating were unenthusiastic about a plan controlled by whites. The African Company in Boston, for example, supported African emigration, but they took exception to Thornton's officious approach: "We do not approve of Mr. Thornton's going [to] settle a place for us. We think it would be better if we could charter a vessel and send some of our own blacks."[4]

Thus even as a majority of free African Americans in the late 1820s remained committed to staying in the United States and seeking full citizenship there, they did not necessarily oppose the efforts of those individuals and groups who supported emigration plans directed and controlled by African Americans themselves. Nor, as we shall see, did they object in various cases to the resettlement of individuals such as freed slaves, even when carried out with white assistance, when these actions were not part of a larger, white-dominated plan.

From the outset, the editors of *Freedom's Journal* demonstrated that they recognized and appreciated these distinctions. An August 1827 news item, for example, mentioned the success of emigrants to "the western parts of Upper Canada" in cultivating and exporting tobacco. And even though African Americans' interest in resettling in Haiti had declined from its peak in the mid-1820s, positive stories about Haitian emigration occasionally appeared in the paper. In December 1827, for example, Russwurm reprinted an announcement from Benjamin Lundy's *Genius of Universal Emancipation* notifying "such humane and philanthropic slave holders as are desirous to give their slaves an opportunity to obtain their freedom" that Lundy would soon "dispatch a vessel to Hayti" for the purpose of transporting these newly freed slaves there. A January 1829 article also reprinted from the *Genius of Universal Emancipation* noted that a Maryland slaveholder intended to "take all his slaves . . . to the Republic of Hayti, with the view of settling them there" and that others "propose[d] to send theirs with him." The article specifically indicated the benefits of Haitian emigration over African colonization, remarking that many of those who had already emigrated were "doing exceedingly well," living "completely 'redeemed[,] regenerated, and disenthralled,' from the prejudices of the white race."[5]

Freedom's Journal's editors did not promote resettlement in Haiti, yet their inclusion of these articles demonstrates that they, like other African Americans of the time, separated Haitian emigration from African colonization. Even though in these stories white Americans—namely slaveholders—were directing the relocation of freed slaves, their efforts did not suggest the large-scale implications of colonization to Africa under the auspices of the powerful and racist ACS. Although they were committed to the notion that African Americans deserved rights in the United States, the editors clearly drew a distinction between individual actions and proposals that would potentially affect all blacks, slave and free.

In this vein, emigration to Africa was at times treated positively by *Freedom's Journal*'s editors even before Russwurm's change of perspective. In installments appearing in their first five issues, they published the "Memoirs of Capt. Paul Cuffee," reprinted from the *Liverpool Mercury* of 1812. Born in 1759, Paul Cuffe became a prosperous ship captain.[6] He was a devout Christian as well as a racially conscious community leader; he and his brother John, we will recall, were among the five African Americans in Dartmouth, Massachusetts, who in 1780 petitioned their state legislature to protest their taxation without representation. By the early nineteenth century, Cuffe had become interested in the welfare of Africa. The captain believed that Africa was in need of spiritual redemption, but he also was interested in his own commercial interests and in promoting trade, particularly between African Americans and blacks living in the British colony of Sierra Leone. To this end, he proposed to recruit African Americans who would, as colonists, bring both commerce and the Gospel to Africa. He visited the colony in 1811, as Floyd Miller explains, for the purpose of "investigating the suitability of Sierra Leone for American black settlement," exploring its "potential as a commercial depot for whatever cargoes he might carry to the area," and "assessing the religious and moral temper of the colony."[7] In December 1815, he and thirty-eight emigrants set sail for Sierra Leone. Soon after, he was contacted by white Americans interested in colonization. Although the aims of Cuffe, a supporter of emancipation and a racially aware businessman who hoped to provide opportunities for blacks, differed greatly from those of many white colonizationists, he nonetheless endorsed their efforts.

Written for a British periodical three years before his 1815 expedition and his subsequent alliance with white colonizationists, the biographical series about Cuffe reprinted by Cornish and Russwurm did not discuss Cuffe's transporting of emigrants to Sierra Leone or explicitly address the issue of white-dominated colonization. Yet readers of the series in *Freedom's Journal* would of course have been aware of events occurring in the intervening years. The fact that Cornish and Russwurm published this positive piece about Cuffe in the context of the late 1820s, even as both editors avowed their disapproval of the ACS and African colonization, gives us insight into the complexity of many African Americans' views about emigration and colonization.

The series began with a news report from the *Edinburgh Review* of August 1811 about the arrival at Liverpool of "a vessel" with a "cargo from Sierra Leone; the owner, master, mate, and whole crew of which are free blacks." That a free African American, "the son of an American slave," and not white businessmen or philanthropists, was in control of this voyage was further underscored: "It must have been a strange and animating spectacle to see this free and enlightened African, entering as an independent trader with his black crew into that port, which was so lately the *nidus* of the slave trade."[8] Readers of *Freedom's Journal* would of course have been proud of Cuffe's direction of his own affairs, but many would no doubt have perceived an additional significance to this description of his plans. In the context of Cuffe's clear management of his own affairs and his direction of his voyages to Africa, his subsequent transportation of colonists to Sierra Leone would have appeared not as acquiescence to white-dominated colonization schemes but as an extension of his self-directed philanthropy and enterprise.

Description of Cuffe's 1811 stay in Sierra Leone in the last installment of the article series emphasized his control of his connections to Africa. He "turned his attention to the colony of Sierra Leone" in the early nineteenth century, the piece related, "and was induced to believe from the communications from Europe and other sources, that his endeavours to contribute to its welfare, and that of his fellow men, might not be ineffectual." Readers learned that Cuffe also gave important roles to other blacks. His nephew, Thomas Wainer, was captain of the *Traveller*, the ship that made the voyage to Sierra Leone, and Cuffe left him "in the colony" to further his "primary intention" of fostering links with the residents there and bettering their lives. He brought back to England "Aaron Richards, a native of Sierra Leone, with a view of educating him, and particularly of instructing him in the art of navigation."[9] The editors' publication of this series made it clear that even for those opposed to colonization, Cuffe was a hero whose efforts should be celebrated. Indeed, their inclusion of these positive articles about a supporter of African colonization demonstrates the depth of perspective even among those who publicly and strongly opposed the ACS and believed that African Americans should fight for their rights as Americans. Even though Cuffe had aligned himself with the ACS, his plans could be viewed apart from white influence, and his goals of furthering African-American and African commerce and bringing Christianity to Africa were not tainted by the racist assumptions—and, in many cases, the proslavery aims—of the ACS and its white supporters. As Floyd Miller asserts, "rejecting what the white colonizationists were proposing" did not necessarily mean that African-American leaders "were turning their backs on Cuffe," whose plans were based on "Christian humanism and racial awareness."[10]

The distinction between colonization and emigration was also apparent in *Freedom's Journal*'s coverage of African-American missionary activity in Africa. As we have discussed in the previous chapter, African Americans of the late 1820s supported the evangelism of those who desired to promote the Gospel in Africa. In the columns of *Freedom's Journal*, the editors and contributors made it clear, either implicitly or explicitly, that one could strongly oppose colonization and at the same time endorse the exertions of those African Americans who chose to emigrate to Africa and undertake missionary work there.

In their first issue, Cornish and Russwurm reprinted an article from the *New-York Observer* noting "the painful fact, that during the year preceding the last Report of the [London-based] Church Missionary Society, no less than *seven* of its missionaries in West Africa had been removed by death." As a result, the Society was "turning their attention to the United States for a supply of Missionaries for these stations; and to *people of color*, as being less exposed than other persons to suffer from the insalubrity of the climate." The article contained an 1826 letter from Edward Bickersteth, the secretary of the Church Missionary Society, to the Right Reverend William White, Presiding Bishop of the Episcopal Church in the United States, outlining the required duties and the proposed compensation.[11]

Cornish and Russwurm did not add any editorial comments encouraging potential African-American missionaries; yet neither did they discourage anyone who might be interested. Their inclusion of this article suggests that even though they opposed and were offended by white-dominated colonization plans, missionary activity—even that sponsored by white philanthropists—was a different matter. Individuals who felt called to emigrate to spread the Gospel were guided by their desire to share their faith and to aid Africans, rather than by the belief that there was no future for people of color in the United States.

In a June 1827 editorial, Cornish and Russwurm distinguished explicitly between colonization and the emigration of missionaries. Reiterating their "oppos[ition] to colonization in principle, object, and tendency," they argued that there were better ways of achieving the goals of "emancipation; the salvation of Africa; and the extermination of the slave trade." "We doubt not," they asserted, "but a Missionary family . . . would effect more in ten years, and at far less expense, towards the conversion of the natives, than our colony in twenty." Other staunch foes of colonization drew similar distinctions. Contributor Investigator, for example, authored three articles which were published in the newspaper in August, September, and October 1827 and which expressed a strong anti-colonization position. As we shall see, Investigator refuted the claims of colonizationists and exposed their racist premises; yet Investigator drew a clear distinction between emigration for missionary purposes and the ACS's plans:

> If [Liberia] be considered as a Missionary station . . . we give it our decided approbation. But if it be considered as an Asylum for the free coloured population of this country, we protest against it. . . . That it is not a Missionary station is plain, from the fact that no missionary society have ever considered it as such; neither have there ever been any efforts made, by its patrons, to procure qualified missionaries for the society.[12]

The distinctions made by the editors from the outset between colonization and self-directed and/or individual emigration, even to Africa, provide an important context for examining articles published in 1829, after Russwurm had decided to become a colonist in Liberia. As we will explore in some detail, Russwurm's coverage of colonization shifted to favor more positive articles about Liberia and about the ACS. Yet the inclusion of other favorable articles late in the periodical's run, particularly about missionary work in Africa, did not constitute a change in the newspaper's overall perspective. In February and March 1829, for example, Russwurm published the constitution of the African Mission School Society, an organization formed by the Episcopal Church to "establish & maintain a school for the instruction of suitable persons of African extraction, with reference to their becoming missionaries, catechists, and schoolmasters in Africa, under the direction of the Domestic and Foreign Missionary Society of the Protestant Episcopal Church." A letter to the editor of *Freedom's Journal* noted that the "school has been for some months in operation," although "very few applications have been received."[13] Although Russwurm had, by the time these articles were published, announced his support for the ACS, we cannot jump to the conclusion that he included these pieces merely because of his personal opinions. Positive information about African emigration motivated by individual desires or religious conviction was always featured in the periodical, and African Americans held complex views about the issues of colonization and emigration, distinguishing among various plans and assessing their utility in furthering the goals of freedom, self-determination, and independence.

"THAT THEY MAY JUDGE FOR THEMSELVES": PRO-COLONIZATION RHETORIC

Cornish and Russwurm remarked that from the outset, they had invited those supportive of colonization to submit their views to *Freedom's Journal*:

> In soliciting patronage to our Journal among Colonizationists, we expressed ourselves to many of them, as opposed to colonization . . . yet, if we were wrong, our minds were open to conviction, and we wished to see the subject discussed; they were generally pleased with the idea. If the Colonization Society possess any merits, it cannot lose by investigation: but if the motives of its founders will not bear investigation, it ought to sink: every good man will say the same.[14]

Some proponents of colonization took Cornish and Russwurm at their word, as we shall see, writing pieces for the newspaper; and the editors honored their commitment by publishing them. At times, Cornish and Russwurm made editorial comments refuting the pro-colonization arguments they published; yet they wanted readers to be exposed directly to the claims of colonizationists.

Cornish and Russwurm, as we have noted, believed that the ultimate result of their open editorial policy would be to strengthen the anti-colonization position. In fact, they implied, colonizationists' own rhetoric often afforded the strongest arguments against their cause. In their September 7, 1827, issue, Russwurm remarked of the editors' inclusion of a pro-colonization letter from correspondent Wilberforce, "We place '*Wilberforce*,' before our readers, in order, that they may judge for themselves, what liberal ideas our Colonization friends . . . entertain of us generally. It is a fact, worthy of notice, that our bitterest enemies think not more contemptibly of us, than do Colonizationists generally. . . ."[15] Publishing the arguments of colonizationists, Cornish and Russwurm believed, would allow readers to "judge for themselves" both the merits of colonization and the motives and beliefs of its supporters.

Examining the pro-colonization articles in *Freedom's Journal*, we discover aspects of the antebellum debate over colonization that have been hitherto unexamined. Although the resistance of most antebellum African Americans to African colonization is well documented, historians have generally not considered the pro-colonization material that they would have encountered. *Freedom's Journal* demonstrates that antebellum African Americans did not merely learn about the ACS and its supporters from the rhetoric of those who opposed colonization; they read—as well as commented on and, as we shall explore in the next section, critiqued—the arguments of colonizationists themselves. In addition, because some of the pro-colonization articles in *Freedom's Journal* were written for the periodical, it is a source of a particular type of pro-colonization rhetoric that has not yet been explored by historians: arguments created specifically to persuade African Americans, rather than the numerous sermons and tracts written by white colonizationists for other white readers.[16] Thus, although the number of contributions written by white ACS supporters specifically for the columns of *Freedom's Journal* is limited—the editors published two letters and a ten-part series of articles, all of them in 1827—they are worthy of close reading.

If they were to attempt to persuade readers of the merits of the ACS's plans, pro-colonization contributors to *Freedom's Journal* had to overcome several significant obstacles. If colonization held such promise for African Americans, for example, why did so many oppose it? This dilemma would not necessarily have been considered by many whites arguing for white audiences; in the paternalistic rhetoric of many ACS supporters, the sentiments and opinions of people of color were not relevant. Yet an author writing for *Freedom's Journal* could hardly have hoped to be effective without acknowledging the views of African Americans. Correspondent Wilberforce assured the editors, "I am persuaded that you feel deeply, and mean well, and that you would not, willingly, be instrumental in retarding the progress of a cause which is worthy of your best affections and labours." Yet he must take "the Junior Editor" to task, he noted, for attacking the ACS, "this best friend of black men." The ACS was the true supporter of African Americans, he claimed, and those who opposed it were not; reading Russwurm's anti-colonization remarks, Wilberforce commented, he "was forcibly reminded of an old proverb—'Save me from my friends, and I will take care of my enemies.'" African Americans' opposition to colonization was, in Wilberforce's view, a result of their inability to distinguish between their true allies, the colonizationists, and misguided friends, like the editors, who worked against "the progress of *African rights* in all their extent" by criticizing the ACS.[17]

In a series of essays written for *Freedom's Journal* in 1827, John H. Kennedy, the assistant to ACS corresponding secretary R. R. Gurley, made a similar claim. African Americans, he argued, must take into account "the characters of those who *befriend*" the ACS. Kennedy chastised those who did not recognize that these supporters of the ACS had African Americans' best interests in mind: "When men truly virtuous and enlightened . . . evince a decided and continued approval of an enterprise, we ought not hastily to denounce it as wicked or chimerical." African-American opposition to colonization, Kennedy maintained, was not only a rash but an irrational response arising from emotion rather than an objective examination of the ACS's merits. This passion was perfectly understandable, but it needed to be redirected: "Can we expect to find men in a mood for dispassionate argumentation, whose every right has been trampled on [?] . . . A little over-boiling of feeling and of expression, only indicates a fire beneath, that promises much, when properly tended. . . ."[18] On their own, Kennedy and Wilberforce implied, African Americans could not be expected to make a fair judgment of the ACS; these white writers were compelled to step in to help them see who their true friends were.

Yet if they were to convince readers to accept colonizationists as allies, contributors to *Freedom's Journal* could not avoid two other difficult, and related, questions: If those who endorsed the ACS's plans had the best interests of African Americans at heart, why were prominent slaveholders among the organization's members and supporters? And why was the rhetoric of many ACS supporters so blatantly racist? Those who addressed the readers of *Freedom's Journal* offered possible answers. An August 1827 letter from a subscriber whose language—"your race," "your people"—indicated a white writer, maintained,

> Though [people of color] may find some enrolled as [ACS] members, and even as its officers who are slaveholders, and who now mean to die such, yet will they not recollect that even such are controlled by public opinion, and may yet be induced to emancipate and prepare their now abject slaves to become freemen in the land of their fathers? Shall the consideration that comparatively few of the patrons of the Society, are insincere, induce you to . . . check the exertions of thousands who are actuated by the most disinterested motives in your cause?

Kennedy suggested that the ACS's founders had pragmatic reasons for seeking slaveholders' support: "Their ultimate destination was the slave states. Success was not to be attained without the co-operation of these states. . . . The founders of this society . . . acted wisely. . . . They selected for officers many who were slave-holders." As for the offensive rhetoric of many ACS propagandists, Kennedy did not deny it; any "enlightened advocate of the

Society," he remarked, "must regret" the aspersions cast on free people of color, who were described as *"pests* and *nuisances."* Like the aforementioned subscriber, though, he asked that the society as a whole not be judged by these, but instead by the *"mass* of those composing it." As a whole, he was "pretty well convinced that the motives of the institution are pure."[19]

Contributors to *Freedom's Journal* also addressed a specific concern many readers might have had about the colonization plan. Even though the ACS claimed that emigration would be voluntary, many African Americans, as we have noted, feared the employment of coercion or even force. Kennedy insisted that these worries were unfounded: "It compels no one to go, it offers no insult to those who stay, nor after his arrival on the coast of Africa need any one remain, unless he find brighter prospects than those he has abandoned." Wilberforce similarly assured readers that the ACS used "no coercion" toward "free coloured people," although he admitted that for slaves the notion of choice was somewhat questionable: "The poor slaves will, no doubt prefer Liberia to a slave-ship—or a slave plantation."[20]

In addition to these assurances aimed at dispelling African Americans' doubts about the motivations and potential methods of those who favored colonization, pro-colonization contributors to *Freedom's Journal* offered arguments defending the ACS's goals and plans. Colonization supporters frequently asserted that African Americans could not rise in the United States to any level of equality with whites, and various contributors to the periodical echoed this contention. Yet they did not take the approach of much pro-colonization rhetoric which, as we have seen, presented free African Americans as degraded, prone to criminal behavior, and unable to contribute to society. The August 1827 letter from a white subscriber maintained that "the idea that Africans could rise to the dignity of freemen, found and transmit to their posterity republican institutions, has been regarded by the mass of our population as chimerical in the extreme." This correspondent, though, avoided any suggestion that African Americans were actually inferior, noting instead that a man of color in the United States inevitably faced the "deeply rooted prejudices" of whites "who, though no better than himself, would gladly trample him in the dust." Calling prejudice against African Americans "an evil" and a "noxious influence," Kennedy insisted that the ACS was not founded "upon the implied inferiority of the coloured man, and his unfitness for the society of the white men." Asking readers again to judge the ACS as a whole, Kennedy noted that even though "some individuals" in the ACS may have held such views, the organization itself "appends not its Amen to those prejudices."[21]

But why, given this prejudice, was colonization the answer? Why not try to attack racism itself or to pursue equal opportunity for African

Americans, allowing them to attain positions of respect and exercise the responsibilities of citizenship? The goal of "elevating the coloured community, even in this country," Kennedy argued, "is not to be attained by argument, but by a silent influence of another sort." Direct rhetoric, then, was not the answer; instead, successful colonization would be implicitly persuasive: "When a respectable colony is established, and the coloured merchant shall visit our shores, argument in the case will be superseded. The coloured man at home, will imperceptibly rise in influence and respectability, through the indirect influence of those from the Colony." The aforementioned subscriber made a similar claim:

> The promoters of colonization have confidently believed, they should not only bless degraded Africa, but gradually revolutionize public sentiment in this country in regard to the condition of our coloured population. For, if Providence should continue to smile on that colony—if it were apparent that these Africans from our land could be influenced by the true spirit of freemen—govern themselves and by industry become independent, no longer could the slave-holder assert that it would be cruel to emancipate his slaves, because they were incapable of governing themselves.[22]

Readers might have found some contradictions in these assertions about racism; indeed, as we shall see, they discovered many discrepancies in the arguments of colonizationists. If prejudice was so recalcitrant that whites would see even those who were "no better than themselves" as inferior, how could a prosperous colony counteract its force? If the ultimate goal of the ACS was to remove all people of color from the United States, would not the goal of eradicating prejudice or elevating African Americans be moot? These inconsistencies notwithstanding, it is notable that these colonizationist writers even tackled the remedy for prejudice at all. In many sermons and speeches given to white audiences, colonizationists accepted prejudice as an inevitable part of American society, without proposing or even noting the need for any remedy.[23] Such an approach is not surprising, given the racism of most antebellum white Americans, who would have seen no need to eliminate the oppression people of color faced. Those who attempted to persuade *Freedom's Journal's* African-American readers adopted a different strategy clearly aimed at the hearts and minds of those who, by contrast, had an interest in eliminating prejudice.

The claim that successful colonization would counteract slaveholders' opposition to emancipation was connected to another prominent set of arguments of the ACS and its supporters: colonization would have a positive effect on slavery and/or the slave trade. From its founding, as we have seen, the ACS did not take a position on slavery, and Kennedy echoed this party line in his *Freedom's Journal* series, noting that "the Society, according to its original avowal, intermeddles not with slavery *di-*

rectly." Indeed, Kennedy strongly answered the "objection" that colonization was "an abolition scheme," apostrophizing slaveholders who may
make such an argument: "we mean not to wrest your slaves from you,
and of this we give you abundant security in the selection of our officers
and the location of our Society." It is curious that Kennedy addressed
slaveholders' potential concerns in *Freedom's Journal*, particularly since he
acknowledged, apparently unaware of the irony, that "the readers of the
'JOURNAL' probably did not feel the *force* of this objection" to the ACS.
For whatever reason, though, Kennedy emphasized in his contributions
to *Freedom's Journal* that the ACS was not an antislavery organization.[24]

Nonetheless, he suggested that colonization could indirectly influence
slavery in two important ways. First, he noted, the "operations" of the ACS
would "tend to *alleviate the miseries of those who remain in servitude."* If "the
presence in slave states of *free* people of colour" was "a principal reason alleged" by masters "for the rigours of slavery," the ACS's plans to remove
them might decrease this harsh treatment. Kennedy assured readers that
he did not "advocat[e] the policy" that dictated that "the rigorous treatment of the slave" be "always in proportion to the number of free people
of colour resident in the community," yet, practically speaking, any "enlightened well-wisher to them and to the slaves, cannot but desire their removal." More importantly, though, Kennedy addressed how the ACS
would affect "the *number* of those who are in servitude"—in other words,
its impact on emancipation. Even though the ACS professed neutrality on
slavery from the outset, he argued, "its collateral bearing on the cause of
emancipation was contemplated and predicted. . . . It was urged as an argument in favour of the institution about to be organized, that it would afford facilities for emancipation which did not then exist." In fact, Kennedy
asserted, colonization could counter slavery in ways that the arguments of
abolitionists could not. Although he did not oppose "the legitimate exercise of argument," Kennedy contended that "the slave States" could not
"be ultimately *argued* into the emancipation of people of Color." In fact, he
asserted, argument was moot: "I have resided for years among slave holders, and have conversed fully with them on the subject, and yet I never
found one who pretended to defend slavery on principle."[25]

Kennedy would no doubt have been aware that many apologists did in
fact "defend slavery on principle," yet his representation of the moral sentiments of slaveholders allowed him to set up a strong contrast between
colonization and abolition. Because slaveholders already knew slavery
was wrong but persisted in it, he asserted, abolitionist arguments would
be useless; worse, "the chains of *many*" might be "tightened through the
well meant interference of the Abolition Society." Even if slaveholders
saw the institution as "a moral marsh which spreads pestilence in every
direction," they would be "apprehensive of an inundation, should its wa-

ters be instantly discharged." Colonization, thus, was the answer to their dilemma, providing "a dyke . . . for their gradual removal."[26] Although the argument that colonization would facilitate emancipation was not universal among colonizationists and was often contradicted by other claims (as we have seen, some supporters of the ACS felt colonization would shore up slavery), it was common in pro-colonization rhetoric. It was thus natural for Kennedy to emphasize this point in writing for the audience of *Freedom's Journal*. Yet Kennedy added an argument that would have appealed directly to readers of *Freedom's Journal* who would have supported a more direct antislavery approach. Readers should put their support behind the colonizationists rather than the abolitionists, he argued, because the former would be more effective in ultimately eradicating slavery.

Contributors also offered the related argument that colonization could have an effect on the international slave trade. Wilberforce claimed that the ACS hoped "to put a stop to the nefarious traffic in human blood which is still carried on upon the whole coast of Southern Africa, by teaching the natives the guilt of this traffic, and by furnishing an asylum for the recaptured slaves." Wilberforce was not specific either about how colonists or ACS members would educate "the natives" or about who exactly the "recaptured slaves" were, but Kennedy offered more detail about the potential effect of colonization on the slave trade. The colony would exert the "direct and indirect influence of moral suasion," serving "as a 'city set on a hill'" and demonstrating the "advantages" of freedom. The colony's authority would also be economic. Kennedy described in detail Africans' participation in the slave trade, and he indicated that "some powerful tribes" were "desirous to abandon it" but could not make the necessary "sacrifice" of forgoing "all foreign commodities," while others were wary of anything that would interfere with "their *present* gains." The colony would convince them that "lawful traffic" could "soon yield them a harvest of those very blessings of which they now obtained the dishonest gleanings." Furthermore, the colony would be "a place of *depot*, for those articles that are now obtained in exchange for slaves." Kennedy specified the incentives of such direct trade: "Is it to be supposed that the Africans will sell each other, when they can obtain the same articles in an honourable way, and at *one-fifth* of the price they now pay for them!"[27]

Supporters of colonization frequently offered the argument that a successful colony would counteract the slave trade through moral and economic means,[28] yet Kennedy would likely have been aware that references to Africa's future would have been of special significance to readers of *Freedom's Journal* who, as we have seen, were deeply interested in the "uplift" and "civilization" of Africa. Kennedy appealed to his readers' concerns for Africa throughout his series. In his first article, he assured readers that he was "not knowingly hostile to African interests," and he referred to the scriptural prophecy "Ethiopia may stretch forth her hands unto God"—which, as we have seen, held great power for antebellum African Americans—as "a promise and petition he sometimes pleads and offers." Kennedy invoked the special concern that many African Americans felt for Africa's welfare in urging them to favor colonization, remarking that because the colonists would be to those living in Africa "a people of the same colour, her sons restored," they would have a unique potential to "civilize the aborigines." The August 1827 letter from a subscriber similarly appealed to African Americans' hopes for Africa's future, although in a different way, describing colonization as a form of reparations, a way "to attempt repaying in part the immense debt due to injured Africa."[29]

For readers who might have been skeptical of the various theoretical and political reasons offered for supporting the ACS, perhaps no better argument could have been offered than the purported success of the Liberian colony. "Never has a colony founded under so embarrassing circumstances, been so prospered as that of Liberia," the enthusiastic subscriber noted in the August 1827 letter. Kennedy acknowledged that at first there were some "afflictions that befel" the colony—"diseases" and lack of "shelter, of wholesome nourishment, of medical attendance"—yet he remarked that the American colonists experienced much greater hardships. These difficulties had been addressed, and now, Kennedy affirmed, "wages are high, industry is general, commerce already begins to thrive, education diffused, morality and religion predominate." In fact, he argued, the emigrants were in a better situation than "the mass of free coloured people in this country." Although Kennedy asked only that African Americans "lend a friendly ear" to the "expositions" of those who have chosen to "*befriend*" this institution and left to them "the liberty of judging ultimately," he was convinced that anyone who had "the benefit" of their free brethren at heart would themselves "berfriend [*sic*] the American Colonization Society."[30]

"PRETENDED FRIENDS":
ARGUMENTS AGAINST COLONIZATION

If writers like Kennedy assured *Freedom's Journal*'s readers that colonizationists were their friends, most contributors saw the matter differently. In August 1827, correspondent Investigator responded to the aforementioned subscriber's defense of the ACS published that month, particularly the claim that those African Americans who opposed colonization, like the editors, would "sadden the hearts of their most ardent friends; and prevent them from struggling on in their cause, with the expectations of being able ultimately to abolish slavery." "As to discouraging your friends," Investigator assured the editors, "they are friends from principle, and until their principles are changed, cannot abandon your cause: except it be in their efforts in behalf of the Colonization Society, in which particular, we would say, '*save us from our friends.*'"[31] Far from trying to appease white supporters of colonization, Russwurm declared in the newspaper the week after he assumed full responsibilities as editor that he would expose their racism. After Professor Samuel Miller of Princeton Seminary wrote the editors of the *New-York Observer* to criticize *Freedom's Journal's* anti-colonization stance, Cornish and Russwurm responded in a letter to the *Observer's* editors. Part of it appeared in that periodical; Russwurm subsequently reprinted it in full in *Freedom's Journal*. "Ecclesiastical censure," the editors affirmed, "shall not compel us to relinquish our pens. We will arraign the motives of all pretended friends—we will strive all in our power to open the eyes of our brethren, upon all subjects which concern them. . . ."[32]

Cornish and Russwurm's letter to the *Observer* made it clear that there was actually no need to "open the eyes" of the majority of African Americans and their true allies: "Our active friends throughout the country, three to one, are directly opposed to it, considering it, as warring with our best interests. That our people do not wish to be colonized in any country whatever should be sufficient reason against the *scheme*, if Liberia were even a paradise." This message—that African Americans' opposition to colonization should be taken seriously—was repeated by various commentators in *Freedom's Journal's* columns. James Forten, writing under the name "A Man of Colour," mentioned a Philadelphia meeting of "nearly three thousand" African Americans "all opposed to colonization in any foreign country whatever." Voicing African Americans' general sentiments about the ACS, Investigator asserted, "we protest against it," describing their plans as "an unwarrantable meddling with the rights and interests of a large portion of our citizens." "The measures of the Colonization Society," Investigator declared, "have not only been contrary to the wishes of our brethren, but against their repeated remonstrances."[33]

Investigator's implication that the ACS and its supporters should not presume to speak for or determine what was best for African Americans was made explicit by various contributors. The educator and author William Watkins—writing to the editors in July 1827 under the pseudonym "A Coloured Baltimorean"—remarked of the ACS, "We know little or nothing of them, but what we gather from their writings. . . ." The ACS did not bother to consult African Americans, Watkins suggested; what they wanted from people of color was acquiescence rather than true exchange of ideas: "Why is it that they would have us yield, with implicit credulity, without the exercise of our own judgment, to whatever they propose for our happiness?" Watkins was even more forthright in an 1828 letter originally published in the *Genius of Universal Emancipation*, in which he declared that the colonizationists' strategy of "tak[ing] upon themselves to represent, prejudicially the interests of thousands who had never delegated them any such power" represented "a most unwarrantable assumption of power." The expectation of colonizationists that African Americans would unquestionably endorse their views was not only insulting but also suspicious. "Does not the dread of liberal enquiry," Watkins asked in his 1827 correspondence, "indicate something radically wrong in their principles? . . . So true it is, that 'truth loses nothing by investigation.'" A correspondent using the pseudonym "A Free Coloured Virginian" offered a similar observation: "That cause must be wretched indeed, which shrinks from investigation, for truth loses nothing by enquiry. How comes it that the advocates of colonization, are so sensitive on the subject of having any thing said in opposition to them?"[34]

Yet Watkins demonstrated that if the ACS believed he and other African-American leaders would not assume the agency to speak for themselves and to challenge colonizationists, they were mistaken: "They should ever bear in mind, that if it is their prerogative to devise, it is ours to investigate. We are all interested." Russwurm, too, vowed that African Americans would voice their opinions on this crucial issue. Commenting in the August 17, 1827, issue on the supporters of colonization in New Haven, Russwurm stated, "The [American Colonization] Society has been very zealous and successful in imposing upon the public, the foolish *idea* that we are all longing to emigrate to their land of '*milk* and *honey*' . . . I deem it high time that our friends, in different parts of the Union, should know the truth of the matter—that we are all, to a man, opposed, in every shape, to the Colonization Society. . . ." He was even less charitable toward the ACS in an installment of his "Travelling Scraps" series published more than a year later. "We have always been candid on the subject," he maintained, "and wherever we have found open ears have always been ready to state our reasons for dissenting from our learned dictators."[35] The palpable anger and resentment in these statements toward those who patronizingly deemed to determine and dictate what was best for them reveals the strength and determination of African Americans in the late 1820s and the power *Freedom's Journal* gave them to resist being spoken for by others. They refused to be silenced by the tactics of white leaders who did not consult them; who wished them to follow blindly those who professed to be friends; or who, like Kennedy and Wilberforce, dismissed their opinions as irrational or uninformed.

The appeals of pro-colonization commentators notwithstanding, many contributors to *Freedom's Journal* considered the participation of slaveholders in the ACS a serious indictment of the organization. Cornish and

Russwurm put the matter bluntly in a June 1827 editorial: "What confidence can we have in members who express so much concern for the free men of colour, and yet hold their brethren in the most cruel bondage?" The editors acknowledged that "many admit this objection; and tell us, though our enemies are not actuated by good motives, yet their evil will be overruled for good," but they suggested that any "friends" who offered this defense of the ACS should remember that "good men have no right to compromise with injustice." Watkins—who noted that in his view "a philanthropic slaveholder is as great a solecism as a sober drunkard"— similarly asked "how these men can desire so ardently, and labour so abundantly, for the exaltation of the free people, thousands of whom they have never seen, and feel so little concern for those who are held in bondage by themselves." Until they "commence by proclaiming deliverance to their own captives," he remarked, African Americans would "continue to question the genuineness of their benevolence."[36]

The example of the ACS's president Bushrod Washington—slaveholder, Supreme Court justice, and nephew of George Washington—was particularly revealing. Far from freeing his slaves, Bushrod Washington sold fifty-four of them in 1821, a fact that the editors highlighted by reprinting an account of the sale from the Baltimore *Morning Chronicle*. Offering an ironic piece of advice to supporters of the ACS, Investigator implied that the endorsement of prominent slaveholders such as Washington exposed its true motives: "If the objects of the Society were emancipation, and the establishment of an asylum for the emancipated, why not tell Judge Washington, and a host of its slaveholding worthies, that they may abandon it at once? It is not fair that they should be deceived, and kept ignorant of its true motives."[37]

Investigator's point, of course, would not have been lost on *Freedom's Journal*'s readers. Slaveholders were hardly being "deceived." On the contrary, they were being deceptive; as Forten indicated in his aforementioned letter, the ACS and certain of its supporters "carefully disguised their intentions," which were in fact favorable to slaveholders. As contributor Veritas commented in a February 1828 article, if the effect of the ACS's proposals ran counter to the interests of slaveholders, why would many "citizens of *slave-holding states*" favor "a design so *perilous* to themselves"? Various contributors explicitly noted what they considered likely to be the actual result of colonization: if free people of color were removed from the United States, slavery would be strengthened. It was not only "erroneous and fallacious" to expect "anything of a beneficial nature, likely to result to the slaves" from the ACS's plans, contributor Clarkson affirmed; in reality, "a contrary effect will unavoidably follow the separation of their brethren, neighbours and friends, the free blacks." Not all colonizationists had such base motives; Cornish and Russwurm noted in a

June 1827 editorial that there were supporters of colonization who truly desired "emancipation; the salvation of Africa; and the extermination of the slave trade." Yet they were mistaken in thinking that colonization would have help achieve these goals. By contrast, the editors asserted, "the natural tendency of colonization is to retard emancipation."[38]

Contributors explained in detail the ways that the ACS's plans would serve to strengthen slavery. In a November 1827 letter to the newspaper, Richard Allen, prominent Philadelphian and Bishop of the African Methodist Episcopal Church, asked, "Is it not for the *interest* of the slave holder, to select, the free people of colour out of the different states, and send them to Liberia? Will it not make their slaves uneasy to see free men of colour enjoying *liberty*?"[39] Slaveholders, Allen revealed, feared the direct and indirect influence of free African Americans on slaves and saw colonization as a way to remove this potential threat to the institution. Russwurm suggested that colonization was a response to white fears of revolt and resistance by slaves and/or free people of color, noting that the "removal from this country" of free African Americans would increase slaveholders' "personal safety" as well as allow for "the better security of their slaves." Making explicit Russwurm's allusion, correspondent S**** B— apostrophized the ACS: "You are not ignorant that many [free blacks] are so far enlightened, as to know that they are unjustly, in this land of liberty, denied the rights and privileges of free citizens. . . . [I]f they continue to increase . . . the day *cannot* be far distant, when they will be able to obtain their natural rights by physical force. *This* is what you fear, and to prevent this, is the sole object in sending them out of this country."[40]

By removing free African Americans, colonization would also make slaves more valuable. A letter from a British abolitionist outlined the economic argument: "If their numbers increase, their labours will come into competition with the labour of the slaves, and in the end would destroy slavery itself. Is it not the feeling, that this scheme insures the existence of slavery, which causes it to be patronized by the slave holders?" Yet the value of slaves was maintained not only by limiting competition for their labor but also by keeping slaves from attaining knowledge. Literacy and liberty were intimately connected; slaveholders knew well that their power over an educated or literate slave was greatly diminished. Clarkson explained that "the suppression . . . of all intelligence and knowledge among slaves" was "universally considered necessary by masters to strengthen their security, and the general system of slavery." To get rid of free African Americans—or, for that matter, educated slaves—was to lessen the chances that their knowledge would be spread. Clarkson described "the danger apprehended by the masters from the diffusion, or existence of knowledge among the slaves" and remarked that colonization would "effectually arrest its further dissemination by the removal of those who possess it, no matter whether free blacks or slaves," who might "mingle with that class intended to be kept in abject bondage."[41]

The ACS's rhetoric as well as its plans could function to impede emancipation and to strengthen prejudices against African Americans. Members of the ACS, Clarkson indicated, "in common with a large majority of our citizens . . . view [people of color] . . . as an inferior race. . . ." The ACS's arguments, *Freedom's Journal*'s contributors emphasized, were insulting; as Watkins remarked, "We are, they say, 'an inferior race . . . a nuisance.' Not, indeed, that we have made ourselves so by our crimes,—no: but . . . because the Creator of all things . . . has thought proper, in his infinite wisdom, to tincture us with a darker hue than that of our white brethren." Such statements were threatening as well as offensive to African Americans. "Any plan," Investigator noted, "which implies in our brethren or their descendants, inferiority, or carries with it the idea that they cannot be raised to respectable standing in this country . . . is wholly at war with our best interests, and we cannot view the Advocates of such sentiments, in any other light, than that of enemies, whatever their principles may be." Those who, "from the press and the pulpit," described the "degradation of the coloured population," were "increasing prejudice" and "retarding the cause of emancipation." In addition, even those colonizationists who claimed prejudice was wrong but insisted on its intractability were apologizing for—and thereby enabling—racism. Investigator did not mince words when discussing the pro-colonization argument that African Americans could never attain their "rightful standing" in the United States: "Is this not deifying prejudice, and paying homage at the shrine of one of the grossest sins, that ever disgraced the human family?"[42]

Contributors to *Freedom's Journal* also pointed out two fundamental contradictions in the ACS's descriptions of African Americans. Clarkson explained, "The advocates of the colony at Liberia are endeavouring to acquire support, by representing in the first place, the total unfitness of our free coloured people to rise from their present ignorant condition and debasement in this country; and depicting in glowing colours, the future civilization and mental advancement of a whole continent through this establishment. . . . Here, then we have a contradiction in terms. . . ." Veritas similarly remarked that the colonizationists called African Americans "the most degraded, the most abandoned race on the earth," yet at the same time proposed that they should be "sent . . . to civilize and christianize the benighted Africans; to be the virtuous missionaries when in Africa, to awaken remorse among the natives for their crimes and idolatry." A related contradiction undermined the argument made by colonizationists, as we have seen, that the elevation of the colonists would help change public opinion in the United States, thereby lessening prejudice and allowing African Americans to gain more opportunities. Russwurm assessed this line of reasoning: "The man of colour while here can be nothing—but send him to the Elysian fields of Africa, and he returns to America, in two or three years a man of first rate intelligence; worth thousands."[43] The inconsistencies in their rhetoric exposed, colonizationists seemed to have neither the best interests of African Americans nor the natives of Africa at heart. Instead, they appeared to be opportunists who alternately presented blacks as degraded hindrances to American society and as potential saviors of Africa, as incapable of elevation and as potentially great merchants, all in an effort to persuade their various audiences—white racists, white philanthropists, or potential African-American emigrants—to accept their cause.

In addition to exposing the contradictions in pro-colonization rhetoric as evidence of hypocrisy, *Freedom's Journal*'s editors and contributors also used colonizationists' inconsistent claims to confront them with the limits of their philanthropy. Questioning the ACS in particular about their dedication to education, Watkins asked, "How much benevolence has been displayed by that philanthropic society, in preparing any of the emigrants that have left the country, for usefulness in the colony whither they have repaired? Would it not be more congenial with the professed object of that society to educate, pretty liberally, in this country, some portion of the emigrants. . . ?"[44] Watkins painted with a broad brush here; there were, in fact, efforts among some groups within the ACS to organize schools to prepare potential emigrants, and Jehudi Ashmun, the society's chief agent in the colony, reported the need for educated colonists.[45] Yet, as we have seen, many prominent ACS members declared publicly that African Americans should not be educated or given other opportunities to rise in America. And Watkins's challenge was clear: if colonizationists simultaneously argued that African Americans were "degraded" and that they were the key to Africa's future, should not the ACS's first priority be expanded educational opportunities for people of color in the United States?

Indeed, because they neglected the primary concerns of African Americans, Clarkson indicated, colonizationists' "professions of disinterested friendship for the African race" appeared shallow and insincere. Why, he inquired, did they not "pursue a course similar to that invariably followed by individuals and societies, whose great aim is to improve their condition . . . by appropriating part of its means in affording instruction . . . teaching them morality and religion; assisting and encouraging them in learning and pursuing the mechanic arts . . . [and] influencing the public sentiment in their favour"? Even those who did not believe that colonizationists' priorities were the result of malice or disingenuousness still regretted that their focus on colonization distracted them from truly seeking reform. An author of a February 1828 commentary, who "considered the education of the rising generations . . . of the highest importance," "lamented that philanthropists should be so misled" as to squander "vast sums" on "Colonization, which will never profit but the few" rather than spending money wisely on education, which "would bring about a new era in the history of [the] coloured population."[46]

In addition to offering philosophical and ideological objections to colonization, articles in *Freedom's Journal* presented practical concerns about the colony itself. African Americans were appropriately suspicious of the glowing reports of its supporters. In January 1828, Russwurm reprinted part of a letter to the senior editor of the *New-York Statesman*, written from the ship *Ontario*, in Port Mahon, Minorca. The writer noted that they were next "bound to Cape Mesurado" in Liberia—the correspondent's "third visit" there—"the El Dorado of some very worthy but enthusiastic people, who would not have heart to send their state-prison convicts to such a clime, still less our national ships, if they but knew half its horrors." The letter did not give details of these "horrors," but the author noted the difficulty of finding any authentic information about the colony, remarking that on this subject "an impartial man is nigri similis cygno"—like a black swan, or extremely rare—"if he is any way interested in the Augean task of changing our national complexion by the boasted specific African colonization."[47]

Russwurm echoed this skepticism in an editorial published two weeks later, in which he commented on a "long address from the happy citizens of Liberia" published in the previous month's issue of the *African Repository*. "Though opposed to the plans of the American Colonization Society," Russwurm affirmed, he was glad "to hear of the welfare of [his] brethren in all quarters of the globe" and "pleased to learn [the colonists'] progress in life." Yet he wondered if reports written by such interested sources could be trusted: "We do not deny that we have monthly reports from this *'paradise of bliss,'* but from what quarter do they emanate? From the pens of impartial men, or from those, who having formed visionary theories, are determined to try the experiment, no matter how many lives are sacrificed[?] With the writer on board the U. S. Ship Ontario, we believe . . . that an impartial man in this affair is 'nigri similis cygno.'" Even African-American emigrants themselves, correspondent Veritas noted in an article published the following month, were "persons interested" whose accounts may be biased. Veritas hypothesized that they "have possessed influence at home, and . . . on account of this fact being known, there have been dressed up with a little brief authority in Africa, received appointments, made Librarians &c. with salaries attached to them—and thus dazzled and gulled, write flaming epistles to their friends in America, persuading them to emigrate."[48]

Countering these pro-colonization accounts, contributors to *Freedom's Journal* cited specific concerns about the colony. Unlike Kennedy, Veritas did not downplay the deaths among colonists, noting that "the bill of mortality at the Colony in Africa, exceeds anything of the kind in so small a period of time I ever read of." Watkins compared the information of ACS secretary Gurley to that provided by a letter from "an intelligent Colonist from Baltimore" named Remus Harvey. Gurley lauded the schools in the colony, while Harvey noted that "education is at a very low ebb." Gurley declared the colony to have "resources . . . nearly adequate to its subsistence"; Harvey reported that "the colony experiences no small inconvenience *for want of the necessaries of life.*" Those who might wish to "judg[e] . . . these conflicting statements," Watkins maintained, should "bear in mind that Mr. Harvey is in Africa, and Mr. Gurley in America: and that it is more probable that Mr. Gurley should be misinformed than that Mr. Harvey should give a false statement." The aforementioned "Free Coloured Virginian" expressed concern about the future of the colony and the relationships between its different constituencies:

> What is to become of this colony, when it becomes sufficiently rich to tempt the rapacity of foreign governments? What to protect it from piratical despera-does? What are they to do, if having to contend, not only with external but internal foes? For to suppose that the natives will ever consider them in any other light than intruders, and consequently as enemies, is as fanciful as false.[49]

Considering the subsequent history of Western exploitation of Liberia and the troubled relationship between the indigenous people of Liberia and the colonists and their descendants, these concerns were strikingly prescient.

Above all, the objection of many African Americans to colonization was based on their identity as Americans and as part of a community that was committed to both its free and enslaved members. As we have seen, one of the newspaper's fundamental goals was to affirm African Americans' right to be active civic participants in American life and to empower them to do so. Challenging the ACS's contentions, Watkins proclaimed where his allegiances lay: "We are told that we can never be men, unless we abandon the land of our birth, 'our veritable home,' and people an uncongenial clime, the barbarous regions of Africa." African Americans' claim to the United States went beyond birth; they had contributed to the welfare and prosperity of the nation. The ACS "trifle[s] with the liberties of five hundred thousand freemen of colour," Investigator asserted, "whose rights to the country are equally as good as theirs, or any other citizens [*sic*], and many of whose fathers fought and bled for the liberty we enjoy." Noting the hypocrisy of a country to which "thousands of foreigners emigrat[ed] . . . every year" but that wished to "send the *first tillers* of the land away," Richard Allen emphatically claimed, "This land which we have watered with *our tears* and *our blood*, is now our *mother country* and we are well satisfied to stay where wisdom abounds, and the gospel is free."[50]

To accept colonization, furthermore, was for many not only to reject America and the struggle for full citizenship for free African Americans but also to abandon the slaves and the struggle for their liberty. "We can assure our friends of Liberia," Russwurm remarked in an editorial published in January 1828, "that . . . our views . . . extend not only to the improvement of our own condition, but to the ultimate emancipation of our brethren who are in bondage: and never shall we consent to emigrate from America, until their prior removal from this land of their degradation and suffering."[51] Many readers would no doubt have appreciated this sentiment and would have continued to hold it even after, a little over a year later, Russwurm informed them that he no longer did.

"A FREE MAN": RUSSWURM'S ENDORSEMENT OF COLONIZATION

The August 29, 1828, installment of Russwurm's "Travelling Scraps" column contained a brief account that, although it must have seemed unremarkable to readers at the time, appears more significant in hindsight. Describing his tour of the nation's capital, Russwurm commented on his "visit to the Secretary of the Colonization Society," R. R. Gurley. He offered some positive observations, noting that "the office . . . contains many articles of African ingenuity from Liberia and the surrounding country, worthy of inspection" and remarking that "for the agent of the Society [he has] always entertained the highest sentiments." Yet the article did not indicate any public change of sentiment on Russwurm's part; in contrast, as we have seen, he reaffirmed his editorial stance against colonization, maintaining that the criticism he had received for it confounded him and describing colonizationist leaders as "learned dictators."[52]

These strong words notwithstanding, in retrospect we can make certain observations. We need not discredit Russwurm's criticism of colonization and the ACS in this column to find evidence of a continuing interest in Liberia and a potential openness to changing his perspective about the colony. Russwurm had, as we have explored, previously entertained the notion of emigrating to Haiti and to Liberia, corresponding with ACS secretary Gurley in 1827 about a potential position. It was also Gurley to whom Russwurm applied in January 1829, asking for employment in the colony; as we have noted, his decision was the result of much introspection and investigation. It appears that Russwurm kept up his relationship with the ACS secretary, taking the time to visit him and to see the ACS office while in Washington. Of course, Russwurm did so as *Freedom's Journal*'s editor, providing readers with an account of the society's activities, but it is likely that he had a personal curiosity as well.

Perhaps the most compelling evidence that Russwurm's views began to change after August 1828 lies in the newspaper's columns. In issues subsequent to the one reporting this visit, Russwurm began to publish more positive news items about the colony, often reprinted from ACS publications. As we have seen, it was not unusual to find items from colonizationist sources in the newspaper from its beginning—the articles about African history explored in the previous chapter, for example, and the pieces contributed by Kennedy and other ACS members or supporters—yet a subtle but notable shift in editorial tone is present starting in the last few months of 1828. Russwurm began increasingly to choose to reprint informational items highlighting the success of the colony itself. Whereas earlier articles that contained positive accounts were published as part of the editorial commitment to allowing both sides to give their arguments, these accounts seem to demonstrate Russwurm's increasing attraction to Liberia and the ACS's colonial project rather than a concern with even debate.

In September 1828, for example, we find a brief article about the death of the ACS agent Jehudi Ashmun; an announcement of the society's appointment of a Colonial Agent to Liberia; and a reprinted account of a Georgia slaveholder who "recently sought aid of the Colonization Society, to remove the whole number of his slaves (43) to Liberia." The contrast between the latter piece and earlier contributions is notable. Articles about slaveholders freeing slaves in order to allow emigration to Haiti were, as we have seen, published previously in the newspaper, yet this piece highlighted the role of the ACS. Since pro-colonizationists asserted that the ACS's plans facilitated emancipations, the inclusion of this piece seems to connote at least a willingness on Russwurm's part to entertain this argument. The following month, Russwurm printed in the newspaper a report from Gurley of a meeting of the ACS's Board of Managers outlining the terms of trade between "such colonists, as are desirous of carrying on trade with the United States in Liberian vessels."[53] Perhaps Russwurm published this statement to validate the ACS's claims about how the colony would facilitate trade, particularly among those African Americans who chose to emigrate; perhaps he was doing Gurley a favor by publicizing the ACS's activities; perhaps he simply found the account interesting and wanted to share it with others. In any event, it appears that Russwurm was giving consideration to the ACS's plans and publications, and he felt that his readers should be aware of them as well.

As we have discovered, Russwurm had determined by January 1829 that he would leave the United States for Liberia after he had completed the second year of *Freedom's Journal*'s run. Although he did not announce this decision to the newspaper's readers until February 14, it is clear that his personal plans affected his editing, as the number of published accounts from Liberia and ACS reports increased. Reprinted articles described emigrants leaving the United States for Liberia, reported on masters' emancipating slaves to emigrate to the colony and on the generosity of donors who gave funds to the society, and invited potential colonists to apply to the ACS.[54] Written for the white press rather than specifically for *Freedom's Journal*, these accounts did not demonstrate the attempts to appeal to African Americans' views that were evident in the original contributions to the newspaper of Kennedy and other ACS supporters. Instead of taking into account that many African Americans were opposed to colonization, for example, a reprinted piece from the *African Repository* asserted confidently that "the disposition to remove is daily increasing among the free people of colour, and hence all who desire the improvement of their condition, or Africa's redemption, should go forward with more burning zeal and mightier resolution." An article originally published in the *Ontario Repository* announcing a donation to the ACS quoted the sentiments of the donor, Philadelphia bookseller and printer Matthew Carey. Hardly a friend to African Americans, as we have seen by his denigration of the heroic black nurses during the 1793 yellow fever epidemic, Carey speculated about the probable "increase of the coloured population of the United States . . . unless some efficient measures of prevention be adopted" and asked, "Who can regard this increase without affright?"[55]

The issue of February 14, 1829, as we have discussed, made public what Russwurm had already informed Gurley: his "views" on colonization were "materially altered." Since *Freedom's Journal*'s last issue was published on March 28, 1829, Russwurm had only seven issues in which to openly advocate colonization. In addition to continuing to reprint news items about Liberia and ACS reports,[56] Russwurm devoted much of his commentary to defending his altered position. In his editorial announcing his changed outlook, Russwurm maintained, "We consider it mere waste of words to talk of ever enjoying citizenship in this country: it is utterly impossible in the nature of things: all therefore who pant for these, must cast their eyes elsewhere." In this statement, the common pro-colonization argument that African Americans could never enjoy equality in the United States took on a different tone from that of white ACS supporters, capturing the personal frustration of an educated and talented man who was discouraged by the "limited" nature of "the different plans now in operation for [African Americans'] benefit." Russwurm's editorials published the following weeks were similarly infused with emotion. In the United States, he remarked, African Americans "cannot enjoy the privileges of citizens, for certain reasons known and felt daily"; "the man of colour . . . must be sensible of the degraded station he holds in society; and from which it is impossible to rise, unless he can change the Ethiopian hue of his complexion." Although he endorsed the ACS's plans, he fervently declared his desire for self-determination and pride, noting that in Africa, his brethren "may enjoy all the rights of freemen . . . [they] may not only feel as men, but . . . [they] may also act as such."[57]

Russwurm offered readers other reasons to support colonization as well, similar to those put forth by white colonizationists. He rejected the argument "that Southern interests completely guide the plans" of the ACS and "that all their movements tend to fetter more closely the chains of the enslaved." In contrast, he argued, many emancipations had been inspired by the society. Liberia was a rich, abundant land, he asserted, downplaying reports of disease; the colony would not only flourish itself but "in progress of time, [it] may be the means of disseminating civilization & christianity throughout the whole of that vast continent." Russwurm maintained as well that prejudice in the United States was an intractable and permanent force: "Should each of us live to the age of Methusalah, at the end of the thousand years, we should be exactly in our present situation: a proscribed race, however, unjustly—a degraded people, deprived of all the rights of freemen; and in the eyes of the community, a race, who had no lot nor portion with them."[58]

Ultimately, though, Russwurm's editorials following his statement of his conversion relied more on his passion and commitment than on particular logical appeals to make his case. In fervent, even religious language, he invited readers to feel the power of his own belief in the colony and its promise. In his editorial of March 7, Russwurm declared,

> Have we any young men, whose constant prayer is to be useful in their day, and who are in want of a situation: "we point to Liberia." Have we any middle aged men with families, who are anxious that their children should enjoy all the rights of freemen . . . we point to Liberia as our promised Land; from whose borders shall issue in progress of time thousands who shall go forth, as pioneers of civilization and heralds of the Cross, into the vast regions of that hitherto unexplored quarter of the globe.

He reasserted his belief that emigration to the colony was the key to an independent and meaningful future for African Americans in his editorial published the following week: "Can any consider it a mark of folly, for us to cast our eyes, upon some other portion of the globe . . . where the Man of Colour freed from the fetters and prejudice and degradation, under which he labours in this land, may walk forth in all the majesty of his creation—a new born creature—a *Free Man!*"[59]

The fact that most of his readers would have remained unconvinced did not diminish Russwurm's powerful advocacy of the cause. Indeed, his fervor about his view after his conversion as well as before demonstrates that, as George Walker asserts, for antebellum African Americans, "with the single exception of slavery, no other question was capable of evoking such an intense and widespread emotional response as colonization."[60] Like his former partner Cornish, like various contributors to the newspaper, Russwurm faced the issues of colonization directly and passionately, never shying away from the implications of either support or rejection of the cause, always realizing just how challenging, complex, and controversial the issue was and would remain.

NOTES

1. Wright, "Progress," in Woodson, *Negro Orators*, 87–88.
2. Samuel E. Cornish and John B. Russwurm, "To Our Patrons," *FJ*, 16 March 1827; Samuel E. Cornish and John B. Russwurm, "Colonization Society," *FJ*, 14 September 1827.
3. Russwurm to Gurley, New York, 26 January 1829.
4. V. P. Franklin, *Black Self-Determination*, 89–90; Samuel Stevens for the African Company to the African Union Society [Newport, Rhode Island], Boston, 1 June 1787, in Sterling, *Speak Out*, 6. On the distinction between plans dominated by whites and those controlled by African Americans, see also Vincent Thompson, *Africans*, 203–4; Saillant, "Circular," 486. On Thornton, see also Horton and Horton, *In Hope*, 179–180; Floyd Miller, *Search*, 9–12.
5. "Negro Enterprize," *FJ*, 3 August 1827; "Removal of Slaves to Hayti," *FJ*, 21 December 1827; "More General Philanthropy," *FJ*, 16 January 1829.
6. This biographical sketch of Cuffe draws from Floyd Miller, *Search*, 21–53; Thomas, *Rise*; Sheldon Harris, *Paul Cuffe*. In some accounts, Cuffe is spelled Cuffee.
7. Floyd Miller, *Search*, 28.
8. "Memoirs of Capt. Paul Cuffee," *FJ*, 16 March 1827.
9. "Memoirs of Capt. Paul Cuffee," *FJ*, 13 April 1827. The immediate fate of Richards upon arriving in Liverpool, although not mentioned in the article, was less heartening (and no doubt less flattering to British public opinion). He was, explains Lamont Thomas, "taken captive by a press gang" and detained by British authorities; and the intervention of British philanthropists, including Thomas Clarkson, was necessary to free him (*Rise*, 58–59; see also Cuffe's journal entries in Sheldon Harris, *Paul Cuffe*, 89–93, 97–99).
10. Floyd Miller, *Search*, 49.
11. "Missions to Africa," *FJ*, 16 March 1827.
12. Samuel E. Cornish and John B. Russwurm, "Colonization Society," *FJ*, 8 June 1827; Investigator, "Colonization Society. No I," *FJ*, 7 September 1827.
13. "African Mission School Society," *FJ*, 28 February 1829; "For the Freedom's Journal," *FJ*, 7 March 1829.
14. Cornish and Russwurm, "Colonization Society," *FJ*, 8 June 1827.
15. Junior Editor [John B. Russwurm], "Wilberforce," *FJ*, 7 September 1827.
16. Most historical accounts emphasize the rhetoric of African-American leaders who opposed colonization and/or the arguments made by white members of

the ACS and their supporters for white audiences. See, for example, Kinshasa, *Emigration vs. Assimilation*; Castiglia, "Pedagogical Discipline"; Davis, "Northern Colonizationists"; Rosen, "Abolition." Floyd Miller mentions the publication in *Freedom's Journal* of the rhetoric of John H. Kennedy, assistant to ACS corresponding secretary R. R. Gurley (*Search*, 86), yet he does not explore Kennedy's arguments in detail.

17. Wilberforce, letter to editors, *FJ*, 7 September 1827.

18. John H. Kennedy, "American Colonization Society. No. III," *FJ*, 28 September 1827; J[ohn] H. K[ennedy], "American Colonization Society. No. I," *FJ*, 14 September 1827. Kennedy signed the first two installments with his initials, subsequently using his full name. In a headnote to the third of the series, Russwurm included a letter from Kennedy stating that he had decided to use his full name for two reasons: "1. In case of opposition, that the arguments might be met with calmness, a more likely case where the adversary stands confessed. 2. A conviction that the arguments . . . which else will be laid aside without a perusal, or after a very cursory one, would be seriously pondered by many coloured persons, who know the writer as one who has always felt and manifested a sympathy in their sorrows."

19. A Subscriber, "Colonization Society" [letter to editors], *FJ*, 24 August 1827; J[ohn] H. K[ennedy], "American Colonization Society. No. II," *FJ*, 21 September 1827.

20. Kennedy, "American Colonization Society. No. III"; Wilberforce, letter.

21. A Subscriber, "Colonization Society"; Kennedy, "American Colonization Society. No. III"; John H. Kennedy, "American Colonization Society. No. IV," *FJ*, 5 October 1827.

22. Kennedy, "American Colonization Society. No. III"; Subscriber, "Colonization Society."

23. See, for example, [Burgess], *Address*, 28; McMurray, *Sermon*; Philip Hay, *Our Duty*.

24. John H. Kennedy, "American Colonization Society. No. V.—(Concluded.)," *FJ*, 19 October 1827; John H. Kennedy, "American Colonization Society. No. VI," *FJ*, 26 October 1827.

25. John H. Kennedy, "American Colonization Society. No. V," *FJ*, 12 October 1827; Kennedy, "American Colonization Society. No. V—Concluded."

26. Kennedy, "American Colonization Society. No. V," 12 October 1827.

27. Wilberforce, letter; Kennedy, "American Colonization Society. No. IV."

28. See, for example, [Burgess], *Address*, 12–13, 27; *Proceedings of a Meeting of the Friends of African Colonization*, 9–10.

29. Kennedy, "American Colonization Society. No. I"; Kennedy, "American Colonization Society. No. IV"; A Subscriber, "Colonization Society."

30. A Subscriber, "Colonization Society"; Kennedy, "American Colonization Society. No. III."

31. A Subscriber, "Colonization Society"; Investigator, "Colonization Society" [letter to editors], *FJ*, 31 August 1827.

32. Samuel E. Cornish and John B. Russwurm, letter to editors of the *New-York Observer*, *Freedom's Journal*, 21 September 1827. We can conclude that this letter was written by both Cornish and Russwurm even though it appeared in *Freedom's*

Journal in the first issue that Russwurm edited on his own; it referred to *Freedom's Journal*'s "editors" and distinguished the "junior Editor." A headnote to the full text in *Freedom's Journal* provided an arch comment on the decision of the *Observer*'s editors to print only part of Cornish and Russwurm's correspondence: "We transfer the whole to our columns, believing, that had the Doctor's [Miller's] communication [to the *Observer*] been twice its present length, the whole would have been inserted."

33. Cornish and Russwurm, letter to editors of the *New-York Observer*; A Man of Colour [James Forten], letter to editors, *FJ*, 18 May 1827; Investigator, "Colonization Society. No. I." A decade after its publication in *Freedom's Journal*, Cornish reprinted the letter from "A Man of Colour" in the *Colored American*, 13 May 1837, specifying that it was written by Forten (I am indebted to Julie Winch's *A Gentleman of Color*, 205, for bringing this identification to my attention).

34. A Coloured Baltimorean [William Watkins], "Colonization Society" [letter to editors], *FJ*, 6 July 1827; A Coloured Baltimorean [William Watkins], "American Colonization Society," *FJ*, 11 July 1828; A Free Coloured Virginian, "For the Freedom's Journal," *FJ*, 6 July 1827. Bettye Gardner identifies Watkins as the author of the first letter; Watkins used this pseudonym in various letters to the *Genius of Universal Emancipation* and the *Liberator* as well ("Opposition to Emigration"; see also Bacon, *Humblest*, 52; Ripley et al., *Black Abolitionist Papers*, vol. 3, 96).

35. A Coloured Baltimorean [Watkins], "Colonization Society"; John B. Russwurm, "To the Senior Editor—No. III," *FJ*, 17 August 1827; John B. Russwurm, "Travelling Scraps," *FJ*, 29 August 1828.

36. Cornish and Russwurm, "Colonization Society," 8 June 1827; A Coloured Baltimorean [Watkins], "Colonization Society."

37. "From the Baltimore Morning Chronicle," *FJ*, 14 September 1827; Investigator, "Colonization Society. No I."

38. A Man of Colour [Forten], letter; Veritas, "Colonization Society," *FJ*, 29 February 1828; Clarkson, "Colonization Society. No. II," *FJ*, 19 October 1827; Cornish and Russwurm, "Colonization Society," *FJ*, 8 June 1827.

39. Richard Allen, "Letter from Bishop Allen" [letter to editor], *FJ*, 2 November 1827. Russwurm explained in a headnote to the letter that it was written at the editor's "*request, to contradict certain reports, of [Allen's] having become a convert to the colonization* scheme." As we have seen, Allen endorsed Haitian emigration in the mid-1820s; he also had been a supporter of Cuffe and had seemed willing during the previous decade to consider other African colonization ventures. Yet he opposed the white-dominated ACS. See Floyd Miller, *Search*, 48–51, 74, 78.

40. John B. Russwurm, "To the Senior Editor—No. III," *FJ*, 17 August 1827; S**** B—, "Colonization Society," *FJ*, 9 November 1827.

41. J**** C******, letter to editors, *FJ*, 10 August 1827; Clarkson, "American Colonization Society," *FJ*, 30 November 1827.

42. Clarkson, "American Colonization Society"; A Coloured Baltimorean [Watkins], "Colonization Society"; Investigator, "Colonization Society," *FJ*, 31 August 1827; Investigator, "Colonization Society. No. II," *FJ*, 5 October 1827.

43. Clarkson, "American Colonization Society. No. IV," *FJ*, 16 November 1827; Veritas, "Colonization Society," *FJ*, 7 March 1828; John B. Russwurm, "To Rev. Samuel E. Cornish," *FJ*, 2 November 1827.

44. A Coloured Baltimorean [Watkins], "Colonization Society."

45. See Vincent Franklin, "Education."

46. Clarkson, "American Colonization Society. No. IV"; untitled and unsigned response to F.A., letter, *FJ*, 15 February 1828.

47. "Extract of a Letter to the Senior Editor of the New-York Statesman, Dated U. S. Ship Ontario Mahon, 12th October 1827," *FJ*, 11 January 1828.

48. John B. Russwurm, "Liberian Circular," *FJ*, 25 January 1828; Veritas, "Colonization Society," *FJ*, 29 February 1828.

49. Veritas, "Colonization Society," *FJ*, 29 February 1828; A Coloured Baltimorean [William Watkins], "American Colonization Society Continued," *FJ*, 18 July 1828.

50. A Coloured Baltimorean [Watkins], "Colonization Society"; Investigator, "Colonization Society. No. I"; Allen, "Letter."

51. Russwurm, "Liberian Circular."

52. Russwurm, "Travelling Scraps," *FJ*, 29 August 1828.

53. "Death of Mr. Ashmun," *FJ*, 12 September 1828; "The African Colony," *FJ*, 26 September 1828; "Liberality," *FJ*, 26 September 1828; R. R. Gurley, report of Board of Managers of the ACS, 6 October 1828, *FJ*, 17 October 1828.

54. "Expedition to Liberia," *FJ*, 2 January 1829; "Emigrants to Liberia," *FJ*, 7 February 1829; "Emancipation and Colonization," *FJ*, 2 January 1829; "American Colonization Society," *FJ*, 24 January 1829; untitled account of donation to ACS, *FJ*, 31 January 1829; "Expedition to Liberia," *FJ*, 9 January 1829.

55. "Expedition to Liberia," *FJ*, 2 January 1829; "American Colonization Society," *FJ*, 24 January 1829.

56. See, for example, "Migration to Liberia," *FJ*, 14 February 1829; ACS, "Ann. Meeting of the Colonization Society," *FJ*, 7 March 1829; ACS, "Plan of Civil Government for the Colony of Liberia," *FJ*, 28 March 1829; "Latest from Liberia," *FJ*, 28 March 1829.

57. John B. Russwurm, "Liberia," *FJ*, 14 February 1829; John B. Russwurm, "Liberia," *FJ*, 21 February 1829; John B. Russwurm, "Our Vindication," *FJ*, 7 March 1829.

58. Russwurm, "Liberia," 21 February 1829; Russwurm, "Our Vindication"; John B. Russwurm, "Colonization," *FJ*, 14 March 1829.

59. Russwurm, "Our Vindication"; Russwurm, "Colonization."

60. George Walker, "Afro-American," 272.

8

~

"Our Brethren Who Are Still in Bondage": Slavery and Antislavery

A s we have discovered, the broad coverage of diverse subjects in *Freedom's Journal* renders any description of the newspaper as solely an antislavery periodical reductive. Yet slavery was very much on the minds of its editors, contributors, and readers. Cornish and Russwurm asserted in their opening editorial the fundamental connection between free African Americans and slaves: "We would not be unmindful of our brethren who are still in bondage. They are our kindred by all the ties of nature; and though but little can be effected by us, still let our sympathies be poured forth, and our prayers in their behalf, ascend to Him who is able to succour them." It is clear that African Americans throughout the free states felt the link to slaves that Cornish and Russwurm described. *Freedom's Journal* reprinted an 1827 report, for example, about the celebration of the abolition of slavery in New York in one (unnamed) town. The people of color there "seem[ed] not to have forgotten that a part of their race are still in bondage," the account related, "and instead of firing as many guns as there are states in the Union, fired only the number of those that acknowledge the African's right, as well as the white man's, to breathe the air of liberty."[1]

Free African Americans also, in many cases, had concrete connections to slavery; they or their parents might have been slaves, for example, or a family member might still have been in bondage. In addition, as we have seen, they faced the threats of kidnapping and enslavement, whether or not they were actually fugitives. Naturally, then, slavery was a significant topic for news and commentary in *Freedom's Journal*.

In fact, as Russwurm declared in an early 1829 editorial, no other subject was more critical:

> Give as much importance as we may to other subjects, to us SLAVERY is the all absorbing one—before it all others fall into insignificance: and the reason is obvious; nearly TWO MILLIONS of HUMAN BEINGS are held in a state never designed by their Creator, in this Republic . . . we are bold therefore, in denouncing Slavery as an unnatural state, and one upon which a beneficent Being can never look with complacency.[2]

To fully investigate the coverage of slavery in *Freedom's Journal* and the ways that the editors and contributors sought to resist its power and to explore its abolition, we must not limit our perceptions of how antebellum African Americans viewed slavery and what, for them, constituted resistance. Historians have traditionally dated the beginning of abolitionist activity in the United States in the early 1830s, starting with the publication in 1831 of William Lloyd Garrison's *Liberator*.[3] As we have explored—and as recent scholarship demonstrates—these accounts are incomplete. African Americans, both individually and in community organizations, opposed and fought slavery long before white Americans became radicalized.[4] By the 1820s, African Americans were arguing intensely and forcefully against slavery; indeed, their efforts influenced the later work of their white colleagues.

To place the coverage of slavery in *Freedom's Journal* in its proper context, we must view antislavery activity and rhetoric expansively. We cannot, for example, restrict our investigation to organizations devoted solely to abolition or texts that argued explicitly for an immediate end to slavery. For African Americans, antislavery concerns were addressed in religious organizations and self-help groups; and the questions of civil rights and equality that were the focus of much activism were linked, both explicitly and implicitly, to resistance to slavery.[5] The interrelatedness of various forms of oppression influenced the coverage of slavery in *Freedom's Journal*, in which slavery and antislavery were considered in articles about a range of concerns. Reports both of the gruesome realities of enslavement and the practical ways that African Americans opposed it also linked free black readers to slaves. In addition, the newspaper's editors and contributors sought to uncover the ideological bases for slavery and to refute proslavery rhetoric and the assumptions—scriptural, economic, and political—on which it was based. Although these examinations often did not explicitly address the question of abolition, they, too, constituted attacks on slavery and its power.

The coverage of slavery in *Freedom's Journal*, as we shall see, is wide-ranging, varied, and powerful. Yet there is an aspect of it that, at first glance, might seem problematic. Cornish and Russwurm's declaration that their readers could do "but little" except offer "sympathies" and "prayers" might appear to have been a tepid response compared to the rhetoric of African-American and white abolitionists of the 1830s who advocated immediate abolition. Indeed, although a few articles in *Freedom's Journal* expressed support for a direct and rapid end to the system, many contributors either proposed a gradual approach as the only practical method of abolition or offered no concrete plans for ending slavery. Yet we must resist the temptation to judge the coverage of slavery in *Freedom's Journal* anachronistically as somehow inferior to the abolitionist texts which followed it. For a variety of reasons, as we shall discuss, gradual abolition may have seemed to be the only feasible approach to ending slavery (or at least the only method that it was safe for the newspaper to endorse).

In addition, to deem *Freedom's Journal*'s coverage of slavery conciliatory or inadequate is to diminish its role in the antislavery movement. Traditional formulations that posit that only explicitly immediatist rhetoric was militant and that other antislavery argumentation was necessarily compromised are reductive. We shall see that there were many forceful antislavery texts in *Freedom's Journal* that did not advocate a particular plan for immediate abolition, even many that did not specifically address methods for ending the institution, that were nonetheless adamant in condemning slavery and insisting that African Americans resist its power. We must not forget that the immediatist rhetoric of African-American and white abolitionists of the 1830s and beyond was built on the impressive foundations laid by the editors of and contributors to *Freedom's Journal*.

"BLESSINGS OF SLAVERY": DOMESTIC AND INTERNATIONAL NEWS

As we have noted, in fulfilling their promise to bring readers "all the principal news of the day," Cornish and Russwurm offered them alternatives to white press coverage, which generally either disregarded or disparaged African Americans. Reports about slavery were particularly significant, since, as we have seen, white editors in the North often attempted to suggest that nothing could be done about slavery, to ignore it altogether, or to defend it. In white newspapers and other popular texts of the time, slavery's supporters asserted that slaves were well cared for and treated kindly. Indeed, proslavery writers from the colonial period onward had argued that slaves enjoyed pleasant, happy lives, free of the burdens and cares of most human beings. Eighteenth- and nineteenth-century defenses of the institution proposed that slavery was beneficial to Africans, some even deeming it a "blessing."[6] In the words of American apologist Robert

Walsh Jr. in his 1819 *Appeal from the Judgments of Great Britain Respecting the United States of America*, the "physical condition" of slaves was "on the whole, not comparatively alone, but positively good"; indeed, he argued, slaves were "exempt from those racking anxieties—the exacerbations of despair, to which the English manufacturer and peasant are subject to in the pursuit of their pittance."[7]

The cruelty, oppression, and dehumanization of slavery, of course, put the lie to any claim that slaves were content or well treated. Providing accounts of these realities, *Freedom's Journal* offered readers a counterweight to proslavery claims and an alternative to the general reluctance and neglect of many white editors about the topic of slavery. *Freedom's Journal* brought to light the truths that many Americans would rather avoid and constantly reminded free African Americans of the oppression faced by their "brethren who were still in bondage." Publishing such information about slavery was thus a means of connecting free African Americans and slaves, a way of activating the "sympathies" to which the editors referred in their opening editorial. If, as the editors proposed, free African-American readers and slaves were "kindred by all the ties of nature," the stark and often gruesome details in these accounts would have been powerful to readers, strengthening their resolve to oppose slavery on emotional as well as theoretical and practical levels.[8] Since, as we have discussed, there was not a clear demarcation in newspapers of the time between articles providing news and those offering opinions, reports about slavery were at times included in essays that argued a particular point of view or were combined with commentary from the editors and contributors.

Accounts in *Freedom's Journal* of the horrors of slavery were brief at times, yet they vividly revealed the system's brutality and capriciousness. Two men "recently killed a slave in North-Carolina, because he could not travel further on account of debility" and "left him lying on the public highway"; a slave was "killed by one Clark, for taking the part of his master, during a quarrel between them"; a Kentucky slave was "murdered by his master and another man, without any material provocation." Other narratives provided more detail. An 1827 article titled "Horrible! Most Horrible!"—originally published in the *Genius of Universal Emancipation*—described the gruesome lynching of an Alabama slave (indeed, as we have noted, it is the first known newspaper report of a lynching). After "a neighboring planter" suspected the slave of theft and "seized him," the "sable culprit" stabbed him. Handed over to a mob by a justice of the peace, the captive was "immediately executed by being *burnt to death*."[9]

An article reprinted from the *Richmond Compiler* described the excruciating death of a slave at the hands of his master. As a means of "punishing him for some offence," the master ordered the slave to be put on a chair in a smoke house with a rope around his neck. The slave "strangled to death." Although the Southern newspaper's report did not condemn the act—it noted, in fact, that the "Jury are said to be of opinion, that [the master] intended no injury to the boy"—the gruesome description revealed otherwise. An additional message was conveyed through the reprinting of this article in *Freedom's Journal* with its commentary about the jury's excuse for the act: the atrocities of slavery were tolerated by Southerners. An account titled "Hunting Men" made the point explicit: "It is stated in a Savannah paper, as if it were an affair of ordinary occurrence, that a runaway negro had been apprehended and sent to jail, though 'he did not surrender until he was considerably maimed by the dogs that had been set upon him.'"[10]

The dehumanizing effects of slavery were displayed vividly in the newspaper through reports of the domestic slave trade. This commerce was flourishing in the late 1820s, particularly from the Upper South and Eastern Shore of the country to the Deep South.[11] Information about those who were the most visible participants in this business—the slave traders—naturally made its way into *Freedom's Journal*. Despite the tolerance of slavery in many parts of the nation, antebellum Americans, in the South as well as the North, slaveholders included, claimed to disapprove of slave dealers, and frequently described them in highly negative terms.[12] Thus it would not have been unusual for readers of antebellum newspapers to encounter criticisms of those engaged in this profession. Yet the negative rhetoric about slave traders and the insistence that they were hated and condemned, as Frederic Bancroft explains in his classic *Slave Trading in the Old South*, actually "served as a shield." While the character of the slave trader "was made the scapegoat for the conspicuous evils of slave-selling" in Southern rhetoric, those dealers who were prosperous were accepted in Southern society, advertising publicly in newspapers and enjoying prominent social standing.[13] In addition, slave traders carried out their work because they were encouraged, supported, and assisted by numerous others, from the slaveholders who sold to or bought from them to the officials, lawmakers, and jurists who protected them. The accounts reprinted and summarized by *Freedom's Journal*'s editors called attention to slave trading in a way that powerfully revealed these ugly truths that many antebellum Americans would rather not have examined.

Notably, the accounts provided to *Freedom's Journal*'s readers indicated that slave dealers were not solely responsible for the evils of the trade, calling attention to those who enabled and defended them. An 1827 notice that "John Smith, the well known Slave dealer has been confined some time in the gaol of Hartford for debts principally due in Massachusetts, to the amount of $80,000," for example, noted that "a desperate attempt was made to liberate him by 4 men." Although they were unsuccessful, it was clear that Smith had assistants or supporters.[14]

An article ironically titled "Baltimore Justice!!" similarly placed a slave trader named Austin Woolfolk into a larger context. A Baltimorean from a family engaged in the business, Woolfolk was one of the most notorious slave dealers of his time—so much so that his name, or the variation "Woldfolk," was used by some slaves to refer to any trader. When, in January 1827, Benjamin Lundy described Woolfolk as a "monster in human shape" and an "Ishmaelite" in the pages of the *Genius of Universal Emancipation*—adding, "Hereafter, let no man speak of the humanity of Woolfolk"—Woolfolk physically attacked Lundy in the street.[15] The slave dealer was arrested and convicted, but the sentence of one dollar revealed the judge's dismissal of the crime.[16] The article in *Freedom's Journal* noted the judge's comments:

> Chief Justice Brice, in pronouncing sentence, took occasion to observe that he had never seen a case in which the provocation for a battery was greater than the present—that if abusive language could ever be a justification for battery, this was the case—that the traverser was engaged in trade sanctioned by the laws of Maryland . . . that the trade itself was beneficial to the state, as it removed a great many rogues and vagabonds . . . that Lundy had received no more than a merited chastisement for his abuse of the traverser, and but for the strict letter of the law, the Court would not fine Woodfolk [*sic*] any thing.[17]

This account—and the ironic title under which it was published—made it clear that not only Woolfolk was blameworthy. The "laws of Maryland" and those who enforced them were on his side, to the extent that the victim became, in the judge's opinion, the offender.

Other accounts of slave trading drew attention to the impact on the human beings subjected to public examination and sale as well as on the nation that tolerated this commerce. An article in the first issue of the newspaper described a slave named William, "a very pious, humble Christian," sold to a trader—a "detestable person"—"for about $265." This article, originally published in the New York *Christian Advocate*, a publication of the Methodist Episcopal Church, noted William's Christian resignation to his fate, but it did not downplay the harsh realities that he faced, the likelihood that he would be sold "far, very far from his native place," and the possibility that he would "fall into the hands of some hard, tyrannical master." An 1828 article included the description from "an inhabitant of a southern state" of a group of slaves, "torn from" their loved ones, "chained together like wild beasts," "driven by inhuman monsters in the shape of men," and soon "to be sold to inhuman task masters." "My feelings revolted, and my soul sickened at the sight," the Southerner reflected. "I exclaimed, can this be a 'land of liberty.'"[18]

Perhaps the most glaring example of the duplicity this Southern witness identified was the presence of slave dealing in the very capital of a nation ostensibly devoted to liberty. Recounting his visit to Washington in an August 1828 article, Russwurm noted that it was "disgraceful that in the Capital of a Republic which boasts of the enjoyment of more liberty than other states or kingdoms," human beings were sold, "in the face of open day, under the sanction of a constitution which proclaims that *'we hold these truths to be self-evident, that all men are created equal, and endowed by their Creator with certain inalienable rights; that among these are life, LIBERTY, and the pursuit of happiness.'*" A reprinted article from the *Albany Daily Advertiser* highlighted the stark contradiction:

> Nothing is more common than to be entertained in the capitol by the impassioned eloquence of a Virginian or South Carolinian orator on the subject of the equal rights of men, and upon leaving the house and descending from Capitol Hill, to meet in Pennsylvania Avenue, droves of slaves, who have been sold in the Washington market, chained to a bar of iron, and who are to be driven in a condition worse than brutes, by the lash of a monster in human form, to the more southern plantations.

The author made it clear that the fault lay not with Southerners alone, noting with dismay that a New York assemblyman opposed a resolution expressing "disapprobation" of the slave trade in the District.[19]

The national complicity implied in these accounts was noted explicitly in a reprinted account from the *Genius of Universal Emancipation*, whose title—"Blessings of Slavery in Baltimore, MD.!!"—evoked ironically both the notion of slavery's "blessings" to the enslaved advocated in proslavery rhetoric and the phrase "the blessings of liberty" from the Constitution.[20] As we have noted, for African Americans to rewrite and revise the meanings of dominant phrases in ironic fashion is a powerful rhetorical strategy, a form of signifying.[21] The irony was underscored in the article itself. "On last sabbath," the author Y. related, "a day which we should remember to keep holy . . . was seen marching in solemn procession through this *republican*, nay *christian* city, a wretched train of human beings, men, women and children, (about 27) chained and handcuffed!!!" Y. harshly criticized the nation for its insincere commitment to freedom: "But on this subject you are not to say a word—You must hush these things into silence, and join with those who can tell us on the 4th July . . . that 'oppression is no where heard in all our happy land,' that 'the voice of liberty resounds from the centre to the circumference. . . . May God save you from such consummated hypocrisy and such glaring inconsistencies." Shifting from "you" to "we," Y. emphasized the nation's collective complicity and guilt:

> It is not to be expected that we, who encourage, in any way, the barbarous slave trade, shall escape those judgments which are congregating in the

stores of heaven. . . . We are aware that the statute book of Maryland, so far from denouncing such flagrant violations of the law of God, sanctions this iniquitous traffic, thus affording encouragement to the slave traders. . . . Shall we license the slave trader to buy and sell his fellow man, and tell him he shall be indemnified?[22]

As Y.'s reference to the laws of Maryland indicated, beneath the everyday horrors and atrocities of slavery lay the complex system of laws and judicial decisions that enabled them. Reprinting a variety of reports about legal issues, *Freedom's Journal's* editors exposed these foundations and helped readers to understand how the nation's courts as well as state and national laws justified, strengthened, and perpetuated slavery. An article reprinted from the *Genius of Universal Emancipation* described "a *domestic slave ship*" transporting "200 souls" from Baltimore to New Orleans, in which the slaves were "chained in pairs in the hold." The author noted the legal hypocrisy: because the international slave trade to the United States had been outlawed, "the utmost vengeance of the law [was] meted" out to any American citizen participating in "the horror of the African slave trade"; yet domestic commerce in slaves was sanctioned by the "lame and relaxed" laws that permitted it. Other laws shored up slavery's power. Another article with the same biting title as Y.'s account—"Blessings of Slavery"—remarked on the passage of a bill in the South Carolina legislature "to prohibit the instruction of people of colour in reading and writing." The author's description of the reasons for this proscription demonstrated how masters maintained their power over slaves: "The slave holders at the south are conscious that 'knowledge is power,' and that the diffusion of light among their slaves would rouse up a host of armed men, ready to give the dreadful retribution of emancipated bondage."[23]

Freedom's Journal's editors were also interested in international news about slavery. They featured articles that reported on particular aspects of slavery in other regions of the world, in effect placing American slavery into a global context. Although judgments about whether slavery was more or less "harsh" or "mild" in some regions of the world than in others are problematic in many ways, they served certain purposes. By informing readers that slaves in various other countries were treated more humanely than those in the United States or given some rights not experienced by their American counterparts, the editors put the lie to the notion that American slavery could be excused as simply a manifestation of a perpetual system that was an inevitable part of human societies, past and present, throughout the world. In addition, such comparisons highlighted American hypocrisy, since the nation that professed to champion equality and liberty was more repressive in its treatment of slaves than certain monarchies.

In November 1827, for example, Russwurm reprinted an article from the *Genius of Universal Emancipation* about slavery in Cuba that noted particular aspects of the institution. Slaves in Cuba were provided an "official protector" by law; regulations dictated that masters who "use their slaves ill, may be compelled to sell them"; and some slaves (*coartados*) could engage in a process which allowed them to purchase their freedom. In an editorial, Russwurm reflected on the implications of these distinctions: "It becomes not slave-owners, who style themselves Republicans, to allow the subjects of so despotic a sovereign as Ferdinand, to treat their slaves with greater clemency in every respect. . . . [I]t must be evident . . . that in no respect, do our brethren of the South, in bondage, possess one quarter of the privileges enjoyed in Cuba." A reprinted article from a British antislavery periodical which described aspects of slavery in the Spanish colonies, particularly the treatment of slaves and the conditions under which they may earn or gain their freedom, remarked that the Spanish system "may well put to shame both the law and the practice of Slavery in the British Colonies, and in the United States."[24]

Other articles, though, highlighted the harshness of slavery around the world. Taking the editor of the *New-York Evening Post* to task for apologizing for slavery both in the United States and the West Indies, Cornish and Russwurm emphasized the similarities in the institution in the two regions. The *Post*'s editor's defense, they asserted, was "derived not from experience, but from free conversation with ladies and gentlemen of the South, and from a volume written by a 21 years Resident of the West-Indies." Of course, these sources were "blinded by interest" and thus could not be trusted. In fact, both American and West Indian slaves wished to be free of their bondage, as was illustrated by advertisements for runaway slaves in Jamaican newspapers and the personal experiences of the editors with former American slaves, none of whom "preferred a state of bondage to that of freedom" or "regretted his emancipation." Other pieces called attention to the particular horrors of slavery in the British colonies. An article which the editors published under the heading "Happiness of Being Flogged"—a phrase reminiscent of the ironic titles about slavery's "blessings"— provided an extract from a Trinidad newspaper which declared that the whip is necessary to the "COMFORT, WELFARE, and HAPPINESS of [the] labouring classes" of that island and gave a detailed description of how and when it was used.[25] Articles also reported on particular cruelties of the international slave trade.[26] News about this international commerce reminded readers that although American participation in it had been legally abolished (even though, as we have seen, its domestic counterpart was flourishing), Africans continued to suffer its horrors.

One particular form of news emphasized strongly the consequences of slavery both for individuals enmeshed in the system and the nation that fostered and enabled the institution. Reports of slaves' resistance did more than counter the argument that slaves were happy and well off; they revealed that those Americans who believed these myths were fooling themselves, often with dire results. In June 1827, Cornish and Russwurm reprinted under the title "Blessings of Slavery!" two short but striking accounts, one describing a "most dangerous and extensive insurrection of the blacks" in Macon, Georgia, the other noting that a Virginia man was "murdered recently in his field by several of his slaves." The same title was used in 1828 as a heading to a brief account of a Kentucky slave dealer killed by one of the slaves in his power.[27] These accounts deepened the irony of the contention that slaves were fortunate; whites who believed this claim might (literally) find themselves tragically mistaken. The oppressed would ultimately claim their humanity, whatever the consequences. As the notion of the "blessings of slavery" collapsed, then, so too did the ideological foundations of slavery, suggesting that the system could and ultimately would be destroyed.

TRAVELERS, SOJOURNERS, RESIDENTS, AND FUGITIVES: SLAVERY AND THE LAW

One of the goals of *Freedom's Journal*, as we have discussed, was to provide an education in civics and the American legal system. Because slavery was based on and regulated by a complex system of laws and judicial decisions that occasionally restricted but usually bolstered slavery's power in the nation, it was important for the newspaper's readers to learn about and understand their implications. One legal question was particularly significant, having consequences for definitions of liberty, civil rights, personhood, and national unity: Under what circumstances might slaves who set foot on free soil become liberated? Reading *Freedom's Journal*, we discover that African Americans of the late 1820s were interested in and informed about the intricate and at times contradictory decisions of judges and lawmakers on this question. Articles on the subject educated readers about the legal manifestations of slavery, linked free African Americans to slaves, and demonstrated how the meaning of freedom and the status of people of color in the nation were shaped by the intersection of slavery and the law.

In 1827, *Freedom's Journal* reported on two important decisions from British courts, the 1772 case *Somerset v. Stewart* and the 1827 case of the slave Grace. James Somerset, a slave of Virginian Charles Stewart, traveled with his master to England in 1769. After Somerset ran away from Stewart, was recaptured, and was put aboard a ship to be taken to Jamaica to be sold as a slave, British abolitionist Granville Sharp aided him in bringing his case before Lord Mansfield, chief justice of the Court of King's Bench. Mansfield ordered him released on the basis of "two narrow points of English law," as William Wiecek elucidates: "a master could not seize a slave and remove him from the realm against the slave's will, and a slave could secure a writ of habeas corpus"—which would allow him or her to appear before a judge—"to prevent that removal." Even though Mansfield and others "disavowed" that the case had "broad implications," Wiecek notes, many took his decision as an extensive antislavery statement. In particular, certain words attributed to Mansfield in the decision were used frequently to argue that slavery fundamentally contradicted natural law: "The state of slavery is of such a nature, that it is incapable of being introduced on any reasons, moral or political. . . . It's so odious, that nothing can be suffered to support it, but positive law."[28]

This decision had a great impact in the American colonies and subsequently in the United States. At the least, the Somerset precedent established that slaves in free jurisdictions could appeal to the courts to prevent their removal; broadly considered, it proposed that a slave who entered a region where there were no laws regulating slavery became free. On a theoretical level, it provided opponents of slavery with a strong statement that the institution violated natural law.[29] These general antislavery implications would no doubt have resonated deeply for readers of *Freedom's Journal*. In November 1827, Russwurm reprinted an excerpt from Prince Hoare's 1820 *Memoirs of Granville Sharp* which discussed the case. Describing the appeal to Lord Mansfield, Hoare declared, "The cause of liberty was now no longer to be tried on the ground of a mere special indictment, but on the broad principle of the essential and constitutional right of every man in England to the liberty of his person, unless forfeited by the laws of England." Hoare's summary of Mansfield's decision similarly suggested its broad application: "Mr. Mansfield . . . contended, that if the Negro Somerset was a man—and he should conclude him one till the court should adjudge otherwise—it was impossible he could be a slave in England, unless by the introduction of some species of property unknown to our constitution."[30]

This summary of the case—and the fact that Russwurm wanted readers to be exposed to it—emphasized its significance for all Americans opposed to slavery and for African Americans in particular, quite apart from the particulars of what the decision actually achieved or what Mansfield intended. Indeed, Wiecek remarks, the case and the "rhetoric of liberty" surrounding it had an impact on African Americans soon after the decision, when it was publicized in the colonies. Because the Somerset case influenced subsequent American legal decisions about slavery, it was a valuable part of readers' education in the American legal system, particularly the ways it defined and controlled personal liberty. Russwurm also no doubt wanted readers to be aware of how the Somerset decision fit into antislavery discourse. As Wiecek explains, the case represented "a cloud over the legitimacy of slavery in America" and "revitalized notions of natural or fundamental law and infused them into American case law."[31] As we shall discuss, natural law was an important part of American thought and abolitionist argumentation of the late 1820s; Somerset's invocation of this tradition solidified its antislavery power. In addition, Russwurm's publication of Hoare's description of the case would have had additional significance for African-American readers. The affirmation that slaves were unequivocally *men* would, in light of the gendered rhetoric of the periodical that equated manhood and liberty, confirm their right to freedom and establish that all African-American men were entitled to assert themselves in ways that white society tried to suppress.

An 1827 decision in England, though, revised and limited the Somerset precedent. Grace, a domestic slave in the West Indies, came to England with her mistress in 1822, returning to Antigua with her in 1823. In 1825, a customs official seized her, declaring that she was free as a result of the residence in England; the Court of Antigua disagreed and in 1826 remanded her to her mistress. The case was appealed to the crown. Deciding the case in 1827, Lord Stowell affirmed the ruling. Grace "was not a free person," Stowell declared; she could not claim a "violation of right" to freedom "conveyed by a mere residence in England," because this was a "right she possessed no longer than whilst she resided in England, but which had totally expired when that residence ceased and she was imported into Antigua."[32]

In January 1828, Russwurm published a short account of the decision with his commentary in order to provide readers "a correct idea of the subject." Strongly criticizing the decision, Russwurm declared, "If the laws of the mother country are not to have weight in her West India Colonies, we cannot perceive why they should at home: for if the slave who obtains his liberty by setting his foot in England, becomes to all intents and purposes an Englishman; as one, by the operation of her laws, he is at liberty to travel unmolested to any part of the kingdom or the colonies pertaining to it." Grace, then, should have been free to "return at her own time" to England. It is noteworthy that Russwurm considered that readers should be aware of this case so soon after it was decided. As Paul Finkelman notes, the decision in fact "was not immediately incorporated into American law" because it raised certain "unanswered questions"; yet it did develop an influence, most famously in the Dred Scott case.[33] Russwurm, it seems, was ahead of his time in assigning this case significance for American jurisprudence.

In the antebellum American context, the question of when residence in a free state conferred freedom raised questions about how the North and

South would deal with cases that rested on conflicts between national unity and sectional interests. In particular, potential clashes arose when Southerners resided for periods in the North with their slaves. Various statutes allowed for those Southerners who were sojourning, or living in free states for limited periods—six months in Pennsylvania, for example, and nine months in New York—to retain the slaves they brought with them. Cases that arose from these laws had important consequences, establishing whether and to what extent slavery would be protected by the Constitution and allowed to encroach upon free states.[34]

In 1827 and 1828, Russwurm featured various reports in *Freedom's Journal* that informed readers about recent decisions and their implications. A reprinted article from the *African Observer* titled "Important" described a Pennsylvania case in which a master was "accompanied by his slave into one of the free states." "Upon application to Judge Washington for a certificate to authorise his removal," the master was informed "that, as the slave did not escape from another state or territory into this, he had no authority to direct his return." Judge Bushrod Washington's decision in this 1823 case, *Ex Parte Simmons*, did indeed free the slave of a Mr. Simmons of South Carolina. After residing in Pennsylvania for eleven months with his slave, Simmons appealed to the Fugitive Slave Act of 1793 for authorization to return to the South with his slave. Washington ruled that the Act did not apply, since it "relate[d] to fugitives from one state or territory to another" and not to a person "having been voluntarily brought by his master into [Pennsylvania]"; thus, he would not consent to the removal of the slave, declaring that he had "no cognizance of the case." The judge added that since Simmons had exceeded the sojourning period, he was "of opinion that the alleged slave [was] free."[35]

An "extract of a letter from a gentleman in Illinois to his friend in Philadelphia," originally published in the *Genius of Universal Emancipation*, described the decision in the 1827 Missouri case *Merry v. Tiffin and Menard*. John Merry, a Missouri slave, sued his owners, Tiffin and Menard, claiming his freedom since he was born in Illinois after the passage of the Northwest Ordinance of 1787, which stipulated that no one born in the Northwest Territory should be a slave. The Missouri Supreme Court held that Merry "was not property; and at the time of his birth, he could not be property."[36] This decision, the Illinois writer maintained, provided hope that the "foul blot" of slavery in the free states would "be immediately washed out, and the friends of man [would] have a new cause to felicitate themselves on the progress of correct principles, and on the restoration of his long lost rights."[37]

Readers, to be sure, would have rejoiced with this correspondent, but they would also have understood that his optimism needed to be tempered with the awareness that slavery's power did indeed reach into the

North. An October 1828 article reprinted from the *Albany Daily Advertiser* related the case of "Maria Howard, a colored girl, claimed as a slave, and her brother." The proprietor of a boarding house, who had "connections in Baltimore," claimed them as slaves and wanted to sell them. Two questions were raised: Was "the claimant of these two children" a "resident," in which case her slaves were free? And, even if this was the case, could she continue to assert a right to the children's labor under the 1817 "Act Relative to Slaves and Servants"? The 1817 statutes extended the tenets of the 1799 Gradual Abolition Act to slaves brought into New York with their masters. Slaves born after July 4, 1799, under this standard, would be "deemed and adjudged to be born free" but would "be the servant of the legal proprietor of his or her mother until such servant, if a male, shall arrive at the age of twenty-eight years, and if a female, at the age of twenty-five years." The judgment set the children free, most likely because even if the claimant could prove she had a right to their services, the 1817 statute prohibited the sale of slaves and the exporting of slaves and servants out of the state and set free any who were either "exported" or "attempted to be exported." Yet the legal complexities of the case reminded readers that de facto if not de jure liberty in New York could, in some cases, be limited.[38]

In addition, a curious aspect of the article shed light on slavery's sinister presence in the state. The account mentioned that Maria Howard actually was willing to "remain in the service of her mistress any term of years or during life." The prospect of sale, though, was terrifying; her "principal dread was falling into the hands of a fellow of the name of Wolfhawk"—presumably Woolfolk—and "being sold into the Georgia market . . . beyond the reach or the reclamations of humanity."[39] Such transactions, although illegal, were a common way that slaveholders aimed to profit from the Gradual Abolition Act by selling those held in bondage to traders who would then put them on the Southern market.[40] Despite the positive judgment in this case, then, the article highlighted specific ways in which slavery continued to pervade life in New York even after emancipation. Freedom in New York may not always have meant actual liberty from servitude, this case revealed, and a person who was technically free but who found herself in this legal limbo might have been faced with the threat of sale into Southern bondage.

In other cases, legal judgments affirmed slavery's reach, particularly when fugitives were apprehended. The week after the letter from Illinois was published, in fact, Russwurm reprinted a short piece from the Unitarian *Christian Register* that reported on a case from New York State, in which "a female slave belonging to a southern gentleman, and accompanying him and his family on a journey to Niagara falls," escaped, "was apprehended, and, after a long and able argument before Judge Chapin," was "given up to her master." Criticizing the decision, the article expressed a decidedly antislavery perspective; it was the author's "opinion, that those slaves who travel with their masters ought to be free on a free soil; and if retained in bondage to their masters, it ought to be a moral bondage merely—the service to which they are bound by choice and affection."[41] Unfortunately, of course, this correspondent's judgment was contradicted by the Fugitive Slave Law as well as by ordinances regulating sojourning.

The variety of articles in *Freedom's Journal* about slavery, law, and the courts revealed to readers the complicated legal underpinnings of slavery and educated them about the ways the institution influenced North as well as South. They also served another important antislavery purpose. As the articles informed readers that decisions in cases about slavery varied and were the subject of antislavery commentary and critique, they demystified the legal foundations of slavery's power. The law, readers learned, could be at once a tool of oppression and a weapon in the hands of the oppressed, who should be aware of its use and its implications.

ANTISLAVERY RHETORIC, SACRED AND SECULAR

To truly inform readers about slavery's power and about the ways they could counter it, it was necessary to provide them not only with news about slavery and the specific legal decisions regulating it but also with more theoretical antislavery texts. It might be "obvious" to readers, as Russwurm remarked, that slavery was "an unnatural state, and one upon which a beneficent Being can never look with complacency,"[42] but there was a formidable array of beliefs and arguments in early-nineteenth-century America dedicated to espousing the opposite view. Antebellum African Americans needed to know how to counter this discourse with solid antislavery rhetoric.

Throughout the newspaper's run, the editors published explicitly persuasive articles that established the immorality and impracticality of slavery and took on the traditional defenses—religious, historical, political, and economic—of the institution. Often, these pieces were reprinted from other sources, including the writings of British abolitionists; other articles were penned specifically for the periodical. Although the arguments offered were not always unique, they are important examples of the antislavery rhetoric that both was created by and influenced African Americans in the period. Through the columns of *Freedom's Journal*, the editors exposed readers to a wide range of antislavery thought and perspectives, in effect giving them a broad education about the theoretical foundations of slavery and how they could be attacked. The newspaper also served as a forum for African Americans who wished to craft their own antislavery persuasion. *Freedom's Journal* gives us a sense of the ways various components of antislavery thought were articulated by, passed along to, and in some cases reshaped by African Americans of the late 1820s, setting the stage for the antislavery rhetoric of subsequent decades.

Proslavery commentators often turned to the Bible for justification. The Old Testament was frequently cited by apologists, particularly two claims: that Africans were destined to be slaves according to Noah's curse on Canaan; and that, because biblical patriarchs held slaves and the Bible outlined instructions for their treatment, the institution was sanctioned in Scripture.[43] The former contention depended upon a particular reading of Genesis 9:25, in which Noah declared that Ham's son Canaan would be "a servant of servants . . . unto his brethren." Because biblical scholars held that Africans were descendants of Ham, this argument proposed that slavery was sanctioned in Scripture for all those of African descent.

Texts published in *Freedom's Journal* demonstrated that opponents of slavery could accept that Scripture was authoritative yet counter the proslavery interpretation of Noah's curse. In May 1827, for example, the editors reprinted an article from the *New-York Observer* titled "The Curse of Canaan." Noah's prophecy was meant to be fulfilled, the author argued, but it was only intended to apply to the descendants of Canaan, "the person designated in the prophecy." Canaan's descendants indeed experienced "oppressions that accord well with the predictions"; "most of them *were* destroyed or brought into subjection in the days of Joshua . . . and the rest were brought into subjection in the days of David." Yet Misriam and Cush were also Ham's sons; as we have seen, the Egyptians and the Ethiopians were regarded as their descendants. Was the prophecy supposed to include them? The author of "The Curse of Canaan" contended that it was not: "The Egyptians . . . were once a powerful people. . . . The same may be said of Ethiopia under some of its kings, and for a considerable period." The greatness of Egypt and Ethiopia—an important theme for African Americans of the late 1820s, as we have explored—demonstrated that Noah's curse could not be considered binding on all of Ham's descendants or, by extension, on all Africans. Those who argued otherwise, the author remarked, were "attempt[ing] to suit the text to the condition of the African part of Ham's family"—in other words, to justify the enslavement and oppression of Africans.[44]

But what of the facts that the patriarchs held slaves; that slavery was recognized, permitted, and regulated in the Hebrew Scriptures; and that Paul's epistles outlined the proper conduct of slaves and masters? Did not these texts provide biblical sanction for American slavery? Articles opposing slavery in *Freedom's Journal* did not reject biblical passages that seemed to authorize slavery outright; indeed, many nineteenth-century opponents of slavery acknowledged that some instances of slaveholding were indeed given divine acceptance. Yet they argued that Scripture was being misinterpreted and misapplied by proslavery commentators. The American institution, they insisted, was not sanctioned by God—indeed, it violated basic Judeo-Christian precepts set down in the Bible.

Avoiding judgments of slavery as practiced by the patriarchs of the Old Testament, antislavery commentators proposed that this system was *fundamentally different* from American slavery and as such could not be used to defend the contemporary institution. The four-part "History of Slavery," originally published in the *African Observer* and reprinted in *Freedom's Journal* in 1827, argued this position. This series of articles, we will recall, distinguished between American slavery and the bondage "to which the descendants of Jacob were subjected during their residence in Egypt"; similarly, the author proposed that the "species of slavery" that "existed during the patriarchal ages" should not be considered a precedent for the institution of the contemporary South. Citing particular passages of Scripture, numerous examples were offered to demonstrate the essential differences between the two forms of servitude: the slaves of Abraham "were treated with a degree of confidence, to which the slavery of our day affords but few parallels"; they were made "part of the patriarchal household, equally with the sons an object of religious care"; the Hebrews were prohibited from stealing human beings or holding slaves that were stolen; Mosaic law assumed that slavery was of a *"limited duration"* rather than "perpetual and hereditary." This last distinction was particularly significant; a master who knew a slave would be eventually free would have more cause to follow regulations than one without this incentive, since the "servant, if abused, might when free demand and enforce restitution."[45]

If the Old Testament contained instances in which slavery seemed to be sanctioned, it also provided precedent for God's vengeance against those who held slaves. In particular, the biblical plight of the Israelites was linked by African-American Christians to the sufferings of American slaves; the South was an Egypt in which God's people endured harsh bondage.[46] Correspondent S**** B— described the ultimate outcome suggested by this parallel: "The Southern people . . . are, like the Egyptians, cruel and oppressive; and they harden their hearts, that they will not let the Africans go. . . . The groans, the tears, the anguish of the sufferers, have reached the throne of Mercy: the God of justice will pour out his wrath, upon their oppressors, without mixture of mercy."[47]

Certain contributors to *Freedom's Journal* were less concerned with particular injunctions or examples from Scripture than with the antislavery force of Christ's ministry and teaching. In a letter to Russwurm, correspondent Aristides dismissed those who would argue that "slavery, at least, in a qualified sense, was sanctioned by the Jewish law": "This single law, which fell from the lips of Him, who 'spake as never man spake,'—'As ye would that men should do unto you, even so do ye to them,' has levelled the odious system of slavery forever." In an October 1828 editorial, Russwurm noted that although some "advocates have endeavoured to prove that several passages of the New Testament had a peculiar reference to the condition of master and slave," these were "doubtful interpretations." Russwurm did not specify or counter these proslavery readings of Scripture; for him, the teachings of Christ served as a sufficient antislavery argument: "We have always been at a loss to conceive how ministers of the gospel, who are, or should be, followers of our meek and lowly Saviour, can reconcile the subject of slavery to their consciences. For in nothing does slavery agree with his precepts. . . ."[48] Aristides and Russwurm appealed to the centrality of Christ's identification with the oppressed and the promise of ultimate freedom in African-American Christianity.[49] They affirmed the authenticity of their view of Christ as liberator in contrast to the dominant culture's disingenuous attempts to cast Christ as at best indifferent to and at worst a supporter of slavery. As C. Eric Lincoln and Lawrence H. Mamiya remark, "The black Christians who formed the historic black churches . . . knew implicitly that their understanding of Christianity . . . was more authentic than the Christianity practiced in white churches."[50]

Although Christian arguments would have been particularly powerful for the many religious readers of *Freedom's Journal*, one did not have to rely specifically on Christian precepts to demonstrate that slavery was, as Russwurm described, an "unnatural state" in opposition to the divine order. As the term "unnatural" suggests, the theory of natural law—that humans have rights given to them by God and that moral conduct should be judged against this standard—was used by white and African-American abolitionists to critique slavery.[51] An 1827 series of articles signed with the initials S. F. D., reprinted from the *Christian Spectator*, cited the argument of the British abolitionist Thomas Buxton that only "the black man" had a right "to his own body," given to him by "nature" and "the grant of God." The "claim of the white man" to it was founded on "robbery, violence, inconceivable wickedness." For American abolitionists, natural law had a particular power, since the concept was a foundation of the Declaration of Independence. Correspondent Aristides suggested the basis of American civil liberties in natural law, which is intrinsically antislavery: "Opposed to slavery in any form, stand reason, justice, mercy. . . . Reason decrees that 'all men are born equal.'" A report from the Abolition Society of Stark County, Ohio, similarly combined the theory of natural rights with the language of the Declaration to question the basis upon which any person could hold another as "property": "Liberty is the unalienable right of every man; and whether by violence or by villainy it has fallen into the hands of another, the original owner . . . has an everlasting title to demand it."[52]

Through the Declaration, the language of one particular slaveholder became a tool of those who opposed the institution. The incongruity between Jefferson's ownership of slaves and his words on behalf of freedom itself constituted an antislavery argument, highlighting conspicuously the clash between American ideals and reality. Jefferson's "eloquent appeal" that "all men possess certain unalienable rights—among which are life, *liberty*, and the pursuit of happiness," Aristides maintained, "has rendered his name immortal." "But what strange inconsistency is here?" Aristides demanded. "In one hand, the 'Sage of Monticello,' presents this declaration of *rights*; in the other, he grasps the chains which hold in perpetual bondage five hundred of his fellow-men!!! No man's patriotism appears better on *paper*, but how is it developed upon his plantation?"[53]

Jefferson's hypocrisy, in Aristides's view, called attention to slavery's infringement of natural law. Jefferson's writings, indeed, indicated an awareness of this contradiction. A piece written in 1820 that the editors reprinted in *Freedom's Journal* in September 1827 noted that Jefferson, although an owner of slaves, saw clearly that slavery was not "consistent with sound morality, and Christian principles." The article cited perhaps the most famous Jeffersonian proclamation about slavery in his *Notes on the State of Virginia*, predicting a confrontation between slavery and freedom: "I tremble for my country when I reflect that God is just: that his justice cannot sleep forever: that considering numbers, nature and natural means only, a revolution of the wheel of fortune, an exchange of situation, is among possible events. . . The Almighty has no attribute which can take side with us in such a contest." The reprinted article in *Freedom's Journal* remarked that Jefferson, although a slaveholder, "trembl[ed] under an apprehension of divine justice and rebellion" and anticipated that in "the eventual struggle, which must ultimately take place between masters and slaves; 'The Almighty has no attribute which can take side with us in such a contest.'"[54] In Jefferson's life was embodied the fundamental paradox of America's founding, its professed commitment to divine providence and natural law and its tolerance of slavery; in his rhetoric, the struggle between these elements threatened the nation that ignored the inevitable triumph of freedom over bondage.[55]

Not only was slavery ultimately doomed; it also was a destructive moral force on the society that tolerated it. In a series of articles reprinted in 1828 which were originally published in the British antislavery periodical the *Anti-Slavery Monthly Reporter*, slavery's corrupting influence was elucidated. Slave women were sexually exploited by British men; those who owned slaves were led to view fellow humans not as people, but as property, tainting their relationships with "the whole working class"; slaves became deceitful, shameless, and motivated by "no consideration but that of fear"; their masters became "tyrants." Presumably written by a British abolitionist, the series elaborated at much greater length about the effect on the humanity of the masters than that of the slaves. Indeed, the author contended that a "slave has, in fact, no character," denying, in effect, that slaves possessed the ability to make moral choices.[56] Yet even given this racist perspective, the article would have been useful to readers of *Freedom's Journal*, demonstrating that there were advocates for black freedom in other countries as well as in the United States and providing them with examples of potential appeals to the consciences of white Americans. In subsequent generations, as abolitionists attempted to persuade white audiences, discussions of slavery's debasing effects on white Americans became commonplaces of their rhetoric. In addition, African-American readers of *Freedom's Journal*, urged by the editors from the outset to remember their "brethren who are still in bondage," would have been moved even by the relatively brief focus on the sufferings of slaves. White abolitionists might have emphasized the consequences for the masters of their abuse of slaves, but African-American readers would not have forgotten those who endured their cruelties.

For numerous white Americans, of course, religious and ethical antislavery arguments would have been futile. After all, all too many self-proclaimed Christians and patriots supported the institution; power and profit clearly were quite persuasive forces. If readers of *Freedom's Journal* were to be armed with the full range of antislavery appeals needed to convince a complicit nation, they required articles based on practical considerations such as economics and self-interest. S. F. D.'s 1827 series from the *Christian Spectator* argued that slavery was responsible for the deterioration and impoverishment evident throughout the South: "It curses every thing which it touches. It sheds a blight over all the departments of national prosperity." S. F. D. noted in detail the ways that the institution destroyed the Southern economy: planters took too much risk and went into debt; slavery used fear to motivate workers, and thus discouraged industry. S. F. D., it should be noted, did not believe that slaveholders would respond to these arguments or be eager "to surrender" their "love of power." But those opposing slavery could appeal to others—"men at a distance"—who could "judge of what is for the true interest of planters, better than the planters can for themselves."[57]

Also in 1827, the editors reprinted two series of articles that argued the economic case for free over slave labor. In six installments, they featured an important antislavery argument written by British economist and abolitionist Adam Hodgson, which was originally published as a letter to the French economist Jean-Baptiste Say in an appendix to Hodgson's 1823 *Remarks During a Journey Through North America in the Years 1819, 1820, and*

1821. Although Say opposed slavery, he argued in his *Treatise on Political Economy*, first published in French in 1803 with its first American edition appearing in 1821, that slave labor may be more profitable than free labor.[58] In his letter, Hodgson noted that he had "much concern" about Say's treatment of "the subject of the comparative expense of free and slave labour": "I cannot but regret deeply, that opinions so much calculated to perpetuate slavery should have the sanction of your authority; and that, while you denounce the slave-system as unjustifiable, you admit that in a pecuniary point of view it may be the most profitable." Hodgson sought "to controvert" Say's position, citing authorities from Pliny to Adam Smith and featuring examples from ancient Rome to the contemporary United States. Presenting complex and detailed arguments, he compared the costs expended to maintain free laborers and slaves, the work output of these two classes, the worth of land in slave and free regions, and the value of estates before and after emancipation. Hodgson, too, acknowledged planters' unwillingness to abandon the system, but he did not see this as evidence that slavery was beneficial to them. Rather, he argued that "the practice of a planter, like that of other men, may be at variance with his interest—especially if in unison with his prejudices and his inclinations."[59]

In a series of articles from the *Alexandria Gazette*, Quaker cleric Samuel Janney also marshaled economic evidence to argue against slavery. Janney's articles outlined the perspectives of the Benevolent Society of Alexandria for Ameliorating and Improving the Condition of the People of Colour, an organization which he helped create and which, in his words, sought "to rescue from the possession of the slave traders, persons illegally held in bondage and to enlighten the public mind in regard to the evils of slavery." As did Hodgson, Janney built a logical economic case, demonstrating that slavery was less efficient and made goods more expensive (for the producer and consumer) and land less valuable than free labor. He was, however, more hopeful than either S. F. D. or Hodgson that slaveholders could be persuaded that an end to slavery would advance their future and "even their present interests."[60]

Whether or not slaveholders had ignored economic self-interest, they would likely have paid attention to claims about danger to themselves and their families. News about the resistance of particular slaves thus constituted a potentially powerful antislavery argument. In addition, such reports reminded readers, as we have seen, that the enslaved could and did struggle against their bondage, reinforcing their humanity and underscoring the precariousness of the system. Opponents of slavery often made this argument directly. S. F. D. noted the irony of the claim that discussions of abolition would "excite the slaves to insurrection": "I ask if there is now no danger? If every slave owner feels as safe when he goes to bed as if he were surrounded by a free peasantry? If not, what mean those pistols under his pillow, and that loaded rifle over it?" Southerners were indeed ignoring historical precedent. In an article reprinted from the *Genius of Universal Emancipation*, correspondent Z. remarked, "They seem willing to close their eyes to passing events—for them the page of history is not suffered to unfold itself . . . and nothing will arouse them from this lethargic slumber, but the bursting asunder of those chains, with which they have fettered, that unfortunate part of the human family." Z. referred not only to the obvious example of Haiti but also to revolutions in France, Colombia, and Mexico, in which the "common people," "despised and ill treated," overthrew oppressors. The consequences of Southerners' "ignorance and stupidity" could be deadly.[61]

PROPOSALS FOR ABOLITION

Although Cornish and Russwurm maintained that readers could do "but little" except offer "sympathies" and "prayers" on behalf of slaves, various plans for ending slavery—both speculative and concrete—were in fact presented in the columns of *Freedom's Journal*. The proposals most often offered favored gradualist approaches rather than immediate methods of ending slavery, yet it is important to place this aspect of the newspaper's coverage in context. Alice Dana Adams's study of white antislavery reformers in the early nineteenth century demonstrates that most favored gradual abolition, often in conjunction with colonization, until the early 1830s.[62] News in *Freedom's Journal* of white abolitionist organizations or activities often reflected this perspective. Although, as we have discussed, African-American abolitionists were ahead of white reformers in many areas of antislavery thought and activism, it is not surprising that to some extent they would share their white colleagues' belief that it was not possible or practical to anticipate an immediate end to slavery. Thus texts written by African Americans that were published in *Freedom's Journal* often avoided advocating immediate abolition as well. As Richard Newman notes, however, we should not view African Americans' espousal of gradual abolition in the early nineteenth century as "assimilationist"; on the contrary, the antislavery arguments of these black activists assumed that African Americans could become "valued citizens while also maintaining an autonomous social and cultural identity."[63]

The abolition of slavery in New York through gradual measures also may have contributed to a sense that a pragmatic approach was necessary and could ultimately be effective. Various articles in the newspaper around July 4, 1827—the day slavery officially ended in that state—as well as on its anniversary a year later celebrated the institution's demise.[64]

In addition, as Frankie Hutton remarks, for the editors to have gone farther in their antislavery rhetoric "would have been to risk the survival of a black publication and the lives of those connected with it."[65]

Consider, for example, Janney's 1827 series about the Benevolent Society of Alexandria for Ameliorating and Improving the Condition of the People of Colour. The goals of this organization, as Janney's aforementioned description implied, were based on antislavery sentiment but were not immediatist; and Janney specified that members of the Benevolent Society had "no intention of interfering with the constitutional rights of slave-holders." Instead, he explained that they wished to persuade them to support "a judicious course of gradual manumission and colonization." At once cautious and optimistic, Janney shied away from offering any plans for even this measured approach, noting that "it would be premature in this stage of the investigation, to propose a remedy for the evil" but declaring that "there is much to cheer the heart of the philanthropist." In the United States, he declared, "the march of public sentiment" towards ending slavery, "though gradual . . . is steady and must ultimately prove victorious."[66]

For many American reformers, the work of British abolitionists in the 1820s who were calling for parliamentary intervention to ameliorate and eventually abolish slavery in the colonies was a particular source of antislavery inspiration and precedent. In 1828, Russwurm published numerous reports in *Freedom's Journal* of these efforts.[67] In addition to giving readers an international context for American antislavery efforts, such accounts had potentially ironic implications—if citizens of Great Britain, the monarchy against which the American Revolutionists had rebelled for freedom, were making efforts to end slavery, Americans would either have to follow suit or have their hypocrisy exposed.[68] It is also important to realize that the influence suggested by these articles went two ways. Not only did they imply that British antislavery could have some bearing on American policies, but they also suggested the role of American, and particularly African-American, activists as important colleagues of British abolitionists. In November 1827, Russwurm published a letter from British abolitionist Thomas Pringle, secretary to the Society for the Mitigation and Gradual Abolition of Slavery, noting that he had received "several numbers of your able and meritorious Journal, and [had] submitted them to the committee of the Society." In a headnote, Russwurm commented on the letter, "We . . . publish it, to let our friends at home, know that the Abolitionists of Great Britain are yet alive to the interests and cause of our enslaved brethren." Readers were part of an international community of activists; abolitionists across the sea were learning from them through the pages of the newspaper as they gained knowledge of strategies and tactics that were shaping British policy. In this context, reports from Britain were part of an ongoing collaboration between reformers in the two nations in which African Americans played a significant role.[69]

While many white abolitionists in the late 1820s may have seen slave-holders' purported "rights" to their "property" as an impediment to abolition in many regions, there was one notable exception. The District of Columbia, as Alice Dana Adams notes, was under the "complete control" of Congress, "should it choose to exercise it"; and starting in 1809, abolitionists began to petition for laws that would bring about emancipation there. People throughout the United States had a say in the District; in the words of the editor of the *New-England Inquirer*, featured in *Freedom's Journal* in November 1828, it was "owned . . . by the *Non*-slave-holding, as well as the slave-holding States." In addition, the symbolic—and highly visible—contradiction of slavery in the capital of a country purportedly built on freedom demanded a national response. An address of the American Convention for Promoting the Abolition of Slavery, published in *Freedom's Journal* in December 1828, maintained that "the honor of the nation" was "implicated, by the toleration of slavery in the District of Columbia." "Slavery is certainly disgraceful in any part of the Union," Russwurm asserted, "but more particularly within the limits of the District of Columbia, under the immediate notice of Congress, and Ministers from the different governments of Europe." A reprinted article from the *Genius of Universal Emancipation* encouraged the citizens of "every State, to circulate memorials and petitions . . . for signature." There should be no equivocation or compromise, the author declared: "The most suitable time . . . is *now*, NOW. . . . Let petitions, memorials, addresses, and remonstrances be poured into the capital . . . until our national Legislatures shall *feel* the blushes of shame to encrimson their cheeks!"[70] *Freedom's Journal's* columns featured reports from the various organizations, such as the American Convention for Promoting the Abolition of Slavery and New York's Manumission Society, advocating abolition in the nation's capital as a primary goal, as well as an example of a petition to Congress from citizens of Washington and Alexandria.[71]

Early-nineteenth-century abolitionists had attacked the foreign slave trade, but after the abolition of the international slave trade to the United States in 1808, they turned to its domestic counterpart which, as we have noted, was thriving in the late 1820s. Various reports of antislavery activity in *Freedom's Journal* focused on abolishing this commerce as well as stopping the related crime of kidnapping and enslaving free people of color. "As an incipient step to the abolition of slavery," a report of an October 1827 meeting of the American Convention for Promoting the Abolition of Slavery advised, abolitionists should make "immediate application . . . to the Legislatures of states where slavery exists, to prohibit the sale of slaves out of state." A committee of the Convention was appointed "to consider of and report to this convention what measures are necessary to be taken to promote the abolition of the domestic slave trade and to protect free persons of colour from being kidnapped."[72]

The response of this committee, also published in *Freedom's Journal*, was instructive. They hoped that Congress could be persuaded to "procure some wholesome restraint upon a traffick fraught with such aggravated evil, and productive of such complicated misery." Yet they also concluded that "the intimate connexion between the Domestic Slave Trade, and the system of slavery generally, precludes the expectation of applying a very efficient check to the one except by a reduction in the other."[73] This link was crucial, demonstrating that even as abolitionists of the period often proposed that efforts had to be limited to ending the slave trade rather than slavery itself, many were beginning to realize that partial measures were inadequate.

Even those who advocated only the abolition of the slave trade revealed in their rhetoric the necessity of abolishing slavery as well. Consider, for example, a late 1828 account that Russwurm reprinted from the *Georgetown Columbian*, which was signed with the name Wilberforce. The article described the frequent "exhibition of droves of negroes" through the streets of the District of Columbia, on their way "to be enslaved by strangers." Problematically, Wilberforce supposed that slaves were in a "happy condition at their natal home," argued that "negroes in general, are better situated as slaves, when well treated, than they would be if free," and was concerned not with ending slavery itself but rather with abolishing the slave trade and its separation of family and friends. Yet Wilberforce's descriptions suggested that this abhorrent trade was an inextricable component of slavery. "The avarice of the master" led him "to obtain that, the love of which is declared in holy writ, to be the root of all evil"; if they would not admit to be motivated by money, slaveholders excused their actions in selling slaves by citing "the bad conduct of a slave, either real of imaginary."[74] If, as readers would no doubt agree, the slave trade and slavery were interconnected, to condemn one naturally called the other into question.

In fact, as Russwurm asserted in an editorial in October 1828, only when Americans focused on the domestic slave trade would they be able to address the dangers of slavery fully. He implied that for Americans to focus on the foreign slave trade was a strategy of denial that allowed them to look beyond rather than within their borders for the evils of slavery: "We may declaim as much as we please upon the horrors of the foreign slave trade, but we would ask, are the horrors of the internal trade less— are the relations of life less endearing in this country than in Africa—are the Wood-folks of the South less cruel than the slavers on the coast? Surely not—surely the natural heart of man is the same wherever he has the power to domineer over his fellow-man, to bind him hand and foot, and sell him like beasts of burden, and when he pleases, to destroy him." These "horrors of the internal trade" were clearly terrors inherent to slavery as well: dominance, oppression, and the threat of destruction. Russwurm clarified the link between slavery and the commerce in human beings within the United States as he moved naturally from the slave trade to slavery. Following his description of the domestic slave trade, he asserted that it was his "earnest wish, that the subject of domestic slavery may continually be placed before the public."[75]

While the antislavery articles and reports in *Freedom's Journal* highlighted the evils of slavery and the need to take steps to eradicate it, they generally did not call for immediate abolition, the central tenet of the antislavery movement of the following decades. Yet there were some notable exceptions. Reports of the Abolition Society of Stark County, Ohio, for example, championed what it called "radical Abolition" or "radical emancipation." Specific plans were not delineated, but the organization's assertions that "all men are born equal, and freedom is the natural right of all" suggested the injustice of gradual measures which left some in bondage. The report also indicated that the Society had no desire to negotiate with slaveholders and their representatives, denouncing the "artifice of the Southern states in exciting prejudice and fears with regard to the blacks" and the "visionary dangers and evils, which emancipation might carry into the free states." While not explicitly stating that only immediate abolition should be tolerated, these declarations implied that antislavery plans must free all slaves without delay or compromise to be morally defensible.[76]

Other statements in *Freedom's Journal* endorsed immediate abolition more specifically. S. F. D., in the aforementioned 1827 series of articles reprinted from the *Christian Spectator*, affirmed, "It is time to do something; neither can the urgency of the case be satisfied with any half-way measures. We may as well . . . make up our minds that the point to be aimed at is the entire and speedy *abolition* of slavery." "Leav[ing] it to wiser heads . . . to mature a plan for this purpose," S. F. D. nonetheless established that immediatist principles must be followed: the eradication of slavery must be "a *national* business," attended to by all politicians as well as the president. If nothing "can be done under the constitution as it now is," it must "be amended"; abolition must not depend upon the goodwill of slaveholders and must not include compensation to them.[77]

In particular, S. F. D. disavowed gradualism on two counts. The argument that abolition should "wait until the negroes are *fit* to be freemen" was spurious; as S. F. D. declared, "Nothing but freedom itself will fit a man to be free." In addition, gradual measures such as those proposed by Jefferson or those that were taken in the North were not solutions considering the scale of slavery in the South: "The man who drinks drams, may perhaps control his appetite so as to leave it off by degrees. The drunkard must break off at once, or not at all. . . . To say all in one word, the measures to be taken must be aimed at the root." A toast from a gathering of New York African Americans to celebrate the abolition of slavery in the state succinctly and powerfully proclaimed, *"Emancipation* without *emigration,* but equal rights on the *spot;* this is *republicanism."*[78] While such strong statements were the exception rather than the rule, they reveal that immediate abolition was an emerging current of thought among antebellum African Americans before most white abolitionists advocated this approach. African-American rhetoric of the late 1820s that called for a swift and direct end to the institution of slavery, such as these arguments in *Freedom's Journal,* laid the groundwork for the radical efforts of abolitionists, both black and white, in subsequent decades.

"PRACTICAL ABOLITION"

In addition to antislavery arguments and proposals for abolition, we discover in the pages of *Freedom's Journal* reports of antislavery activism that we might describe as concrete rather than theoretical. Historical accounts often emphasize the work of abolitionist organizations which attacked slavery systemically, yet African-American abolitionists throughout the antebellum period felt that specific acts against slavery—most notably, efforts to obtain the freedom of particular slaves—were also crucial components of the antislavery struggle. The remarks of David Ruggles, the secretary of the New York Committee of Vigilance, an organization created in 1835 to prevent kidnappings of free African Americans, aptly reflected this perspective. Noting that the Committee's members "admired and embraced the principles of the American Anti-Slavery Society" although they were not officially connected to the group, Ruggles explained in the Committee's first annual report that they felt they needed to "call forth the energy of their hands" to bring "the noble principles of the Anti-Slavery Constitution . . . into operation." Ruggles described the central role of concrete action to the larger struggle:

> To effect a mighty revolution, such as the general abolition of slavery, requires agents, and funds, and time, and influence . . . but while we long and labor for the accomplishment of this noble cause, let us not lose sight of the minor evils, which tend in the aggregate to make up that monstrous system of iniquity; let us in every case of oppression and wrong, inflicted on our brethren, prove our sincerity, by alleviating their sufferings, affording them protection, giving them counsel, and thus in our individual spheres of action, prove ourselves practical abolitionists.[79]

Reports of such "practical abolition"—particularly preventing kidnapping and facilitating the freedom of particular slaves—were published in the newspaper. As Ruggles's description suggests, African Americans saw these efforts as blows against slavery, and the coverage of them in *Freedom's Journal* would have exemplified for readers antislavery activity. In addition, as they encountered information about concrete action, readers would have been inspired and empowered to see themselves as fundamentally connected to their "brethren who are still in bondage" and to take whatever actions they could to aid them as well as to protect themselves and others from the dangers posed by kidnapping and the hunting of fugitives. *Freedom's Journal*, then, not only publicized but furthered various antislavery efforts, giving readers models for activism, providing a forum for to them to publicize their efforts and seek assistance, and warning African Americans of the dangers that slavery posed to all people of color.

There were, in a general sense, two methods practical abolitionists could use to free the enslaved. They could work through underground channels, defying the laws and encouraging, supporting, and assisting fugitives, or they could operate within the legal and economic system. The former approach needed to be treated carefully in the pages of *Freedom's Journal*. To include any specific information about those who escaped from slavery and those who assisted them would obviously have compromised their efforts and put them in danger, so it is not surprising that particular accounts were not featured in the newspaper. Russwurm remarked, in fact, that he "could tell many an interesting anecdote of the dangers [fugitives] had to encounter—of their plan of escape, &c.—did not the glorious cause of Freedom, dearer to me than life itself, require me to be silent." Yet Russwurm did not hide his support for those who had fled slavery, and he used the pages of *Freedom's Journal* to assist them. Describing life in Baltimore in his "Travelling Scraps" column in 1828, Russwurm related that "both in Baltimore and Washington, they have authorized agents, with a list of runaway slaves, who make it their sole business to visit our different northern cities for the purpose of apprehending them." He indicated that these operatives were "frequently successful, through the treachery of our own brethren, and the imprudence of the runaways, in invariably taken [*sic*] care to settle in our largest and most commercial cities" and offered an implicit warning: "One would think, after escaping, they would be very careful in choosing their places of abode."[80]

Remarking on the arrests of various people of color accused of being runaways in October 1828, Russwurm issued a more explicit caution to fugitives in New York: "It would be well if all our brethren who have been so lucky as to escape from bondage, would pay particular attention to this notice, and leave the city, or the more frequented parts of it, for awhile, at least, as there are many from the South now in daily search of them." He echoed this warning in editorials published over the ensuing weeks, lamenting that frequently African Americans had turned in runaways "for the sake of paltry lucre"—a comment that also served implicitly to put fugitives on their guard and to deter any who considered making money by betraying them. Instead of settling in cities such as New York, Boston, or Philadelphia—"places which are visited every year by hundreds from the South"—Russwurm advised escaped slaves to find "some sequestered country village, where they would be out of danger of losing that liberty which is their inherent right by Nature." Because they had to be on their guard against betrayal by people of color, fugitives could not "trust even their most intimate friends on a subject in which they are so deeply interested." Russwurm also printed names of kidnappers and those who conspired with them so that his "brethren may be on the alert against their base and infamous practices" and "keep a look-out for these villains" in order to apprehend them. It was also possible that some would-be captors or their assistants were deterred by this exposure of their identities. African Americans who aided slave-hunters would suffer particular consequences: "It is an indisputed fact, that such vile traitors should not be suffered to associate with us. . . ."[81]

Various articles published in January 1829 informed fugitives and their allies that they would be especially safe in Canada. In 1826, Secretary of State Henry Clay had asked Albert Gallatin, American Minister to the British Court of St. James, to ask the British government to agree to the "mutual surrender of all persons held to service or labor under the laws of one party, who escape into the territories of the other." In other words, the American government wanted those slaves who reached Canada to be returned. The British government would not agree. Russwurm reprinted in *Freedom's Journal* Henry Clay's December 1828 report, which included official correspondence about the American government's unsuccessful requests to the British. He also commented on the subject in his editorial of January 16, 1829: "We rejoice to find the members of the British Cabinet so firm and positive. . . . [T]he British Government could not disgrace themselves by the delivering up of persons who have taken shelter in their dominions for the enjoyment of liberty. We are sure that they have proved themselves to be good and industrious members of society to Canada. . . ."[82] Russwurm affirmed the right of slaves and those who would assist them to defy American law and seek freedom. He also conveyed an important message to anyone involved in this form of activism: Canada was a refuge beyond the power of American slavery.

Although it would have been unwise and unsafe to discuss the details of escapes or to identify those who assisted fugitives, exactly the opposite was true of efforts that operated within the law. For individuals and organizations who aided those free African Americans who had been kidnapped and sold into slavery or whose loved ones had suffered this fate—as well as for all people of color who faced this threat—the publicizing of specifics was beneficial. A notice in various issues called attention to the work of the "Protecting Society of the city and county of Philadelphia, for the preventing of kidnapping and man-stealing, auxiliary to the Abolition Society of the above city." Dire circumstances had given rise to this organization: "Of the many evils to which we as fallible creatures are liable, none is more to be dreaded and execrated than the system of kidnapping free persons of Colour, which has been carried on even in this city by a set of unprincipled men, for some years past." The announcement not only reported on the work of the organization; it also alerted readers in Philadelphia to this threat to their safety and linked those who had been affected by this crime to assistance: "Persons desirous of assistance in the recovery of their friends, who have been kidnapped, must make application personally or by letter *post paid*, addressed to the Secretary of the Society." Readers were encouraged to support the organization's efforts by "us[ing] their best endeavours to carry the benevolent views of the Society into operation." This organization's work also served as a model for activists in other cities. In a December 1828 editorial, Russwurm lamented the fact that "the business of arresting our brethren as runaways is still daily occurring in [New York] and suggested that "perhaps the formation of such a society as the Protecting Society, of Philadelphia for the preventing of kidnapping and man-stealing; might be of incalculable benefit."[83]

Freedom's Journal publicized the efforts of particular individuals as well, allowing African Americans and white allies to seek assistance in specific cases. Such articles had the potential to lead to the apprehension of criminals and the freedom of their victims. Consider, for example, a notice published by the editors in the issue of May 4, 1827: "Mrs. Betsey Wallis, a free woman of colour, of Baltimore, offers a reward of $100 for the recovery of her son, John Wallis who has been missing since the 8th of March.—There is reason to believe that he has been kidnapped."[84]

A reprinted article from the *Literary Cadet and Rhode-Island Statesman*, published in *Freedom's Journal* in February 1828, described the death of James Dailey in the Philadelphia Almshouse. Dailey had previously been kidnapped from Philadelphia and taken south to endure the cruelty of "a merciless master." Although he was subsequently rescued from bondage through the efforts of the city's High Constable Samuel Garrigues and returned to Philadelphia, the abuse he had endured proved too much, and he "yielded up this mortal tabernacle, to that God who gave it." Noting that this case was not anomalous—that indeed "there are hundreds in the Southern States who have been torn from their houses by the kidnappers"—the piece provided important information about similar cases:

We know of several free blacks, belonging to the neighbourhood of Wilmington, Delaware, who are now held as slaves in the South Western States and who were kidnapped and torn from their homes and families. If they are yet living, and we doubt not that they are, they can be easily returned, and should any citizen of Delaware, feel sufficiently interested, to induce him to make an effort to procure their redemption, if he will address a note to the editor of the Literary Cadet, Providence, Rhode Island, the residence of the kidnapped slaves will be pointed out, and every information be given, necessary to their redemption. We can also point to one, who was kidnapped in the city of New York—sold in Norfolk, Virginia, and afterwards transported to Alabama. Should any citizen of New York feel disposed to be informed in relation to the last mentioned kidnapped boy, by addressing us, he can be directed how to proceed, to save the sufferer from a life of slavery.[85]

The forum provided by a national newspaper such as *Freedom's Journal* was a crucial tool in recovering kidnapped loved ones and gaining assistance for the freeing of slaves.

Specific reports also served as warnings by publicizing both the names of suspected kidnappers and the ways in which they operated. A short article reprinted from the *New-York Spectator* in 1828, for example, related that a "man named Andrew O'Conner, was brought up to the police office a few days since, suspected of being engaged in kidnapping" after he "attempted to take a little coloured boy, under the pretext that he had run off from Newark." Although O'Conner was "discharged" because "the proof was not positive," the announcement added that "it is believed that a number of coloured children have recently been kidnapped, and taken from the city." Readers were thus warned about O'Conner and his modus operandi specifically and about the general danger to African-American children in New York. Russwurm also alerted New Yorkers to another potential scenario: "Their success of late, has rendered slave holders, quite forgetful, that they are in a free State. . . . [I]n two, if not three cases, they have been bold enough during the evening to enter the dwellings of our brethren without any authority or civil process whatever, but mere physical, force having four or five men in company, and carry them off without a hearing or trial." As he advised runaways to be careful about the potential of betrayal by African Americans, so too Russwurm counseled free people of color to be equally cautious, since he "believe[d] any man of colour who will betray one who is a runaway, would not hesitate one moment towards assisting to kidnap those who are free." "*Beware of such,*" he warned all African Americans of these traitors, "*they are snakes in the grass, charming unwary birds.*"[86] In addition to raising the public's awareness of specific dangers, these articles conveyed a general sense of the precariousness of freedom for African Americans and the oppression that threatened them continually. The coverage, thus, likely stirred activism as it provided information.

There was also an approach, albeit controversial, that could be taken by abolitionists who wished to free those already enslaved but who wished to work within the system. Slaves' freedom could be purchased, and such initiatives were publicized in the newspaper. As we have discussed, readers were notified in 1828 about campaigns to raise money to free the children of Abdul Rahahman, the former prince of Futa Jallon who had been enslaved in the South before his master freed him on the condition that he would return to Africa. In June 1828, the newspaper ran an announcement of a lecture that would be given in Philadelphia by the Reverend George Erskine. A Presbyterian minister and former slave who had been manumitted in 1815, Erskine traveled to various cities, speaking and preaching in order to raise money to liberate his children. At the Philadelphia engagement, the notice indicated, "a collection" would be "taken up to aid him in redeeming his children who are at this time in bondage in East Tennessee."[87]

While at least some of Erskine's and Rahahman's children obtained freedom, a similar effort to buy the liberty of the poet George Moses Horton failed. A North Carolina slave who taught himself to read and write, Horton became known for his poetry among students at the University of North Carolina and eventually his fame spread. Various philanthropists helped publicize his work, and efforts in the North and South were undertaken to purchase his freedom from his master. African Americans throughout the nation became involved. Detailing the case in an August 1828 letter, the newspaper's North Carolina correspondent noted that although it might have seemed that "a sum like 4 or $500 might soon be gathered" in the region, in the case of "the emancipation of a fellow being," few would offer aid. *Freedom's Journal*, the writer suggested, could help raise the necessary funds. In the following months, Russwurm appealed to readers. "A little can be spared towards effecting the liberation of one who bids fair to be an honour to our race," he urged in a September 1828 piece. "*Something must be done—George M. Horton must be liberated from a state of bondage.* Were each person of colour in this city to give but one penny, there would be no danger about obtaining his liberty. But as it is impossible to obtain even this little sum from all, will not all who feel disposed to give a little send us their names. . . ." Unfortunately, these efforts to free Horton did not prove successful.[88]

Of course, the purchasing of slaves' freedom was, at some level, problematic and contradictory. Was it not conciliating slaveholders to compensate them? Did it not convey, at some level, that they had a "right" to their "property"? It could be argued that this approach not only did not attack the institution of slavery but perhaps even furthered it by participating in the buying and selling of human beings. On the other hand, such efforts brought freedom to some who might not otherwise gain it.[89]

Even those who stood firmly against the system of slavery, such as Russwurm and the militant abolitionist and *Freedom's Journal* agent David Walker, supported efforts to purchase the freedom of Rahahman's children and George Moses Horton.[90] A reprinted article from the British *Manchester Gazette* that advocated forming a society to redeem slaves in the British colonies articulated the dilemma clearly while taking a firm stand in favor of the practice. "Though I conceive the principle of compensation to the slave holders, to be exactly similar to that which would indemnify the receivers of property they have wrongfully obtained," the author Phileleutherus declared, "yet I am exceedingly unwillingly [*sic*] that any portion of my fellow subjects should remain in slavery, because they cannot now be set at liberty in the way I should most approve. If the existing slaves are to taste the sweets of freedom, every available method must at once be emplyed [*sic*] for their deliverance." Even those who "on *principle*, feel a repugnance to this method," Phileleutherus observed, "will probably consent to adopt it, rather than suffer their slave brethren to linger and perish in captivity, while waiting the slow progress of legislative enactment." Phileleutherus also suggested that the redemption of slaves should not take the place of other abolitionist activism. The observation that, even in the face of valid objections to buying individuals' freedom, slaves must be freed by "every available method" would no doubt have rung true for Russwurm and for many readers.[91]

Indeed, in general, the sense that abolitionists needed to be creative and flexible, using all tactics, pervaded the coverage of slavery and antislavery in *Freedom's Journal*. Theory and practice, politics and religion, legal and extralegal efforts, cooperative ventures with white abolitionists and separate projects—all contributed to this immense and vital struggle. In the pages of *Freedom's Journal*, on slavery as well as on other vital issues, the editors, contributors, and readers of *Freedom's Journal* defined their concerns in diverse and powerful ways, laying the groundwork for the efforts of those who would follow them.

NOTES

1. Samuel E. Cornish and John B. Russwurm, "To Our Patrons," *FJ*, 16 March 1827; untitled item in "Domestic News" column, *FJ*, 20 July 1827.

2. John B. Russwurm, "Freedom is the Brilliant Gift of Heaven," *FJ*, 16 January 1829.

3. See, for example, Dumond, *Antislavery*; Lawrence J. Friedman, *Gregarious Saints*; Barnes, *Antislavery Impulse*; Kraditor, *Means and Ends*; Walters, "Boundaries"; Walters, *Antislavery Appeal*; Scott, "Abolition"; Perry, *Radical Abolitionism*; Arkin, "Federalist Trope."

4. Quarles, *Black Abolitionists*; Pease and Pease, *They Who Would Be Free*; Levesque, "Black Abolitionists"; Dick, *Black Protest*; Donald Jacobs, *Courage and Conscience*; Yee, *Black Women Abolitionists*; Logan, *"We Are Coming"*; Ripley et al., *Black Abolitionist Papers*; Hinks, *To Awaken*; Swartz, "Emancipatory Narratives," 347–52; Bacon, *Humblest*.

5. See Ripley et al., *Witness for Freedom*, 12; Bacon, *Humblest*, 23–24, 27.

6. Tise, *Proslavery*, 32–36; 97–102. Tise argues against the traditional "positive good theory of slavery" favored by many historians, which asserts that during the 1820s "there was a significant shift in proslavery thinking" out of which grew the argument that slavery benefited African Americans. In contrast, Tise demonstrates that this view was a component of defenses of slavery from the colonial period.

7. Walsh, *Appeal*, 409–10.

8. Cornish and Russwurm, "To Our Patrons."

9. "Summary" column, *FJ*, 6 July 1827; "Summary" column, *FJ*, 8 June 1827; "Horrible! Most Horrible!" *FJ*, 3 August 1827.

10. "From the Richmond Compiler of July 24," *FJ*, 3 August 1827; "Hunting Men," *FJ*, 6 July 1827.

11. Calderhead, "Role," 196; Dickson Preston, *Young Frederick Douglass*, 74–75; Tadman, *Speculators and Slaves*, 29–31; Gudmestad, *Troublesome Commerce*, 20.

12. Bancroft, *Slave Trading*, 366–69; Calderhead, "Role," 195; Gudmestad, *Troublesome Commerce*, 152–53.

13. Bancroft, *Slave Trading*, 367–81; see also Gudmestad, *Troublesome Commerce*, 154–57.

14. Untitled item in "Domestic News" section, *FJ*, 30 March 1827.

15. Benjamin Lundy, editorial comments on article "Execution of William Bowser," *Genius of Universal Emancipation*, 2 January 1827. Lundy described the attack in "The Late Assault," *Genius of Universal Emancipation*, 20 January 1827.

16. Calderhead, "Role"; Dickson Preston, *Young Frederick Douglass*, 76–80; Tadman, *Speculators and Slaves*, 29–31; Bancroft, *Slave Trading*, 39–43; Gudmestad, *Troublesome Commerce*, 25–30, 155–56.

17. "Baltimore Justice!!" *FJ*, 27 April 1827.

18. "Effects of Slavery," *FJ*, 16 March 1827; "Slavery at Home," *FJ*, 26 September 1828.

19. John B. Russwurm, "Travelling Scraps," *FJ*, 29 August 1828; Howard, "Slavery in the District of Columbia," *FJ*, 28 February 1829.

20. Although the notion of slavery as a blessing was a commonplace of eighteenth- and nineteenth-century proslavery thought, I have been unable to determine the exact origins of the phrase "blessings of slavery," either as an ironic description or a defense of slavery, although examples of both usages can be found throughout the antebellum period.

21. On this mode of signifying, see Gates, *Figures*, 17, 236; Gates, *Signifying*, 103–24.

22. Y., "Blessings of Slavery in Baltimore, MD.!!" *FJ*, 31 October 1828.

23. "Domestic Slavery," *FJ*, 7 November 1828; "Blessings of Slavery," *FJ*, 18 January 1828.

24. "Cuba," *FJ*, 30 November 1827; John B. Russwurm, "Slavery in Cuba," *FJ*, 30 November 1827; "Extracts, from the Supplement to the Anti-Slavery Monthly Reporter, for June, 1828," *FJ*, 14 November 1828.

25. Samuel E. Cornish and John B. Russwurm, "Slavery in the West-Indies," *FJ*, 11 May 1827; "Happiness of Being Flogged," *FJ*, 5 October 1827. Other news items on slavery in the British colonies included "West India Negro Whip," *FJ*, 26 October 1827 and "Slavery in the Colonies," *FJ*, 4 April 1828.

26. See, for example, "From a Sierra Leone Paper," *FJ*, 25 May 1827; "Slave-Trade," *FJ*, 27 July 1827; "Slave Trade," *FJ*, 14 September 1827; "Rio Janeiro," *FJ*, 11 April 1828; "The Slave Trade," *FJ*, 12 December 1828.

27. "Blessings of Slavery!" *FJ*, 22 June 1827; "Blessings of Slavery!" [in "Summary" column], *FJ*, 29 June 1827; "Blessings of Slavery" [in "Summary" column], *FJ*, 22 February 1828.

28. Wiecek, *"Somerset,"* 87–88; Catterall, *Judicial Cases*, vol. 1, 15. Wiecek and Finkelman note that there is dispute over whether Mansfield actually made various statements attributed to him in the most frequently cited account of the case by Capell Lofft. Regardless of its accuracy (which Wiecek defends), the strong statement about the conflicts between slavery and natural law was widely quoted and associated with the case for abolitionists in Britain and the United States. See Wiecek, *"Somerset,"* 141–46; Finkelman, *Imperfect Union*, 39.

29. Finkelman, *Imperfect Union*, 38–45; Finkelman, *Dred Scott*, 20–21; Wiecek, *"Somerset"*; Fehrenbacher, *Dred Scott*, 53–56. On *Somerset v. Stewart* and its implications for American slave law, see also Finkelman, *Slavery*, 19–25; Wiecek, *Sources*, 28–39; Catterall, *Judicial Cases*, vol. 1, 4–5, 14–18; Cover, *Justice Accused*, 87–88; Higginbotham, *In the Matter*, 333–55; David Brion Davis, *In the Image*, 196–98; Hunter, "Geographies"; Nash, *Unknown American Revolution*, 120–21.

30. [Prince Hoare], "Case of Somerset," *FJ*, 30 November 1827.

31. Wiecek, *"Somerset,"* 88, 113–15.

32. Catterall, *Judicial Cases*, vol. 1, 34. For further discussion of the case of the slave Grace, see Catterall, *Judicial Cases*, vol. 1, 6–8, 34–37; Finkelman, *Dred Scott*, 21; Finkelman, *Imperfect Union*, 185–87; Higginbotham, *In the Matter*, 360–63; Wiecek, *"Somerset,"* 111; Wiecek, *Sources*, 36–37.

33. "Lord Stowell's Decision Concerning the Slave Grace," *FJ*, 11 January 1828; Finkelman, *Imperfect Union*, 185–235.

34. Finkelman, *Imperfect Union*, 46–100.

35. "Important," *FJ*, 25 January 1828; Catterall, *Judicial Cases*, vol. 4, 279–80. On this case, see also Finkelman, *Imperfect Union*, 242–43.

36. "Important Decision," *FJ*, 14 December 1827; Catterall, *Judicial Cases*, vol. 5, 114–15, 128–29. On *Merry v. Tiffin and Menard*, see also "History of Freedom Suits in Missouri"; Elley, "Missouri's Dred Scott Case."

37. "Important Decision."

38. "From the Albany Daily Advertiser," *FJ*, 3 October 1828; Act Declaring 1827 as the End of Slavery in New York, 1817, in Gellman and Quigley, *Jim Crow*, 70–71; Gradual Abolition Act, 1799, in Gellman and Quigley, *Jim Crow*, 53; "An Act Relative to Slaves and Servants," March 31, 1817, in *Laws of the State of New-York*, 138–39.

39. "From the Albany Daily Advertiser."

40. McManus, *History*, 175–77; Gellman and Quigley, *Jim Crow*, 67.

41. "Ranaway [sic] Slave," *FJ*, 21 December 1827. Although I have searched at length, I have been unable to determine the particulars of this case or locate any other accounts that match it. However, the New York courts frequently upheld the

rights of slaveholders to fugitives; see Finkelman, *Imperfect Union*, 75–76; Catterall, *Judicial Cases*, vol. 4, 353.

42. Russwurm, "Freedom is the Brilliant Gift."

43. On these justifications, see Frederickson, *Black Image*, 60–61; Shanks, "Biblical Anti-Slavery Argument," 136; Sanders, "Hamitic Hypothesis," 523; Jenkins, *Pro-Slavery Thought*, 6, 58, 119, 201–07; Haynes, *Noah's Curse*, 6–8; Bacon, *Humblest*, 25, 159; Goldenberg, *Curse of Ham*, 175–76.

44. "The Curse of Canaan," *FJ*, 4 May 1827.

45. "History of Slavery," *FJ*, 13 July 1827; "History of Slavery," *FJ*, 20 July 1827; "History of Slavery," *FJ*, 27 July 1827; "History of Slavery," *FJ*, 3 August 1827.

46. Raboteau, "African-Americans"; Coleman, *Tribal Talk*, 128.

47. S**** B—, "For the Freedom's Journal" [letter to editors], *FJ*, 14 September 1827.

48. Aristides, "Slavery" [letter to editor], *FJ*, 28 September 1827; John B. Russwurm, "Christianity and Slavery," *FJ*, 31 October 1828.

49. See Lincoln and Mamiya, *Black Church*, 3–4; Coleman, *Tribal Talk*, 179–82; Cone, *God*, 32–33, 108–22.

50. Lincoln and Mamiya, *Black Church*, 4; see also Coleman, *Tribal Talk*, 181–82.

51. See, for example, Finseth, "David Walker," 350; Blanck, "Seventeen Eighty-Three"; Gordon, *Black Identity*, 93.

52. S. F. D., "People of Colour," *FJ*, 23 March 1827; Aristides, "Slavery"; "General Views of the Abolition Society of Stark County, Ohio, Adopted at a Regular Meeting, held November 3, 1827," *FJ*, 7 December 1827. On S. F. D.'s article, see also Ernest, *Liberation*, 290–91.

53. Aristides, "Slavery."

54. Jefferson, *Notes*, 163; "For the Freedom's Journal," *FJ*, 7 September 1827.

55. See Bacon, *Humblest*, 84–93, 103–4.

56. "On the Demoralizing Influence of Slavery," *FJ*, 11 April 1828; "On the Demoralizing Influence of Slavery," *FJ*, 18 April 1828; "On the Demoralizing Influence of Slavery," *FJ*, 25 April 1828.

57. S. F. D., "People of Colour," *FJ*, 27 April 1827.

58. Say, *Treatise*, 130, 206–8. On Say's views and writings about slavery and slave labor, see Palmer, *J.-B. Say*, 61–65; Drescher, *Mighty Experiment*, 63–70.

59. Adam Hodgson, "A Letter, to M. Jean Baptiste Say, on the Comparative Expense of Free and Slave Labour," *FJ*, 10 August 1827; Adam Hodgson, "A Letter, to M. Jean Baptiste Say, on the Comparative Expense of Free and Slave Labour," *FJ*, 17 August 1827; Adam Hodgson, "A Letter, to M. Jean Baptiste Say, on the Comparative Expense of Free and Slave Labour," *FJ*, 24 August 1827; Adam Hodgson, "A Letter, to M. Jean Baptiste Say, on the Comparative Expense of Free and Slave Labour," *FJ*, 31 August 1827; Adam Hodgson, "A Letter, to M. Jean Baptiste Say, on the Comparative Expense of Free and Slave Labour," *FJ*, 7 September 1827; Adam Hodgson, "A Letter, to M. Jean Baptiste Say, on the Comparative Expense of Free and Slave Labour," *FJ*, 14 September 1827. Seymour Drescher notes that Say's reply to this correspondence "thanked Hodgson for his interest" and affirmed "that slavery was incompatible with advanced industry and would someday disappear," but he "retracted none of the calculations and conclusions" of the *Treatise* (*Mighty Experiment*, 68).

60. [Samuel M. Janney], "Views of the Benevolent Society of Alexandria for Ameliorating and Improving the Condition of the People of Colour. No. I," *FJ*, 25 May 1827. Samuel M. Janney, *Memoirs of Samuel M. Janney, Late of Lincoln, Loudoun County, Va., A Minister in the Religious Society of Friends (Written by Himself)*, in *Documenting the American South* [electronic archival collection], 28; [Samuel M. Janney], "Views of the Benevolent Society of Alexandria for Ameliorating and Improving the Condition of the People of Colour. No II," *FJ*, 1 June 1827; [Samuel M. Janney], "Views of the Benevolent Society of Alexandria for Ameliorating and Improving the Condition of the People of Colour. No. III," *FJ*, 8 June 1827; [Samuel M. Janney], "Views of the Benevolent Society of Alexandria for Ameliorating and Improving the Condition of the People of Colour. No IV," *FJ*, 15 June 1827; Although these articles were published without any author's name, Janney noted in his *Memoirs* that "on behalf of" the Benevolent Society he wrote in 1827 "a series of essays on slavery and the domestic slave trade" for publication in the *Alexandria Gazette* (28). *Freedom's Journal* indicated that the series was reprinted from this source; the articles were first published in the *Gazette* from April 30, 1827, to May 28, 1827.

61. S. F. D., "People of Colour," *FJ*, 6 April 1827; Z., "Slavery," *FJ*, 30 November 1827.

62. Adams, *Neglected Period*, 16–28; see also Quarles, *Black Abolitionists*, 11.

63. Newman, "Chosen Generation," 76–77.

64. "Abolition of Slavery," *FJ*, 20 April 1827; "Abolition of Slavery in the State of New-York," *FJ*, 4 May 1827; "Abolition of Slavery," *FJ*, 22 June 1827; "Abolition of Slavery," *FJ*, 6 July 1827; "Celebration of the Second Anniversary of the Abolition of Domestic Slavery in the State of New-York," *FJ*, 11 July 1828.

65. Hutton, *Early Black Press*, 39.

66. "Views of the Benevolent Society of Alexandria for Ameliorating and Improving the Condition of the People of Colour. No. I." Janney noted in his *Memoirs*, written in 1881, that he later changed his mind about colonization (29). He also recollected that the gradualist views he expressed in the late 1820s did not reflect his own opinion. Speaking of a petition presented to Congress by the Benevolent Society for the abolition of slavery in the District of Columbia, he maintained, "For my part, I was in favor of immediate and unconditional emancipation, and did not hesitate to say so; but knowing the prejudice against it in the minds of the people, I only asked for gradual emancipation" (33). (The context suggests that he referred to "immediate and unconditional emancipation" in the District of Columbia; it is unclear whether he supported immediate abolition throughout the United States.)

67. "Anti-Slavery Society," *FJ*, 27 June 1828; "Anti-Slavery Society. (Continued)," *FJ*, 4 July 1828; "Anti-Slavery Society. (Concluded)," *FJ*, 11 July 1828; "Abolition of Slavery," *FJ*, 29 August 1828; "Abolition of Slavery," *FJ*, 19 September 1828; "Slavery," *FJ*, 5 December 1828; "Slavery. (Continued)," *FJ*, 12 December 1828. On British antislavery, see Walvin, "Propaganda"; Walvin, *Black Ivory*, 259–74; Drescher, *Econocide*.

68. Ironic comparison of policies toward slavery in Britain and America constituted an important theme in antebellum African-American antislavery rhetoric; see Bacon, *Humblest*, 93–97.

69. "England," *FJ*, 9 November 1827. African-American abolitionists and their British counterparts continued throughout the antebellum period to collaborate, with prominent black activists such as Frederick Douglass and Charles Lenox Remond visiting and gaining support from their colleagues in Great Britain. See Quarles, *Black Abolitionists*, 117–18, 129–42; Pease and Pease, *They Who Would Be Free*, 48–67; Fisch, *American Slaves*; Rice, *Radical Narratives*, 172–74; Bacon, *Humblest*, 93.

70. Adams, *Neglected Period*, 16; untitled comments of the editor of *New-England Inquirer*, *FJ*, 7 November 1828; "Address from the American Convention for Promoting the Abolition of Slavery, &c. &c," *FJ*, 19 December 1828; "The District of Columbia," *FJ*, 7 December 1827.

71. "Minutes, &c., of the American Convention," *FJ*, 1 February 1828; "Minutes, &c., of the American Convention. [Continued]," *FJ*, 8 February 1828; "Minutes, &c., of the American Convention. [Continued]," *FJ*, 15 February 1828; "Minutes, &c., of the American Convention. [Concluded]," *FJ*, 22 February 1828; "Circular. From the Corresponding Committee of the Manumission Society of New-York," *FJ*, 2 May 1828; "Circular. From the Corresponding Committee of the Manumission Society of New-York. (Concluded)," *FJ*, 9 May 1828; "To the Honourable the Senate and House of Representatives of the United States of America, in Congress Assembled," *FJ*, 1 February 1828.

72. "Minutes, &c., of the American Convention," 1 February 1828; "Minutes, &c., of the American Convention. [Continued]," 15 February 1828.

73. "Minutes, &c., of the American Convention. [Concluded]," 22 February 1828.

74. Wilberforce, "Slavery in the District of Columbia," *FJ*, 14 November 1828.

75. John B. Russwurm, "Domestic Slave Trade," *FJ*, 17 October 1828.

76. "For Freedom's Journal," *FJ*, 19 September 1828; "General Views of the Abolition Society of Stark County, Ohio."

77. S. F. D., "People of Colour," *FJ*, 13 April 1827; S. F. D., "People of Colour," *FJ*, 20 April 1827.

78. S. F. D., "People of Colour," 27 April 1827; "For the Freedom's Journal," *FJ*, 20 July 1827.

79. New York Committee of Vigilance, *First Annual Report*, 10–13.

80. John B. Russwurm, "Travelling Scraps," *FJ*, 15 August 1828.

81. John B. Russwurm, "Worthy of Notice," *FJ*, 31 October 1828; John B. Russwurm, "Self Interest," *FJ*, 7 November 1828; John B. Russwurm, "Self-Interest," *FJ*, 14 November 1828.

82. "Fugitive Slaves," *FJ*, 16 January 1829; "Fugitive Slaves. (Concluded)," *FJ*, 24 January 1829; Russwurm, "Freedom is the Brilliant Gift." On the communication between the American and British governments about fugitive slaves taking refuge in Canada, see E. Delorus Preston, "Genesis," 163–64; Fehrenbacher, *Slaveholding Republic*, 102–3.

83. "Notice," *FJ*, 25 April 1828; John B. Russwurm, "Land of Liberty," *FJ*, 5 December 1828. The former also appeared in other issues.

84. Untitled item in "Summary" column, *FJ*, 4 May 1827.

85. "Horrors of Slavery," *FJ*, 15 February 1828. Although the source for this article was noted in *Freedom's Journal* as the "*Providence, R. I. Lit. Gaz.*," it seems to

have been a misprint. There was no paper published in Providence at this time with the name *Literary Gazette*; in addition, the comment in the article that correspondence should be sent to the editor of the *Literary Cadet* suggests it was this periodical.

86. "Kidnapping," *FJ*, 8 August 1828; Russwurm, "Land of Liberty"; Russwurm, "Self-Interest," *FJ*, 14 November 1828.

87. Announcement of lecture by George Erskine, *FJ*, 13 June 1828. On Erskine, see Robert Booker, "Knoxville Had Link to Liberia," *News Sentinel*, 19 August 2003; Apperson, "George M. Erskine." Although some of Erskine's children were liberated through his efforts, it is not clear whether they all obtained their freedom.

88. "Extract," *FJ*, 29 August 1828; John B. Russwurm, "George M. Horton," *FJ*, 12 September 1828. On Horton, see Horton and Horton, *In Hope*, x–xi; Sherman, *Black Bard*, 1–14; Richmond, *Bid the Vassal Soar*, 105–8; Bruce, *Origins*, 169–71.

89. These questions became even more controversial during the subsequent decades leading to the Civil War, as abolitionists became more militant in their insistence that slavery must be abolished immediately and systemically. See, for example, "Buying a Mother's Freedom," *North Star*, 13 July 1849; "Buying Persons Out of Slavery," *Frederick Douglass' Paper*, 16 July 1852; "Meeting of Colored Citizens at the City Hall," *Frederick Douglass' Paper*, 31 August 1855; "A Mother Pleading for Her Son," *Frederick Douglass' Paper*, 18 September 1855; Harriet Jacobs, *Incidents*, 187. Indeed, these dilemmas remain highly relevant in the twenty-first century, as those seeking to abolish slavery in the Sudan and other regions debate these very issues, with some individuals and groups supporting the redemption of slaves and others opposing it. See Bok, *Escape*, 150–51; Arrowsmith, "Slave Redemption"; Davan Maharaj, "Panel Frowns on Efforts to Buy Sudan Slaves' Freedom," *Los Angeles Times*, 28 May 2002; Miniter, "False Promise"; Christine Gardner, "Slave Redemption."

90. Articles in the paper noted Walker's support for these efforts; see "Public Dinner in Boston," *FJ*, 24 October 1828; John B. Russwurm, "George M. Horton," *FJ*, 3 October 1828.

91. Phileleutherus, "Redemption of Slaves," *FJ*, 11 April 1828.

PART III

9

~

"Echoes and Re-Echoes": The Impact and Legacy of *Freedom's Journal*

If *Freedom's Journal* was, to return to the metaphor suggested by Theodore Wright in 1837, a powerful storm, appearing "with a clap of thunder" and affecting all who came in contact with it during its short but intense tenure, we would expect it to alter the environment radically. And indeed it did, in a variety of ways. To grasp its influence, consider the comments of Uriah Boston in an 1840 letter to the *Colored American*:

> There is no one means connected with our enterprise which is so much cal-
> culated to do so much good, and is so effective abroad as the press; and I re-
> joice that . . . we have an organ through which we can communicate with
> each other, and correspond upon all the different subjects which demand our
> attention in all parts of the free states; yes, and I may say, in the slave states
> and throughout the civilized world. . . .
>   These things of themselves, rightly considered, ought to be sufficient to in-
> duce every man and woman to take the Colored American. . . . And thus our
> people . . . all say, in tones of thunder, which sound from Maine to Georgia,
> and the sound echoes and re-echoes, long live the Colored American![1]

Although Boston described the *Colored American* specifically, his comments reveal how fundamentally *Freedom's Journal* had transformed
African-American life, letters, and activism. The central role of the press
in the African-American community was established, fostering national
communication and cooperation. It allowed its editors and contributors to
hone their rhetorical skills and to examine and articulate their views
about the role of people of color in and beyond America. It gave voice to
the concerns of African Americans about issues that affected them and the

nation, such as colonization and slavery, in ways that influenced black and white abolitionists and reformers. If, by 1840, African Americans could affirm the power of the press "in tones of thunder," it was in large part because of *Freedom's Journal's* powerful precedent and pioneering influence. A groundbreaking effort that changed African-American life and letters, *Freedom's Journal* truly created "echoes and re-echoes."

These waves reverberated in the lives of those who were associated with the periodical; the work of those who were influenced by it; and the African-American press of the nineteenth, twentieth, and twenty-first centuries. Cornish and Russwurm both continued their public work as well as their editing, each striving in his own fashion (although not without difficulties) to further the empowerment that was reflected and fostered in *Freedom's Journal.* That two men who worked together on a groundbreaking periodical would take such divergent paths after its demise is significant, revealing that the complex questions faced by African-American activists, from their time to ours—about assimilation, separation, nationalism, identity—can provoke various responses. The abolition movement that gained ground in the 1830s and that led to organizations like the AASS was built on the foundation that was laid by *Freedom's Journal.* Activists who had worked on and/or written for the periodical played important roles in the movements against slavery and colonization, helping to shape the views of white abolitionists. Black editors who followed Cornish and Russwurm built on the principles they had established and confirmed: that the press was fundamental to the struggle against oppression, that a variety of views should be represented on issues, that African Americans had the right and the duty to speak for themselves, and that they needed a forum in which they could do so independently and forcefully. Let us examine these developments, beginning with the editors' later careers.

"I SHALL LIVE AND DIE IN AFRICA": JOHN RUSSWURM

Russwurm arrived in Liberia in November 1829.[2] In a letter published in the *African Repository and Colonial Journal* five months later, which Russwurm wrote to "a young man of colour" who was "preparing himself for missionary efforts in Africa," he expressed enthusiasm about the prospects for him and the colony: "What my sensations were upon landing I can hardly describe. This town contains double the number of houses I expected. . . . The colonists here, (at Monrovia,) appear to be thriving. . . . You here behold coloured men exercising all the duties of office of which you can scarcely believe, many fulfill the important duties with much dignity."[3] It seemed that Russwurm had found what he sought, a place where he and other men of color could prosper, be independent, and rise to positions of leadership. As superintendent of the schools, Russwurm dedicated himself to the welfare of the colony. In March 1830, he revived the *Liberia Herald*, a newspaper that was founded in 1826 but ceased publication when its previous editor died. Also in 1830, Russwurm was elected colonial secretary. He married in 1833 and entered into a business partnership with Joseph Dailey, a colonist from Virginia. It certainly appeared that Russwurm's dreams had come true.

In the *Liberia Herald*, Russwurm published ACS reports, material originally published in colonizationist periodicals, international news, advice, historical sketches, and reprinted articles from American newspapers. In his editorial remarks, Russwurm defended the ACS and the colonization venture, and spoke glowingly about the colony, which he deemed a "land of true equality." "Colonization . . . must go on and prosper," he asserted in an 1831 commentary. "Every year has gained it advocates among the wise of the land. . . ." In an 1832 editorial, he provided a positive report of Liberia's "advanc[ement] in commerce and agriculture and population" and noted its "peace and happiness" despite the "internal commotions" that "have been the lot of more civilized portions of the globe."[4]

In reality, though, the situation was not as promising as it seemed, either for Russwurm or for the colonists as a whole. The ACS had sent white officials to oversee the government of the colony, and the settlers were not pleased that they were given so little control in their affairs. In an 1835 letter to his half-brother Francis Edward, Russwurm was candid about his bitter disappointment with those who held power in the colony: "More fanaticism, bigotry & ignorance I never saw amongst men, not excepting the two last agents of the A. C. S." Russwurm was not alone in believing that various ACS representatives were racist; other colonists drew similar conclusions. Dailey described colonial agent Joseph Mechlin, for example, who governed the colony from 1829 to 1833, as an "insidious hypocrite" who ruled as "a complete monarch" over "his cringing subjects, *or slaves*, to use a fitter expression." There was also conflict between the settlers and the natives—the beginnings of the longstanding tension between the "Americo-Liberians," the African-American colonists and their descendants, and the indigenous population—due to resentment of the natives about the settlers' presence, the colonists' condescending attitude toward the Africans, African participation in the slave trade, and wars between African tribes. The latter, as Russwurm remarked to Francis Edward, damaged trade with the natives.[5]

Russwurm's positive portrayals of the colony in the *Herald* were contradicted by accounts of other settlers. Writing to African-American abolitionist Robert Purvis from Liberia in 1833, Dailey related that "Public improvements are suspended & deteriorating" and asserted that "were it not for the mercantile & mechanical enterprise of a number of the citizens, the Colony wd. present a desolate spectacle." "The local resources of the Colony with regard to agriculture is not in proportion to one-quarter of our population," he maintained, "& if the Colonization Society continues to pour in emigrants as they have done the past year, untold sufferings must follow. . . ." So many colonists had fallen ill that the hospitals were overcrowded, Dailey lamented, and many were dying. In correspondence written the following year, white abolitionist Simeon Jocelyn echoed this judgment, noting that "a recent letter from Joseph Dailey at Liberia . . . describes the last year as one of great mortality." Russwurm's own health had declined severely. Jocelyn remarked that "Russwurm is so emaciated that [Dailey] says I should scarcely know him," and Russwurm indicated in an 1835 letter to his half-brother that he had been suffering from rheumatism for "the last two years."[6]

Russwurm also suffered professional setbacks. His letters to Francis Edward in 1834 and 1835 described business as "dull" as a result of tribal conflict. Dailey was more personal in his assignment of blame. "Russwurm's apathy and listlessness" had made him a weak partner, he related in his correspondence to Purvis, complaining, "I am compelled to labor like a slave to avoid any miscarriage." As he had as editor of *Freedom's Journal*, Russwurm encountered criticism of his management of the *Liberia Herald*. While generally praising Russwurm's editing, the *African Repository* wished for "a larger proportion of matter from his own pen," echoing concerns of his earlier critics. In an 1831 letter to William Lloyd Garrison, James Forten accused Russwurm of inaccurate reporting about the colony: "I have this moment received a letter from Liberia from an old friend of mine, he mentions . . . a [settler] family . . . of 31 persons . . . all of whom died but one—Russwurm states in his paper, that only two had died and they were children—mark his deception. . . ." Of course, Forten and Garrison, as opponents of colonization, would have been apt to criticize positive reports of the colony, but the suggestion that Russwurm was a mouthpiece for the ACS was echoed by others. Dailey—who, due to his disillusionment with both Russwurm and the colonial project, should also be considered a partial observer—noted that "all that emanates" from Russwurm in the *Herald* "(to use Garrison's expression) are a few 'pop guns' at the Liberator, in defense of the [American Colonization] Society."[7]

While it was true that the *Herald* put forward the ACS's positions, Russwurm was not always pleased to have to defend the organization. Increasingly, he found it difficult to negotiate his position between the black colonists, hoping for power in the colony, and the ACS. In 1835, the settlers staged protests against the policies of colonial agent John Pinney, a Baptist minister and Mechlin's successor. Pinney issued a proclamation that the colonists were in a state of insurrection and demanded that Russwurm print it in the *Herald*. After advising Pinney against making the declaration public, Russwurm reluctantly published the letter, enraging the colonists, who damaged the press that printed the *Herald*. Russwurm was subsequently removed from his position as colonial secretary and as the *Herald*'s editor. In an 1835 letter to Gurley, Russwurm complained that despite his efforts at preventing unrest, "the whole blame" for the disorder was "cast upon" him. It is not surprising that his 1835 letter to his half-brother expressed weariness and despair: "I suppose I shall live and die in Africa, but I hope not in Liberia."[8]

Soon, Russwurm was presented with the opportunity to get out from under the ACS's power. The plans of the Maryland Colonization Society offered an appealing alternative to those of the national organization; in 1832, Maryland had granted money to the organization and two years later it had founded a colony at Cape Palmas, south of Monrovia on the West African coast. In 1836, the Maryland Society's board appointed Russwurm governor. Russwurm encountered difficulties—shortages of food, disagreements with other officials, currency problems, resentment of his policies by some settlers, conflicts with indigenous people—but he persisted. Heartened by Liberia's independence from the ACS in 1847, Russwurm hoped for the same for his colony. His death in 1851 prevented him from seeing the independent republic of Maryland in Liberia in 1854, which was annexed to the Liberian Republic three years later.

SAMUEL CORNISH, EDITOR AND ACTIVIST

Shortly after the demise of *Freedom's Journal*, Cornish resumed editorial work. On May 29, 1829, the first issue of his newspaper the *Rights of All* was published.[9] The venture was short-lived, however; only six monthly issues appeared, with the last published on October 9, 1829. Yet as when he resigned from *Freedom's Journal*, Cornish did not exit public life when the *Rights of All* ceased publication. During the 1830s he worked diligently against slavery and prejudice and for the improvement of life and education for African Americans. At the First Annual Convention of the People of Colour in September 1830—the initial gathering of the convention movement, which continued until 1864—he was elected "to collect funds" for a proposed manual labor college for African Americans.[10] He was active in the Phoenix Society, an organization designed to promote African-American education and literacy, which ran a high school,[11] as well as in the New York Committee of Vigilance, the organization of "practical abolitionists" noted in the previous chapter who worked to prevent kidnappings of free blacks. He served terms on both the Board of Managers and the Executive Committee of the AASS, founded in December 1833. Cornish continued to argue against slavery and colonization, publishing articles (both on his own and in conjunction with other members of the Executive Committee) in antislavery organs such as the *Emancipator* and the *Liberator*.

A few African-American newspapers appeared briefly in the early and mid-1830s, as we shall see, but it was not until 1837 that Cornish resumed editing. In March of that year, he became the editor of the two-month-old *Weekly Advocate*, previously edited by Philip A. Bell, changing its name to the *Colored American*. After a year, he gained an assistant, James McCune Smith, a writer and physician. Financial problems plagued the newspaper, due in part to the delinquency of payments by its subscribers. A libel suit precipitated by an 1837 article cost the newspaper precious funds and placed a strain on Cornish as editor. In October 1837, Cornish printed a letter from Joseph Gavino to David Ruggles, Secretary of the New York Committee of Vigilance, which accused a John Russell, "a colored man and seaman's landlord," of helping a sea captain kidnap "three native Africans" in order to sell them in New Orleans. Russell, the letter alleged, had "forced" the men "on board the vessel." Ruggles had forwarded the letter to Cornish with assurances—which were printed in a headnote to Gavino's letter—that he was "satisfied as to its authenticity and truth." Russell sued the *Colored American* and Ruggles for libel and won. The damages and costs came to almost 600 dollars, as Cornish noted in the paper in November 1838, but the Vigilance Committee and its secretary—who should rightly, Cornish argued, bear the financial burden—did not respond to requests. A July 1839 report even accused Ruggles of withholding "monies which were paid to him to be applied towards aiding [the *Colored American*] to pay [its] expenses." By this time, Cornish and Smith were no longer editors of the paper, having left in June 1839. They were succeeded by "Charles B. Ray & Co.," a designation Ray explained in an October 1839 notice to readers: "During the absence of Mr. Ray, the editorial department is conducted by the gentleman for whom the word Co. stands for—namely P[hilip] A Bell." Ray also informed readers that Cornish and Smith left because "the patronage of the paper was not sufficient to allow us to employ them any longer."[12]

Although active in various causes throughout the 1830s, Cornish came into conflict with other reformers, at times quite publicly in the columns of the *Colored American*. Working closely with white abolitionists, particularly his colleagues in the AASS, he—like other African-American abolitionists—resented their condescension, racist beliefs, and attempts to dictate the parameters of antislavery activism; and he was not afraid to say so.[13] In a May 1837 editorial titled "Difficulties of Abolition," Cornish gave white abolitionists credit for their efforts, asserting that "the colored man who does not hold the person, the character and the doings, of American Abolitionists in the highest estimation, is unworthy . . . the standing he holds among the reputable of his race." Yet while "conced[ing] to them every thing which constitutes purity of motive, and zeal, in prosecution," Cornish declared that "with the wise and good Reformers of every age, they have much to investigate, and much to learn," particularly with respect to their treatment of their African-American colleagues:

> Our friends should judge of us as they do of other men, or they never can succeed.
>
>   . . . We would have our friends and brethren know, unless our moral and intellectual attainments be measured by the same rule, and brought, to the same standard by which our white brethren are tried and estimated, we cannot occupy the same place in society, nor be held in the same repute.
>
> We want NO FAVOURS in this matter—we wish not to be carried forward with any of our imperfections. We feel ourselves under the same obligations, and capable of the same moral and intellectual responsibilities.[14]

Cornish and other African-American abolitionists also found some of the philosophical positions of white abolitionists problematic. Garrison and his followers were staunch critics of the clergy, held that political action was inherently corrupt, and linked antislavery with issues such as women's rights. As a minister, Cornish could hardly be blamed for chafing at the Garrisonians' anticlericalism. He also felt that it was imprudent to alienate potentially supportive white ministers. Believing that "political action . . . should be left as a matter of conscience" and that issues such as women's rights should not "have anything to do with . . . Anti-Slavery efforts," he criticized Garrison's approach. Many African Americans, particularly in New England, continued to support Garrison, leading to divisions, which Cornish lamented in an 1839 editorial: "The threatening difficulties with some of our New England brethren, to every colored man and every true abolitionist, are matters of deep concern. . . . Why then make governments or anti-governments—resistance or non-resistance—women's rights or men's rights—Sabbaths or anti-Sabbaths, a bone of contention?"[15]
Cornish may have regretted debates with his fellow African-American reformers, but he certainly did not avoid them. Indeed, by blaming "New England brethren" for the struggles within the ranks of African-American abolitionists, he accused them of injuring the cause. Cornish was also critical of the American Moral Reform Society, an organization that had grown out of the 1835 national African-American convention, and of his Philadelphia colleagues who dominated it. He dismissed the organization as unproductive and overly focused on irrelevant issues, claiming that it "occupie[d] the time" and "waste[d] the means, the strength and the talents of wise and good men, who, but for its existence, would surely appropriate them to better purposes." He did not spare the "leading members of the

Society," particularly Robert Purvis and William Whipper, whom he described as "vague, wild, indefinite and confused in their views." He criticized those people of color who took the advice of white abolitionists to avoid "political strife":

> We always believed, and always said, it was a bad and ruinous policy. No man nor body of men, ever gained anything by yielding up their manhood. Why colored citizens should ever have been advised by their friends to keep from the polls, we cannot tell, and we are at a much greater loss to account for their weakness in following such advice. . . . That man who conceives himself so insignificant as to be socially or politically unimportant in the community, is in great danger of being morally and mentally so.[16]

Cornish clashed publicly with Ruggles, their relationship already strained by the aforementioned libel suit. Cornish and other members of the New York Committee of Vigilance disapproved of Ruggles's management of the organization's funds and his willingness to take bold and at times extralegal action to assist fugitives.[17]

Cornish also disagreed with African-American and white political reformers because although he supported political activism, he did not approve of creating an antislavery political party. When abolitionists at a national antislavery convention in Albany in August 1839 adopted a resolution proposing that no candidate should be supported who was not in favor of immediate abolition, the *Colored American* took the side of those who countered it. Although Cornish was no longer editor at this time, he would no doubt have agreed with the paper's view and its opposition to a third party (such as the Liberty Party, created the following year). The description of the controversy and the newspaper's editorial position in it evokes debates among reformers who, in our nation's past and present, have discussed the merits of third-party candidacies:

> Say some, [voting for a third-party candidate] is better than sustaining slavery by our votes, for to vote for either party who do not go for immediate abolition is only choosing between two evils. We deny this. . . . [S]hould there be two candidates, the one much worse than the other, and whose election depended upon the neutrality of abolitionists, and his defeat upon their votes being placed in the other end of the scale, we ask, in such a case, would not abolitionists be bound to PREVENT THE GREATER EVIL by voting for the better man?

The paper argued that supporting third-party candidates was not only wrong but impractical: "Vote for the men of whatever party, who will do most for emancipation and equal rights, but do not over-shoot the mark, and tie up your hands in disfranchisement."[18]

By the time Cornish left the *Colored American* in 1839, some felt that his views were no longer relevant. Ray, for example, dismissed Cornish just a few months after succeeding him as the editor of the newspaper as "an old School man" who "stands by the old paths but does not inquire for the new" and "embraces every true principle, but goes but *just halfway*."[19] In spite of these conflicts and animosities, though, Cornish did not leave the public realm. In the 1840s and 1850s, he continued his clerical work; helped to organize missionary associations; attended public meetings; and wrote an important anticolonization pamphlet with Theodore Wright, *The Colonization Scheme Considered*. He joined with eight other African Americans, all clergymen, who were among the founding members of the American and Foreign Anti-Slavery Society, created as an alternative to the Garrisonian AASS in 1840, serving on its Executive Committee.[20] He died in 1858.

FREEDOM'S JOURNAL, ABOLITION, AND ANTEBELLUM REFORM

Influence, of course, is difficult to establish definitively, but it is clear that *Freedom's Journal* had a significant impact on antebellum reform in general and on the abolition movement in particular, both directly and indirectly. The connections among African-American leaders in different cities that were created by *Freedom's Journal* led to important developments. In the newspaper's columns, African Americans realized their goal of speaking for themselves, not merely in reaction to white America's classifications of them but in order to assert their opinions, voice their concerns, and explore questions of identity. *Freedom's Journal* established, as Martin Dann explains, that "the black press provided one of the most potent arenas in which the battle for self-definition could be fought and won" and that African-American newspapers could educate, connect, empower, foster "racial pride," and help readers realize "the promise of self-fulfillment." Richard Newman calls the newspaper "a stepping stone for key second-generation black activists" who rose to prominence in the Jacksonian era.[21] On such a foundation, much could be built.

By establishing that independent African-American voices were central to defining the experiences and perspectives of people of color—and providing a forum in which they could develop their rhetorical skills and circulate their persuasion—*Freedom's Journal* was instrumental in fostering national connections. The African-American convention movement, for example, grew out of the national consciousness that was cultivated in *Freedom's Journal* and brought together many of the activists who had worked as contributors and agents to explore issues that the periodical had raised, such as slavery, colonization, education, and moral reform. It also was an arena for the assertive, independent, and forceful public rhetoric that distinguished *Freedom's Journal*.[22]

Freedom's Journal helped create a generation of writers, orators, and activists whose impact on society was significant. In addition to Cornish, many who were associated with the periodical as agents and contributors went on to play important roles in fighting slavery and oppression. As I. Garland Penn pointed out, the periodical's "agents and contributors . . . were remarkable men" who continued to "work in behalf of the Afro-American."[23] One of the most famous was Boston agent David Walker. Walker's 1829 *Appeal to the Coloured Citizens of the World*, as we have discussed, denounced slavery and colonization; called for immediate abolition, even if violence was necessary to bring it about; and used vivid and vehement language to issue a prophetic appeal for justice for the oppressed. As our examination of *Freedom's Journal* has shown, the militancy of Walker's text should not be considered anomalous; others created forceful arguments as well in the late 1820s. Yet Walker's *Appeal* caused quite a reaction, with authorities in the South (unsuccessfully) trying to keep it out of the hands of African Americans there and even whites who opposed slavery disavowing its radical message. The *Appeal* has been linked by scholars to *Freedom's Journal* and the convention movement as a defining force in the empowerment of African Americans in the public sphere and the development of the organized antislavery movement of the 1830s and beyond.[24]

It can be argued, in fact, that *Freedom's Journal* helped make the *Appeal* possible. As Donald Jacobs asserts, "as a result" of his association with *Freedom's Journal*, "Walker quickly came to realize the power of the printed word in the shaping of popular opinion." Peter Hinks notes that various arguments in *Freedom's Journal*—such as the "essential interrelatedness of blacks throughout the world"—are central themes in the *Appeal*.[25] Walker's work, in turn, had a notable impact on white as well as African-American abolitionists. Although he stated that he "deprecated [the *Appeal*'s] spirit," William Lloyd Garrison was clearly influenced by its forceful call for immediate abolition. Calling it "one of the most remarkable productions of the age," Garrison noted that "it contains . . . many valuable truths and seasonable warnings."[26] Garrison's fiery editorials, full of prophetic language and sharp condemnations of slaveholders and those who supported them, suggest Walker's effect on the influential abolitionist and journalist, who previously had been a supporter of colonization.

Theodore Wright, *Freedom's Journal*'s Princeton agent and Cornish's successor to the pulpit of the First Colored Presbyterian Church in New York, was involved in numerous reform efforts with white and African-American colleagues. Garrison mentioned in his correspondence that he occasionally attended Wright's church. With Cornish, Wright was active in the AASS, the Phoenix Society, and the New York Committee of Vigilance.[27] Baltimore agent Hezekiah Grice initiated the convention movement, writing in 1830 to various African-American leaders about the possibility of organizing a national gathering. An associate of Garrison and Lundy, Grice organized a Legal Rights Association in the early 1830s, described in an 1859 article as "entirely composed of colored men" with "the purpose of ascertaining the legal status of the colored man in the United States."[28] Another member of Grice's Legal Rights Association was William Watkins, the "Colored Baltimorean" whose powerful writings in *Freedom's Journal* we have explored. Watkins's anticolonization arguments were also published in the late 1820s in the *Genius of Universal Emancipation*, linking him to Garrison, who worked on the newspaper at the time. Watkins frequently corresponded with Garrison and was a subscription agent for the *Liberator* in Baltimore.[29] Garrison's sons Wendell Phillips Garrison and Francis Jackson Garrison proposed in their biography of their father that "some of [Garrison's] colored friends in Baltimore" convinced him to reject colonization; it seems likely that Watkins and Grice were among this group.[30]

Many of those associated with *Freedom's Journal* were also notable, in Penn's words, as the "fathers of public-spirited descendants."[31] This next generation included Charles Lenox Remond and Sarah Parker Remond, the children of Salem agent John Remond, who himself was a member of the Massachusetts Anti-Slavery Society. Charles was an agent for the *Liberator* and a founding member of the AASS; both he and Sarah became part of the AASS's team of traveling lecturers and were influential antislavery orators at home and abroad in the 1840s and 1850s.[32] Rochester agent Austin Steward's daughter Barbara Ann Steward was an educator and antislavery orator who spoke throughout New York and New England during the 1850s.[33] William Watkins's son William J. Watkins and niece Frances Ellen Watkins Harper also argued in print and on the platform on behalf of abolition.[34]

This legacy leaves no doubt that *Freedom's Journal* had a direct and indirect impact on the views and activism of many abolitionists, African Americans and whites, men and women. At a time when most white reformers who opposed slavery also supported the colonization of those who were freed, *Freedom's Journal* presented the arguments of African Americans who, for the most part, opposed colonization. Even though the newspaper also printed procolonization pieces—including, ultimately, Russwurm's reversal of the newspaper's anticolonization position—the numerous articles in which African Americans articulated why colonization was offensive and problematic allowed them to speak for themselves about their future and their role in the nation as well as to educate white reformers. It is notable, for example, that New Yorker Gerrit Smith, who became an influential abolitionist and supporter of African-American civil rights, was a subscriber to *Freedom's Journal*.[35] Although at the time of his subscription he supported colonization and, as we have seen, was troubled by the newspaper's opposition to the ACS, Smith was undoubtedly influenced by the strong arguments in its columns and his association with its editor. An 1859 article in the *Anglo-African Magazine* supported this assumption, relating that "Samuel E. Cornish . . . had the distinguished honor of reasoning Gerrit Smith out of colonizationism."[36]

It is likely that other white abolitionists who were influenced by African Americans' opposition to colonization also read or learned of the anticolonization rhetoric in the columns of *Freedom's Journal* and found it compelling. As we discussed in chapter 8, white supporters of colonization wrote specifically for *Freedom's Journal*, suggesting they were, if not regular readers of the periodical, at least quite familiar with its contents. It is reasonable to assume that the arguments in *Freedom's Journal* were part of the process through which various white abolitionists such as Garrison and Arthur Tappan, with whom Cornish served on the AASS's Executive Committee, came to relinquish their support for colonization in the early 1830s. In commentary written in 1837, Cornish reinforced the connection: "Intelligent colored people never had but one view of Colonization. They have always been opposed to it, as being at war with all their sacred rights, and interests. . . . This doctrine is neither Tappan nor Garrisonism. It is Bibleism, and we claim some instrumentality in teaching it to both of these good men (Tappan and Garrison)."[37] Indeed, "the essential message" of Garrison's 1832 *Thoughts on African Colonization*, as C. Peter Ripley et al. note, was provided by Garrison's African-American colleagues. John B. Vashon, one of *Freedom's Journal*'s Pennsylvania agents, and other African-American activists distributed numerous copies of Garrison's pamphlet to whites.[38] He or others might have similarly passed along copies of *Freedom's Journal* a few years earlier.

Even though, as we have explored in the previous chapter, most of the antislavery rhetoric in *Freedom's Journal* was not explicitly immediatist, it is clear that the editors and contributors were thinking about slavery broadly, investigating its effect on society, considering creatively the advantages and disadvantages of various approaches to abolition, and giving practical advice to those who wanted to take direct action. In this way, they were not only ahead of many white reformers who were generally considering only cautious, gradual approaches; they were also laying the groundwork for the organized abolition movement that began in the 1830s. In an 1855 letter to *Frederick Douglass' Paper*, New York physician and abolitionist James McCune Smith corrected the view that white abolitionists led passive African Americans in adopting antislavery principles. Even though he and other black abolitionists might have been apt to "stand aloof" from white reformers by the mid-1850s due to various tensions between the two groups, Smith argued that African Americans inspired and, to a great extent, created the antislavery movement:

> The colored people . . . almost began the present movement; they certainly anti-dated [*sic*] many of its principles. . . . And they did this in spite of the earnest remonstrances of the abolitionists of that day. In 1813, when Pennsylvania was about to enact a law requiring every colored person to be registered, the law was opposed in a series of brilliant letters, written by "a man of color," letters containing sentiments promulgated twenty years afterwards as new Anti-Slavery truth. They may be found reprinted in the *Freedom's Journal* for March, 1828, a paper edited by Rev. S. E. Cornish and J. B. Russwurm, colored men. . . . William Lloyd Garrison and the *Liberator* owe their evangel to the free colored people. . . . Mr. Garrison came on one platform, and remains on it, in this matter, in which the eloquence of words belongs to him, of action to us: our action antedating his words, and giving force to them: our action embracing a new principle. . . . It is the principle of resisting oppression on the spot, against all odds. . . .[39]

Smith may have given Garrison credit for his "eloquence of words," but it is clear that he viewed *Freedom's Journal* and the arguments it published—like James Forten's "brilliant letters," the 1813 *Series of Letters by a Man of Color*—as the rhetorical and ideological foundation on which Garrison and his white colleagues built. "As a result of reading" *Freedom's Journal*, Timothy Patrick McCarthy notes, "a good number of whites . . . were increasingly sympathetic to the antislavery cause." Garrison did not inspire, create, or manage the activism of African-American abolitionists; on the contrary, as Smith asserted, "when in 1830-31, Mr. Garrison came among them, he found the Colored People already a 'power on earth.'" Smith suggested the dual influence on Garrison's *Liberator* of *Freedom's Journal*, which established the power of appeals to African-American readers and created a subscriber base.[40]

Because one of the goals of *Freedom's Journal* was to encourage debate on important subjects, we find in the pages of *Freedom's Journal* multifaceted discussions of issues that white abolitionists would not take up until subsequent decades. Issues such as women's role in reform and in the public sphere, the use of physical resistance and extralegal action, and the reliance on or rejection of political institutions were all, as we have seen, explored from different angles in *Freedom's Journal*. The fact, too, that *Freedom's Journal* did not devote itself solely to one cause or viewpoint also distinguishes it from periodicals such as the *Liberator* which, although they contained articles on other subjects, were generally devoted to a particular perspective. Readers concerned about slavery could also learn about a variety of other issues and concerns in the columns of *Freedom's Journal*.

This approach helped shape the perspectives of African-American abolitionists, whose approach to slavery and abolition was broader and more nuanced than that of their white colleagues. As Ripley et al. explain,

> Black abolitionism possessed a seamless quality, fusing a variety of concerns, which gave the movement a practical and intellectual continuity that few white reformers appreciated. A black temperance gathering could adjourn and immediately reconvene as an antislavery meeting with no change in tenor or participants. . . . A black vigilance committee, while aiding fugitives, could also organize a petition campaign for black voting rights. The range and continuity of these activities helped broaden the meaning of black abolitionism to include much of northern black life, institutions, and culture.[41]

Many white abolitionists never were able to realize the importance of fighting prejudice as well as slavery, frustrating their African-American colleagues. Speaking to the New York State Anti-Slavery Society in 1837, Theodore Wright reminded abolitionists,

> It is an easy thing to talk about the vileness of slavery at the South, but to call the dark man a brother . . . that is the test. . . . A healthful atmosphere must be created, in which the slave may live, when rescued from the horrors of slavery. . . . I am alarmed sometimes, when I look at the constitutions of our societies. . . . I have seen constitutions of abolition societies, where nothing was said about the improvement of the man of color! They have overlooked the giant sin of prejudice . . . which is at once the parent and offspring of slavery.[42]

As did Cornish's criticism of his white colleagues, Wright's comments suggested the frustration and desire for independence from white abolitionists that led many African-American abolitionists by the late 1830s to seek independence from white reformers. This development, too, can be seen as part of *Freedom's Journal's* legacy. *Freedom's Journal* had allowed African Americans to articulate their views for themselves and to define their concerns. To some extent, they continued to do so in the pages of Garrison's *Liberator*, a periodical that, as we shall see, frequently featured the writings of men and women of color. Yet white abolitionists such as Garrison often expected their African-American colleagues to take direction from them, and, as James McCune Smith's aforementioned comments suggested, to allow whites to take credit for the movement.[43] *Freedom's Journal* not only demonstrated that African Americans *could* speak for themselves but that they *must* and *would* do so, regardless of whites' discomfort or criticisms. *Freedom's Journal* had established that an independent, national black newspaper was a central component of the struggle for freedom, agency, and self-definition.

FREEDOM'S JOURNAL AND THE AFRICAN-AMERICAN PRESS

On May 29, 1829, the first issue of the *Rights of All*, edited by Cornish, appeared. It seems that Cornish had planned to resume editing even before *Freedom's Journal*'s demise. Writing to Gurley in February 1829, Russwurm noted that he "expect[ed] 'Freedom's Journal' will be continued under the care of Mr. Cornish."[44] Yet Cornish decided instead to create a new periodical; although the *Rights of All*, as we shall see, carried on the work of its predecessor, it is inaccurate to see it as merely a continuation of *Freedom's Journal* under a different name.[45] Renowned historian of the black press Armistead Pride argues, "*Rights of All* ... turned out to be more than a change in name [from *Freedom's Journal*]; an entirely new publication had come to life with a new set of serial and page numbers, thus allowing *Freedom's Journal* to come to a halt with its last page. To emphasize the newness of the *Rights of All* Cornish identified the issue of May 29, 1829 as 'the first number of this paper.'" Cornish also stressed that the creation of the periodical should not be considered merely as a reaction to Russwurm's change of heart about colonization. In an article in the second issue titled "An Error Corrected," Cornish lamented that the *New-York Observer* had the previous week described the *Rights of All* as "having been issued merely in consequence of the change of the 'Freedom's Journal,' in respect to African Colonisation." Cornish rectified this mistake, describing his objectives broadly: "The improvement of society is our object, and were there not a coloured man in America, save the Editor of this paper ... we should feel it our duty to issue this *publication*."[46]

Although it should be viewed as a new periodical, the *Rights of All* had similar goals, in many respects, to those of its predecessor. In his opening editorial, Cornish stressed the paper's role in informing African Americans and inspiring them to seek advancement: "It will be the constant aim of the Editor, as far as in his power, to ... promote habits of industry and economy, and to inculcate the importance of an improved education. ... Virtuous characters, instances of laudable ambition, attractive science &c. &c. will constantly be through these columns presented to his readers, with the view of exciting the spirit of emulation, in every thing noble, every thing virtuous and good." Cornish indicated, too, that, like its predecessor, the *Rights of All* would focus on the advancement of African Americans and present accurate information about them: "The patriot and the christian who desires the education and improvement of our coloured people; who wish at all times a correct knowledge of the condition and morals of this people, is humbly solicited to patronize 'THE RIGHTS OF ALL.'" The periodical, he asserted, "will at all times, give a correct representation" of African Americans, allowing them to define their own concerns "in opposition to the persecuting, slanderous accounts, too often presented to the publick eye."[47]

The newspaper was also an educational tool. Describing the paper's "Literary Department" in the first issue, Cornish indicated that it would provide "readers something in science in each number—some phenomenon or description of the natural world." Remarking that it was "much to be desired" that African Americans "should become more acquainted with men and things," Cornish linked this goal—and the newspaper's role in it—to community literacy: "We purpose also as soon as a sufficient number of subscribers to defray the expences shall have been obtained, to open a Reading Room, where will be kept, most of the approved journals of the day, the best selections of history, and works on natural sciences, maps, &c." Like *Freedom's Journal*, a broad range of material was published in *Rights of All*, including biographical sketches of notables such as Benjamin Lundy and British abolitionist Daniel O'Connell; accounts of organizations, public meetings, and speeches; articles on education, slavery, and colonization; domestic and international news; and poetry. As *Freedom's Journal* had for most of its run, the *Rights of All* took a decided stance against the ACS and its colonization proposals but did not condemn self-directed emigration. Cornish argued in the first issue,

> My views, and the views of the intelligent of my brethren generally, are the same as ever in respect to colonization; we believe it may benefit the few that emigrate, and survive, and as a missionary station, we consider it as a grand and glorious establishment. . . . But as it respects three millions that are now in the United States, and the eight millions that in twenty or twenty five years, will be in this country, we think it in no wise calculated, to meet their wants or ameliorate their condition.[48]

The list of agents for the *Rights of All* published at the end of each issue indicates that, with a few exceptions, those who solicited supporters for *Freedom's Journal* continued to do so for its successor throughout the United States, Canada, England, and Haiti. Many advertisements that had appeared in *Freedom's Journal* were repeated in the *Rights of All* as well. Cornish proposed in the first issue that the paper would be issued weekly; however, he was only able to publish it monthly because of the lack of payment by many subscribers. A year's subscription to the three-column, eight-page paper was two dollars. As with *Freedom's Journal*, half the yearly cost was to be paid in advance, yet clearly these terms were rarely met; Cornish noted in the August 1829 issue of the paper that he had only received "36 dollars 50 cents" although he had sent out eight hundred copies each month. In a message published the same month, the paper's stockholders (the group that owned the periodical) appealed to all African Americans to support the paper, noting that although Cornish had "promised to publish monthly for a year though it should be at his own expense," he hoped it would eventually be published "at least weekly."[49]

This goal was never realized, and only six monthly issues appeared, with the last published on October 9, 1829.[50]

It was not until 1837, with the appearance of the *Weekly Advocate* (shortly renamed the *Colored American*), as Pride explains, that another "Black newspaper of any consequence" was published. "We know from contemporaries of the period that the urge to publish Black newspapers had not lessened," Pride notes, "but posterity has been denied anything more than sketchy traces of any papers that did appear. It is safe to observe that during the intervening seven years, no newspaper came forth with the appeal, the reach, and the impact of *Freedom's Journal* or its successor." Certain publications are known to have been issued. A few copies of John G. Stewart's *African Sentinel and Journal of Liberty*, published in Albany, New York, in 1831, have survived. In his 1852 *Condition, Elevation, Emigration and Destiny of the Colored People of the United States*, Martin Delany mentioned the *Struggler*, edited by Philip A. Bell, as the newspaper "out of which the Colored American took its origin." The minutes of the First Annual Convention of the People of Colour recorded a resolution that "this Convention approves and highly appreciates the laudable intention of (Junius C. Morel and John P. Thompson,) to establish a weekly Journal in the city of Philadelphia, in aid of the cause of our oppressed brethren." Morel and Thompson published a proposal for the paper, which was to be called the *American*, in Garrison's *Liberator*; yet we have no evidence that the periodical was ever established.[51]

During this period without a major black newspaper, African Americans backed William Lloyd Garrison's *Liberator*, the first issue of which was published on January 1, 1831. Strongly influenced by the views of African Americans, as we have seen, Garrison was embraced at the time by people of color, whose support was crucial to the initial success of the *Liberator*. African Americans worked as agents and placed advertisements in the paper. In its early years, African Americans were a large majority—eighty percent at the outset and, by 1834, nearly seventy-five percent—of the subscribers.[52] "Viewing the *Liberator* as their voice," Ripley et al. maintain, "blacks also contributed hundreds of essays and letters to its columns." Indeed, Garrison described the *Liberator* as "belong[ing] especially to the people of color—it is their organ." African-American leaders initially agreed. In a March 1831 letter to Garrison, James Forten asserted, "[The *Liberator*] has roused up a Spirit in our Young People, that had been slumbering for years, and we shall produce writers able to vindicate our cause."[53] In fact, such writers were already available and well prepared, empowered by *Freedom's Journal* to take advantage of the opportunity provided by the *Liberator*.

In addition to African-American men, women of color frequently submitted pieces to the *Liberator*, which in its early years were published in a special section of the periodical called the "Ladies' Department" and subsequently integrated into the main portion of the paper's offerings.[54] Indeed, women's writing frequently appeared in the *Liberator*, a presence that, as we have seen, was rare in *Freedom's Journal*. Garrison's view of women's rights as part of the abolition cause—a point of view, as we have seen, not shared by all his colleagues—likely influenced him to solicit and publish material by women. It would also seem that by creating a particular forum for women's writings, the *Liberator* allowed women who might have been reluctant to assert themselves publicly in a newspaper to voice their concerns in a seemingly circumscribed sphere. Yet although African-American women's rhetoric appeared in the *Liberator* as it had not in *Freedom's Journal*, we must not dismiss the latter's importance in creating the atmosphere that nurtured these female writers. In addition to providing, as we have seen, a forum for discussing gender fully and, at times, in ways that offered women empowering alternatives to restrictive roles, *Freedom's Journal* also shaped the lives and views of a generation of women. Like their male counterparts, African-American female activists of the 1830s had come of age in an era in which *Freedom's Journal*'s impact was crucial.

By the late 1830s, as we have discussed, African-American abolitionists became frustrated and discouraged in their efforts in white-dominated organizations, and changes at the *Liberator* were a part of this disillusionment. Writing to *Frederick Douglass' Paper* in 1855, James McCune Smith recalled that two decades earlier, after African-American agents had helped build the *Liberator*'s audience, their "names were erased from its columns" and replaced with those of white agents. Smith angrily suggested that white abolitionists had patronized African Americans and refused to grant them authority and independence: "Where are the colored gentlemen agents now? Out of the forty who had stood by the *Liberator* and upheld it in the day of its struggling adversity, was there no one fit for the office of agent when that office *paid*? There were dozens, but they were passed over whenever money began to flow in, and white men placed in their stead. . . ."[55] By the late 1830s, many African Americans must have begun to question whether the *Liberator* was still "their organ" or whether they needed to create one that would truly be their own.

The latter path was chosen in January 1837 with the appearance of the first issue of the *Weekly Advocate*, founded by Philip A. Bell and published in New York. Bell's opening editorial specifically addressed the need for a paper that was edited and managed by African Americans:

> The addition of another Paper to the list of those already before the Public, may be, and is probably considered, by some persons of common observation and superficial reflection, as unnecessary and uncalled for; but . . . it is believed by

many of our people, that there is still a vacancy to be supplied. . . . If the Press, a 'FREE PRESS,' be a foe to the tyrant—if its blessings be so great and innumerable the Question naturally presents itself, why may we not have one of our own? We now have a Press and Paper under our own entire control. . . .

The Advocate will be like a chain, binding you together as ONE. Its columns will always be the organ of your wishes and feelings, and the proper medium for laying your claims before the Public. . . . [H]ow often have we been insulted and degraded, and how frequently do we feel the want of an ADVOCATE among us?

In his prospectus, published the following week, Bell distinguished the *Weekly Advocate* from papers that were under the control of whites: "Where is *that paper* you can emphatically call *your own*?—We give you the Advocate, for little more than the expense of its weekly delivery at your doors."[56]

At the end of February, Bell announced that Cornish "had been invited to take charge of the Editorial department, and has consented to do so." Robert Sears would continue to print the paper, while Bell would "promote the *circulation* of the paper." Bell explained that the name of the paper will also be changed: "Now I am advised, and upon reflection am satisfied, that 'THE COLORED AMERICAN' will be a better name. It is short, emphatic, and distinctive. We are *Americans*,—*colored* Americans, brethren, and let it be our aim to make the title '*Colored American*,' as honorable, and as much respected before the world, as '*white* Americans,' or any other." In the first issue under the new name, published on March 4, 1837, Cornish noted that he chose the name for various reasons: because he wished to emphasize that people of color were Americans, "in spite of [their] enemies, who would rob [them] of [their] nationality"; because African Americans needed to "be known and [their] interests presented in community . . . by some distinct, specific name"; and because the terms "*Negroes*, *Africans*, and *blacks*" all "have been stereotyped, as names of reproach." As did Bell in the *Weekly Advocate*, Cornish emphasized the need for African Americans to use the power of the press themselves and not be satisfied with others' direction of their efforts: "No class of men, however pious and benevolent can take our place in the great work of redeeming our character and removing our disabilities. They may identify themselves with us, and enter into our sympathies. Still it is ours to will and to do . . . in the doing of which, this journal *as an appropriate engine*, may exert a powerful agency."[57]

The four-page, four-column format of the *Weekly Advocate* was carried over to the *Colored American*, as was the price, one dollar and fifty cents, although the terms of payment changed slightly. Notices in the *Weekly Advocate* stated that subscribers owed one dollar in advance and could pay the remaining fifty cents within six months; as of the name change to the

Colored American, the full amount was due up front. The newspaper printed advertisements like those featured in *Freedom's Journal* from grocers and other small businessmen, educators, and owners of boarding houses. In November 1837, the newspaper announced that it had between 1,200 and 1,500 subscribers; in December, the publishing agent Charles B. Ray noted that the "subscription book" contained "the names of 1650 subscribers." By April 1838, Cornish stated, "We strike off, weekly, 2,250 copies—2000 of which we send to subscribers, and the remainder we use in exchange with other journals." The price of a subscription to the periodical was raised to two dollars per year in June 1838. In an appeal to readers for support in December of the following year, Ray indicated, "We had at the commencement of this year, more than 2000 subscribers, since that time we have lost in various parts of the country, nearly 800, and have received an accession in Pennsylvania and Ohio of about 300. . . ."[58]

Many subscribers were not paying what they owed, and, like its predecessors, the *Colored American* experienced continual financial troubles. In a July 1837 request to readers and supporters, Bell related the plan of African-American clergyman, educator, and abolitionist Lewis Woodson to raise funds for the *Colored American.* Appealing to "friends and brethren," Bell reported that the newspaper could not "meet [its] expenses" and that Cornish's "services up to [July 1, 1837] have been gratuitous." Some African Americans assisted, including "forty-nine noble brothers who came forward, voluntarily, and pledged themselves for 50 cents a week, individually, whenever it was wanted." Yet the delinquency of many subscribers was a significant problem. In a scathing indictment published in April 1838, Cornish declared, "If our people be taken as a body, and their patriotism judged of, by their support of the ONLY PAPER conducted by themselves, and consecrated to their interest, every intelligent mind would say, they mostly deserve to be slaves." He offered a remedy to those unhappy with his editing: "We say to all such, APPOINT YOUR MAN, and that moment you bring into the field more talent and experience, we will gladly yield our place, and pledge towards the salary of our successor, at least $50 annually. But until they do this, we demand their support, and brand them as imbecile, impolitic and cowardly if they withhold it."[59] Frequent announcements of this kind—albeit not so harsh—appeared throughout the paper's run, which ended in 1842.

Cornish proposed at the outset that the *Colored American* would be "a journal of facts and of instruction . . . freighted with information for all,"[60] and in its pages were news stories, persuasive articles on important issues, and correspondence. Given the general opposition to colonization of most African Americans, it is not surprising that many articles argued against the ACS and its plans and that the paper often featured resolutions adopted by anticolonization gatherings throughout the United

States. News from Liberia was generally negative, emphasizing the desolation of the colony and the hardships endured by the settlers.[61] The paper condemned slavery sharply, publicized the activities of abolitionists, and endorsed immediate abolition. Because by this time many African-American abolitionists were in favor of political action, as we have discussed, articles frequently supported this course. Yet, notably, contributions endorsing the actions of abolitionists such as Garrison, who were against political means, were also published, as were accounts of the "practical abolitionism" we examined in the previous chapter.[62] It seems that the broad approach to slavery of *Freedom's Journal* continued (without the gradualism of the previous decade), and that the editors and readers of the *Colored American*, like those of its predecessor, valued the expression of diverse opinions.

The emphasis on literacy of the first African-American periodical also carried on, with an important modification. Elizabeth McHenry explains that "whereas *Freedom's Journal* had primarily encouraged black communities to form literary societies and avail themselves of their benefits, the *Colored American* acted as a coworker of these societies." Reading was still presented as crucial to improvement and uplift, but as a result of the "improved literary skills and changing needs of black readers," more "sophisticated debates" took the place of the "sensational domestic tragedies and international trivia" often published in *Freedom's Journal*.[63]

By the late 1830s, the power of the African-American press as a tool in building community and fighting oppression was established. Various periodicals were created throughout the North in the decades that followed, including the *Mirror of Liberty*, edited by David Ruggles, founded in New York in 1837; the *National Reformer*, edited by William Whipper in Philadelphia, which appeared in 1838; Stephen Myers's *Northern Star and Freeman's Advocate*, published in Albany beginning in 1842; the *Ram's Horn*, a New York City weekly launched in 1847 by Willis A. Hodges; and the *Weekly Anglo-African*, edited by Thomas Hamilton in New York starting in 1859.[64] Hamilton's assertion in his first issue of the *Weekly Anglo-African* was reminiscent of Cornish and Russwurm's declaration of their purpose: "We need a Press—a press of our own. We need to know something else of ourselves. . . . Our *cause* . . . demands our own advocacy." As African Americans rallied to support these newspapers, their words, too, echoed statements made in *Freedom's Journal*. At meetings in 1838 supporting the *Mirror of Liberty*, New York African Americans affirmed that "the Liberty of Speech is unquestioned and indisputable, and Printing only gives circulation to what might be freely spoken"; resolved that "the triumphant success of our cause depends, under God, upon the tremendous and inconceivable power of the free and independent press"; and "hail[ed] the Mirror of Liberty as a powerful auxiliary in behalf of the dumb, and against the power of the oppressor." In

Philadelphia, African Americans praised the *Colored American*'s "fearless and independent tone" and acclaimed the "Mirror of Liberty, and other papers, periodicals, &c., as powerful auxiliaries in advocating the civil and political rights of our colored brethren."[65]

Perhaps the most well-known African-American editor of the antebellum period was Frederick Douglass. Born a slave in Maryland, Douglass escaped in 1838 and in the 1840s became an abolitionist orator. In 1847 he established the *North Star*; it was followed by *Frederick Douglass' Paper*, published from 1851 to 1860, and *Douglass' Monthly*, published from 1858 to 1863.[66] In his opening editorial in the *North Star*, Douglass asserted, "It has long been our anxious wish to see, in this slave-holding, slave-trading, and negro-hating land, a printing-press and paper, permanently established, under the complete control and direction of the immediate victims of slavery and oppression." African-American journalists, Douglass declared, had a central role in the fight against slavery and oppression: "In the grand struggle for liberty and equality now waging, it is meet, right and essential that there should arise in our ranks authors and editors, as well as orators, for it is in these capacities that the most permanent good can be rendered to our cause."[67]

Some white abolitionists, not surprisingly, were threatened by the independent spirit of the African-American press. In 1839, for example, Philip Bell reported that a meeting of the New York State Anti-Slavery Society had denounced the *Colored American* and told its members to withhold patronage from it because, in Bell's words, it "*dared* to admit an article differing from the known opinions of the New York State Anti-Slavery Society." The ostensible subject of the controversy was political abolition, but African-American abolitionists recognized that the true problem for their white colleagues was their assertiveness. "We are not surprised," Bell remarked, "we always knew that such was the spirit with which the white man would act toward his 'colored brethren.' . . . As long as we let them think and act for us; as long as we will bow to their opinions, and acknowledge that their 'word is counsel, and their will is law;' so long will they outwardly treat us as men, while in their hearts they still hold us as slaves." Cornish was similarly incensed that the "president of the State Society" would respond to an African-American writer who "dare[d] to utter an honest opinion, differing from his own" by attempting to "shackle him, and put down the only legitimate organ of the colored man in this country."[68] Cornish's description of the *Colored American* is of note here. Garrison's *Liberator* may have been worthy of praise, but Cornish and other African-American abolitionists no longer found it to be the forum for their voices that they had anticipated.[69]

Douglass's editorial projects similarly caused conflict with white editors. Douglass's creation of the *North Star* was opposed by William Lloyd Garrison and other white abolitionists, who suggested that he should publish his views in white antislavery periodicals instead of creating what they perceived as competition for their publications. Their patronizing comments about Douglass's project in correspondence demonstrate all too plainly that they wished to keep him under their control and were offended when he took independent action. "Garrison feels badly that F. Douglass never consulted him about the matter," Samuel Joseph May related in an 1847 letter to John Bishop Estlin. May's complaints about Douglass in correspondence to Estlin written the following year were revealing, suggesting that Douglass would fail without the guidance of white abolitionists and chastising him condescendingly for not keeping to his place:

> [Garrison and other white abolitionists] could not let it be understood that they would come forward & back up "the North Star," or any other new paper, when all its capital was gone. . . . Moreover, in order to give [Douglass] every opportunity to write & communicate, they said he should have the entire use and control of 2 columns weekly in the [*Anti-Slavery Standard*, published by the AASS]. . . . It was a wise & friendly offer. . . . F. D. thought, however, differently and established his paper.[70]

Yet antebellum African-American editors did not back down. The legacy of *Freedom's Journal* is clear in the responses of these editors to challenges from white leaders. They affirmed the need for the African-American press; were empowered to assert themselves on its behalf, even in the face of opposition; and would not be deterred by the efforts of white colleagues to control or patronize them. "Sooner than abate one jot or tittle of our right to think, speak and act like men," Bell proclaimed, "we will suffer our enterprise to perish, and the Colored American to be numbered with the things that were. . . We think we know what course should be pursued to benefit the colored man better than any of our white brethren . . . and while we think so we shall always freely and without reserve give publicity to our thoughts."[71] Always irritated by the control white abolitionists tried to exert over his writing and speaking,[72] Douglass was unwavering in his first editorial. Although he did not doubt the "zeal, integrity or ability" of white abolitionists, Douglass declared that African Americans needed to be "their own representatives and advocates": "Such a Journal would do a most important and indispensable work, which it would be wholly impossible for our white friends to do for us. . . . [T]he man STRUCK is the man to CRY OUT. . . . Our mind is made up, and we are resolved to go forward."[73]

Douglass and other African-American editors throughout the nineteenth and twentieth centuries and into the twenty-first have indeed gone forward, carrying on the legacy of *Freedom's Journal*. As various historians and journalists have noted, the issues raised in *Freedom's Journal* have been discussed in the African-American press in various forms since its publication. The goals of the first black newspaper remain relevant even as editors face new challenges posed by the competition from mainstream periodicals which increasingly purport to cover issues of concern to African Americans, the rising costs of production, and changing relationships with advertisers.[74] White press coverage of minority communities may have improved since Cornish and Russwurm's time, but mainstream newspapers still tend to portray African Americans in negative ways, focusing on crime and poverty and offering patronizing solutions.[75] In many media outlets, African-American leaders are treated with disrespect and their ideas distorted, while issues of concern to people of color are misrepresented and trivialized.[76] Press coverage of Africa in many major newspapers is frequently inaccurate and racist.[77] As did *Freedom's Journal*, African-American newspapers continue to report stories that are ignored in the mainstream white-dominated media, to interpret news in ways that make it relevant to people of color, to educate and empower, and to critique the nation and challenge it to live up to its ideals.[78] The latter function remains important; even given the progress that the nation has made since the early nineteenth century, much remains to be done. In the words of John J. Oliver Jr., president of the National Newspaper Publishers Association, a coalition of more than 200 African-American newspapers in the United States, "Today, as it was in the past, it is Black newspapers . . . that continue to remind America that she has a long journey before she reaches her full potential and truly becomes 'one nation under God, indivisible with liberty and justice for all.'"[79]

And as editors and journalists associated with the black press continue the legacy of *Freedom's Journal*, they pay tribute to the first African-American newspaper, acknowledging its influence and allowing the words in its columns to continue to resonate. As contemporary journalists build on *Freedom's Journal*'s foundation, they recall Cornish and Russwurm's groundbreaking statements in their opening editorial. In a 1998 commentary in *Speakin' Out News* of Huntsville, Alabama, Howard Ball maintained, "The first editorial in this premier newspaper, *Freedom's Journal*, spoke to an objective that many of our black newspapers, including *Speakin' Out News*, still emphasize: 'We are there to plead our own cause. Too long have others spoken for us.'" Describing the functions of the contemporary black press, Ball reaffirmed the general goals laid out by Cornish and Russwurm: "We chronicle specific events happening in the black community many of which are not considered news worthy by the general press. . . . We point to weaknesses in our social systems as education and health care. We cry out against the tyranny that attacks public welfare and housing. . . . We take on sensitive racial issues." "The Black Press remains as necessary today as it was in 1827," a May 2000 editorial in the *Philadel-*

phia Tribune asserted. "What was true in the past remains true today and will be true in the future—we can not allow others to speak for us."[80]

Freedom's Journal gave much to those who followed: for editors and journalists from communities of color, a foundation to build on and an empowering example; for historians, a rich source for understanding African-American life and rhetoric of the late 1820s in new and vital ways; for activists, a confirmation that when those who are marginalized are given a forum to voice their concerns, society can be forever changed. For all who believe in the power of the press and the links among rhetoric, protest, and social change, the resounding words of the first editorial of *Freedom's Journal* remain relevant not only as a statement of purpose but also as a call to action. As Oliver maintains, "The act of speaking up for ourselves is both legacy and mandate."[81] In the African-American press now as it will in the future, the spirit of *Freedom's Journal*'s declaration of independence echoes and re-echoes.

NOTES

1. Uriah Boston, "Long Live the Colored American" [letter to editor], *CA*, 28 November 1840.

2. In addition to the primary sources cited throughout this section, my account of Russwurm's later life and work draws on Wolseley, *Black Press*, 17; Nordin, "In Search," 128; Borzendowski, *John Russwurm*; Shick, *Behold*, 37–39, 61; Ripley et al., *Black Abolitionist Papers*, vol. 3, 82–83; Campbell, *Maryland in Africa*; Laughon, "Administrative Problems"; Wiley, *Slaves No More*, 2–7; Burrowes, "Press Freedom," 333–34; Sagarin, *John Brown Russwurm*; Huberich, *Political and Legislative History*, 392–93, vol. 1, 466–94; Clegg, *Price of Liberty*, 144–45; Beyan, *African American Settlements*.

3. Russwurm, "Mr. Russwurm's Letter." C. Peter Ripley et al. indicate that Edward Jones, the second African-American college graduate (Amherst College, August 23, 1826) and an Episcopal priest in training for African missionary work, was "the likely recipient of Russwurm's letter" (*Black Abolitionist Papers*, vol. 3, 79).

4. John B. Russwurm, "Arrival of Emigrants," *Liberia Herald*, 22 December 1831; John B. Russwurm, "To Our Readers," *Liberia Herald*, 22 February 1832.

5. John Brown Russwurm to Francis Edward Russwurm, 27 September 1835, *John Sumner Russwurm Papers*; Joseph R. Dailey to Robert Purvis, Liberia, 12 April 1833, Boston Public Library Anti-Slavery Collection, Ms. A.1.2, vol. 3, no. 39; John Brown Russwurm to Francis Edward Russwurm, 31 March 1834, *John Sumner Russwurm Papers*. Although Dailey did not mention Mechlin by name, it is clear that he was describing the agent in charge of the colony, Mechlin's position at the time the letter was written.

6. Dailey to Purvis, 12 April 1833; S[imeon] S. Jocelyn to George Benson, New York, 6 May 1834, Boston Public Library Anti-Slavery Collection, Ms. A.1.2, vol. 4, no. 37; John Brown Russwurm to Francis Edward Russwurm, 27 September 1835.

7. John Brown Russwurm to Francis Edward Russwurm, 31 March 1834; John Brown Russwurm to Francis Edward Russwurm, 27 September 1835; "Liberia Herald"; James Forten to William Lloyd Garrison, Philadelphia, 20 October 1831, Boston Public Library Anti-Slavery Collection, Ms. A.1.2, vol. 1, no. 40; Joseph R. Dailey to Robert Purvis, Liberia, 15 August 1833, Boston Public Library Anti-Slavery Collection, Ms. A.1.2, vol. 3, no. 57.

8. Russwurm quoted in Huberich, *Political and Legislative History*, vol. 1, 494; John Brown Russwurm to Francis Edward Russwurm, 27 September 1835.

9. In addition to the primary sources cited throughout this section, my account of Cornish's later life and work draws on Wesley, "Negroes of New York," 77–87; Wesley, "Negro in the Organization," 231–33; Gross, "First National," 435; Tripp, *Origins*, 28–40; Bryan, "Negro Journalism," 11–13; Dann, *Black Press*, 17–18; Swift, *Black Prophets*, 42–48, 56–66, 84–112; Swift, "Black Presbyterian"; Ripley et al., *Black Abolitionist Papers*, vol. 3, 95–96; Quarles, *Black Abolitionists*, 68, 109; Pride, "*Rights of All.*"

10. *Minutes and Proceedings*, 7. On the proposals for the manual labor college and their outcome, see Ripley et al., *Black Abolitionist Papers*, vol. 3, 114.

11. On the Phoenix Society, see Leslie Harris, *In the Shadow*, 186–88; Porter, "Organized," 565–66; Tappan, *Life*, 158–62; Mabee, *Black Education*, 58–59.

12. David Ruggles and Joseph Gavino, "Humanity Weeps," *CA*, 7 October 1837; Samuel E. Cornish, "Libel Suit," *CA*, 3 November 1838; Charles B. Ray, "David Ruggles' Meeting," *CA*, 27 July 1839; Charles B. Ray, "To Correspondents," *CA*, 12 October 1839. On the libel suit, see also Pease and Pease, *They Who Would Be Free*, 210–11.

13. For a full discussion of the biased and paternalistic attitudes of many white abolitionists—and African Americans' commentary about them—see Bacon, *Humblest*, 27–33; Pease and Pease, "Black Power," 19–20; Quarles, *Black Abolitionists*, 47–51; Robert Hall, "Massachusetts Abolitionists," 82.

14. Samuel E. Cornish, "Difficulties of Abolition," *CA*, 27 May 1837.

15. Samuel E. Cornish, "Controversy with Eastern Brethren," *CA*, 11 May 1839.

16. Samuel E. Cornish, "Moral Reform Convention," *CA*, 26 August 1837; Samuel E. Cornish, "Our Brethren of Pennsylvania," *CA*, 3 March 1838.

17. Samuel E. Cornish, "To the Thoughtless Part of our Colored Citizens," *CA*, 15 August 1837; Samuel E. Cornish, "Agent of the Vigilance Committee," *CA*, 26 January 1839; Ray, "David Ruggles' Meeting"; G. M. Tracy et al., statement of New York Committee of Vigilance, *CA*, 23 November 1839; Pease and Pease, *They Who Would Be Free*, 209–11.

18. Charles B. Ray, "The Signs of the Times," *CA*, 17 August 1839; "Political Action," *CA*, 19 October 1839.

19. Charles B. Ray, untitled editorial, *CA*, 9 November 1839.

20. The split in the abolitionist ranks that led to the formation of the American and Foreign Anti-Slavery Society in 1840 is often attributed by historians solely to disagreement over women's rights and participation within the movement. For those African-American abolitionists who left the AASS, though, the causes of the division were more complex; see Bacon, *Humblest*, 19–20.

21. Dann, *Black Press*, 13–14; Newman, "Protest," 195. On the political influence of the black press, see also Wilder, "Black Life," 233–35.

22. On the links between the conventions and the African-American press in general and *Freedom's Journal* in particular, see also Bell, *Minutes*, iii; Dann, *Black Press*, 17; Dick, *Black Protest*, 3; Swift, *Black Prophets*, 56.

23. Penn, *Afro-American Press*, 30.

24. Dick, *Black Protest*, 3; Nordin, "In Search," 128; McHenry, *Forgotten Readers*, 41; Swift, *Black Prophets*, 56.

25. Donald Jacobs, *Courage*, 9; Hinks, *To Awaken*, 179, 191; see also Levine, "Circulating," 26; Burrow, *God*, 21.

26. William Lloyd Garrison, "Walker's Pamphlet," *Liberator*, 1 January 1831; William Lloyd Garrison, comments on Leo, "Walker's Appeal" [letter to editor], *Liberator*, 29 January 1831.

27. Ripley et al., *Black Abolitionist Papers*, vol. 3, 187–88; Swift, *Black Prophets*, 50–71.

28. "The First Colored Convention"; see also Cromwell, *Early Negro Convention*, 4–5; Bragg, *Men of Maryland*, 59–60.

29. Bacon, *Humblest*, 52; Ripley et al., *Black Abolitionist Papers*, vol. 3, 96–97.

30. Garrison and Garrison, *William Lloyd Garrison*, vol. 1, 147–48. On the crucial role African-American opposition to colonization played in altering Garrison's views, see also Goodman, *Of One Blood*, 36–42; Sernett, *North Star Country*, 25; Michael Bennett, *Democratic Discourses*, 3.

31. Penn, *Afro-American Press*, 30.

32. Bacon, *Humblest*, 52; 167; Ripley et al., *Black Abolitionist Papers*, vol. 3, 318–19, 374.

33. Bacon, *Humblest*, 48, 165–66; Ripley et al., *Black Abolitionist Papers*, vol. 4, 297.

34. Bacon, *Humblest*, 53, 167; Ripley et al., *Black Abolitionist Papers*, vol. 4, 155–56, 405–6.

35. Friedman, *Gregarious Saints*, 96–126; Stauffer, *Black Hearts*.

36. "The First Colored Convention."

37. Samuel E. Cornish, "Colored People Always Opposed to Colonization," *CA*, 13 May 1837. Like Garrison, Tappan was persuaded to give up his earlier support for colonization by African Americans (Tappan, *Life*, 134–38).

38. Ripley et al., *Black Abolitionist Papers*, vol. 3, 11.

39. Communipaw [James McCune Smith], "From Our New York Correspondent" [letter to editor], *Frederick Douglass' Paper*, 26 January 1855.

40. Timothy Patrick McCarthy, "To Plead," 120. Communipaw [James McCune Smith], "From Our New York Correspondent" [letter to editor], *Frederick Douglass' Paper*, 16 February 1855. On the role of *Freedom's Journal* in articulating the "agenda of radical abolition" that was created among African Americans in the early nineteenth century, see Sinha, "Black Abolitionism," 243; on the influence of *Freedom's Journal* on the *Liberator*, see also Fanuzzi, *Abolition's Public Sphere*, 105.

41. Ripley et al., *Witness for Freedom*, 12.

42. Wright, "Progress," in Woodson, *Negro Orators*.

43. On the strain between white and African-American abolitionists beginning in the late 1830s, see Ripley et al., *Black Abolitionist Papers*, vol. 3, 20–26; Bacon, *Humblest*, 32–33.

44. Russwurm to Gurley, New York, 24 February 1829.

45. Many historians have incorrectly described the *Rights of All* as the same paper as *Freedom's Journal* except for the name change; see Bryan, "Negro Journalism," 10; Tripp, *Origins*, 22; Penn, *Afro-American Press*, 30; Wolseley, *Black Press*, 18; Detweiler, *Negro Press*, 36; Clint Wilson, *Black Journalists*, 29; Barrow, "Our Own Cause," 121; Nordin, "In Search," 128; Emery and Emery, *Press*, 181; Dann, *Black Press*, 17.

46. Pride, "*Rights of All*," 129; Samuel E. Cornish, "An Error Corrected," *RA*, 12 June 1829. Pride's identification of the *Rights of All* as a new and unique publication has been echoed by other scholars; see Vincent Thompson, *Africans*, 141; Swift, *Black Prophets*, 41; Swift, "Black Presbyterian," 129; George Walker, "Afro-American," 115.

47. Samuel E. Cornish, "To Our Patrons, and the Publick Generally," *RA*, 29 May 1829; Samuel E. Cornish, "The Rights of All," *RA*, 29 May 1829.

48. Samuel E. Cornish, "Literary Department," *RA*, 29 May 1829; Cornish, "To Our Patrons." Cornish also criticized colonization in "The Old Hobby, Colonization," *RA*, 18 September 1829 and "American Colonization Society," *RA*, 16 October 1829.

49. Cornish, "Rights of All," 29 May 1829; Cornish, "*Rights of All*," 14 August 1829; Thomas L. Jennings [*sic*] and P[eter] Williams [on behalf of stockholders], "To the People of Colour Throughout the United States," *RA*, 14 August 1829.

50. Penn stated that "the *Rights of All* suspended publication in 1830" (*Afro-American Press*, 30). Pride notes, however, that "the surviving file of this paper stops with the October 9, 1829 issue" and that "Penn is alone in indicating that *Rights of All* was published beyond this date" ("*Rights of All*," 131). I follow Pride's conclusion here; as we have seen, Penn's account, although extremely valuable, contains certain inaccuracies.

51. Pride and Wilson, *History*, 25–26; Delany, *Condition*, 127; *Minutes and Proceedings*, 10; Junius C. Morel and John P. Thompson, "The American," *Liberator*, 2 July 1831.

52. Pride and Wilson, *History*, 26; Ripley et al., *Black Abolitionist Papers*, vol. 3, 9. On African-American support for the *Liberator*, see also Fanuzzi, *Abolition's Public Sphere*, 102–9.

53. Ripley et al., *Black Abolitionist Papers*, vol. 3, 9; Garrison quoted in Ripley et al., *Black Abolitionist Papers*, vol. 3, 9; James Forten to William Lloyd Garrison, Philadelphia, 21 March 1831, Boston Public Library Anti-Slavery Collection, Ms. A.1.2, vol. 1, no. 19.

54. The "Ladies' Department" appeared in the paper from 1832 to 1837. For a full discussion, see Bacon, "*Liberator*'s 'Ladies' Department.'"

55. Communipaw [Smith], "From Our New York Correspondent," *Frederick Douglass' Paper*, 26 January 1855.

56. Philip A. Bell, "Our Undertaking," *Weekly Advocate*, 7 January 1837; Philip A. Bell, "Our Prospectus," *Weekly Advocate*, 14 January 1837.

57. P[hilip] A. Bell, "New Arrangements," *Weekly Advocate*, 25 February 1837; Samuel E. Cornish, "Title of this Journal," *CA*, 4 March 1837; Samuel E. Cornish, "Why We Should Have a Paper," *CA*, 4 March 1837.

58. Thomas L. Jinnings and Charles B. Ray, "To Our Patrons and Friends," *CA*, 11 November 1837; C[harles] B. Ray, "To the Agents and Friends of this Paper,"

CA, 30 December 1837; Samuel E. Cornish, "Our Noble Committee," CA, 12 April 1838; Charles B. Ray, Philip A. Bell, and Stephen H. Gloucester, "To the Public, and the Subscribers of the COLORED AMERICAN," CA, 2 June 1838; Charles B. Ray, "The Last Number of the Colored American," CA, 7 December 1839.

59. Philip A. Bell, "To the Public, and the Friends of the Colored American," CA, 22 July 1837; Samuel E. Cornish, "Our Noble Committee," 12 April 1838.

60. Cornish, "Why We Should Have a Paper."

61. See, for example, "Latest from Liberia," CA, 2 October 1841; "Liberia and the Slave Trade," CA, 2 November 1839.

62. See, for example, Thomas Cole, "Voting" [letter to editor], CA, 26 December 1840; "Anniversary of the American A. S. Society," CA, 15 May 1841; "Kidnapped Freemen—High Handed Cruelty," CA, 2 January 1841; Charles B. Ray, "Moral Abolition," CA, 16 November 1839; "Fruits of Abolition," CA, 12 October 1839.

63. McHenry, Forgotten Readers, 104–106.

64. Further discussion of these publications can be found in Pride and Wilson, History, 44; Bryan, "Negro Journalism," 30–33; Tripp, Origins, 44–56; Wolseley, Black Press, 19–24.

65. Thomas Hamilton, "Our Paper," Weekly Anglo-African, 23 July 1859; "Adjourned Meeting," CA, 15 September 1838; "The Mirror of Liberty," CA, 8 September 1838; "Public Meeting of the Colored Young Men of Philadelphia," CA, 13 October 1838.

66. Douglass and Gerrit Smith opted in 1851 to merge the North Star with Smith's Liberty Party Paper, creating Frederick Douglass' Paper. Douglass' Monthly was issued for foreign subscribers. For further discussion of these newspapers, see Wolseley, Black Press, 21–24; Detweiler, Negro Press, 40–42; Clint Wilson, Black Journalists, 36–38; Penn, Afro-American Press, 67–70.

67. Frederick Douglass, "Our Paper and Its Prospects," North Star, 3 December 1847.

68. P[hilip] A. B[ell], "Proscription," CA, 5 October 1839; Samuel E. Cornish, "A Vestige of Pro-Slavery," CA, 5 October 1839.

69. Neglecting Ruggles's Mirror of Liberty and Whipper's National Reformer, Cornish also seemed to disparage these periodicals by implication. The omission was not surprising given Cornish's contentious relationship with these two editors and his criticisms of their work.

70. Samuel Joseph May to John Bishop Estlin, Boston, 31 October 1847, Samuel Joseph May Papers, Boston Public Library/Rare Books Department; Samuel Joseph May to John Bishop Estlin, Boston, 31 October 1848, May Papers. See also William Lloyd Garrison to Helen E. Garrison, Cleveland, 20 October 1847, Letters of William Lloyd Garrison, 532–33; William Lloyd Garrison, untitled comments on letter from Frederick Douglass, Liberator, 23 July 1847; Pease and Pease, "Boston Garrisonians," 36; Quarles, "Breach," 147–48; Ernest, Liberation, 285.

71. Bell, "Proscription."

72. Bacon, Humblest, 30–33.

73. Douglass, "Our Paper and Its Prospects."

74. Finkle, Forum for Protest, 20; Lerone Bennett, Before the Mayflower, 174; Lerone Bennett, Shaping, 129; Daniel, Black Journals, ix; "Black Newspapers: A History of Making the Invisible Visible," Jacksonville Free Press, 11 February

2004; Carol McGruder, "The Black Newspaper—More Precious Than Gold," *Sacramento Observer*, 2 July 2003; "Celebrating 176 Years of the Black Press," *Atlanta Inquirer*, 22 March 2003; Vernon Jarrett, "The Black Press: A Voice Still Needed," *Chicago Defender*, 4 May 2002; Todd Steven Burroughs, "Black Press Serves Black Aspirations," *Michigan Citizen*, 30 March 2002.

75. Males, "With Friends Like These"; James Wright, "94 Percent of Blacks Not in Prison," *Afro-American Red Star*, 9 December 1995.

76. James Wright, "White Press Again Misquotes Dr. Elders," *Afro-American Red Star*, 10 September 1994; Mary Rhodes Hoover, "The White Press vs. Ben Chavis," *Afro-American Red Star*, 17 September 1994; James L. Reed, "Farrakhan Calls for Unity—But White Press Reads It Different," *New York Beacon*, 4 February 1994; Bacon, "Disrespect"; Bacon, "Reparations."

77. "Black Publishers Go to Troubled Nigeria," *Atlanta Inquirer*, 7 October 1995; Allimadi, "Inventing Africa"; Bacon, "Sins of Omission and Commission"; Toufe, "Let Them Eat Cake."

78. Wolseley, *Black Press*, 3–8; Fearn-Banks, "African-American Press Coverage"; Owens, "Entering the Twenty-First Century"; Ward, "Black Press"; Hatchett, "Black Press"; Bacon, "Different Race."

79. Oliver, "Black Press."

80. Howard G. Ball, "Your Newspaper—Yesterday, Today and Tomorrow," *Speakin' Out News*, 24 March 1998; "Black Press Remains Voice for Community," *Philadelphia Tribune*, 17 March 2000.

81. Oliver, "Black Press."

Bibliography

PRIMARY SOURCES

Manuscripts and Manuscript Collections

Boston Public Library Anti-Slavery Collection. Boston Public Library/Rare Books Department, Boston.

BV Diary, 1821–1824. New-York Historical Society, New York.

Grellet, Stephen. Manuscript collection. Library Company of Philadelphia, Philadelphia.

May, Samuel Joseph (1810–1899). Papers. Boston Public Library/Rare Books Department, Boston.

Miscellaneous American Letters and Papers. New York Public Library, Schomburg Center for Research in Black Culture, New York.

Pennsylvania Abolition Society Papers. Historical Society of Pennsylvania, Philadelphia.

Presbytery of New York. Minutes, 15 April 1822–13 August 1828. Presbyterian Church (U.S.A.), Department of History and Records Management Services, Philadelphia.

Presbytery of Philadelphia. Minutes, 1806–1837. Presbyterian Church (U.S.A.), Department of History and Records Management Services, Philadelphia.

Microfilm Collections

The Arthur A. Schomburg Papers. Bethesda: University Publications of America, 1991. Originals in the Schomburg Center for Research in Black Culture, the New York Public Library.

The Records of the American Colonization Society. Washington: Library of Congress Photoduplication Service, 1971. Originals in the Library of Congress Manuscript Division, Washington, DC.

Black Abolitionist Papers, 1830–1865. Sanford, NC: Microfilming Corporation of America, 1981.

John Sumner Russwurm Papers. Nashville: Tennessee State Library and Archives, 1968. Originals in the Tennessee State Library and Archives, Nashville.

Electronic Archival Collections

An American Time Capsule: Three Centuries of Broadsides and Other Printed Ephemera. Washington: Library of Congress, Rare Book and Special Collections Division. www.memory.loc.gov/ammem/rbpehtml/pehome.html.

African American Perspectives: Pamphlets from the Daniel A. P. Murray Collection, 1818–1907. Washington: Library of Congress, Rare Book and Special Collections Division. www.memory.loc.gov/ammem/aap/aaphome.html.

Documenting the American South. Chapel Hill: Academic Affairs Library, the University of North Carolina at Chapel Hill. www.docsouth.unc.edu.

Newspapers

Alexandria Gazette, 30 April 1827–28 May 1827.
Colored American, New York, 4 March 1837–2 October 1841.
Frederick Douglass' Paper, Rochester, New York, 16 July 1852–18 September 1855.
Freedom's Journal, New York, 16 March 1827–28 March 1829.
Genius of Universal Emancipation, Baltimore, 2 January 1827–28 June 1828.
Liberator, Boston, 1 January 1831–23 July 1847.
Liberia Herald, Monrovia, 22 December 1831–22 February 1832.
National Advocate, New York, 3 August 1821–21 September 1821.
New-York American, 22 November 1827.
New-York Enquirer, 19 September 1826–24 April 1827.
New-York National Advocate, 2 March 1825–18 March 1825.
North Star, Rochester, 3 December 1847–13 July 1849.
Pennsylvania Gazette, Philadelphia, 25 November 1789.
Rights of All, New York, 29 May 1829–16 October 1829.
Statesman, New York, 1 December 1826.
Weekly Advocate, New York, 7 January 1837–25 February 1837.
Weekly Anglo-African, New York, 23 July 1859.

Books, Tracts, Articles, Speeches, and Collections

American Colonization Society. *A View of Exertions Lately Made for the Purpose of Colonizing the Free People of Colour, in the United States, in Africa, or Elsewhere*. Washington, 1817.

Aptheker, Herbert, ed. *A Documentary History of the Negro People in the United States*. Vol. 1: *From Colonial Times Through the Civil War*. New York: Citadel Press, 1951.

Bell, Howard Holman, ed. *Minutes of the Proceedings of the National Negro Conventions 1830–1864*. New York: Arno Press, 1969.

[Burgess, Ebenezer]. *Address to the American Society for Colonizing the Free People of Colour of the United States*. Washington, 1818.

Carey, Mathew. *A Short Account of the Malignant Fever, Lately Prevalent in Philadelphia: With a Statement of the Proceedings That Took Place on the Subject, in Different Parts of the United States*. 4th ed. Philadelphia, 1794.

Clay, Henry. *Speech of the Hon. Henry Clay, Before the American Colonization Society, in the Hall of the House of Representatives, January 20, 1827*. Washington, 1827.

Delany, Martin Robison. *The Condition, Elevation, Emigration, and Destiny of the Colored People of the United States*. Philadelphia, 1852.

Denham [Dixon], [Hugh] Clapperton, and [Walter] Oudney. *Narrative of Travels and Discoveries in Northern and Central Africa, In the Years 1822, 1823, and 1824*. 2 vols. 1826. Reprint, London: Drake Publishers Limited, 1985.

Ducas, George, and Charles Van Doren, eds. *Great Documents in Black American History*. New York: Praeger Publishers, 1970.

"The First Colored Convention." *Anglo-African Magazine*, October 1859.

Foner, Philip S., and Robert James Branham, eds. *Lift Every Voice: African American Oratory, 1787–1900*. Tuscaloosa: University of Alabama Press, 1998.

Forten, James, and Russell Parrott. *Address of the Free People of Colour in Philadelphia*. Pp. i–iv in *Minutes of the Proceedings of a Special Meeting of the Fifteenth American Convention for Promoting the Abolition of Slavery and Improving the Condition of the African Race*. Philadelphia, 1818.

Gallaudet, T[homas] H[opkins]. *A Statement with Regard to the Moorish Prince, Abduhl Rahhahman*. New York, 1828.

Garrison, Wendell Phillips, and Francis Jackson Garrison. *William Lloyd Garrison, 1805–1879: The Story of His Life Told by His Children*. 4 vols. New York, 1885–1889.

Garrison, William Lloyd. *The Letters of William Lloyd Garrison*. Ed. Walter M. Merrill. 5 vols. Cambridge, MA: Belknap Press of Harvard University Press, 1971–1981.

Gellman, David N., and David Quigley, eds. *Jim Crow New York: A Documentary History of Race and Citizenship, 1777–1877*. New York: New York University Press, 2003.

Grégoire, H[enri]. *An Enquiry Concerning the Intellectual and Moral Faculties, and Literature of Negroes*. Trans. D. B. Warden. 1810. Reprint, ed. Graham Russell Hodges. Armonk, NY: M. E. Sharpe, 1997.

Griffin, Edward D. *A Plea for Africa: A Sermon Preached October 26, 1817, in the First Presbyterian Church in the City of New-York, Before the Synod of New-York and New-Jersey, at the Request of the Board of Directors of the African School Established by the Synod*. New York, 1817.

Herodotus. *Histories*. Trans. Aubrey de Sélincourt. Ed. A. R. Burn. 1972. New York: Penguin Books, 1980.

Harper, Robert Goodloe. *A Letter from General Harper, of Maryland, to Elias B. Caldwell, Esq., Secretary of the American Society for Colonizing the Free People of Colour, in the United States, With Their Own Consent*. Baltimore, 1818.

Hay, Philip C. *Our Duty to Our Coloured Population. A Sermon for the Benefit of the American Colonization Society, Delivered in the Second Presbyterian Church, Newark, July 23, 1826*. Newark, 1826.

Jacobs, Harriet A. *Incidents in the Life of a Slave Girl: Written by Herself.* Ed. Lydia Maria Child. 1861. Reprint, ed. Jean Fagan Yellin. Cambridge, MA: Harvard University Press, 1987.

Jefferson, Thomas. *Notes on the State of Virginia.* 1787. Reprint, ed. William Peden. Chapel Hill: University of North Carolina Press, 1955.

Jones, Absalom, and Richard Allen. *A Narrative of the Proceedings of the Black People, During the Late Awful Calamity in Philadelphia, in the Year 1793: And a Refutation of Some Censures, Thrown Upon Them in Some Late Publications.* Philadelphia, 1794.

Laws of the State of New-York, Passed at the Fortieth Session of the Legislature, Begun and Held at the City of Albany, the Fifth Day of November, 1816. Albany, 1817.

"Liberia Herald." *African Repository and Colonial Journal,* November 1831.

McMurray, William. *A Sermon, Preached in Behalf of the American Colonization Society, in the Reformed Dutch Church, in Market-Street, New-York, July 10, 1825.* New York, 1825.

Minutes and Proceedings of the First Annual Convention of the People of Colour. Philadelphia, 1831.

Moses, Wilson Jeremiah, ed. *Classical Black Nationalism: From the American Revolution to Marcus Garvey.* New York: New York University Press, 1996.

Needles, Edward. *An Historical Memoir of the Pennsylvania Society, for Promoting the Abolition of Slavery; the Relief of Free Negroes Unlawfully Held in Bondage, and for Improving the Condition of the African Race.* Philadelphia, 1848.

Newman, Samuel P. *Address Delivered Before the Benevolent Society of Bowdoin College, Tuesday, Sept. 5, 1826.* Portland, ME, 1826.

New York Committee of Vigilance. *The First Annual Report of the New York Committee of Vigilance, for the year 1837, Together with Important Facts Relative to Their Proceedings.* New York, 1837.

New-York Evangelical Missionary Society. *The Fifth Annual Report of the Directors of the New-York Evangelical Missionary Society, at Their Anniversary Meeting. On Monday, December 3, 1821.* New York, 1821.

New-York Evangelical Missionary Society of Young Men. *A Brief View of Facts, Which Gave Rise to the New-York Evangelical Missionary Society of Young Men, Together With the Constitution.* New York, 1817.

Porter, Dorothy, ed. *Early Negro Writing 1760–1837.* Boston: Beacon Press, 1971.

Proceedings of a Meeting Held at Princeton, New-Jersey, July 14, 1824. To Form a Society in the State of New-Jersey, to Cooperate With the American Colonization Society. Princeton, 1824.

Proceedings of a Meeting of the Friends of African Colonization, Held in the City of Baltimore, on the Seventeenth of October, 1827. Baltimore, 1828.

The Proceedings of the Free African Union Society and the African Benevolent Society, Newport, Rhode Island 1780–1824. Ed. William H. Robinson. Providence: Urban League of Rhode Island, 1976.

Ripley, C. Peter, et al., eds. *The Black Abolitionist Papers.* 5 vols. Chapel Hill: University of North Carolina Press, 1985–1992.

Russwurm, John B. "Mr. Russwurm's Letter." *African Repository and Colonial Journal,* April 1830.

Say, Jean-Baptiste. *A Treatise on Political Economy; Or, the Production, Distribution & Consumption of Wealth.* New American ed. Trans. C. R. Prinsep. Philadelphia, 1880.

Sterling, Dorothy, ed. *Speak Out in Thunder Tones: Letters and Other Writings by Black Northerners, 1787–1865*. Garden City, NY: Doubleday, 1973.

St. John de Crevècoeur, J. Hector. *Letters from an American Farmer*. 1782. New York: Fox, Duffield & Company, 1904.

Tappan, Lewis. *The Life of Arthur Tappan*. New York, 1870.

Walker, David. *David Walker's Appeal, in Four Articles; Together with a Preamble, to the Coloured Citizens of the World, But in Particular, and Very Expressly, to Those of the United States of America*. 3rd ed. 1830. Reprint, ed. Charles M. Wiltse. New York: Hill and Wang, 1965.

Walsh, Robert, Jr. *An Appeal from the Judgments of Great Britain Respecting the United States of America. Part First, Containing an Historical Outline of their Merits and Wrongs as Colonies; and Strictures upon the Calumnies of the British Writers*. 1819. Reprint, New York: Negro Universities Press, 1969.

Woodson, Carter G. *Negro Orators and Their Orations*. Washington: Associated Publishers, 1925.

SECONDARY SOURCES

Newspapers

Afro-American Red Star, Washington, 10 September 1994–9 December 1995.

Atlanta Inquirer, 7 October 1995–22 March 2003.

Boston Globe, 1 September 2002.

Chicago Defender, 4 May 2002.

Jacksonville Free Press, 11 February 2004.

Los Angeles Times, 28 May 2002.

Michigan Citizen, Highland Park, 30 March 2002.

News Sentinel, Knoxville, TN, 19 August 2003.

New York Beacon, 4 February 1994.

Philadelphia Tribune, 17 March 2000.

Sacramento Observer, 2 July 2003.

Speakin' Out News, Huntsville, AL, 24 March 1998.

Books and Articles

Adams, Alice Dana. *The Neglected Period of Anti-Slavery in America (1808–1831)*. 1908. Reprint, Gloucester, MA: Peter Smith, 1964.

Adams, James Truslow. "Disenfranchisement of Negroes in New England." *American Historical Review* 30 (1924–25): 543–47.

Adefila, Johnson A. "The Black Press and Africa in the 19th Century Black American Struggle for Equality." Pp. 29–43 in *Critical Perspectives on Historical and Contemporary Issues about Africa and Black America*, edited by Tunde Adeleke. New York: Edwin Mellen Press, 2004.

Adeleke, Tunde. *UnAfrican Americans: Nineteenth-Century Black Nationalists and the Civilizing Mission*. Lexington: University Press of Kentucky, 1998.

Alderson, Robert. "Charleston's Rumored Slave Revolt of 1793." Pp. 93–111 in *The Impact of the Haitian Revolution in the Atlantic World*, edited by David P. Geggus. Columbia: University of South Carolina Press, 2001.

Allen, James Egert. *The Negro in New York*. New York: Exposition Press, 1964.

Alford, Terry. *Prince among Slaves*. New York: Harcourt Brace Jovanovich, 1977.

Allimadi, Milton. "Inventing Africa: *New York Times* Archives Reveal a History of Racist Fabrication." *Extra!* August/September 2003.

Andrews, Dee. "The African Methodists of Philadelphia, 1794–1802." *Pennsylvania Magazine of History and Biography* 108 (1984): 471–86.

Apperson, George M. "George M. Erskine: Slave * Presbyterian Minister * Missionary." *Presbyterian Voice*, December 2001, 10.

Aptheker, Herbert. "Militant Abolitionism." *Journal of Negro History* 26 (1941): 438–84.

———. *"One Continual Cry": David Walker's Appeal to the Colored Citizens of the World (1829–1830), Its Setting & Its Meaning*. New York: Humanities Press, 1965.

Arkin, Marc M. "The Federalist Trope: Power and Passion in Abolitionist Rhetoric." *Journal of American History* 88 (2001): 75–98.

Armstrong, Erica R. "A Mental and Moral Feast: Reading, Writing, and Sentimentality in Black Philadelphia." *Journal of Women's History* 16 (2004): 78–102.

Arrowsmith, Martin. "Slave Redemption Has a Role in Combating Slavery in Sudan." Pp. 45–48 in *Slavery Today*, edited by Auriana Ojeda. Farmington Hills, MI: Greenhaven Press, 2004. First published as "Slave Redemption: A Tactic of Last Resort," in *Satya*, December 2002/January 2003.

Austin, Allan D. *African Muslims in Antebellum America: A Sourcebook*. New York: Garland Publishing, 1984.

Austin, Allan D. *African Muslims in Antebellum America: Transatlantic Stories and Spiritual Struggles*. New York: Routledge, 1997.

Bacon, Jacqueline. "A Different Race: The Black Press Reveals Gaps in Mainstream Election Coverage." *Extra!* November/December 2004, 14–18.

———. "Disrespect, Distortion and Double Binds: Media Treatment of Progressive Black Leaders." *Extra!* March/April 2003, 27–29.

———. *The Humblest May Stand Forth: Rhetoric, Empowerment, and Abolition*. Columbia: University of South Carolina Press, 2002.

———. "The *Liberator*'s 'Ladies' Department,' 1832–1837: Freedom or Fetters?" Pp. 3–19 in *Sexual Rhetoric: Media Perspectives on Sexuality, Gender, and Identity*, edited by Meta G. Carstarphen and Susan C. Zavoina. Westport, CT: Greenwood Press, 1999.

———. "Reparations and the Media: A Slanted Arena for Discussions of Slavery Recompense." *Extra!* May/June 2002, 21–22.

———. "Rhetoric and Identity in Absalom Jones and Richard Allen's *Narrative of the Proceedings of the Black People, During the Late Awful Calamity in Philadelphia*." *Pennsylvania Magazine of History and Biography* 125 (2001): 61–90.

———. "Sins of Omission and Commission: Press Coverage of Liberian History." *Extra!* November/December 2003, 16–18.

Bacon, Jacqueline, and Glen McClish, "Descendents of Africa, Sons of '76: Exploring Early African-American Rhetoric." *Rhetoric Society Quarterly* 36 (2006): 1–29.

———. "Reinventing the Master's Tools: Nineteenth-Century African-American Literary Societies of Philadelphia and Rhetorical Education." *Rhetoric Society Quarterly* 30, no. 4 (Fall 2000): 19–47.

Baldasty, Gerald J. *The Commercialization of News in the Nineteenth Century.* Madison: University of Wisconsin Press, 1992.

Bancroft, Frederic. *Slave-Trading in the Old South.* Baltimore: J. H. Furst Company, 1931.

Barnes, Gilbert Hobbs. *The Antislavery Impulse 1830–1844.* New York: D. Appleton-Century, 1933.

Barrow, Lionel C. "'Our Own Cause': *Freedom's Journal* and the Beginnings of the Black Press." *Journalism History* 4 (1977–1978): 118–22.

Bay, Mia. "See Your Declaration Americans!!! Abolitionism, Americanism, and the Revolutionary Tradition in Free Black Politics." Pp. 25–52 in *Americanism: New Perspectives on the History of an Ideal,* edited by Michael Kazin and Joseph A. McCartin. Chapel Hill: University of North Carolina Press, 2006.

———. *The White Image in the Black Mind: African-American Ideas about White People, 1830–1925.* New York: Oxford University Press, 2000.

Bellegarde-Smith, Patrick. *Haiti: The Breached Citadel.* Boulder, CO: Westview Press, 1990.

Belt-Beyan, Phyllis M. *The Emergence of African American Literacy Traditions: Family and Community Efforts in the Nineteenth Century.* Westport, CT: Praeger, 2004.

Bennett, Lerone, Jr. *Before the Mayflower: A History of Black America.* 5th ed. 1982. New York: Penguin, 1984.

———. *Confrontation Black and White.* Baltimore: Penguin Books, 1965.

———. "Founders of the Black Press." *Ebony* 42.4 (February 1987): 96–97, 100.

———. *Pioneers in Protest.* Chicago: Johnson Publishing Company, 1968.

———. *The Shaping of Black America.* Chicago: Johnson Publishing Company, 1975.

Bennett, Michael. *Democratic Discourses: The Radical Abolition Movement and Antebellum American Literature.* New Brunswick, NJ: Rutgers University Press, 2005.

Berardi, Gayle K., and Thomas W. Segady. "The Development of African-American Newspapers in the American West: A Sociohistorical Perspective." *Journal of Negro History* 75 (1990): 96–111.

Berlin, Ira. "The Revolution in Black Life." Pp. 349–82 in *The American Revolution: Explorations in the History of American Radicalism,* edited by Alfred F. Young. DeKalb: Northern Illinois University Press, 1976.

Berry, Mary Frances, and John W. Blassingame. *Long Memory: The Black Experience in America.* New York: Oxford University Press, 1982.

Bethel, Elizabeth Rauh. "Images of Hayti: The Construction of an Afro-American *Lieu De Mémoire.*" *Callaloo* 15 (1992): 827–41.

———. *The Roots of African-American Identity: Memory and History in Free Antebellum Communities.* New York: St. Martin's Press, 1997.

Beyan, Amos J. *African American Settlements in West Africa: John Brown Russwurm and the American Civilizing Efforts.* New York: Palgrave Macmillan, 2005.

Blackwell, James E. *The Black Community: Diversity and Unity.* New York: Dodd, Mead & Company, 1975.

Blanck, Emily. "Seventeen Eighty-Three: The Turning Point in the Law of Slavery and Freedom in Massachusetts." *New England Quarterly* 75 (2002): 24–51.

Bloch, Herman D. *The Circle of Discrimination: An Economic and Social Study of the Black Man in New York.* New York: New York University Press, 1969.

Bok, Francis, with Edward Tivnan. *Escape from Slavery: The True Story of My Ten Years in Captivity—and My Journey to Freedom in America.* New York: St. Martin's Press, 2003.

Booker, Christopher B. *"I Will Wear No Chain!" A Social History of African American Males.* Westport, CT: Praeger, 2000.

Borzendowski, Janice. *John Russwurm.* New York: Chelsea House Publishers, 1989.

Bowers, John Waite, and Donovan J. Ochs. *The Rhetoric of Agitation and Control.* New York: Random House, 1971.

Boylan, Anne M. "Benevolence and Antislavery Activity among African American Women in New York and Boston, 1820–1840." Pp. 119–37 in *The Abolitionist Sisterhood: Women's Political Culture in Antebellum America,* edited by Jean Fagan Yellin and John C. Van Horne. Ithaca, NY: Cornell University Press, 1994.

Bragg, George F. *Men of Maryland.* Baltimore: Church Advocate Press, 1914.

Brewer, William M. "John B. Russwurm." *Journal of Negro History* 13 (1928): 413–22.

Brooks, Joanna. *American Lazarus: Religion and the Rise of African-American and Native American Literatures.* Oxford, UK: Oxford University Press, 2003.

Brown, Richard D. *Knowledge Is Power: The Diffusion of Information in Early America, 1700–1865.* New York: Oxford University Press, 1989.

Bruce, Dickson D., Jr. "National Identity and African-American Colonization, 1773–1817." *Historian* 58 (1995): 15–28.

———. *The Origins of African American Literature, 1680–1865.* Charlottesville: University Press of Virginia, 2001.

Bryan, Carter. "Negro Journalism in America before Emancipation." *Journalism Monographs* 12 (1969): 1–33.

Burrow, Rufus, Jr. *God and Human Responsibility: David Walker and Ethical Prophecy.* Macon, GA: Mercer University Press, 2003.

Burrowes, Carl Patrick. "Press Freedom in Liberia, 1830–1847: The Impact of Heterogeneity and Modernity." *Journalism and Mass Communication Quarterly* 74 (1997): 331–47.

Calderhead, William. "The Role of the Professional Slave Trader in a Slave Economy: Austin Woolfolk, a Case Study." *Civil War History* 23 (1977): 195–212.

Campbell, Penelope. *Maryland in Africa: The Maryland State Colonization Society, 1831–1857.* Urbana: University of Illinois Press, 1971.

Carby, Hazel V. *Reconstructing Womanhood: The Emergence of the Afro-American Woman Novelist.* New York: Oxford University Press, 1987.

Carson, Emmett D. *A Hand Up: Black Philanthropy and Self-Help in America.* Washington: Joint Center for Political and Economic Studies Press, 1993.

Castiglia, Christopher. "Pedagogical Discipline and the Creation of White Citizenship: John Witherspoon, Robert Finley, and the Colonization Society." *Early American Literature* 33 (1998): 192–214.

Catterall, Helen Tunicliff. *Judicial Cases Concerning American Slavery and the Negro.* 5 vols. Washington, DC: Carnegie Institution, 1926–1937.

Cincinnati, Edward F. "Belleville—A Black Abolitionist's Garden of Eden." *New Jersey Historical Commission Newsletter,* February 1978, 3.

Clegg, Claude A., III. *The Price of Liberty: African Americans and the Making of Liberia*. Chapel Hill: University of North Carolina Press, 2004.

Cmiel, Kenneth. *Democratic Eloquence: The Fight over Popular Speech in Nineteenth-Century America*. New York: William Morrow, 1990.

Cockrell, Dale. *Demons of Disorder: Early Blackface Minstrels and Their World*. Cambridge: Cambridge University Press, 1997.

Cole, Hubert. *Christophe: King of Haiti*. New York: Viking Press, 1967.

Coleman, Will. *Tribal Talk: Black Theology, Hermeneutics, and African/American Ways of "Telling the Story."* University Park: Pennsylvania State University Press, 2000.

Condit, Celeste Michelle, and John Louis Lucaites. *Crafting Equality: America's Anglo-African Word*. Chicago: University of Chicago Press, 1993.

Cone, James H. *God of the Oppressed*. Minneapolis: Seabury Press, 1975.

Cooper, Frederick. "To Elevate the Race: The Social Thought of Black Leaders." *American Quarterly* 24 (1972): 604–25.

Copher, Charles B. "The Black Presence in the Old Testament." Pp. 146–64 in *Stony the Road We Trod: African American Biblical Interpretation*, edited by Cain Hope Felder. Minneapolis: Fortress Press, 1991.

Cornelius, Janet Duitsman. *"When I Can Read My Title Clear": Literacy, Slavery, and Religion in the Antebellum South*. Columbia: University of South Carolina Press, 1991.

Cottrol, Robert J. *The Afro-Yankees: Providence's Black Community in the Antebellum Era*. Westport, CT: Greenwood Press, 1982.

Cover, Robert M. *Justice Accused: Antislavery and the Judicial Process*. New Haven, CT: Yale University Press, 1975.

Cromwell, John W. *The Early Negro Convention Movement*. Washington: American Negro Academy, 1904.

Crouthamel, James L. *James Watson Webb: A Biography*. Middletown, CT: Wesleyan University Press, 1969.

Curry, Leonard P. *The Free Black in Urban America, 1800–1850: The Shadow of the Dream*. Chicago: University of Chicago Press, 1981.

Dabel, Jane E. "'I Have Gone Quietly to Work for the Support of My Three Children': African-American Mothers in New York City, 1827–1877." *Afro-Americans in New York Life and History* 27, no. 2 (July 2003): 7–27.

Dain, Bruce. "Haiti and Egypt in Early Black Racial Discourse in the United States." *Slavery and Abolition* 14 (1993): 139–61.

———. *A Hideous Monster of the Mind: American Race Theory in the Early Republic*. Cambridge, MA: Harvard University Press, 2002.

Daniel, Walter C. *Black Journals of the United States*. Westport, CT: Greenwood Press, 1982.

Dann, Martin E., ed. *The Black Press, 1827–1890: The Quest for National Identity*. New York: G. P. Putnam's Sons, 1971.

Davis, David Brion. "Impact of the French and Haitian Revolutions." Pp. 3–9 in *The Impact of the Haitian Revolution in the Atlantic World*, edited by David P. Geggus. Columbia: University of South Carolina Press, 2001.

———. *In the Image of God: Religion, Moral Values, and Our Heritage of Slavery*. New Haven, CT: Yale University Press, 2001.

———. "The Emergence of Immediatism in British and American Antislavery Thought." *Mississippi Valley Historical Review* 49 (1962): 209–30.

Davis, Hugh. "Northern Colonizationists and Free Blacks, 1823–1837: A Case Study of Leonard Bacon." *Journal of the Early Republic* 17 (1997): 651–75.

Davis, Susan G. *Parades and Power: Street Theatre in Nineteenth-Century Philadelphia.* Philadelphia: Temple University Press, 1986.

Detweiler, Frederick G. *The Negro Press in the United States.* Chicago: University of Chicago Press, 1922.

Dewberry, Jonathan. "The African Grove Theatre and Company." *Black American Literature Forum* 16 (1982): 128–31.

Dick, Robert C. *Black Protest: Issues and Tactics.* Westport: Greenwood Press, 1974.

———. "Negro Oratory in the Anti-Slavery Societies: 1830–1860." *Western Speech* 28 (1964): 5–14.

Dicken-Garcia, Hazel. *Journalistic Standards in Nineteenth-Century America.* Madison: University of Wisconsin Press, 1989.

Dixon, Chris. *African America and Haiti: Emigration and Black Nationalism in the Nineteenth Century.* Westport, CT: Greenwood Press, 2000.

———. "'A True Manly Life': Abolitionism and the Masculine Ideal." *Mid-America* 77 (1995): 267–90.

Dodson, Howard, et al. *The Black New Yorkers: The Schomburg Illustrated Chronology.* New York: John Wiley & Sons, 2000.

Dorsey, Bruce. "A Gendered History of African Colonization in the Antebellum United States." *Journal of Social History* 34 (2000): 77–103.

Drake, St. Clair. *Black Folk Here and There: An Essay in History and Anthropology.* 2 vols. Los Angeles: Center for Afro-American Studies, University of California, Los Angeles, 1987.

———. *The Redemption of Africa and Black Religion.* Chicago: Third World Press, 1977.

Drescher, Seymour. *Econocide: British Slavery in the Era of Abolition.* Pittsburgh: University of Pittsburgh Press, 1977.

———. *The Mighty Experiment: Free Labor Versus Slavery in British Emancipation.* New York: Oxford University Press, 2002.

Dumond, Dwight Lowell. *Antislavery: The Crusade for Freedom in America.* Ann Arbor: University of Michigan Press, 1961.

Egerton, Douglas R. *He Shall Go Out Free: The Lives of Denmark Vesey.* Madison, WI: Madison House, 1999.

Elley, Christyn. "Missouri's Dred Scott Case, 1846–1857." *Office of the Secretary of State, Matt Blunt, Missouri, State Archives.* February 2002. www.sos.mo.gov/archives/resources/africanamerican/scott/scott.asp (5 May 2004).

Emery, Edwin, and Michael Emery. *The Press and America: An Interpretive History of the Mass Media.* 5th ed. Englewood Cliffs, NJ: Prentice-Hall, 1984.

Ernest, John. *Liberation Historiography: African American Writers and the Challenge of History, 1794–1861.* Chapel Hill: University of North Carolina Press, 2004.

Fabre, Geneviève. "African-American Commemorative Celebrations in the Nineteenth Century." Pp. 72–91 in *History and Memory in African-American Culture,* edited by Geneviève Fabre and Robert O'Meally. New York: Oxford University Press, 1994.

Fanuzzi, Robert. *Abolition's Public Sphere.* Minneapolis: University of Minnesota Press, 2003.

Fearn-Banks, Kathleen. "African-American Press Coverage of Clarence Thomas Nomination." *Newspaper Research Journal* 15, no. 4 (Fall 1994): 98–116.

Fehrenbacher, Don E. *The Dred Scott Case: Its Significance in American Law and Politics.* Oxford: Oxford University Press, 1978.

———. *The Slaveholding Republic: An Account of the United States Government's Relations to Slavery.* Completed and ed. Ward M. McAfee. New York: Oxford University Press, 2001.

Finkelman, Paul. *Dred Scott v. Sandford: A Brief History with Documents.* Boston: Bedford Books, 1997.

———. *An Imperfect Union: Slavery, Federalism, and Comity.* Chapel Hill: University of North Carolina Press, 1981.

———. *Slavery in the Courtroom: An Annotated Bibliography of Cases.* Washington: Library of Congress, 1985.

Finkle, Lee. *Forum for Protest: The Black Press during World War II.* Cranbury, NJ: Associated University Presses, 1975.

Finseth, Ian. "David Walker, Nature's Nation, and Early African-American Separatism." *Mississippi Quarterly* 54 (2001): 337–62.

Fisch, Audrey A. *American Slaves in Victorian England: Abolitionist Politics in Popular Literature and Culture.* Cambridge: Cambridge University Press, 2000.

Foner, Philip S. *History of Black Americans from Africa to the Emergence of the Cotton Kingdom.* Westport, CT: Greenwood Press, 1975.

———. *History of Black Americans from the Emergence of the Cotton Kingdom to the Eve of the Compromise of 1850.* Westport, CT: Greenwood Press, 1975.

———. "John Brown Russwurm, A Document." *Journal of Negro History* 54 (1969): 393–97.

Forbes, Robert P. "'Truth Systematised': The Changing Debate over Slavery and Abolition, 1761–1916." Pp. 3–22 in *Prophets of Protest: Reconsidering the History of American Abolitionism,* edited by Timothy Patrick McCarthy and John Stauffer. New York: New Press, 2006.

Fordham, Monroe. *Major Themes in Northern Black Religious Thought, 1800–1860.* Hicksville, NY: Exposition Press, 1975.

Foster, Charles I. "The Colonization of Free Negroes in Liberia, 1816–35." *Journal of Negro History* 38 (1953): 41–66.

Foster, Frances Smith. "A Narrative of the Interesting Origins and (Somewhat) Surprising Developments of African-American Print Culture." *American Literary History* 17 (2005): 714–40.

———. *Written by Herself: Literary Production by African American Women, 1746–1892.* Bloomington: Indiana University Press, 1993.

Fox, Tom. "From Freedom to Manners: African American Literacy in the Nineteenth Century." Pp. 51–63 in *Contested Terrain: Diversity, Writing, and Knowledge,* ed. Phyllis Kahaney and Judith Liu. Ann Arbor: University of Michigan Press, 2001. First published as "From Freedom to Manners: African American Literary Instruction," in *Forum* 6 (1995): 1–12.

Francis, Wigmoore. "Nineteenth- and Early-Twentieth-Century Perspectives on Women in the Discourses of Radical Black Caribbean Men." *Small Axe* 7, no. 1 (March 2003): 116–39.

Franklin, John Hope, and Alfred A. Moss Jr. *From Slavery to Freedom: A History of African Americans.* 8th ed. New York: Alfred A. Knopf, 2000.

Franklin, V. P. *Black Self-Determination: A Cultural History of the Faith of the Fathers.* Westport, CT: Lawrence Hill, 1984.

———. "Education for Colonization: Attempts to Educate Free Blacks in the United States for Emigration to Africa, 1823–1833." *Journal of Negro Education* 43 (1974): 91–103.

Frederickson, George M. *The Black Image in the White Mind: The Debate on Afro-American Character and Destiny, 1817–1914*. New York: Harper and Row, 1971.

———. "Toward a Social Interpretation of the Development of American Racism." Pp. 240–54 in *Key Issues in the Afro-American Experience*. Vol. I: *To 1877*, edited by Nathan I. Huggins, Martin Kilson, and Daniel M. Fox. San Diego: Harcourt Brace Jovanovich, 1971.

Freeman, Rhoda G. "The Free Negro in New York City in the Era before the Civil War." Ph.D. diss., Columbia University, 1966.

Friedman, Lawrence J. *Gregarious Saints: Self and Community in American Abolitionism 1830–1870*. Cambridge: Cambridge University Press, 1982.

———. "Purifying the White Man's Country: The American Colonization Society Reconsidered, 1816–1840." *Societas* 6 (1976): 1–24.

Gardner, Bettye J. "Opposition to Emigration, A Selected Letter of William Watkins (The Coloured Baltimorean)." *Journal of Negro History* 67 (1982): 155–58.

Gardner, Christine J. "Slave Redemption." *Christianity Today*, 9 August 1999, 28–33.

Gates, Henry Louis, Jr. *Figures in Black: Words, Signs, and the "Racial" Self*. New York: Oxford University Press, 1987.

———. Introduction to *African-American Newspapers and Periodicals: A National Bibliography*, edited by James P. Danky and Maureen E. Hady. Cambridge, MA: Harvard University Press, 1998.

———. *The Signifying Monkey: A Theory of Afro-American Literary Criticism*. New York: Oxford University Press, 1988.

George, Carol V. R. "In the Beginning: Mother Bethel A. M. E. Church." *American Visions* 1.6 (November/December 1986): 43–46.

———. *Segregated Sabbaths: Richard Allen and the Emergence of Independent Black Churches, 1765–1840*. New York: Oxford University Press, 1973.

Giddings, Paula. *When and Where I Enter: The Impact of Black Women on Race and Sex in America*. New York: Bantam Books, 1985.

Gilje, Paul A. *The Road to Mobocracy: Popular Disorder in New York City, 1763–1834*. Chapel Hill: University of North Carolina Press, 1987.

Ginzberg, Lori D. "'The Hearts of Your Readers Will Shudder': Fanny Wright, Infidelity, and American Freethought." *American Quarterly* 46 (1994): 195–226.

Goldberg, Isaac. *Major Noah: American-Jewish Pioneer*. New York: Alfred A. Knopf, 1937.

Goldenberg, David M. *The Curse of Ham: Race and Slavery in Early Judaism, Christianity, and Islam*. Princeton, NJ: Princeton University Press, 2003.

Gomez, Michael A. *Exchanging Our Country Marks: The Transformation of African Identities in the Colonial and Antebellum South*. Chapel Hill: University of North Carolina Press, 1998.

———. "Muslims in Early America." *Journal of Southern History* 60 (1994): 671–710.

———. *Reversing Sail: A History of the African Diaspora*. Cambridge: Cambridge University Press, 2005.

Goodman, Paul. *Of One Blood: Abolitionism and the Origins of Racial Equality*. Berkeley: University of California Press, 1998.

Gordon, Dexter B. *Black Identity: Rhetoric, Ideology, and Nineteenth-Century Black Nationalism.* Carbondale: Southern Illinois University Press, 2003.

Gore, George W. *Negro Journalism: An Essay on the History and Present Conditions of the Negro Press.* Greencastle, IN: Journalism Press, 1922.

Gravely, William B. "The Dialectic of Double Consciousness in Black American Freedom Celebrations, 1808–1863." *Journal of Negro History* 67 (1982): 302–17.

———. "The Rise of African Churches in America (1786–1822): Re-Examining the Contexts." Pp. 301–17 in *African American Religious Studies: An Interdisciplinary Anthology*, edited by Gayraud S. Wilmore. Durham, NC: Duke University Press, 1989.

Gronowicz, Anthony. *Race and Class Politics in New York City before the Civil War.* Boston: Northeastern University Press, 1998.

Gross, Bella. "The First National Negro Convention." *Journal of Negro History* 31 (1946): 435–43.

———. "*Freedom's Journal* and the *Rights of All.*" *Journal of Negro History* 27 (1932): 241–86.

———. "Life and Times of Theodore S. Wright, 1797–1847." *Negro History Bulletin* 3 (1940): 133–38, 144.

Gudmestad, Robert H. *A Troublesome Commerce: The Transformation of the Interstate Slave Trade.* Baton Rouge: Louisiana State University Press, 2003.

Hall, Kim F. *Things of Darkness: Economies of Race and Gender in Early Modern England.* Ithaca, NY: Cornell University Press, 1995.

Hall, Robert L. "Massachusetts Abolitionists Document the Slave Experience." Pp. 75–99 in *Courage and Conscience: Black and White Abolitionists in Boston*, edited by Donald M. Jacobs. Bloomington: Indiana University Press, 1993.

Harding, Vincent. *The Other American Revolution.* Los Angeles and Atlanta: Center for Afro-American Studies, University of California, Los Angeles, and Institute of the Black World, 1980.

Harris, Leslie M. *In the Shadow of Slavery: African Americans in New York City, 1626–1863.* Chicago: University of Chicago Press, 2003.

Harris, Sheldon H. *Paul Cuffe: Black America and the African Return.* New York: Simon and Schuster, 1972.

Harrold, Stanley. *The Rise of Aggressive Abolitionism: Addresses to the Slaves.* Lexington: University Press of Kentucky, 2004.

———. *Subversives: Antislavery Community in Washington, D. C., 1828–1865.* Baton Rouge: Louisiana State University Press, 2003.

Hatchett, David. "The Black Press." *Crisis*, January 1987, 14–19.

Hay, Samuel A. *African American Theatre: A Historical and Critical Analysis.* Cambridge: Cambridge University Press, 1994.

Haynes, Stephen R. *Noah's Curse: The Biblical Justification of American Slavery.* New York: Oxford University Press, 2002.

Higginbotham, A. Leon, Jr. *In the Matter of Color: Race and the American Legal Process. The Colonial Period.* New York: Oxford University Press, 1978.

Hileman, Gregor. "The Iron-Willed Black Schoolmaster and His Granite Academy." *Middlebury College Newsletter* 48, no. 3 (Spring 1974): 6–14.

Hill, Errol G., and James V. Hatch. *A History of African American Theatre.* Cambridge: Cambridge University Press, 2003.

Hine, Darlene Clark, and Ernestine Jenkins. "Introduction: Black Men's History: Toward a Gendered Perspective." Pp. 1–58 in *A Question of Manhood*. Vol. 1: *"Manhood of Rights": The Construction of Black Male History and Manhood, 1750–1870*, edited by Darlene Clark Hine and Ernestine Jenkins. Bloomington: Indiana University Press, 1999.

Hinks, Peter P. *To Awaken My Afflicted Brethren: David Walker and the Problem of Antebellum Slave Resistance*. University Park: Pennsylvania State University Press, 1997.

Hirsch, Leo H., Jr. "The Negro and New York, 1783 to 1865." *Journal of Negro History* 16 (1931): 382–473.

"History of Freedom Suits in Missouri." *St. Louis Circuit Court Historical Records Project*. www.stlcourtrecords.wustl.edu/about-freedom-suits-history.cfm (5 May 2004).

Hodges, Graham Russell. *Root & Branch: African Americans in New York and East Jersey, 1613–1863*. Chapel Hill: University of North Carolina Press, 1999.

Horton, James Oliver. "Freedom's Yoke: Gender Conventions among Antebellum Free Blacks." *Feminist Studies* 12 (1986): 51–76.

———. *Free People of Color: Inside the African American Community*. Washington, DC: Smithsonian Institution Press, 1993.

———. "The Manhood of the Race: Gender and the Language of Black Protest in the Antebellum North." www.law.yale.edu/outside/pdf/centers/sc/Horton-Manhood.pdf (5 May 2004).

———. "Urban Alliances: The Emergence of Race-Based Populism in the Age of Jackson." Pp. 23–34 in *African American Urban Experience: Perspectives from the Colonial Period to the Present*, edited by Joe W. Trotter with Earl Lewis and Tera W. Hunter. New York: Palgrave Macmillan, 2004.

Horton, James Oliver, and Lois E. Horton. *Black Bostonians: Family Life and Community Struggle in the Antebellum North*. Rev. ed. New York: Holmes & Meier, 1999.

———. *Hard Road to Freedom: The Story of African America*. New Brunswick, NJ: Rutgers University Press, 2001.

———. *In Hope of Liberty: Culture, Community, and Protest among Northern Free Blacks, 1700–1860*. New York: Oxford University Press, 1997.

———. "Violence, Protest, and Identity: Black Manhood in Antebellum America." In *Free People of Color: Inside the African American Community*, 80–96. Washington: Smithsonian Institution Press, 1993.

hooks, bell. *Ain't I A Woman: Black Women and Feminism*. Boston: South End Press, 1981.

Huberich, Charles Henry. *The Political and Legislative History of Liberia*. 2 vols. New York: Central Book Company, 1947.

Humphrey, Carol Sue. *The Press of the Young Republic, 1783–1833*. Westport, CT: Greenwood Press, 1996.

Hunt, Alfred N. *Haiti's Influence on Antebellum America: Slumbering Volcano in the Caribbean*. Baton Rouge: Louisiana State University Press, 1988.

Hunter, T. K. "Geographies of Liberty: A Brief Look at Two Cases." Pp. 41–58 in *Prophets of Protest: Reconsidering the History of American Abolitionism*, edited by Timothy Patrick McCarthy and John Stauffer. New York: New Press, 2006.

Hutton, Frankie. "Democratic Idealism in the Black Press." Pp. 5–20 in *Outsiders in 19th-Century Press History: Multicultural Perspectives*, edited by Frankie Hutton and Barbara Straus Reed. Bowling Green, OH: Bowling Green State University Popular Press, 1995.

———. *The Early Black Press in America, 1827 to 1860.* Westport, CT: Greenwood Press, 1993.

———. "Economic Considerations in the American Colonization Society's Early Effort to Emigrate Free Blacks to Liberia." *Journal of Negro History* 68 (1983): 376–89.

Isani, Makhtar Ali. "The Contemporaneous Reception of Phillis Wheatley: Newspaper and Magazine Notices during the Years of Fame, 1765–1774." *Journal of Negro History* 85 (2000): 260–73.

Jacobs, Donald M., ed. *Courage and Conscience: Black and White Abolitionists in Boston.* Bloomington: Indiana University Press, 1993.

Jacobs, Sylvia M. "The Historical Role of Afro-Americans in American Missionary Efforts in Africa." Pp. 5–29 in *Black Americans and the Missionary Movement in Africa,* ed. Sylvia M. Jacobs. Westport, CT: Greenwood Press, 1982.

Jenkins, William Sumner. *Pro-Slavery Thought in the Old South.* Gloucester, MA: Peter Smith, 1960.

Johnson, Sylvester A. *The Myth of Ham in Nineteenth-Century American Christianity: Race, Heathens, and the People of God.* New York: Palgrave Macmillan, 2004.

Jordan, Winthrop D. *White over Black: American Attitudes toward the Negro, 1550–1812.* Chapel Hill: University of North Carolina Press, 1968.

Kachun, Mitch. "Antebellum African Americans, Public Commemoration, and the Haitian Revolution: A Problem of Historical Mythmaking." *Journal of the Early Republic* 26 (2006): 249–73.

———. *Festivals of Freedom: Memory and Meaning in African American Emancipation Celebrations, 1808–1915.* Amherst: University of Massachusetts Press, 2003.

Kessler, Lauren. *The Dissident Press: Alternative Journalism in American History.* Beverly Hills: Sage, 1984.

Kimmel, Michael. *Manhood in America: A Cultural History.* New York: Free Press, 1996.

Kinshasa, Kwando M. *Emigration vs. Assimilation: The Debate in the African American Press, 1827–1861.* Jefferson, NC: McFarland, 1988.

Kleinfeld, Daniel J. "Manuel Mordecai Noah." Pp. 5–10 in *The Selected Writings of Mordecai Noah,* ed. Michael Schuldiner and Daniel J. Kleinfeld. Westport, CT: Greenwood Press, 1999.

Kraditor, Aileen S. *Means and Ends in American Abolitionism: Garrison and His Critics on Strategy and Tactics, 1834–50.* 1969. Reprint, Chicago: Ivan R. Dee, 1989.

Lapsansky, Emma Jones. *Neighborhoods in Transition: William Penn's Dream and Urban Reality.* New York: Garland Publishing, 1994.

———. "'Since They Got Those Separate Churches': Afro-Americans and Racism in Jacksonian Philadelphia." *American Quarterly* 32 (1980): 54–78.

Lapsansky, Phillip. "'Abigail, a Negress: The Role and the Legacy of African Americans in the Yellow Fever Epidemic." Pp. 61–78 in *A Melancholy Scene of Devastation: The Public Response to the 1793 Philadelphia Yellow Fever Epidemic,* edited by J. Worth Estes and Billy G. Smith. Canton, MA: Science History Publications, 1997.

———. "Graphic Discord: Abolitionist and Antiabolitionist Images." Pp. 201–30 in *The Abolitionist Sisterhood: Women's Political Culture in Antebellum America,* edited by Jean Fagan Yellin and John C. Van Horne. Ithaca, NY: Cornell University Press, 1994.

Lasch, Christopher. *Haven in a Heartless World: The Family Besieged*. New York: Basic Books, 1977.

Laughon, Samuel W. "Administrative Problems in Maryland in Liberia—1836–1851." *Journal of Negro History* 26 (1941): 325–64.

Leonard, Thomas C. *News for All: America's Coming-of-Age with the Press*. New York: Oxford University Press, 1995.

Levesque, George A. "Black Abolitionists in the Age of Jackson: Catalysts in the Radicalization of American Abolition." *Journal of Black Studies* 1 (1970): 187–201.

———. "Inherent Reformers—Inherited Orthodoxy: Black Baptists in Boston, 1800–1873." *Journal of Negro History* 60 (1975): 491–525.

Levine, Michael L. *African Americans and Civil Rights: From 1619 to the Present*. Phoenix, AZ: Oryx Press, 1996.

Levine, Robert S. "Circulating the Nation: David Walker, the Missouri Compromise, and the Rise of the Black Press." Pp. 17–36 in *The Black Press: New Literary and Historical Essays*, edited by Todd Vogel. New Brunswick, NJ: Rutgers University Press, 2001.

Lewis, Gordon K. *Main Currents in Caribbean Thought: The Historical Evolution of Caribbean Society in Its Ideological Aspects, 1492–1900*. Baltimore: Johns Hopkins University Press, 1983.

Lincoln, C. Eric, and Lawrence H. Mamiya. *The Black Church in the African American Experience*. Durham: Duke University Press, 1990.

Lindsay, Arnett G. "The Economic Condition of the Negroes of New York Prior to 1861." *Journal of Negro History* 6 (1921): 190–99.

Loewenberg, Bert James, and Ruth Bogin, eds. *Black Women in Nineteenth-Century American Life: Their Words, Their Thoughts, Their Feelings*. University Park: Pennsylvania State University Press, 1976.

Logan, Shirley Wilson. "Literacy as a Tool for Social Action among Nineteenth-Century African American Women." Pp. 179–96 in *Nineteenth-Century Women Learn to Write*, edited by Catherine Hobbs. Charlottesville: University Press of Virginia, 1995.

———. *"We Are Coming": The Persuasive Discourse of Nineteenth-Century Black Women*. Carbondale: Southern Illinois University Press, 1999.

Lott, Eric. *Love and Theft: Blackface Minstrelsy and the American Working Class*. New York: Oxford University Press, 1993.

Mabee, Carleton. *Black Education in New York State: From Colonial to Modern Times*. Syracuse, NY: Syracuse University Press, 1979.

Malcomson, Scott L. *One Drop of Blood: The American Misadventure of Race*. New York: Farrar, Straus & Giroux, 2000.

Males, Mike. "With Friends Like These: Black Youth Stereotyped by Progressive Columnist Bob Herbert." *Extra!* February 2004, 15–16.

Marshall, Herbert, and Mildred Stock. *Ira Aldridge: The Negro Tragedian*. New York: The Macmillan Company, 1958.

Martin, Asa Earl. "Pioneer Anti-Slavery Press." *Mississippi Valley Historical Review* 2 (1916): 509–28.

Martin, Tony. "The Banneker Literary Institute of Philadelphia: African American Intellectual Activism before the War of the Slaveholders' Rebellion." *Journal of African American History* 87 (2002): 303–22.

McAllister, Marvin. *White People Do Not Know How to Behave at Entertainments Designed for Ladies and Gentlemen of Colour: William Brown's African and American Theater*. Chapel Hill: University of North Carolina Press, 2003.

McCarthy, Michael. *Dark Continent: Africa as Seen by Americans*. Westport, CT: Greenwood Press, 1983.

McCarthy, Timothy Patrick. "'To Plead Our Own Cause': Black Print Culture and the Origins of American Abolitionism." Pp. 114–44 in *Prophets of Protest: Reconsidering the History of American Abolitionism*, edited by Timothy Patrick McCarthy and John Stauffer. New York: New Press, 2006.

McGraw, Mary Tyler. "Richmond Free Blacks and African Colonization, 1816–1832." *Journal of American Studies* 21 (1987): 207–24.

McHenry, Elizabeth. "'Dreaded Eloquence': The Origins and Rise of African American Literary Societies and Libraries." *Harvard Library Bulletin*, n.s., 6, no. 2 (Spring 1995): 32–56.

———. "Forgotten Readers: African-American Literary Societies and the American Scene." Pp. 149–72 in *Print Culture in a Diverse America*, edited by James P. Danky and Wayne A. Wiegand. Urbana: University of Illinois Press, 1998.

———. *Forgotten Readers: Recovering the Lost History of African American Literary Societies*. Durham, NC: Duke University Press, 2002.

McKeen, Gayle. "Whose Rights? Whose Responsibility? Self-Help in African-American Thought." *Polity* 34 (2002): 409–32.

McManus, Edgar J. *A History of Negro Slavery in New York*. Syracuse, NY: Syracuse University Press, 1966.

Mehlinger, Louis. "The Attitude of the Free Negro toward African Colonization." *Journal of Negro History* 1 (1916): 276–301.

Meier, August, and Elliot M. Rudwick. *From Plantation to Ghetto: An Interpretive History of American Negroes*. 3rd ed. New York: Hill and Wang, 1976.

Melish, Joanne Pope. "The 'Condition' Debate and Racial Discourse in the Antebellum North." *Journal of the Early Republic* 19 (1999): 651–72.

———. *Disowning Slavery: Gradual Emancipation and "Race" in New England, 1780–1860*. Ithaca, NY: Cornell University Press, 1998.

Miller, Christopher L. *Blank Darkness: Africanist Discourse in French*. Chicago: University of Chicago Press, 1985.

Miller, Floyd J. *The Search for a Black Nationality: Black Emigration and Colonization, 1787–1863*. Urbana: University of Illinois Press, 1975.

Miniter, Richard. "The False Promise of Slave Redemption." *Atlantic Monthly* (July 1999): 63–70.

Mohl, Raymond A. *Poverty in New York, 1783–1825*. New York: Oxford University Press, 1971.

Moore, Moses N. "Righteousness Exalts a Nation: Black Clergymen, Reform, and New School Presbyterianism." *American Presbyterians: Journal of Presbyterian History* 70 (1992): 222–38.

Morris, Aldon D. Foreword to *A Question of Manhood*. Vol. 1: *"Manhood of Rights": The Construction of Black Male History and Manhood, 1750–1870*, edited by Darlene Clark Hine and Ernestine Jenkins. Bloomington: Indiana University Press, 1999.

Morris, Thomas D. *Free Men All: The Personal Liberty Laws of the North, 1780–1861*. Baltimore: Johns Hopkins University Press, 1974.

Moses, Wilson Jeremiah. *Afrotopia: The Roots of African American Popular History*. Cambridge: Cambridge University Press, 1998.

———. *Alexander Crummell: A Study of Civilization and Discontent*. New York: Oxford University Press, 1989.

———. *The Wings of Ethiopia: Studies in African-American Life and Letters*. Ames: Iowa State University Press, 1990.

Murphy, Sharon. *Other Voices: Black, Chicano, and American Indian Press*. Dayton, OH: Pflaum/Standard, 1974.

Murray, Andrew E. *Presbyterians and the Negro—A History*. Philadelphia: Presbyterian Historical Society, 1966.

Nash, Gary B. *Forging Freedom: The Formation of Philadelphia's Black Community, 1720–1840*. Cambridge, MA: Harvard University Press, 1988.

———. *Race and Revolution*. Madison, WI: Madison House, 1990.

———. "Reverberations of Haiti in the American North: Black Saint Dominguans in Philadelphia." *Pennsylvania History* 65 (1998, supplement): 44–73.

———. *The Unknown American Revolution: The Unruly Birth of Democracy and the Struggle to Create America*. New York: Viking-Penguin, 2005.

Newman, Richard S. "'A Chosen Generation': Black Founders and Early America." Pp. 59–79 in *Prophets of Protest: Reconsidering the History of American Abolitionism*, edited by Timothy Patrick McCarthy and John Stauffer. New York: New Press, 2006.

———. "Protest in Black and White: The Formation and Transformation of an African American Political Community during the Early Republic." Pp. 180–204 in *Beyond the Founders: New Approaches to the Political History of the Early Republic*, edited by Jeffrey L. Pasley, Andrew W. Robertson, and David Waldstreicher. Chapel Hill: University of North Carolina Press, 2004.

———. *The Transformation of American Abolitionism: Fighting Slavery in the Early Republic*. Chapel Hill: University of North Carolina Press, 2002.

Newman, Richard, Patrick Rael, and Phillip Lapsansky. "Introduction: The Theme of Our Contemplation." Pp. 1–31 in *Pamphlets of Protest: An Anthology of Early African-American Protest Literature, 1790–1860*, edited by Richard Newman, Patrick Rael, and Phillip Lapsansky. New York: Routledge, 2001.

Nichols, Ashton. "Mumbo Jumbo: Mungo Park and the Rhetoric of Romantic Africa." Pp. 93–113 in *Romanticism, Race, and Imperial Culture, 1780–1834*, edited by Alan Richardson and Sonia Hofkosh. Bloomington: Indiana University Press, 1996.

Nicholls, David. *From Dessalines to Duvalier: Race, Colour and National Independence in Haiti*. Cambridge: Cambridge University Press, 1979.

Nordin, Kenneth. "In Search of Black Unity: An Interpretation of the Content and Function of *Freedom's Journal*." *Journalism History* 4 (1977–78): 123–28.

Oak, Vishnu V. *The Negro Newspaper*. Yellow Springs, Ohio: Antioch Press, 1948.

O'Kelly, Charlotte G. "Black Newspapers and the Black Protest Movement: Their Historical Relationship, 1827–1945." *Phylon* 43 (1982): 1–14.

Oliver, John J., Jr. "The Black Press: Future Tense." *HUArchivesNet: The Electronic Journal of the Moorland-Spingarn Research Center, Howard University*. June 2000. www.huarchivesnet.howard.edu/nnpa1.htm; www.huarchivesnet.howard.edu/nnpa2.htm (4 May 2004).

Ottley, Roi, and William Weatherby, eds. *The Negro in New York: An Informal Social History*. New York: The New York Public Library, 1967.

Owens, Reginald. "Entering the Twenty-First Century: Oppression and the African American Press." Pp. 96–116 in *Mediated Messages and African-American Culture: Contemporary Issues*, edited by Venise T. Berry and Carmen L. Manning-Miller. Thousand Oaks, CA: Sage Publications, 1996.

Palmer, R. R. *J.-B. Say: An Economist in Troubled Times*. Princeton, NJ: Princeton University Press, 1997.

Payne, Aaron Hamlet. "The Negro in New York Prior to 1860." *Howard Review* 1 (1923): 1–64.

Pease, Jane H., and William H. Pease. "Black Power—The Debate in 1840." *Phylon* 29 (1968): 19–26.

———. "Boston Garrisonians and the Problem of Frederick Douglass." *Canadian Journal of History* 11.2 (September 1967): 29–48.

———. *They Who Would Be Free: Blacks' Search for Freedom, 1830–1861*. New York: Atheneum, 1974.

Penn, I. Garland. *The Afro-American Press, and its Editors*. Springfield, MA: Willey and Co., 1891.

Perkins, Linda. "Black Women and Racial 'Uplift' Prior to Emancipation." Pp. 317–34 in *The Black Women Cross-Culturally*, edited by Filomina Chioma Steady. Rochester, VT: Schenkman Books, 1981.

———. "The Impact of the 'Cult of True Womanhood' on the Education of Black Women." *Journal of Social Issues* 39, no. 3 (1983): 17–28.

Perry, Lewis. *Radical Abolitionism: Anarchy and the Government of God in Antislavery Thought*. Ithaca, NY: Cornell University Press, 1973.

Peterson, Carla L. "Black Life in Freedom: Creating an Elite Culture." Pp. 181–214 in *Slavery in New York*, edited by Ira Berlin and Leslie M. Harris. New York: New Press, 2005.

———. *"Doers of the Word": African-American Women Speakers and Writers in the North, 1830–1880*. New York: Oxford University Press, 1995.

Porter, Dorothy. "The Organized Educational Activities of Negro Literary Societies, 1828–1846." *Journal of Negro Education* 5 (1936): 555–76.

Pratt, Mary Louise. *Imperial Eyes: Travel Writing and Transculturation*. London: Routledge, 1992.

Preston, Dickson, J. *Young Frederick Douglass: The Maryland Years*. Baltimore: Johns Hopkins University Press, 1980.

Preston, E. Delorus Jr. "The Genesis of the Underground Railroad." *Journal of Negro History* 18 (1933): 144–70.

Pride, Armistead S. "*Rights of All*: Second Step in Development of Black Journalism." *Journalism History* 4 (1977–1978): 129–31.

Pride, Armistead S., and Clint C. Wilson II. *A History of the Black Press*. Washington, DC: Howard University Press, 1997.

Quarles, Benjamin. *Allies for Freedom: Blacks and John Brown*. New York: Oxford University Press, 1974.

———. "Antebellum Free Blacks and the 'Spirit of '76." *Journal of Negro History* 61 (1976): 229–42.

———. *Black Abolitionists*. New York: Oxford University Press, 1969.

———. *Black Mosaic: Essays in Afro-American History and Historiography.* Amherst: University of Massachusetts Press, 1988.

———. "The Breach Between Douglass and Garrison." *Journal of Negro History* 23 (1938): 144–54.

———. "Freedom's Black Vanguard." Pp. 174–90 in *Key Issues in the Afro-American Experience.* Vol. I: *To 1877,* edited by Nathan I. Huggins, Martin Kilson, and Daniel M. Fox. San Diego: Harcourt Brace Jovanovich, 1971.

Raboteau, Albert J. "African-Americans, Exodus, and the American Israel." Pp. 1–17 in *African-American Christianity: Essays in History,* edited by Paul E. Johnson. Berkeley: University of California Press, 1994.

Rael, Patrick. *Black Identity and Black Protest in the Antebellum North.* Chapel Hill: University of North Carolina Press, 2002.

———. "The Long Death of Slavery." Pp. 111–46 in *Slavery in New York,* edited by Ira Berlin and Leslie M. Harris. New York: New Press, 2005.

Rammelkamp, Julian. "The Providence Negro Community, 1820–1842." *Rhode Island History* 7 (1948): 20–33.

Reed, Harry. *Platform for Change: The Foundations of the Northern Free Black Community, 1775–1865.* East Lansing: Michigan State University Press, 1994.

Rice, Alan. *Radical Narratives of the Black Atlantic.* London: Continuum, 2003.

Richardson, Harry V. *Dark Salvation: The Story of Methodism as It Developed among Blacks in America.* Garden City, NY: Anchor Press/Doubleday, 1976.

Richmond, M. A. *Bid the Vassal Soar: Interpretive Essays on the Life and Poetry of Phillis Wheatley (ca. 1753–1784) and George Moses Horton (ca. 1797–1883).* Washington, DC: Howard University Press, 1974.

Ripley, C. Peter, et al., eds. *Witness for Freedom: African American Voices on Race, Slavery, and Emancipation.* Chapel Hill: University of North Carolina Press, 1993.

Roberson, Susan L. "Advice to Young Men in Nineteenth-Century America." *Journal of the American Studies Association of Texas* 22 (1991): 30–38.

Roberts, Samuel K. *In the Path of Virtue: The African American Moral Tradition.* Cleveland: Pilgrim Press, 1999.

Rosen, Bruce. "Abolition and Colonization, the Years of Conflict: 1829–34." *Phylon* 33 (1972): 177–92.

Rouse, P. Joy. "Cultural Models of Womanhood and Female Education: Practices of Colonization and Resistance." Pp. 230–47 in *Nineteenth-Century Women Learn to Write,* edited by Catherine Hobbs. Charlottesville: University Press of Virginia, 1995.

———. "'We Can Never Remain Silent: The Public Discourse of the Nineteenth-Century African-American Press." Pp. 128–42 in *Popular Literacy: Studies in Cultural Practices and Poetics,* edited by John Trimbur. Pittsburgh: University of Pittsburgh Press, 2001.

Rowe, G. S. "Black Offenders, Criminal Courts, and Philadelphia Society in the Late Eighteenth Century." *Journal of Social History* 22 (1988–89): 685–712.

Royster, Jacqueline Jones. *Traces of a Stream: Literacy and Social Change among African American Women.* Pittsburgh: University of Pittsburgh Press, 2000.

Rury, John L. "Philanthropy, Self Help, and Social Control: The New York Manumission Society and Free Blacks, 1785–1810." Pp. 95–107 in *Freedom's Odyssey: African American History Essays from Phylon,* edited by Alexa Benson Henderson and Janice Sumler-Edmond. Atlanta: Clark Atlanta University Press, 1999. First published in *Phylon* 46 (1985): 231–41.

Ryan, Susan M. *The Grammar of Good Intentions: Race and the Antebellum Culture of Benevolence*. Ithaca, NY: Cornell University Press, 2003.

Sagarin, Mary. *John Brown Russwurm: The Story of* Freedom's Journal, *Freedom's Journey*. New York: Lothrop, Lee, and Shepard, 1970.

Saillant, John. "Circular Addressed to the Colored Brethren and Friends in America." *Virginia Magazine of History and Biography* 104 (1996): 481–504.

Sanders, Edith R. "The Hamitic Hypothesis; Its Origin and Functions in Time Perspective." *Journal of African History* 10 (1969): 521–32.

Sarna, Jonathan D. *Jacksonian Jew: The Two Worlds of Mordecai Noah*. New York: Holmes and Meier Publishers, 1981.

Saxton, Alexander. "Blackface Minstrelsy, Vernacular Comics, and the Politics of Slavery in the North." Pp. 157–75 in *The Meaning of Slavery in the North*, edited by David Roediger and Martin H. Blatt. New York: Garland Publishing, 1998.

Sealander, Judith. "Antebellum Black Press Images of Women." *Western Journal of Black Studies* 6 (1982): 159–65.

Sernett, Milton. *North Star Country: Upstate New York and the Crusade for African American Freedom*. Syracuse, NY: Syracuse University Press, 2002.

Schudson, Michael. *Discovering the News: A Social History of American Newspapers*. New York: Basic Books, 1978.

Scott, Donald M. "Abolition as a Sacred Vocation." Pp. 51–74 in *Antislavery Reconsidered: New Perspectives on the Abolitionists*, edited by Lewis Perry and Michael Fellman. Baton Rouge: Louisiana State University Press, 1979.

Shade, William G. "'Though We Are Not Slaves, We Are Not Free': Quasi-Free Blacks in Antebellum America." Pp. 118–38 in *Upon These Shores: Themes in the African-American Experience, 1600 to the Present*, edited by William R. Scott and William G. Shade. New York: Routledge, 2000.

Shanks, Caroline L. "The Biblical Anti-Slavery Argument of the Decade 1830–1840." *Journal of Negro History* 16 (1931): 132–57.

Shepperson, George. "Mungo Park and the Scottish Contribution to Africa." *African Affairs* 70 (1971): 277–81.

Sherman, Joan R., ed. *The Black Bard of North Carolina: George Moses Horton and His Poetry*. Chapel Hill: University of North Carolina Press, 1997.

Shick, Tom W. *Behold the Promised Land: A History of Afro-American Settler Society in Nineteenth-Century Liberia*. Baltimore: Johns Hopkins University Press, 1977.

Simmons, Charles A. *The African-American Press: A History of News Coverage during National Crises*. Jefferson, NC: McFarland and Co., 1998.

Simonhoff, Harry. *Jewish Notables in America, 1776–1865: Links of an Endless Chain*. New York: Greenberg, 1956.

Sinha, Manisha. "Black Abolitionism: The Assault on Southern Slavery and the Struggle for Racial Equality." Pp. 239–62 in *Slavery in New York*, edited by Ira Berlin and Leslie M. Harris. New York: New Press, 2005.

Sorin, Gerald. *The New York Abolitionists: A Case Study of Political Radicalism*. Westport, CT: Greenwood Publishing Corporation, 1971.

Staudenraus, P. J. *The African Colonization Movement 1816–1895*. New York: Columbia University Press, 1961.

Stauffer, John. *The Black Hearts of Men: Radical Abolitionists and the Transformation of Race.* Cambridge, MA: Harvard University Press, 2001.

Stewart, James Brewer. "The Emergence of Racial Modernity and the Rise of the White North, 1790–1840." *Journal of the Early Republic* 18 (1998): 181–217.

Stoller, Paul. "Back to the Ethnographic Future." *Journal of Contemporary Ethnography* 28 (1999): 698–704.

Stuckey, Sterling. *The Ideological Origins of Black Nationalism.* Boston: Beacon Press, 1972.

Swan, Robert J. "John Teasman: African-American Educator and the Emergence of Community in Early Black New York City, 1787–1815." *Journal of the Early Republic* 12 (1992): 331–56.

Swartz, Ellen. "Emancipatory Narratives: Rewriting the Master Script in the School Curriculum." *Journal of Negro Education* 61 (1992): 341–55.

Sweet, John Wood. *Bodies Politic: Negotiating Race in the American North, 1730–1830.* Baltimore: Johns Hopkins University Press, 2003.

Sweet, Leonard I. *Black Images of America 1784–1870.* New York: W. W. Norton, 1976.

———. "The Fourth of July and Black Americans in the Nineteenth Century: Northern Leadership Opinion within the Context of the Black Experience." *Journal of Negro History* 61 (1976): 256–75.

Swift, David E. "Black Presbyterian Attacks on Racism: Samuel Cornish, Theodore Wright and Their Contemporaries." *Journal of Presbyterian History* 51 (1973): 433–70.

———. *Black Prophets of Justice: Activist Clergy before the Civil War.* Baton Rouge: Louisiana State University Press, 1989.

Tadmun, Michael. *Speculators and Slaves: Masters, Traders, and Slaves in the Old South.* Madison: University of Wisconsin Press, 1989.

Takaki, Ronald. "The Black Child-Savage in Ante-Bellum America." Pp. 27–44 in *The Great Fear: Race in the Mind of America,* edited by Gary B. Nash and Richard Weiss. New York: Holt, Rinehart and Winston, 1970.

Tate, Gayle T. "Free Black Resistance in the Antebellum Era, 1830 to 1860." *Journal of Black Studies* 28 (1998): 764–82.

———. "Political Consciousness and Resistance Among Black Antebellum Women." *Women and Politics* 13 (1993): 67–89.

———. *Unknown Tongues: Black Women's Political Activism in the Antebellum Era, 1830–1860.* East Lansing: Michigan State University Press, 2003.

Terborg-Penn, Rosalyn. "Black Male Perspectives on the Nineteenth-Century Woman." Pp. 28–42 in *The Afro-American Woman: Struggles and Images,* edited by Sharon Harley and Rosalyn Terborg-Penn. Port Washington, NY: Kennikat Press, 1978.

Thomas, Lamont D. *Rise to Be a People: A Biography of Paul Cuffe.* Urbana: University of Illinois Press, 1986.

Thompson, George A. *A Documentary History of the African Theatre.* Evanston, IL: Northwestern University Press, 1998.

Thompson, Vincent Bakpetu. *Africans of the Diaspora: The Evolution of African Consciousness and Leadership in the Americas.* Trenton, NJ: Africa World Press, 2000.

——. "Leadership in the African Diaspora in the Americas Prior to 1860." *Journal of Black Studies* 24 (1993): 42–76.

Tise, Larry E. *The American Counterrevolution: A Retreat from Liberty, 1783–1800*. Mechanicsburg, PA: Stackpole Books, 1998.

——. *Proslavery: A History of the Defense of Slavery in America, 1701–1840*. Athens: University of Georgia Press, 1987.

Toll, Robert C. *Blacking Up: The Minstrel Show in Nineteenth-Century America*. New York: Oxford University Press, 1974.

Toufe, Zeynep. "Let Them Eat Cake: TV Blames Africans for Famine." *Extra!* November/December 2002, 14–17.

Tripp, Bernell. *Origins of the Black Press: New York, 1827–1847*. Northport, AL: Vision Press, 1992.

Vaughan, Alden T., and Virginia Mason Vaughan. "Before Othello: Elizabethan Representations of Sub-Saharan Africa." *William and Mary Quarterly*, 3rd ser., 54 (1997): 19–44.

Vogel, Todd. *ReWriting White: Race, Class, and Cultural Capital in Nineteenth-Century America*. New Brunswick, NJ: Rutgers University Press, 2004.

Walker, Clarence E. "The American Negro as Historical Outsider, 1836–1935." *Canadian Review of American Studies* 17 (1986) 137–54.

——. *Deromanticizing Black History: Critical Essays and Reappraisals*. Knoxville: University of Tennessee Press, 1991.

Walker, George E. "The Afro-American in New York City." Ph.D. diss., Columbia University, 1975.

Walters, Ronald G. *The Antislavery Appeal: American Abolitionism after 1830*. Baltimore: Johns Hopkins University Press, 1976.

——. "The Boundaries of Abolitionism." Pp. 3–23 in *Antislavery Reconsidered: New Perspectives on the Abolitionists*, edited by Lewis Perry and Michael Fellman. Baton Rouge: Louisiana State University Press, 1979.

Walvin, James. *Black Ivory: Slavery in the British Empire*. 2nd ed. Oxford: Blackwell Publishers, 2001.

——. "The Propaganda of Anti-Slavery." Pp. 49–68 in *Slavery and British Society: 1776–1846*, edited by James Walvin. Baton Rouge: Louisiana State University Press, 1982.

Ward, Francis B. "The Black Press in Crisis." *The Black Scholar* 5 (1973): 34–36.

Warren, James Perrin. *Culture of Eloquence: Oratory and Reform in Antebellum America*. University Park: Pennsylvania State University Press, 1999.

Washington, Booker T. *The Story of the Negro: The Rise of the Race from Slavery*. 2 vols. 1909. Reprint, Gloucester, MA: Peter Smith, 1969.

Watson, Marsha. "A Classic Case: Phillis Wheatley and Her Poetry." *Early American Literature* 31 (1996): 103–32.

Welter, Barbara. *Dimity Convictions: The American Woman in the Nineteenth Century*. Athens: Ohio University Press, 1976.

Wesley, Charles H. "The Concept of Negro Inferiority in American Thought." *Journal of Negro History* 25 (1940): 540–60.

——. "The Negroes of New York in the Emancipation Movement." *Journal of Negro History* 24 (1939): 65–103.

——. "The Negro in the Organization of Abolition." *Phylon* 2 (1941): 223–35.

——. "Negro Suffrage in the Period of Constitution-Making, 1787–1865." *Journal of Negro History* 32 (April 1947): 143–68.

White, Arthur O. "The Black Leadership Class and Education in Antebellum Boston." *Journal of Negro Education* 42 (1973): 504–15.

White, Shane. "The Death of James Johnson." *American Quarterly* 51 (1999): 753–95.

——. "Impious Prayers: Elite and Popular Attitudes toward Blacks and Slavery in the Middle-Atlantic States, 1783–1810." *New York History* 67 (1986): 260–83.

——. "'It Was a Proud Day': African Americans, Festivals, and Parades in the North, 1741–1834." *Journal of American History* 81 (1994): 13–50.

——. *Somewhat More Independent: The End of Slavery in New York City, 1770–1810.* Athens: University of Georgia Press, 1991.

——. *Stories of Freedom in Black New York.* Cambridge, MA: Harvard University Press, 2002.

Wiecek, William M. "*Somerset*: Lord Mansfield and the Legitimacy of Slavery in the Anglo-American World." *University of Chicago Law Review* 42 (1975): 86–146.

Wilder, Craig Steven. "Black Life in Freedom: Creating a Civic Culture." Pp. 215–37 in *Slavery in New York*, edited by Ira Berlin and Leslie M. Harris. New York: New Press, 2005.

——. *In the Company of Black Men: The African Influence on African American Culture in New York City.* New York: New York University Press, 2001.

——. *The Sources of Antislavery Constitutionalism in America, 1760–1848.* Ithaca, NY: Cornell University Press, 1977.

Wilentz, Sean. Introduction to *David Walker's Appeal, in Four Articles; Together with a Preamble, to the Coloured Citizens of the World, But in Particular, and Very Expressly, to Those of the United States of America.* 3rd ed. 1830. Reprint, New York: Hill and Wang, 1995.

Wiley, Bell I., ed. *Slaves No More: Letters from Liberia, 1833–1869.* Lexington: University of Kentucky Press, 1980.

Williams, Heather Andrea. *Self-Taught: African American Education in Slavery and Freedom.* Chapel Hill: University of North Carolina Press, 2005.

Williams-Myers, A. J. "Some Notes on the Extent of New York City's Involvement in the Underground Railroad." *Afro-Americans in New York Life and History* 29, no. 2 (July 2005): 73–82.

Wilmore, Gayraud S. *Black Religion and Black Radicalism: An Interpretation of the Religious History of African Americans.* 3rd ed. Maryknoll, NY: Orbis Books, 1998.

Wilson, Carol. "Active Vigilance Is the Price of Liberty: Black Self-Defense against Fugitive Slave Recapture and Kidnapping of Free Blacks." Pp. 108–27 in *Antislavery Violence: Sectional, Racial, and Cultural Conflict in Antebellum America*, edited by John R. McKivigan and Stanley Harrold. Knoxville: University of Tennessee Press, 1999.

——. *Freedom at Risk: The Kidnapping of Free Blacks in America, 1780–1865.* Lexington: University Press of Kentucky, 1994.

Wilson, Clint C., II. *Black Journalists in Paradox: Historical Perspectives and Current Dilemmas.* Westport, CT: Greenwood Press, 1991.

Winch, Julie, ed. *The Elite of Our People: Joseph Willson's Sketches of Black Upper-Class Life in Antebellum Philadelphia*. University Park: Pennsylvania State University Press, 2000.

———. *A Gentleman of Color: The Life of James Forten*. New York: Oxford University Press, 2002.

———. *Philadelphia's Black Elite*. Philadelphia: Temple University Press, 1988.

Wolseley, Roland E. *The Black Press, U. S. A.* Ames: Iowa State University Press, 1971.

Woodson, Carter Godwin. *The Education of the Negro Prior to 1861: A History of the Education of the Colored People of the United States from the Beginning of Slavery to the Civil War*. 1919. Reprint, Brooklyn: A and B, n.d.

Wright, Donald R. *African Americans and the Early Republic, 1789–1831*. Arlington Heights, IL: Harlan Davidson, 1993.

Yee, Shirley J. *Black Women Abolitionists: A Study in Activism, 1828–1860*. Knoxville: University of Tennessee Press, 1992.

———. "Organizing for Racial Justice: Black Women and the Dynamics of Race and Sex in Female Antislavery Societies, 1832–1860." Pp. 38–53 in *Black Women in America*, edited by Kim Marie Vaz. Thousand Oaks, CA: Sage Publications, 1995.

Young, Henry J. *Major Black Religious Leaders: 1755–1940*. Nashville, TN: Abingdon, 1977.

Young, R. J. *Antebellum Black Activists: Race, Gender, and Self*. New York: Garland Publishing, 1996.

Young, Sandra Sandiford. "John Brown Russwurm's Dilemma: Citizenship or Emigration?" Pp. 90–113 in *Prophets of Protest: Reconsidering the History of American Abolitionism*, edited by Timothy Patrick McCarthy and John Stauffer. New York: New Press, 2006.

Zilversmit, Arthur. *The First Emancipation: The Abolition of Slavery in the North*. Chicago: University of Chicago Press, 1967.

Credits

Quotes from the Anti-Slavery Collection and the Samuel Joseph May Collection at the Boston Public Library are reprinted with permission from the Boston Public Library/Rare Books Department. Courtesy of the Trustees.

Quotes from BV Diary, 1821–1824, are reprinted with permission from the New-York Historical Society.

Quotes from the Pennsylvania Abolition Society Papers are reprinted with permission from the Historical Society of Pennsylvania.

Quotes from the Stephen Grellet Papers are reprinted with permission from the Library Company of Philadelphia.

Quotes from James Oliver Horton's online article "The Manhood of the Race: Gender and the Language of Black Protest in the Antebellum North" are reprinted with permission from James Oliver Horton.

Material from chapter 2 appeared in the article "The History of *Freedom's Journal*: A Study in Empowerment and Community," *Journal of African American History* 88 (2003): 1–20, reprinted with the permission of the Association for the Study of African American Life and History.

Index

A. (contributor), 139

AASS. *See* American Anti-Slavery Society (AASS)

abolition of slave trade, 20–21, 232–34

abolition of slavery: African-American abolitionists, 230, 235–36, 246n69, 256–57, 262–64, 271–72, 276n20; British abolitionists, 223, 231–32, 243n28, 246n69; Garrison's *Liberator* and, 54, 60–61, 92, 206n34, 210, 261; gradual approach to, 230–31; influence of *Freedom's Journal* on, 259–64; in North, 14–16, 75, 84, 89–90, 96n55, 126, 209, 222, 230; practical abolition, 235–41; proposals for, 230–35; public celebrations of, 89–90, 106–7, 127–29, 209; radical (immediate) abolition, 234–35, 260; rhetoric on, in 1820s, 25–26; in Saint Domingue, 18; in Sudan, 247n89; in Washington, D.C., 232; white abolitionists, 2, 34n36, 230–32, 256–58, 262–64, 272; whites' opposition to, 27–28; and women's rights, 257, 276n20. *See also* antislavery movement; Garrison, William Lloyd

Abolition Society of Stark County, Ohio, 234

ACS. *See* American Colonization Society (ACS)

Adams, Alice Dana, 230, 232

advertisements, 37, 48, 66n37, 72–73, 92, 266, 270

advertising rates, 48, 66n37

Africa: American Colonization Society (ACS)'s portrayal of, 161; Christianity and, 21, 157, 163–65, 182–84, 196; decline of, 156–59; education in, 199; and education of African Americans, 165; Egypt in, 149–59, 224, 225; Ethiopia in, 19, 149, 155–57, 163, 191, 224; exploration of and travel writings on, 159–61; in *Freedom's Journal*, 60, 92, 147–65; history of, 115–16, 148–59; and identity of African Americans, 20–21, 87; news on, in *Freedom's Journal*, 159–65; poetry from, 160; problems of colonists in, 198–99; Rahahman case and, 161–64, 171; self-help by African Americans and, 116–17; Sierra Leone in, 21, 179, 181–82; slave

309

About the Author

Jacqueline Bacon's research and writing focus on African-American history and rhetoric, issues of race in contemporary culture, and the media. She is particularly interested in the ways that people who are marginalized use the power of language to create positive identities, to fight for civil rights, and to critique institutional and societal oppression. She is the author of *The Humblest May Stand Forth: Rhetoric, Empowerment, and Abolition* (2002), as well as numerous articles in scholarly and popular periodicals. An independent scholar, Bacon lives in San Diego, California with her husband Glen McClish and their two sons. Her website is www.jacquelinebacon.com.